Dragons on Bird Wings

A Combat History of the 812ᵗʰ Fighter Regiment
Volume I: Liberation of the Motherland

Text by Vladislav Antipov and Igor Utkin ©2004

English Translation by James Gebhardt ©2005

1ˢᵗ English Edition, SkyGrid ©2006

ISBN 0-9780696-0-9

Executive Editor • Terry Higgins

Series Russian / English Translation Editor •
Ilya Grinberg

Copy Editing • Terry Higgins, with James Gebhardt,
Ilya Grinberg, and Alexander Rusetski

Scale Drawings • Alexander Rusetski

Maps and Diagrams • Terry Higgins*

Aircraft Colour Profiles • Terry Higgins**

*based on historical materials as supplied by the authors

**based on the scale drawings of Alexander Rusetski (Bf109 and
all Yak types), Arthur Bentley (Hs129 and Fw190), and Terry
Higgins (La-5 and Ju87G)

All photos are from the authors' collections unless credited otherwise

Designed in Canada

Printed in Hong Kong

Published in Canada

Aviaeology, by SkyGrid

123 Church Street

Kitchener, Ontario

Canada N2G 2S3

Fax: (519) 742-2182

Email: info@aviaeology.com

Email: skygrid@bellnet.ca

Aviaeology is an imprint of SkyGrid

Library and Archives Canada Cataloguing in Publication

Antipov, Vladislav, 1976-
Dragons on bird wings : the combat history of the 812th Fighter
Regiment / text by Vladislav Antipov and Igor Utkin ; English
translation by James Gebhardt ; executive editor, Terry Higgins ;
series Russian/English translation editor, Ilya Grinberg.

Translated from the Russian.
Includes bibliographical references and index.
Contents: v. 1. Liberation of the Motherland.
ISBN 0-9780696-0-9 (v. 1)

1. Soviet Union. Raboche-Krestianskaia Krasnaia Armiia.
Fighter Regiment, 812th--History.
2. World War, 1939-1945--Aerial operations, Soviet.
3. World War, 1939-1945--Regimental histories--Soviet Union.
4. Yak (Fighter plane)
I. Utkin, Igor, 1960- II. Gebhardt, James F., 1948- III. Higgins,
Terry, 1962- IV. Grinberg, Ilya, 1955- V. Title.

UG635.S65A68 2006   940.54'4947
C2006-904004-4

Dragons on Bird Wings

Contents

Volume 1: Liberation of the Motherland

Maps and Diagrams

Appendices

Publisher's Note

Translation

The Russian-to-English translation for this book was prepared by the translator to a broadly accepted - and I might add, highly professional - standard. In editing his original English draft we decided to modify certain Russian transliterations for pronunciation and readability. For example, gone is the diacritical mark that would normally have such words as *Artemev*, *dal-nego*, *Oktyabr*, and *Prikhodko* appear in English transcription as *Artem'ev*, *dal'nego*, *Oktyabr'*, and *Prikhod'ko*. Words that in academic English transcription would normally contain "ee" such as *Alekseevka* and *Veremeenko*, or start with an "E" like *Evgeniy* are written as *Alekseyevka*, *Veremeyenko*, and *Yevgeniy*, reflecting the original language's "ye" sound of this specific "e". For the same reason, such words containing "a" followed by "e" as *Kitaev*, *Nikolaenkov*, and *Torgaevka* are written *Kitayev*, *Nikolayenkov*, and *Torgayevka*.

Hopefully, this will be of some benefit to readers unfamiliar with the Russian language and its cyrillic alphabet, even if it might appear to be slightly odd to Russian-English readers. Any mistakes that may have crept in during this process are entirely my own and should not reflect on the excellent translation / editing teamwork of Messrs Gebhardt and Grinberg.

Tone

I would like also to comment briefly on the tone of the cited and quoted material in the narrative. During the Great Patriotic War, a highly discernible patriotism, most often expressed as hatred for the enemy combined with an equally strong love of the homeland, permeated the language of citizens, warriors and leaders. Add to that the need to *toe the party line* under the vigilant eye of Stalinism and you have that uniquely Soviet Red Army tone that pervades the narrative. This is particularly evident in official reports, memoirs, and other documents that might have to cross a political branch commissar's desk or two over the years, before it reached the archives.

Beginning in the *Revolution*, this military-political patriotic tone was fine-tuned in meter, melody and verse by the time Hitler invaded the USSR. It thus formed the very foundation of the lingo spoken and written by Soviet officers and men, reaching a crescendo during the Cold War (when many memoirs were written). This tone should not be construed solely as an author's attempt to revisit the propaganda of a bygone era. Sadly, this ill-conceived perception has *set the tone* in a few reviews of other books drawing on Soviet-era memoirs and literature. In actuality, it is an integral part of the history and should be presented as such. In blending these passages with their general narrative the authors have done their job well, while our translation-editorial duo followed through with appropriate sensitivity: They have preserved the tone of the cited material while ensuring that the general narrative presents every detail as the authors intended.

Measurements

Distance, altitudes, speeds, ranges, etc. originally presented in metric are supplemented herein by approximate imperial equivalent (shown in parenthesis), rounded up or down as appropriate. This level of accuracy is generally accepted as satisfactory in a book of this nature. The exceptions are in engineered measurements (i.e. wingspan) where the reader may benefit from having absolute equivalents.

Profiles

The aircraft colour profiles were prepared especially for this volume and are based on the most recent line drawings available to us prior to publication. In fact, certain views within Alex Rusetski's Yak fighter plans (see pages 134–145) were fine-tuned concurrently with the preparation of the relevant profiles. For their enthusiastic input, research efforts, and in-progress feedback which helped *tighten up* each profile, I extend a sincere thank you to my good friends Alex Rusetski and Ilya Grinberg. I am also most grateful to Ilya's very knowledgeable associates, Mikhail Bykov, Sergey Kuznetsov, and Mansur Mustafin. The level of detail they unearthed on particular production batch peculiarities and factory paint schemes was truly awe inspiring. No less appreciation is due to Alex for loaning his refined Bf109 drawings to the cause, Arthur Bentley for letting me use his excellent Fw190 and Hs129 drawings, the authors for their timely responses to requests for additional reference photos, and my good friends John Bubak and Ed Foerter for digging into the depths of their personal book collections in search of "that certain view" – always needed at the last minute to complete the various Luftwaffe subjects.

Terry Higgins,
Kitchener, Ontario
Canada

The 812th Regiment and its flight crews who came to the Kuban were already a cohesive team. Practically all of them knew each other from their service together in the Far East. Each understood that war is war and losses are unavoidable, but of course no one among the pilots expected that they would be so great, that so many of the enemy would be cunning and crafty. We were like half-trained birds thrown to the wind. All the pilots had flying experience except those who had only recently completed flight training. But in air combat everyone should function automatically. Combat is not a time for reflection; our pilots did not have this type of experience.

The first combat sorties were perceived as training flights. Here the tactics were quite different. One had to select the position for attack that the enemy would not anticipate, so as to have superiority in altitude and speed. We frequently attacked in the following manner: you see the enemy and fly headlong toward him, and then for certain someone is flying higher, and at speed shoots down the attacker. An order is an order, and everyone sortied and tried to accomplish the mission despite the losses. There was not any particular fear. You fired and they fired back at you, and vice versa. All hope was that he would not hit the target and you would. Who would outsmart whom? Often all depended on the leader, on his maneuver.

We understood that it was useless to swim upstream and better to shoot down one or two enemy without any losses of our own than to kill three or four and lose someone in the process. But as a rule we did not think about our losses; our main goal was to kill the enemy. In the evening, after the sorties, everyone assembled for supper and discussed what had happened that day. For us every victory was a celebration. And practically the whole short southern night was spent in discussions. Soon the truck arrived to take us to the airfield. At the airfield, people fell asleep wherever they could until the command was issued to sortie.

On average we flew three or four sorties, but some flew up to five in a day. The intensity was great. Every sortie was different and so was every aerial engagement— different nuances all the time. The conduct of an aerial engagement did not much resemble normal flight. Sometimes I turned the airplane so hard that my vision faded out from G-forces. Everyone had to get used to this. The air crews gained more and more experience with each sortie, and when we had finally learned how to fight, only 15—20 percent of the combat-capable pilots were left. But, in spite of this fact, the regiment accomplished its mission. And for us this was the main thing.

The battles for the Kuban became for the regiment a combat christening and a genuine school for pilots. Those who survived and passed through these battles subsequently became genuinely powerful aerial warriors. The tactics of aerial combat were changing and what is more important, the command took this into consideration during training of the newly arriving pilots, using the experience gained in the Kuban.

I would like to say "thank you" to the young generation represented by the authors for not forgetting. They have not forgotten what we *oldtimers* did during the war. Reading the manuscript of this book, I once again lived through those events and that difficult time. I want most of all that our descendants will not forget any of this. Then there remains a chance that such a war will never be repeated.

Kapitan (retired) Aleksandr Ivanovich Ivanov

Pilot, 534th and 812th IAP.

Flight commander, 408th Detached Liaison Aviation Squadron, 3rd IAK

Pilot of a Yak-1 fighter in the Kuban

Foreword

Veteran of the Regiment
Aleksandr I. Ivanov

Sadly Aleksandr Ivanovich Ivanov passed away before this book went to print. As the last living pilot of the 812th IAP he actively participated in the creation of this work with all his heart and soul.

We hope that his foreword and his memoirs will be a reminder of this great man, pilot and defender of his Motherland.

Foreword

Historian, Curator of the
Smithsonian Institution
National Air and Space Museum
and Author of "Red Phoenix",
Von Hardesty

Hitler's bold plan for the invasion of the Soviet Union, dubbed Operation Barbarossa, targeted the Soviet Air Force as its first victim. On the morning of June 22, 1941, the Luftwaffe attacked a series of key forward Soviet airfields, even as a massive force of infantry and tanks quickly advanced into the Soviet Union. Vast numbers of Soviet aircraft were destroyed in place that day. In the face of such a powerful blow only a modest number of Soviet aircraft managed to get airborne to resist the German advance—most to be shot down by marauding German fighters. At the end of that first day, German General Halder recorded in his diary an unbelievable action summary: the Luftwaffe had destroyed 800 Soviet aircraft at the cost of a mere ten aircraft!

The Luftwaffe's stunning preemptive air strike heralded a concerted effort by the Germans to neutralize Soviet air power as a viable force. By the end of the summer of 1941, the Luftwaffe's control of the air appeared complete and seemingly irreversible, with perhaps as many as 10,000 Soviet aircraft destroyed. This monumental German air triumph (along with impressive gains on the ground) soon proved illusory. The Soviet Air Force came back to fight another day—as did the larger Soviet military—winning decisive victories in 1943 and eventually going on the offensive the following year. By 1945, the Soviet Air Force dominated the skies over Berlin, emerging as the largest tactical air arm in the world.

How the Soviet Air Force achieved this improbable victory remains one of the most dramatic, if neglected, sagas of World War II. The appointment of Alexander Novikov as Soviet air commander in the spring of 1942 signaled the advent of a whole new generation of air force leaders. These freshly minted air commanders often reflected talent, personal initiative, and organizational skill. Over time, Novikov perfected the air component in the emerging concept of combined arms warfare in the Soviet strategy. This fundamental transition was part of Novikov's wartime reforms, which included increased centralization of air power assets and reserves, the creation of air armies, and the elaboration of new tactical operations such as the air offensive.

Faced with total war, the Soviet Union went through the arduous process of relocating its aviation plants in 1941. This task set the stage for the rapid expansion and increased productivity of the aviation sector. During the war years Soviet aviation plants supplied frontline air units with modern fighters and ground attack aircraft. Even as these herculean steps proved decisive, the Soviet military benefitted from the timely and critical support of Lend Lease aid, a program that reinforced the Soviet Air Force with American-made fighters and medium bombers. The trajectory of Soviet war-making initiatives ultimately overwhelmed the Luftwaffe.

This extraordinary history, arguably the least known chapter in World War II, is best told at the regimental and small air unit level. However, it would not be until the fall of the Soviet Union this critical genre of historical literature flourished. Only with the small air unit histories were we able to reconstruct in detail how the Soviets reversed their fortunes in the air. Dragons on Bird Wings: The Combat History of the 812th Fighter Regiment (Book One), written by Vladislav Antipov and Igor Utkin and now in English translation, offers us an intimate inside perspective on the brutal air war that raged on the Russian front. One can follow in remarkable detail the combat air operations through many notable battles, from the defense of Moscow, through the Kuban, to the liberation of the South Ukraine. This same time frame, it should be noted, became the pivotal context for Soviet fighter aviation to make its remarkable recovery and to challenge the Luftwaffe for air supremacy.

For those interested in Soviet aircraft, in particular the Yak-1, Yak-7, and Yak-9 fighters, the Antipov and Utkin narrative offers many insights on their combat use during the war. Mirrored also in this regimental history are the many Luftwaffe counterparts, a formidable array of fighters and bombers that had attempted in vain to secure the skies for the German army as it found itself in permanent retreat. The Luftwaffe is portrayed in this book accurately as a lethal challenge to the reborn

Soviet Air Force throughout the long and difficult war. The book also offers statistical data on aircraft losses by both sides, always a matter of debate and speculation.

The 812th Fighter Air Regiment was first organized in March 1942. In recreating its combat history in the opening years of the war, the authors cover many pivotal combat episodes—all supplemented with vivid anecdotes and personal recollections. These descriptive accounts give a human dimension to the story, showing dramatically the high risks and sacrifices required of Soviet pilots during those fateful years. Soviet losses are not ignored in any sort of one-sided story of wartime Soviet heroism. The reader will find as well candid coverage of errors and injustices that came with the war effort. This undertow of open acknowledgement of the darker side sets the book apart from the "official" histories that appeared prior to the fall of the Soviet Union.

As the body of historical literature on the Soviet Air Force continues to expand, I believe Dragons on Bird Wings will enjoy a long shelf life as one of the more compelling and informed accounts of the air war in the east during World War II.

Von Hardesty

Smithsonian National Air and Space Museum

Washington, D.C.

Acknowledgements

The authors express their gratitude to the following people for the assistance they provided in the completion of this work:

Veterans of the 812th IAP:

A.I. Ivanov, I.L. Deryugin, M.S. Shcheglova, K.P. Aleshin, V.M.Baryshev, G.F. Klichko, P.V. Korneyev, N.P. Pechenin, V.Z. Yemets, K.Ye. Kozak, S.P. Kalugin, P.S. Serezhenko.

To the families of Hero of the Soviet Union I.V. Fedorov, former commander of the 2nd Squadron of the 812th IAP; I.F. Popov, former commander of the 812th IAP; F.G. Usmanov, pilot in the 2nd Squadron of the 812th IAP

To the Councils of Veterans of the 265th Melitopol IAD and 3rd Nikopol IAK; To the Central Museum of the Armed Forces of the Russian Federation, Moscow;

To the School Museum, 3rd IAK, and personally to I.I. Leonova, the director of Moscow School No. 39.

To the School Museum of Combat Glory of the village Uglovoye (Crimea Autonomous Republic) and personally to T.I. Ivanova, director, and A.A. Popova, history teacher.

To G.V. Krivosheyev, veteran of the 31st GIAP;

To Hero of the Soviet Union Ya.D. Mikhaylik, veteran of 54th GIAP.

To Dmitriy Mikhaylov, Valeriy Stolov, Andrey Dikov, Aleksey Pekarsh, Dmitriy Sribniy, Aleksey Andreyev, Sergey Alekseyev, Ilya Grinberg, Mikhail Bykov, Audrius Nairanauskas, John Manhro, Peter Randall, Alex Smart, Franek Grabowski, Sergey Kuznetsov, Aleksandr Rusetski, Mansur Mustafin, Igor Zlobin, Lee Anne Bradley (398th BG Historian) and Ota Jirovec.

Unfortunately, until now there has not been published a detailed history of the combat path of a VVS [voenno-vozdushnye sili (air forces of the Red Army)] aviation regiment. The 812th IAP [istrebitelniy aviatsionniy polk (fighter aviation regiment)] is interesting in this regard because by the results of its combat actions, it surpassed many widely known Soviet fighter regiments that received formal "guards" recognition. The 812th IAP retained its original designation. The pilots of this regiment fought practically all their air battles in Yakovlev fighters (Yak-1, Yak-7 and various modifications of Yak-9); they mastered the new Yak-3 fighters that were being introduced to the forces. And the mastery of the new equipment cost the lives of pilots. It was this regiment that conducted field testing of the Yak-9K fighter [to be introduced in Volume 2], armed with the 45mm aviation cannon. In doing this, the pilots and aviation mechanics of the regiment acquired unique experience in the combat employment of the "flying cannon". By the close of the war, the regiment had destroyed more than 500 enemy aircraft (among them an Me262), and by this measure was **among the top ten most productive units of the Soviet VVS.**

The goal of this work is to inform the reader concerning this unusual combat unit and in doing so, by the example of this unit show how at the price of trial and error the training of the regiment's pilots and ground personnel was conducted, and how methods, tactics, and devices for employing the Yak fighters in aerial combat, patrolling, bomber escort, and attack of ground targets were developed and perfected. The reader will be able to find for himself something new (or not known before) concerning the largest aerial conflict in the skies of the Kuban in 1943, that were later named the "Kuban Meat Grinder". And by the example of the regiment's losses the reader will come to understand why this grandiose air battle had such an unflattering name. In the story of this unit the reader will learn also of the air battles in the skies of southern Ukraine, Crimea, Lithuania, Poland, and Germany.

While working on this book, the authors did not forget that not only machines and engines were fighting in the air. Human beings, with their achievements and shortcomings, various levels of experience and skill, and various temperaments and emotions were guiding them. From this book it is possible to see what motives, passions, and pressures (borne by all people) tested both the pilots of the regiment and its ground personnel during the period of combat employment.

Vlad Antipov

The motivation for our decision regarding the beginning of this quest is simple and understandable. At the present time, detailed information clearly is inadequate. Either it is absent entirely or for various reasons distorted, or sometimes simply unconfirmed. It is sufficient only to say that the names of all the pilots of the 812th Regiment who died, and in a majority of cases a brief description, date, region, and circumstances of their death are published for the first time in this work.

We would like those who read this work to add to their knowledge of the air combat on the Eastern front by example of the history of the combat life of the 812th Fighter Regiment, which, like drops of water, reflects the "ocean" of the combat employment, front-line life, and philosophy of fighter regiments of the Soviet VVS. In this we attempted to avoid any kind of "adornment" and excessive pathos, trying to approach to a description of events with maximum objectivity and consideration.

We wish that enthusiasts and military history afficionados would want, first of all, that we not hurry, that we not jump to conclusions in evaluations until that moment when all the available information about the air war on the Eastern front from the most varied number of sources can be processed and analyzed. Only by avoiding one-sidedness in views, characteristic of the past period of the Cold War, is it possible on the basis of comparing information to arrive at their own original conclusions as to the role and evaluation of the combat employment of equipment and to understand the motives and philosophy of the opposing sides of this most destructive war in the history of humankind. For the people of the last century, twice in one hundred years time was divided into two parts—"wartime" and "pre-wartime". The authors sincerely hope that the readers of this book will never have to measure their own lifetimes by these two periods.

Igor Utkin

Vlad Antipov, Moscow, Russia

Igor Utkin, Kharkov, Ukraine

Full Regiment Title and Battle Honors

812th "Sevastopol" Red Banner, Order of Suvorov III Degree, Fighter Aviation Regiment.

Honorific title "Sevastopol"
Order of the Supreme Commander in Chief No. 136 of 14 May 1944.

Order of the Red Banner
"For exemplary fulfillment of the command's missions in combat with the German invaders during the forcing of the River Berezina, for capture of the town Borisov, and for the valor and courage displayed during these actions."
Order of the Presidium of the Supreme Soviet of the USSR of 10 July 1944.

Order of Suvorov III Degree
Order of the Presidium of the Supreme Soviet of the USSR of 28 May 1945.

The **812th IAP** was one of the standard formation regiments of the VVS that reached the 500-victory level and had to its credit, among the downed enemy aircraft, a victory over the Me262 jet fighter. It is not clear why, but not one of the three regiments of the 265th IAD [istrebitelnaya aviatsionnaya diviziya (fighter aviation division)], including the 812th IAP, received the "guards" rank, though by their indicators they surpassed other regiments who were honored more than once. Five pilots who served in the 812th IAP were awarded the rank Hero of the Soviet Union: Ye. Ye. Ankudinov, D. V. Dzhabidze, P. T. Tarasov, A. T. Tishchenko, and I. V. Fedorov. Five pilots executed a ram during this period: F. K. Svezhentsev (8 May 1943), I. V. Fedorov (10 May 1943), N. A. Konovalov (1 October 1943), S. V. Belkin (31 July 1944), and A. I. Filippov (20 January 1945).

The stylized image of a bird's wing on the Yak cowling became the calling card of the entire 3rd IAK [istrebitelniy aviatsionniy korpus (fighter aviation corps)], including the 812th IAP. This symbol, as well as the callsign of the commander of the 3rd Corps, General-Mayor Ye. Ya. Savitskiy—"Dragon", were known during the time of the basic conflicts of the Great Patriotic War (GPW) on both sides of the front during the battles for the Kuban, southern Ukraine, and Crimea, during the liberation of Belorussia, Lithuania, and Poland, and during the capture of Berlin. And though the callsign of the regiment's pilots was "Skvorets" [Starling], just the same they were genuine "dragons" in the air.

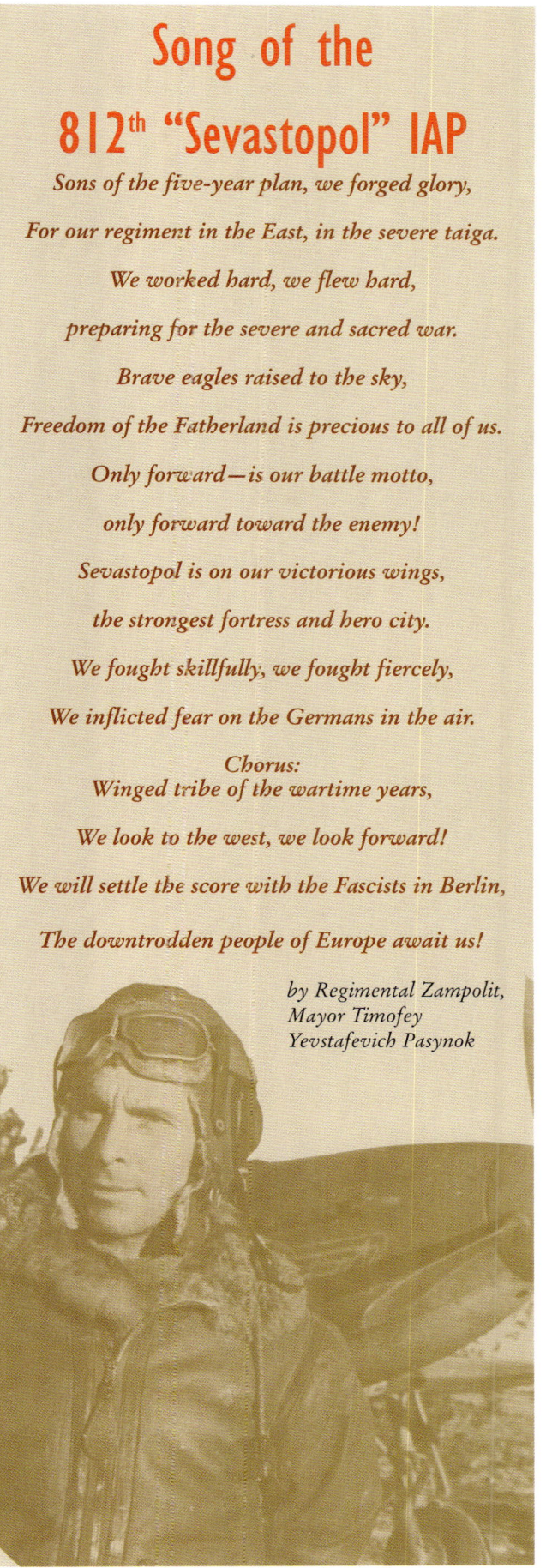

Song of the 812th "Sevastopol" IAP

Sons of the five-year plan, we forged glory,

For our regiment in the East, in the severe taiga.

We worked hard, we flew hard,

preparing for the severe and sacred war.

Brave eagles raised to the sky,

Freedom of the Fatherland is precious to all of us.

Only forward—is our battle motto,

only forward toward the enemy!

Sevastopol is on our victorious wings,

the strongest fortress and hero city.

We fought skillfully, we fought fiercely,

We inflicted fear on the Germans in the air.

Chorus:
Winged tribe of the wartime years,

We look to the west, we look forward!

We will settle the score with the Fascists in Berlin,

The downtrodden people of Europe await us!

by Regimental Zampolit, Mayor Timofey Yevstafevich Pasynok

1942: In Defense of Moscow and Stalingrad

An original Russian map illustrating the Stalingrad counter-offensive

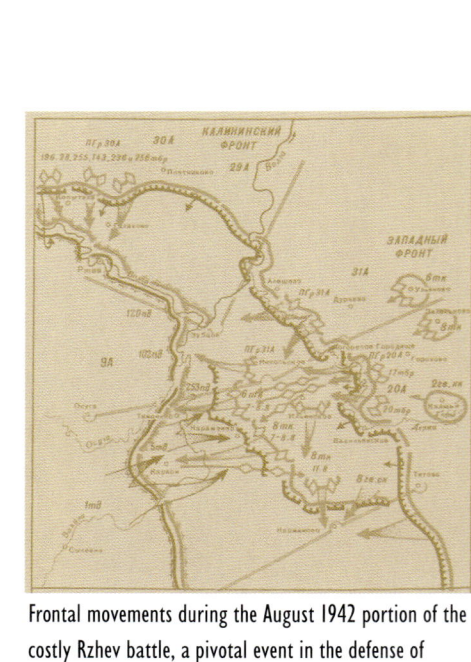

Frontal movements during the August 1942 portion of the costly Rzhev battle, a pivotal event in the defense of Moscow, are depicted on this map

Memorial at Lyubertsy, the site of the former Moscow Military District airfield where the 812th IAP was formed.
Vlad Antipov

Birth in Unequal Battles

The day of the birth and formation of the 812th regiment was Thursday, 26 March 1942. It was formed on the initiative of the commander of the Moscow Military District forces, General Polkovnik P. A. Artemev. Back on 7 March 1942 he had appealed by letter to the commander-in-chief of the Air Forces of the Red Army [VVS], General Polkovnik of Aviation P. F. Zhigarev. In the letter he stated that, "At the present time, the troops of the Moscow defensive zone, who are deployed in fortified regions, are completely exposed to air attack; my long-range artillery does not have forward air controllers, and the Air Forces of the Moscow Military District does not have any combat units assigned to it for coordination with ground forces. I seek your permission to form, by 1 April this year, three fighter air regiments and to locate them at Kubinka, Maloyaroslavets, and Kaluga." In response, on 26 March the commander-in-chief of the Air Forces of the Red Army ordered, "For coverage of the forces located in fortified regions of the Moscow defensive zone, by 1 May 1942 form and train for combat employment the 812th Fighter Aviation Regiment at Kubinka airfield, equipped with Yak-1 aircraft."

Young pilots who had just graduated from flight school began to arrive in the town Lyubertsy [just outside the current Moscow ring road east-southeast of the city], where one of the central airfields of the Moscow Military District was located. Maintenance personnel who had been transferred to the front from reserve regiments arrived at the airfield right behind the flight crews. Mayor I. K. Lokhin was named the first regiment

commander, and Mayor S. V. Lepilin became the chief of staff. The regiment was quickly issued equipment, which consisted of 10 well-worn *Ishaks* [Polikarpov I-16 *Donkeys*] and two Yak-7s for training and familiarization. Although they received such worn-out aircraft, the pilots continued to master the tactics for the conduct of aerial combat. Virtually every pilot familiarized with the Yaks assigned to the regiment.

In May 1942, the personnel of the regiment flew to Shumino airfield, where the long-anticipated Yaks quickly began to arrive. Twenty-two aircraft were flown in from Saratov aviation plant and everyone joked that the regiment had finally become a real combat entity. Having experienced the Yak-7, the pilots quickly mastered the Yak-1. In early June, a command component for the 263rd Fighter Aviation Division [IAD] was established in order to bring together the newly formed 812th, 813th and 814th Fighter Aviation Regiments. The regiment was sent to the front as part of this division on 26 July 1942.

As it turned out, the 812th IAP participated – albeit only briefly – in the two largest battles (measured by the scale of losses) of that difficult year. The first was the Rzhev offensive. To this day, the significance of this battle has not been recognized in the official historiography, though the military actions on the Moscow axis (January 1942 to March 1943) of the central sector of the Soviet-German front can, with full basis, be regarded as among the bloodiest battles of the Great Patriotic War.

To backtrack a little, the situation that unfolded in the course of December 1941 with the counteroffensive of Soviet forces around Moscow, and later during the Rzhev-Vyazma offensive operation (January-April 1942) resulted in the formation of a bulge in the front line on the Moscow axis. Inside this bulge was the most important railroad for the supply of German forces, which connected the two towns Rzhev and Vyazma. German

Irreplaceable chief of staff, 812th IAP Mayor Serafim Vasilyevich Lepilin.

Ivan Fedorov (standing) and Georgiy Churakov, 534th IAP, Pereyaslavka airfield, Khabarovsk kray, late 1941. Note the map of the Pacific Theater and probable enemy - Japan - on the wall. These close friends were part of the initial cadre of "Far Easterners" who became the heart and soul of the 812th. Fedorov survived the war as ace and Hero of the Soviet Union. Six victory ace Churakov was not as fortunate. After his tragic death in the fall of 1943, Fedorov memorialized his good friend and pair leader by having "For Georgiy" painted on the fuselage of his Yak.

Army Group Center created powerful fortifications inside this bulge. Multiple attempts by the Soviet command to liquidate these had failed.

After the conclusion of the exceptionally difficult and bloody first Rzhev-Vyazma operation, preparation began in May and June for a large-scale offensive operation with the goal of destroying the German forces within the bulge. However the events on the southern sector of the Soviet-German front interfered in its conduct. More importantly, the forces of Western and Kalinin Fronts, which had ended up in the enemy's rear after the winter campaign, had to conduct fierce defensive battles against troops of the central German grouping through May and July 1942. After suffering great losses, a portion of the Soviet troops managed to break out of encirclement.

At the end of July 1942, forces of Kalinin and Western Fronts once again attempted to destroy a portion of the enemy forces grouped in the Rzhev-Vyazma bulge. Fierce fighting raged until the end of September. But this, the first Rzhev-Sychevka operation, again concluded in failure. It was here that the 812th IAP received its baptism of fire. For the regiment, the aerial battles on this axis – in contrast to the ground operations of Soviet forces – turned out to be more successful.

On the ground the situation more resembled a long, drawn out nightmare. Skipping ahead, it must be said that only at the end of March 1943 was this dangerous bridgehead close to Moscow finally liquidated. Having lasted from January 1942 until March 1943, the Rzhev battle cost was, by various evaluations, from 1 to 2 million in total personnel losses for the Red Army.

Operating from the Dulovo airfield (the village Dulovo, Kanakovskiy rayon, Tver oblast), which was located in the zone of actions of Kalinin Front, the regiment executed 141 combat sorties and conducted 14 aerial battles during the period 29 July through 8 August 1942. Its pilots destroyed 13 Bf109s, three Ju88s, and one Fw189. The regiment scored its first kill of the Great Patriotic War [GPW] on the first day of its arrival at the front. Here is a note from the combat actions journal for that day:

Upon approach to the airfield Klimovo (8 km from the front line), we spotted an enemy FW-type aircraft. Starshiy Leytenant Nezolya and Leytenant Tolkachev attacked the enemy force. The enemy aircraft was hit and went down in the area

of Aleshki village (13 km northwest of Klimovo). According to testimony of the inhabitants, one of the pilots perished and the second was captured. The aircraft of Nezolya and Tolkachev each received two hits. Confirmation of the destruction of the enemy Focke-Wulf was received from a squadron commander of the 648th IAP and one of his crews.

For Starshiy Leytenant Pavel Nezolya this aerial victory was already his fourth in the early period of the GPW. He had arrived in the 812th IAP from the fabled 6th IAP (subsequently 18th Vitebsk GIAP), with which he had gained three victories: two Fokker D.XXI and one Ju88 in August 1941 on the Northwest axis.

Air battles fought on 2 and 3 August were even more productive. On 2 August two Bf109s were shot down. The following day, the regiment's pilots claimed victories over 11 Bf109s in four group aerial engagements. Starshiy Leytenant V. Veremeyenko, scoring one shared and two individual kills on this day, was particularly

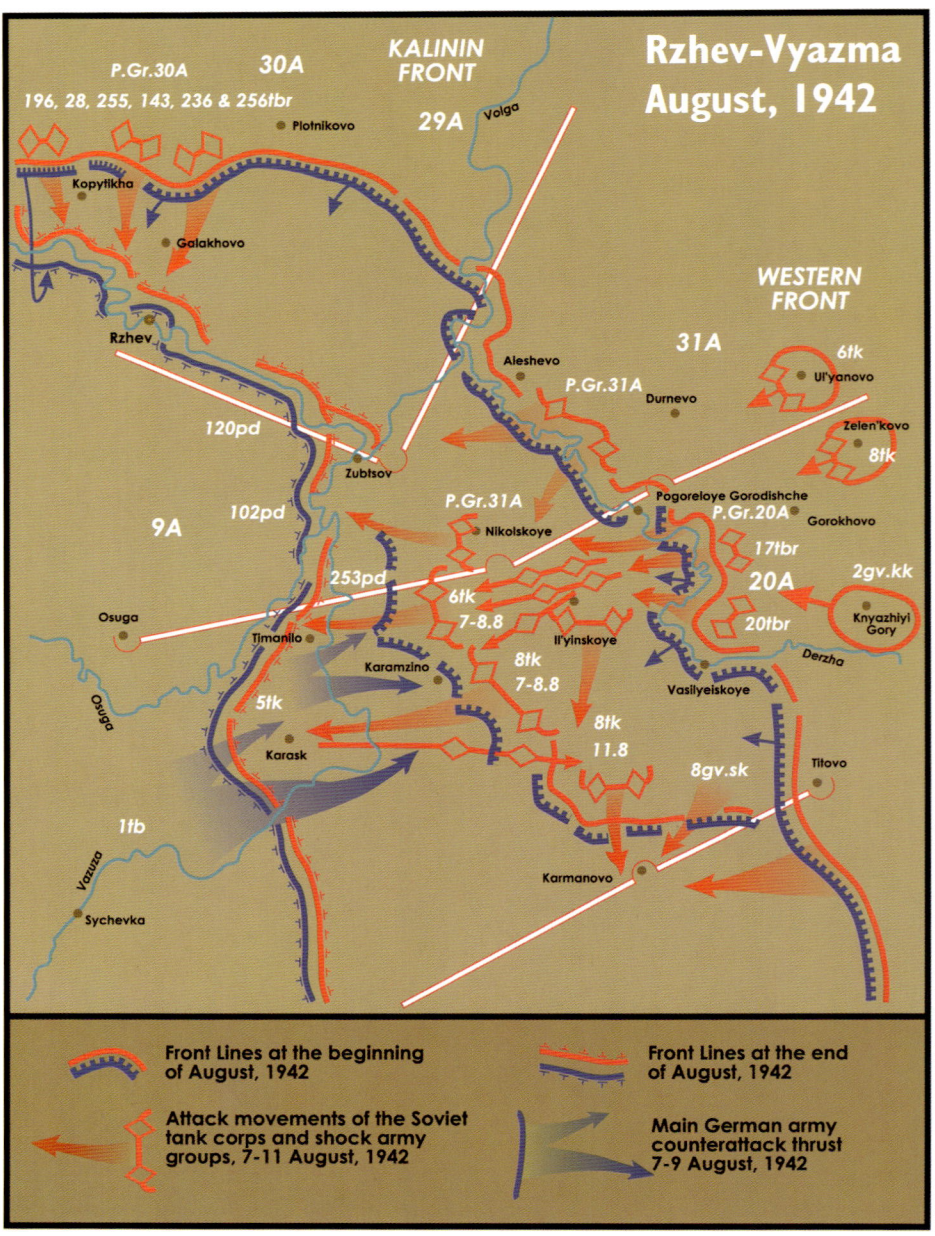

Rzhev-Vyazma August, 1942

KALININ FRONT

WESTERN FRONT

P.Gr.30A 30A
196, 28, 255, 143, 236 & 256tbr

29A
Volga

Plotnikovo

Kopytikha

Galakhovo

Rzhev

Aleshevo

31A

6tk
Ul'yanovo

Durnevo

P.Gr.31A

Zelen'kovo

8tk

120pd

Zubtsov

Pogoreloye Gorodishche
P.Gr.20A

Gorokhovo

9A

102pd

P.Gr.31A

Nikolskoye

17tbr

20A

2gv.kk

253pd

6tk
7-8.8

Il'inskoye

8tk
7-8.8

20tbr

Knyazhiyi Gory

Derzha

Osuga

Timanilo

Karamzino

Vasilyeiskoye

Osuga

5tk

8tk
11.8

Titovo

Karask

8gv.sk

1tb

Vazuza

Karmanovo

Sychevka

Front Lines at the beginning of August, 1942

Front Lines at the end of August, 1942

Attack movements of the Soviet tank corps and shock army groups, 7-11 August, 1942

Main German army counterattack thrust 7-9 August, 1942

For our Soviet Motherland!
USSR
Certificate
For participation in the heroic defense of
Stalingrad
Starshina Korneyev, Pavel Vasilyevich
By decree of the Presidium of the Supreme Soviet of
the USSR
of 22 December 1942 is awarded the medal
For Defense of Stalingrad
On behalf of the Presidium of the Supreme Soviet of
the USSR the medal has been awarded on
3 August 1943.
Commander of the 812th Fighter Aviation Regiment
Mayor Nikolayenkov

GPW participant. Aviation mechanic Pavel Vasilyevich Korneyev, 3rd Squadron, 812th IAP

"All my life my thoughts remained in the war and in this regiment. I arrived at the regiment at age 21 and was with it from the very beginning to the end. This was a very great endeavor!"

P.V. Korneyev

outstanding. Kapitan Andrey Yefremov and Serzhant N. Matveyev each had two kills on Monday, 3 August. The impact of such a large number of German fighters downed in two days can hardly be exaggerated. The primary opponent of the 812th IAP on the Rzhev-Dugino sector of the front, JG51 "Molders", lost 10 Bf109Fs on 2 August. Among the dead and wounded German pilots dispatched to hospitals was the commander of III./JG51, Hauptmann Richard Leppla. On 3 August the Germans lost another seven Bf109Fs. One pilot was killed and three others were wounded (by coincidence, all three were oberleutnants). One of the wounded was Oberleutnant Gottfried Schlitzer, who had 25 victories to his credit. He later died from his wounds in hospital.

This baptism of fire on the Kalinin Front emboldened the young pilots; the more so that the regiment did not suffer any losses. After breaking in their Yak-1s in combat and having learned how to defeat the enemy, the regiment gave up their aircraft and went into VVS reserve on 9 September; with that, they were transferred to an airfield near the village of Stepygino, 50 kilometers from Moscow.

Reforming into a two-squadron table of organization and equipment (TOE), the regiment was assigned to the recently formed 283rd IAD on 24 September.[1] This division, commanded by Polkovnik V. A. Kitayev, included the 431st, 520th, and 563rd IAP with a total of 23 combat aircrews available. Having flown to Altukhov airfield (near Stalingrad), the 812th IAP along with the 520th IAP, located at the same airfield, began combat flight operations on the Stalingrad axis.

Since the 812th IAP fought on the Stalingrad axis as part of the 16th Air Army [VA (vozdushnaya armiya)], it is appropriate to say a few words about this famed air formation of the fall period of 1942. The air army began to be formed on 8 August 1942. General-Mayor of Aviation P. S. Stepanov was named as its temporary commander, with General-Mayor of Aviation S. I. Rudenko as the deputy. Later, on 28 September 1942, General Rudenko assumed command. It began its combat path from Stalingrad to Berlin under his leadership. Formation building

Aircrew Roster of 812th IAP on the Kalinin Front at the Beginning of August 1942

Command
Regiment Commander: Mayor I. K. Lokhin
Regiment Chief of Staff: S. V. Lepilin
Regiment Navigator: Starshiy Leytenant V. T. Veremeyenko

1st Squadron
Commander: Kapitan I. M. Yuzhakov
Deputy Commander and Flight Commander:
    Starshiy Leytenant P. G. Nezolya
Flight Commander: Leytenant A. M. Prikhodko
    Pilots
Mladshiy Leytenant N. A. Tolkachev
Mladshiy Leytenant V. K. Chekanikhin
Starshiy Serzhant N. G. Matveyev
Serzhant B. A. Kvitko
Serzhant V. G. Koledov

2nd Squadron
Commander: Kapitan I. K. Solyannikov
Deputy Commander: Kapitan A. A. Yefremov
Flight Commander: Starshiy Leytenant L. S. Limarenko
Flight Commander: Leytenant V. A. Mishachev
    Pilots
Starshiy Serzhant M. T. Gavrilov
Starshiy Serzhant V. G. Baranov
Starshiy Serzhant I. Ya. Kostrykin
Serzhant I. A. Lukyanov

continued until 4 September. By this time a number of divisions had been transferred to it from the 8th VA, including the 220th IAD of Polkovnik A.V. Utin (43rc, 211th, 237th, 512th, 581st, and 867th IAP, equipped with Yak-1 aircraft, and later the 291st IAP in the LaGG-3) and the 228th ShAD (Ground Attack Aviation Division [shturmovaya aviatsionnaya diviziya]) of Polkovnik V.V. Stepichev, equipped with Il-2 *Shturmoviks*.

At the same time the 283rd IAD (431st, 520th, 563rd, and later,

"Combat Path". This was the unofficial handwritten diary of the 812th IAP. It was maintained, albeit irregularly as dictated by the nature of intensive combat operations, in the regiment during the events described in this book. The page spread shown here contains the text of an order concerning the 8th ZIAP, and shows a photo (see chapter 2) pasted into a rather well drawn ornamental background.

812th IAP, equipped with Yak-1 fighters) under the command of Polkovnik V. A. Kitayev arrived from the Stavka reserve. Also from the reserve came the 291st Composite Aviation Division (SAD [smeshannaya aviatsionnaya diviziya]), under the command of HSU Podpolkovnik A. N. Vitruk, with its constituent 243rd, 245th and 954th ShAPs on Il-2s and 30th Bomber Aviation Regiment (BAP [bombardirovichnyy aviatsionniy polk]) in Pe-2s. This division was later renamed the 291st ShAD with the 30th BAP replaced by the 313th ShAP. At the beginning of September, the 598th and 970th Light Bomber Aviation Regiments (LBAP [legkiy bombardirovochniy aviatsionniy polk]) in Po-2s were also assigned to 16th VA.

Readers should not be misled by the ostentatious moniker *air army* and the multitude of units and formations thus assigned. On 4 September 1942 it had only 152 serviceable aircraft (42 fighters, 79 Shturmoviks, and 31 light bombers) available to it,[2] based on unimproved airfields north of Stalingrad. Altogether, the VVS on the Stalingrad axis, comprising the 8th VA, 16th VA, and 102nd IAD of the Air Defense Forces (PVO [protivo-vozdushnaya oborona]), had available 738 aircraft (113 daylight bombers, 71 night bombers, 241 Shturmoviks, and 313 fighters) at the beginning of September. An additional 150-200 bombers were brought in from Long Range Aviation (ADD [aviatsiya dalnego deystviya]).

The Stalingrad battle continued with uninterrupted growing efforts of the forces of both sides over the course of six and one-half months (from 17 July 1942 until 2 February 1943). Through the first four months, in stubborn defensive battles – first in the great bend of the Don River, later on the approaches to Stalingrad and then in the city itself – Soviet forces exhausted the massive enemy grouping that was reaching toward the Volga River and forced it over to the defensive. In the last two and one-half months the Red Army counteroffensive broke through enemy forces northwest and south of Stalingrad, surrounding, and liquidating its 300-thousand-strong army.

In their fierceness and the numbers of aircraft operating from both sides, the aerial battles that unfolded here differed greatly from those in which the pilots of 812th IAP had fought on the Kalinin Front. On 12 September, when the enemy was approaching Stalingrad from both the west and southwest, the subsequent defense of Stalingrad was entrusted to the 62nd Army of General-Leytenant V. I. Chuykov and the 64th Army of General-Mayor M. S. Shumilov. Fierce street fighting erupted in the outskirts of the city. The regiment's first loss occurred on Friday, 25 September, when the Yak-1 flown by Serzhant Boris Kvitko was shot down. The regiment's pilots, who had never before this moment lost a comrade in battle, realized that a serious enemy was facing them: Ju87 bombers from StG2 and Bf109s from JG3 "Udet".

The regiment staff summary for 29 September reads as follows:

> *Sortie to escort Il-2 in the area of Krasnyy Oktyabr, west of Stalingrad. four Yak-1s sortied at 6:45-7:55. Starshiy Leytenant Veremeyenko shot down 1 Bf109, the pilot of which bailed out. During an aerial engagement near Akhtuba and Dubovka they encountered the Il-2s and covered them to their airfield.*

On the morning of 10 October the combat pair of Yefremov and Baranov shot down Luftwaffe *experte* Erwin Straznicky (Bf109G-2 Wr.N 13663, *Black 16*) 50km (30 mi.) N-NW of Stalingrad. Meanwhile, battles on the near approaches to the city began on 30 September and continued until 12 October. They concluded with the arrival of German forces at the city's defensive ring. On 15 October the enemy managed to break through to the Volga in a narrow sector near the Stalingrad tractor factory. October 1942 arrived, the most difficult month of 1942 for the 812th IAP. On Tuesday, 6 October, the regiment airfield at Altukhov was subjected to a bombing attack by eight Ju87s escorted by five Bf109s. The raid damaged three Yak-1s. Two days later the pilots managed to successfully intercept a group of Stukas from I/StG2 in the area of their airfield.[3]

A Yak-7UTI trainer. Given that many of its early pilots were transitioning from the earlier generation of radial-engined open-cockpit biplanes and monoplanes, the 812th IAP's first Yaks were of this type.

During a mid-November Shturmovik escort mission in the Stalingrad area, four of the 812th's fighters encountered six Bf109s. In the ensuing dogfight, Serzhant Vakhromeyev was forced to bail out of this early-production Yak-1.

Having sortied under the command of Mayor D. Rodin (transferred in from the neighboring 520th IAP and named commander of the 1st Squadron after the death of Kapitan I. Yuzhakov), 10 Yak-1s attacked the bomber formation. The mayor shot down the Ju87D (coded T6+EL) of Feldwebel Ernst Graudenz with a long burst of fire. Bf109s that rushed to the battle scene attacked the fighters of 812th IAP. As a result, Starshiy Leytenant Limorenko was shot down and Serzhant Koledov had to make a forced landing with a dead engine. According to pilot reports, three Bf109s were damaged during this combat.

On the following day, the regiment's pilots shot down three aircraft—1 each Bf109, Ju87 and Ju88—in the areas of Konnaya and Kotluban. On 12 October, three Bf109s conducted a surprise attack on a pair of Yak-1s, destroying 1 Yak (bort 04).[4] On 21 October the regiment destroyed another Ju87. Two days later the Yak-1s of Starshina Baranov and Serzhant Koplev were shot down in aerial engagements with Bf109s. Both pilots survived and soon returned to the regiment. On the following day, a battle between four Yak-1s and four Bf109Fs ended in the downing of the Yak-1 (bort 25) of Serzhant Kulayev. Once again, the pilot survived. The number of aircraft in the regiment continued to fall, while altogether, in October, the pilots of 812th IAP shot down 18 enemy aircraft.

On 10 November the regiment flew to Perfilov airfield, from which they primarily flew escort for groups of Il-2s from the 291st ShAD. Over the Kletskaya area on Saturday, 14 November, the pair of Kapitan V. Veremeyenko shot down a Bf109 that had attempted to attack the two Shturmoviks they were escorting. Staffel 9 of JG3 recorded the loss of the Bf109F-4 of

Unteroffizier Werner Rose in an aerial engagement on this day. The second sortie of the day, again in escort of Shturmoviks, was characterized by heavy combat between four Yak-1s and six Bf109s. As a result of this engagement, the Yak-1 (bort 24) of Serzhant Vakhromeyev was downed and the pilot forced to bail out.

The defensive portion of the Stalingrad battle concluded on 18 November 1942. During the four months of combat between the Don and the Volga, the enemy lost approximately 250,000 men and a large amount of combat equipment. Soviet forces lost more than 640,000 men, of whom approximately 384,000 could not be immediately replaced. The defense of Stalingrad broke Hitler's plan. Nonetheless, the conditions necessary for Soviet forces to go over to a decisive counteroffensive were thus created.

At 0720 on 19 November 1942, the counteroffensive was launched with the opening salvoes from 7,000 guns and multiple rocket launchers. The forces of the Southwest Front, advancing from the Serafimovich and Kletsk areas, broke through the 3rd Romanian Army defenses on the first day and continued moving east toward Kalach and Sovetskiy. At the spearhead of this main effort were the 5th Tank and 21st Armies, supported by aviation from the 2nd and 17th Air Armies. Five Romanian divisions were encircled in the Raspopinskaya area on the third day of the offensive. Battles in the offensive zone of the Don Front, whose forces were supported by the aviation from the 16th Air Army, were extremely intense. By 19 November the 16th VA had 342 aircraft (of which 249 were serviceable)—103 Shturmoviks, 125 fighters, 93 night bombers, seven reconnaissance, and 14 liaison aircraft. Altogether by the beginning of the counteroffensive, the Southwest, Don, and Stalingrad Fronts had 1,350 serviceable

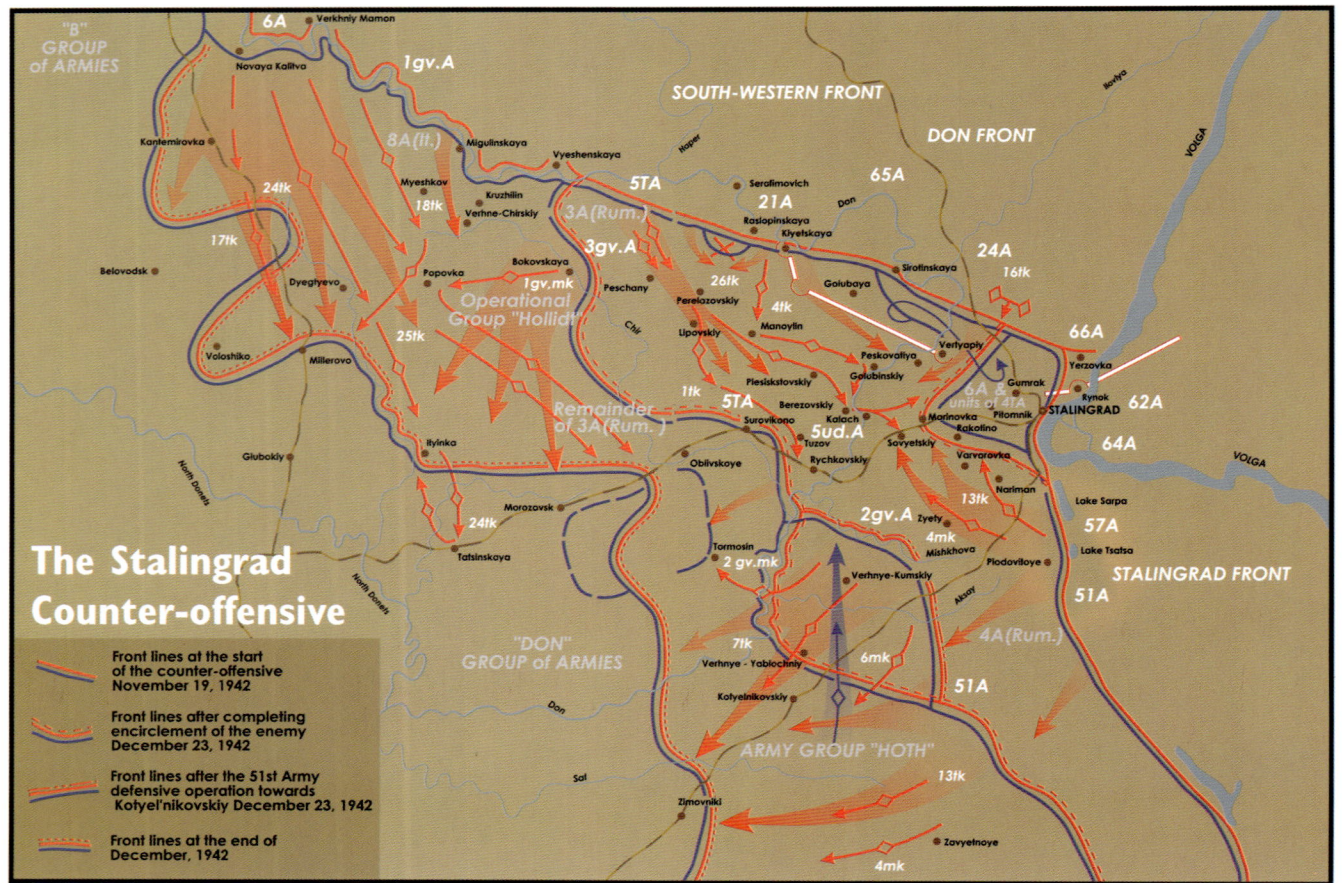

The Stalingrad Counter-offensive

Front lines at the start of the counter-offensive November 19, 1942

Front lines after completing encirclement of the enemy December 23, 1942

Front lines after the 51st Army defensive operation towards Kotyel'nikovskiy December 23, 1942

Front lines at the end of December, 1942

Stalingrad 1942. The original of this photograph is preserved in the documentation center for the most recent history of Volgograd (Stalingrad's presnt-day name) oblast. Photographer unknown.
TsDNIV

German pilots taken captive at Stalingrad. Left to right: Feldwebel Ernst Graudenz and Josef Sauter, gunner of his Ju87D (T6+EL), shot down on 8 October 1942, and three members of a Ju88A bomber crew (V4+HS) from KGI, shot down on 21 October 1942.
Dmitri Karlenko

aircraft (including 308 Po-2, R-5, and SB night bombers).

From 20 November forces of the Stalingrad Front went over to the offensive as well, launching an attack south of Stalingrad. The 62nd Army fought spoiling attacks in the city. The 8th Air Army supported the actions of this front's forces. Having broken the enemy's defense, they surged to the northwest toward Kalach. On 23 November, lead formations of the Southwest Front linked up with units of the Stalingrad Front in the Kalach-Sovetskiy area. The encirclement of the enemy grouping around Stalingrad had been accomplished. In all 22 divisions, plus 160 separate units, were trapped.

By the end of December, forces of the left wing of the Voronezh, Southwest, and Stalingrad Fronts had defeated the enemy across the boundaries of the encirclement, driving the remnants of their formations back some 150–200 km (95–125 mi.). This created favorable conditions for the liquidation of the enemy forces remaining encircled in and around Stalingrad. In December the attempt to organize the supply of the surrounded forces via air was disrupted, destroying approximately 700 enemy aircraft in the process. Altogether from July 1942 until February 1943, the enemy had lost approximately 1 million soldiers and officers between the Don and the Volga. As a result of the Stalingrad battle, the city of Stalingrad — all the structures and services located in the zone of the fierce fighting — was practically destroyed. Continuous miles of ruins, heaps of burned stones, an utterly destroyed infrastructure, mountains of dead bodies, and endless lines of prisoners attested vividly, for a long time thereafter, to the enormity of the tragedy that had occurred here.

One of the last aircraft shot down by the 812th Regiment on the Stalingrad Front was a Bf109. It was destroyed by Kapitan Veremeyenko's group while escorting Il-2s on 28 November 1942. In the second half of the day two Yak-1s on a reconnaissance of Gumrak airfield observed some Bf109Fs coming to intercept them. One of these Bf109s was on skis.

Attacking this Messerschmitt from above, and seeing it begin to smoke, the pair departed for its own airfield.

The upcoming reorganization, and creation of the fighter corps, affected the fate of 812th IAP. Pilots began to be transferred from the regiment to other formations. One of the regiment's veterans, Mayor Dmitriy Ivanovich Rodin (later KIA on 12 January 1943), was transferred to 283rd IAD headquarters. As a member of the division headquarters flight airborne on Monday, 30 November, he participated in the intercept of 17 Ju52s flying along the Bolshaya Rossoshka—Novo-Mikhaylovskiy—Gumrak route. At approximately 1000 the four Yak-1s, led by division commander Polkovnik Kitayev, intercepted the Ju52 group and their escort of four Bf109s. An aerial engagement ensued at an altitude of 400-500 meters (1500-1600 feet), as a result of which five of the transports were shot down and a sixth damaged. Polkovnik Kitayev and Mayor Yeleseyev scored two aircraft each, while Mayor Rodin downed one.

Altogether during the period 22 September to 1 December 1942, the pilots of 812th Fighter Regiment flew 856 combat sorties, conducted 52 group aerial engagements, and destroyed 30 Bf109s, 10 Ju87s, two Ju88s, and two He111s. During these actions the regiment lost five pilots in combat.

2

Spring and Summer 1943:
In the Skies of the Kuban

The command element of the 812th IAP. First row: T. Pasynok, A. Yeremin, S. Lepilin. Second row: D. Nikolayenkov, I. Batychko, F. Svezhentsev.

Bagay-Baranovka airfield, late February 1943. Command and flight crews of 812ᵗʰ IAP, together with leadership of 8ᵗʰ ZIAP. In the first row from left to right: Mayor T. Pasynok, Mayor A. Yeremin, and three of the commanding officers from 8ᵗʰ ZIAP

On Tuesday, 1 December 1942, the 431ˢᵗ and 812ᵗʰ IAPs (of the 283ʳᵈ IAD) turned their aircraft over to other regiments and left for a due-course reconstitution at the 3ʳᵈ Reserve Aviation Brigade (ZAB — zapasnaya aviatsionnaya brigada) located at Bagay-Baranovka airfield [the largest airfield base in the area] in the Volga Military District. In connection with the transition of the regiment to a three-squadron structure, a large number of pilots were transferred to the 520ᵗʰ IAP (56ᵗʰ GIAP).[5] For the former 2ⁿᵈ Squadron deputy commander, Kapitan Andrey Andreyevich Yefremov, this meant he would not see his old regiment again until the victorious year of 1945 on German territory. By that time he would be a mayor and as a member of the 176ᵗʰ GIAP, with 13 personal and 12 shared victories to his credit. Only then would he hear tell of how his former cohort flew and fought. By that time practically no one remained of the original 1942-era regiment wherein he achieved his first victory.

On 12 December 1942, the 534ᵗʰ IAP was partially transferred from the Far East (Pereyaslovka airfield, some 60 kilometers [37 miles] south of Khabarovsk) to the west. Its 32 pilots, under the command of Mayor A.U. Yeremin, arrived at the 13ᵗʰ Reserve Fighter Aviation Regiment (ZIAP [zapasniy istrebitelniy aviatsionniy polk]) base in the city of Kuznetsk. Due partly to the fact that they had flown only Chaikas [I-153 Seagull] and Ishaks (I-16 Donkey) before this, and partly due to bad weather in the 13ᵗʰ ZIAP basing region (i.e. allowing little or no time Yak conversion training), these pilots were immediately transferred to the 8ᵗʰ ZIAP at Bagay-Baranovka airfield. Here they were merged into the air crew roster of 812ᵗʰ IAP. The *second birth* of the regiment had thus begun. This new cohort—the *far easterners*—replaced the fallen and those who had departed to other units. Soon thereafter they would endure their first encounters with the enemy in the *Battle for the Kuban*, as part of the 3ʳᵈ IAK Reserve of the Supreme High Command (RVGK [reserv verkhovnogo glavnokomandovaniya]).[6] This battle would later assume a less pleasant but more descriptive name—*The Kuban Meat Grinder.*

Second Birth

New leadership for the regiment was appointed: Mayor Aleksey Ustinovich Yeremin was named commander, Mayor Serafim Vasilyevich Lepilin was named chief of staff, and Mayor Timofey Yevstafevich Pasynok was named deputy commander for political affairs (zampolit). The *far eastern* pilots, along with maintenance staff called up from the reserve, comprised the foundation of the reconstituted regiment. Leytenant Aleksandr Trofimovich Tishchenko, a flight commander within the 534ᵗʰ IAP's 1ˢᵗ Squadron at that time, recalled:

At the end of 1942, the regiment's pilots gave up their "Chaikas" to new owners, shook hands with all their combat comrades—mechanics, technicians, engine mechanics—and left on the fast train that ran from Vladivostok to Moscow. Shortly before departure changes occurred in the regiment leadership. Mayor Yeremin was named commander. Well-built and quiet, with a demanding bass voice and tough chin, he exuded command presence. Nonetheless, we accepted his arrival without particular enthusiasm. Yeremin was a new person to the regiment; people did not know him and we hadn't had the opportunity to look him over. And we were being sent to the front. Kapitan Nikolayenkov, previously the commander of the Squadron, was named as deputy regiment commander for flight training. Of modest height and smart appearance, he was a good pilot and enjoyed authority among his subordinates. As soon as we crossed Lake Baikal, Mayor Yeremin assembled the leadership personnel and informed them that we were going to a reserve regiment. We would be transitioning to new aircraft. But what aircraft would they give us? Wouldn't it be nice to get Yaks? In the remaining days of our journey we never gave up hope that our dream would be fulfilled. And they were. As soon as we arrived at our new station, they began to transition us to the Yak-1 fighter.[7]

Kapitan Ivan Batychko, commander of the 1st squadron

Instructor and Fighter Pilot Aleksey Mashenkin.
"We 'kidnapped' this experienced, neat, and cultured instructor, Comrade Mashenkin, at the 8th ZAP. He soon became a member of our friendly combat family. Together with us, he passed through the difficult far-eastern school. He dazzled us equally with his piloting skill at low altitude and his fantastic smile, which emphasized his great strength of will."
Regiment staff in "Combat Path."

For the pilots of the 534th IAP, who had acquired good flying habits in piloting the I-15bis, I-153 and I-16, the Yak-1 fighter was an unfamiliar machine. Yet their basis of piloting knowledge enabled them to fly solo after just two or three orientation flights. An 8th ZIAP order recognized the 812th Regiment as an example to other units undergoing training at this same place and time. The pilots particularly liked their instructor, Starshina Aleksey Mashenkin, who also remembered this period:

Winter 1942-43 in Povolzhe was fierce. At times the mercury column fell below 40° [C.]. And despite this, we pilots of the 8th Reserve Fighter Aviation Regiment prepared replacement aviation regiments for the front. At that time our reserve regiment was based, and accomplished its training mission, not far from Saratov. One of the aviation divisions of the 3rd Fighter Corps, commanded by Polkovnik Ye. Ya. Savitskiy, who subsequently would be promoted to the high rank of Marshal and become a Twice Hero of the Soviet Union, arrived at our regiment. This division, and all the regiments of the corps, was from the Far East. They had good habits, were disciplined, and had an unquenchable thirst to depart rapidly for the front in order to engage the enemy. It was my duty, as an instructor pilot of the reserve regiment, to train the pilots of the 812th Fighter Aviation Regiment and help them to master the techniques of piloting the Yak-1 fighter. In the Far East the pilots of this regiment flew the I-153, or "Chaika", as they called their "hawk" in recognition of a unique feature of its construction. The pilots of 812th IAP judged the Yak-1 fighter based on its combat qualities and fervently thanked me when, after several demonstration flights in a
dual-control version of the fighter, I released them to a single-seat combat fighter for solo flight. Even now I can recall their happy, excited faces.

Having made friends among the pilots of the 812th IAP — especially with pilots of Kapitan Ivan Batychko's 1st Squadron — Mashenkin was distressed that soon he would be left behind in the ZIAP, never to see the enemy in the air. After consulting with the zampolit Mayor Pasynok, the pilots decided to assist their instructor, and made requests to have this outstanding pilot assigned to their unit. Several days later Aleksey Mashenkin "disappeared." Someone said that he left to ferry airplanes, but no one was able to say for sure. Some time later it became clear to everyone where Mashenkin had gone. It turned out that someone was needed to deliver documents to General-Mayor Savitskiy at corps headquarters. The corps commander knew, personally, many of the 534th IAP pilots from his own service in the Far East as this regiment belonged to his 29th IAD when he was still a mayor. Timofey Pasynok assigned this mission to Mashenkin, having given him a letter to Savitskiy with a request to keep this "artist of flight" in the regiment. The letter explained who he was and that he would be of greater use at the front than in the rear. Some time later, Savitskiy gave his approval by telegram. Thus, Mashenkin did not return to the training center, and remained with the 812th IAP.

At the same time that pilots were arriving at Bagay-Baranovka, formation of the 3rd Fighter Aviation Corps was already in progress. By the end of the war this corps was one of the most powerful formations in the VVS. It was planned to include two divisions in the corps TOE. One of these was the reconstituted 265th IAD which, by this time, had acquired combat experience.

Having been assigned the 291st, 402nd, and 812th IAPs, the division and regimental headquarters arrived at Lyubertsy airfield and became engaged in the planning for their mutual coordination.

A few words should be said about the two other "far eastern" regiments of the division which, from this day forth, became neighbors of the 812th IAP and with whom they trained together at the 8th ZIAP (Bagay-Baranovka airfield). The 291st IAP, under the command of Mayor V. S. Simonov, received its complete air crew cohort from the 306th IAP of the Far East Front and its maintenance personnel from the reserves. The 402nd IAP, commanded by Mayor V. V. Papkov, received its air crew component from the 301st IAP of the Far East Front and its maintenance personnel from the 8th ZIAP.

The transition training of the air crews passed relatively quickly. The "far easterners" had good flying skills and, more importantly, a sense of urgency to move to a more modern fighter. The re-training of the engineering personnel occurred in somewhat different conditions, as they had to master the peculiarities of servicing aircraft with liquid-cooled engines in severe winter conditions.

The new leadership for the 265th IAD arrived in Bagay-Baranovka at the end of January 1943. Podpolkovnik A. V. Minayev was replaced by Hero of the Soviet Union, Podpolkovnik Pavel Terentevich Korobkov, a veteran of the war in Spain and the fighting at Khalkhin-Gol. The air crews and the leadership element of the maintenance staff of all three regiments assembled in the reserve regiment's club in the evening. After listening to the reports of the unit commanders, Podpolkovnik Korobkov issued the following instructions:

> *Considering the high skill level of the air crews, conduct the training of the regiments in a compressed manner. We have little time and even less gasoline. I have consulted with your commanders and we have decided to give you two or three demonstration flights in a training aircraft in order for you to practice the techniques of piloting and firing in a combat aircraft, and that is all. So do not waste time, study the aircraft thoroughly on the ground, learn all of its idiosyncrasies and the advantages the Yak enjoys over the fascist aircraft. You will fight the enemy in these aircraft.*[8]

These words from the division commander indicating how quickly they would be in combat further encouraged the pilots; the more so because in the regiment they frequently had meetings with pilots who had been in combat. The veterans shared their experiences and did not conceal from them the true nature of combat. This was no "walk in the park on the banks of the Amur."[9] After completing the transition program, the division received its first practical mission—prepare and ferry to the front (in the Stalingrad area) 60 Yak-1 aircraft (20 per regiment). In bad weather conditions the pilots successfully accomplished this mission. They made their landings near Millerovo, which itself had just been liberated from the fascists.

Having delivered the aircraft, they hurried into the town. For many of the "far east" pilots, who had known war only by Sovinformbyuro [Soviet Information Bureau – the only official

265th IAD commander, HSU Polkovnik Pavel Terentevich Korobkov. Veteran of the Spanish Civil War, Khalkhin-Gol, and Finland. Thanks to a detailed analysis of the combat actions in the Kuban, the tactical doctrine that was later named the "Kuban bookshelf" was independently developed in the headquarters of his division.

information agency providing news releases] newsreels and newspaper reports, the sight of a destroyed town and fresh signs of battle left an indelible impression. Soon the 812th IAP received new aircraft and in early March 1943, as part of the 265th IAD, began their transfer along the Bagay-Baranovka—Lyubertsy—Malino (Mikhnevo) route to Stepygino of the Moscow oblast.

There the pilots learned that the 265th IAD had been included in the TOE of the just then forming 3rd IAK RVGK. General-Mayor Ye. Ya. Savitskiy had been named its commander. At this time the corps was reporting directly to the Stavka of the Supreme High Command and consisted of two divisions (265th and 278th IAD), with three regiments in each.

A tragedy occurred at Stepygino airfield on 4 March: While ground-guiding a Yak-1, an 812th IAP engine mechanic, Mladshiy Serzhant Sitrak Galadzhan, took off along with the airplane for some incomprehensible reason. At 50 meters (160 feet) altitude the airplane fell to the ground. The pilot and the engine mechanic were both killed.[10]

3rd Squadron commander Kapitan Fedor Svezhentsev flew this Yak-1b during the Kuban operation. The canopy glazing of early-manufacture Yak-1bs was generally of poor quality, exhibiting optical distortion and "yellowing" after only a short time in service. Pilots thus preferred to keep the canopy open in flight, closing it only when engaged in actual combat. This aircraft is similar to the subtype flown by Yerimin during the mock battle with "Savitskiy's" Bf109.

Bf109G-2/R6 Wr.Nl3903, formerly "White 13" of JG3 "Udet". Having entered service soon after its manufacture in October 1942, this '109, piloted by Heinrich Blaut (8 victories), force landed near Kotluban after combat with Yak-1s on 8 December 1942. By April it was far from the front, being tested by the LII-VVS, its Luftwaffe ID markings oversprayed with local paints. Oddly the upper engine cowl featured the mounting holes unique to tropical Bf109s, but the werke number suggests that it was not a 'trop' airframe. The Red Army aquired many such aircraft in retaking the various airfields in the Stalingrad area. One such "Messer" while still on such an airfield, was flown by General Savitskiy in mock combat against an 812th IAP Yak-I.

The '109 versus the Yak-1

A Bf109 that was flyable provided excellent service in the training of the division's pilots. This aircraft was of great interest to many pilots, including the corps commander himself, General-Mayor Savitskiy.

> Look at this. I was immediately excited: what kind of airplane is this vaunted enemy fighter? What kind of armament does the Messerschmitt have? What are the Messerschmitt's stronger points compared to our aircraft? What are its vulnerabilities? It was not easy to get permission to fly in this unfamiliar machine, but when they finally permitted it, I wanted to fly this aircraft against one of our pilots in a mock combat. Mayor Yeremin, the commander of 812th Regiment, volunteered to be my opponent. He was an excellent pilot. We went out and came back on a meeting course—as equals, like gentlemen, so to speak. I went into a steep bank, pulling the control stick back into my stomach. The Messer inscribed a high-energy turn. This fighter was sufficiently light on the controls, no complaints. The Messerschmitt completed the turn in 26—29 seconds. But our own Yak, thank God, was a first-class airplane for its time. It flew at a speed of 580 kph (358 mph) and could climb to 5,000 meters (16,000 feet) in 5.4 minutes. It could complete that same turn in 20 seconds. Then I look out and see that Yeremin has already gotten on the tail of my Messerschmitt. Time to maneuver. I threw the airplane into a sharp combat turn. For a moment I separate from the Yak, but then it is hanging on my tail again. Then execute a wing-under reverse and race away from Yeremin. This show battle continued until both aircraft ran out of fuel.[11]

By this time, hundreds of eyes were looking up from the ground in rapt attention, following the trace of the two fighters across the sky and back.

> The Yak-1, with the emblem of the bird wing on the cowling, and the yellow-nosed Messerschmitt fought a "battle". They dropped down to roof-top level, then went straight up, both maneuvering with brilliance, trying to get on the other's tail. Now the Messerschmitt, having reached altitude, came rushing down toward the Yak, passed close by it and, dropping a wing sharply, began a turn. The Yak quickly caught up to it in the turn. The distance between the aircraft began to close. At this moment the Messerschmitt departed steeply upward. They repeated this "dance" several times. We felt that experienced pilots were fighting this "battle". Among all those who were intently observing this demonstration from the ground, there was no agreement as to who was the winner.[12]

This is how A. T. Tishchenko remembered this training battle of the regiment commander, Mayor Yeremin, with the *erstwhile* German, General Savitskiy in the Bf109. The young pilots were able to see with their own eyes the weak and strong aspects of the primary German fighter that they soon would encounter in combat. Aleksandr Ivanov (at that time a serzhant), who was also among the observers of this training battle, recalls:

> We noted for ourselves that although the Messer flew away from the Yak in vertical maneuvers and during dives, in horizontal maneuver the Yak was better. Most importantly, the Yak could turn tighter. Overall the Messer seemed somewhat "sickly."

In order to more quickly and effectively prepare the crews for combat, the corps and division command sent pilots who had front-line experience to the regiments. Hero of the Soviet Union Kapitan A. I. Novikov, deputy corps commander for aerial gunnery service, came down to the 812th IAP on more than one occasion. The 812th IAP spent about a month in the Moscow area where the organizational, administrative, and other issues were put to rest while the 265th IAD began preparations for quick movement to the Oboyan area of the Voronezh Front.

A new instruction required the 812th IAP to land at Morshansk airfield en route. An order had been received, "go to the Kuban". The pilots refolded their aeronautical charts and traced a new flight path: Morshansk—Rossosh—Rostov-on-Don—Tikhoretsk—Krasnoarmeyskaya stanitsa.[13] On Saturday, 17 April, they landed at Rostov-on-Don enroute. From there, the last portion of the route lay in areas where they could encounter German fighters. Their Yaks received a full ammunition upload. In the air, the pilots redoubled their observation of the airspace. On the following day the leading teams of maintenance personnel (flown in ahead on transport aircraft) and the flight crews of 265th IAD (in 90 Yak-1s) dispersed on airfields in the Krasnodar basing area under operational subordination to the 4th Air Army. The command elements of 291st IAP settled in at Staronizhnestebliyevskaya airfield, 402nd IAP occupied Pashkovskaya airfield, and 812th IAP with 29 Yak-1s dispersed at Krasnoarmeyskaya airfield.

Commander of the 3rd IAK, General-Mayor Ye. Ya. Savitskiy. "Dragon!" in the air.

OVERVIEW: Combat Actions of 265th IAD in the Kuban

After the successful winter and spring battles for the liberation of the Northern Caucasus conducted by Red Army forces, the enemy had withdrawn and dug in on the Taman peninsula by April 1943. The 265th IAD, as part of the 3rd IAK, was assigned to the 4th Air Army and had available 88 pilots in Yak-1s. Although by now well versed in the techniques of piloting, these flight crews did not have any practical combat experience. Nevertheless, the division's three regiments were given the mission to provide defense to ground forces against enemy air attacks. In addition, they carried out missions for escorting bombers and shturmoviks. Clearly the protection of ground forces was the primary mission, as the regiment flew 551 combat sorties in that task and 327 sorties escorting bombers.

The mission of the Soviet ground forces was to hold a beachhead at Myskhako and thus disrupt the German plan to hold on to the Taman peninsula. Soviet aviation had a threefold mission: to support amphibious forces from the air, to prevent the enemy from bombing them, and to gain and maintain air superiority on a narrow sector of the front. The period from 20 April in the area of Myskhako and Krymskaya stanitsa was characterized by greater aerial activity from both sides. Up to 50 aerial engagements were fought on some days. Enemy bomber aviation conducted raids in groups of 10 to 30 Ju87, Ju88, and He111 bombers escorted by six to 15 fighters. In the majority of cases the fighter support was accomplished by clearing the air in the region of bomber actions, and more rarely by direct escort. Small groups of Bf109 (F and G model) fighters also operated in coverage of ground forces. Pairs and four-ship flights of highly trained pilots (for example, JG52 and JG3 "Udet") took skillful advantage of altitude, sun, and clouds in conducting sudden attacks on Soviet fighters and bombers.

The division carried out its support mission by the patrolling method. At first patrols consisting of 10 to 16 Yak-1s were sent out flying pairs abreast with an interval of 50-100 meters (165-330 feet). Each four-ship flight was separated vertically by an extra 50-100 meters. In addition, the altitude and speed (on the order of 300-350 kph [162-189 knots) of the patrol flight were strictly controlled. And though the groups were divided into containing and attacking elements, the tactically inappropriate arrangement of such a combat formation, the small separation interval along with the low speed all combined to limit the maneuver of friendly formations. Enemy fighters, coming in from high altitude and diving with great velocity, attacked with impunity and then pulled out with another climb to altitude.

As a result, many air crews developed a dangerous opinion regarding the superiority of the technical flight characteristics of the German fighters over their own Yaks, and the impossibility of engaging them in vertical maneuver combat. This then led to the widespread employment of the fallacious practice of forming a defensive circle, which complicated their position even more, thereby permitting a small number of enemy fighters to engage a much larger group of VVS fighters.

Returning from combat. "To our combat christening!" Kapitan Ivan Batychko (left) and Dmitriy Nikolayenkov. Behind them, a Yak-1b with an early variation of the 3rd IAK "Dragon's Wing" adorning its nose.

"Kapitan Batychko personally shot down 7 enemy aircraft in combat. He was an outstanding pilot, a genuine Stalin's Eagle. During an aerial engagement on 7 May 43, in front of his entire group, he expertly got behind a Bf109 and set the enemy aircraft on fire with a burst from 10 meters. For bravery and courage in battles for the Motherland, Kapitan Ivan Dmitrievich Batychko was awarded the Order of the Red Banner." Regiment staff in "Combat Path."

The density of Soviet combat formations was conditioned, to a significant degree, by the poor quality of their radio receiver/transmitter sets. Initially the overwhelming majority of pilots, no matter the rank, regarded radios with persistent disdain. As a consequence, groups were controlled by maneuver and personal example of commanders. This forced the rigid "attachment" of wingman to leader, preventing the pair from executing spatial maneuvers and reducing their ability to make use of sun, clouds, and other means of concealment. Aerial battles took on the nature of melees or carousels in the horizontal plane. Coordination between pairs and four-ship flights was not practiced. As a result of these mistakes, the division suffered great losses. Twelve pilots were lost in the first three days of fighting in the Kuban. These deficiencies were quickly uncovered and, to a significant degree, corrected. Primary attention was given to the matching up of pairs and four-ship flights, to the configuration of the combat formation, and to effective radio communications, ultimately leading to an improvement in combat results. We began to conduct air combat more successfully.

Enemy aviation in the Kuban had to engage various types of fighters: P-39 Airacobras, P-40 Kittyhawks, Spitfires, Yak-1s, Yak-7Bs, and La-5s. Encountering strong and organized resistance from Soviet fighters for the first time in the war, the enemy reacted with frequent changes in tactical action over the battlefield. In the course of operations in the Krymskaya area, VVS fighters managed to inflict heavy air combat losses, significantly reducing Luftwaffe morale. The enemy's level of combat activity was reduced and, on some occasions, paralyzed entirely. In the face of this turn of events, they were faced with a difficult mission—achieve air superiority.

Depending on the situation, German fighter pilots frequently changed their tactics. First of all, they attempted to echelon their combat formation at various altitudes from 1,500 to 7,000 meters (5,000-23,000 feet), with the more experienced and skilled pilots at higher altitudes. Using the sun, their mission was to paralyze Soviet fighters by sudden attacks. In addition, they attempted to achieve numerical superiority over the battlefield by reinforcing their effort in the required airspace, only calling in additional aircraft from neighboring airfields and adjoining regions. Thus,

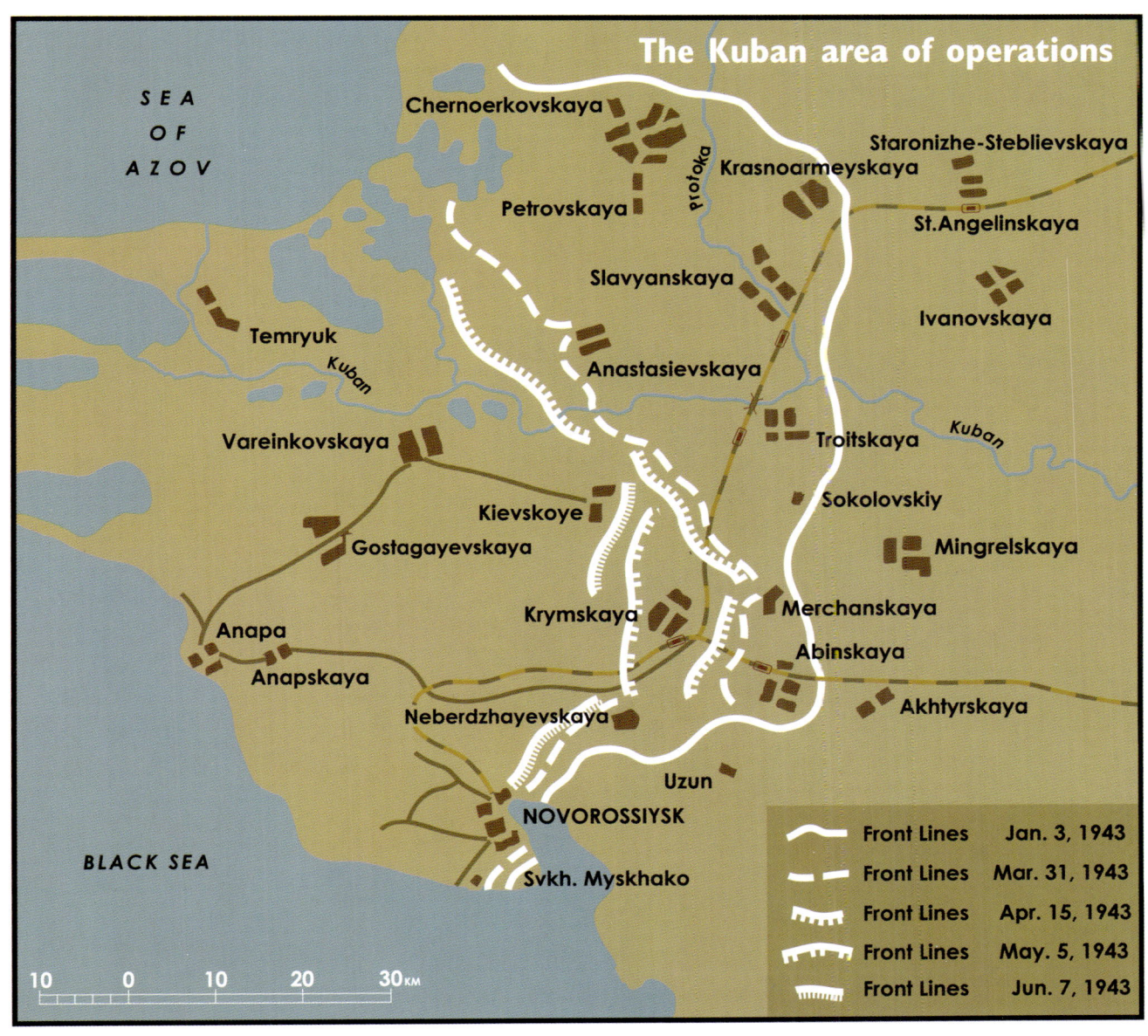

The Kuban area of operations

SEA OF AZOV

BLACK SEA

	Front Lines	Jan. 3, 1943
	Front Lines	Mar. 31, 1943
	Front Lines	Apr. 15, 1943
	Front Lines	May. 5, 1943
	Front Lines	Jun. 7, 1943

in the last days of April, Luftwaffe fighters from the Novorossiysk region were called in to assist with operations in the Krymskaya area.

In the absence of numerical superiority the Germans fought with uncertainty and - especially when against Airacobras and La-5s - very carefully. Knowing full well that the Bf109 had a more powerful engine than the Yak-1 and Yak-7B, the enemy attempted to tie down these fighters at 6,000-7,000 meter (19,700-23,000 foot) altitudes. Initially this method gained the Germans some success, but after some time they were forced to abandon it because of the Airacobras operating at these altitudes.[14] In addition, the Luftwaffe tasked designated aircraft to lure VVS fighters into their rear where they would then come under attack from more powerful groups. The period of April-May, characterized by predominately sunny weather in the Kuban, also saw the Germans fall back to a favorite method of theirs – attacks out of the sun. They did this especially in the afternoon when the sun was more on their side of the front.

The lack of combat experience in the first period of actions, the inappropriate structure of fighter combat formations (lack of sufficient echelonment of the groups by altitude), the approach and presence over the target at low speeds, the absence of coordination between the attack and the cover groups upon entry into an engagement (and in the conduct of the battle itself), improper actions of the ground vectoring station (which frequently hampered the initiative of the group commander in his control of battle)—all these weak elements from the initial sorties were studied by the enemy and used by him to counter Soviet fighters. These deficiencies were the basic causes of the high combat losses suffered by VVS fighter units in the first ten days of combat here.

Just the same, the division accomplished its assigned mission, albeit at a high price. These air battles showed that large groups of fighters, operating in tight formations without echelonment by altitude, were unsuitable for the conduct of air combat with enemy fighters. During the battles enemy tactics were studied and new tactical methods of combating enemy fighters were developed. This ensured victory in the air with minimal losses during the final period of operations, inflicting great losses on the enemy.

Training in Battle

Immediately before the start of battles, corps commander Ye. Ya. Savitskiy received information from the intelligence chief of 4th Air Army, Polkovnik V. F. Voronov.

"One more thing, Comrade General," the intelligence chief caught my attention. "Here, alongside Anapa and Gostalayevskaya stanitsa, are large, well-equipped, and well-defended airfields. These are not primitive landing fields, but complete air bases for combat actions of fighters and bombers of the 4th Air Fleet. These airfields are only 40-50 kilometers (25–30 miles) from Novorossiysk. The enemy is conducting bombing raids from these airfields; he quickly introduces fresh groups of airplanes into the battle, and reinforces in areas where we are gaining the upper

hand. This is a problem for us. Our closest airfields to Novorossiysk are more than twice as far away. The flight time to the battle area is correspondingly greater than the Germans', and our loiter time over the city is less. If our fighters can be in the bridgehead area for 20-25 minutes, then the Germans can be there for 40-50. You will have to take all of this into consideration."[15]

Subsequent events demonstrated that this warning applied not only to the pilots of the corps. The commander-in-chief of VVS of the North Caucasus Front, Leytenant General K. A. Vershinin, received Savitskiy warmly on the same day.

We have been waiting for you! How we have been waiting! You probably have already learned that the Germans are operating approximately 1200 combat aircraft in our zone. Altogether in two air armies (4th VA and 5th VA) I have no more than 450. And even when you add to that number some 70 aircraft of the Black Sea Fleet and 60 bombers from long-range aviation, we have only 580 aircraft. In addition, the flight crews were exhausted in the winter battles. We have suffered great losses, especially in the last three weeks. We are fighting fiercely, but the odds are against us. That is why you have been brought here in such a hurry. From the march into battle, as they say. Your pilots are facing heavy combat.[16]

The pilots of 812th IAP had to fight within the triangle formed by Novorossiysk, Krymskaya, and Abinskaya. The conflagration that would go into history as the Battle for Kuban was beginning on the southern sector of the Soviet-German front. The intelligence section of long-range aviation headquarters also reported on the massing of the forces of German aviation. The ADD special intelligence summary No. 4 for April 1943 noted:

According to information from our agent network, on 11 April at the beginning of the operation, in order to strengthen the Kuban bridgehead and weaken the actions of our fleet, the German command is supporting its ground forces with the 1st Aviation Corps under the command of General of Aviation Ferster (corps headquarters in Simferopol), consisting of the following named aviation units:

III Gruppe, Kampfgeschwader 3 at Kerch airfield
II Gruppe, Kampfgeschwader 27 at Sarabuz airfield
III Gruppe, Kampfgeschwader 27 at Sarabuz airfield
I Gruppe, Kampfgeschwader 51 at Bagerovo airfield
II Gruppe, Kampfgeschwader 51 at Sarabuz airfield
III Gruppe, Kampfgeschwader 51 at Bagerovo airfield
I Gruppe, Kampfgeschwader 55 at Sarabuz airfield
II Gruppe, Kampfgeschwader 55 at Zamorsk airfield
III Gruppe, Kampfgeschwader 55 at Zamorsk airfield
I Gruppe, Sturzkampfgeschwader 3 at Kerch airfield
II Gruppe, Sturzkampfgeschwader 2 at Kerch airfield
III Gruppe, Sturzkampfgeschwader 2 at Kerch airfield
III Gruppe, Sturzkampfgeschwader 3 at Sarabuz airfield
I Gruppe, Jagdgeschwader 3 at Anapa airfield
II Gruppe, Jagdgeschwader 3 at Anapa airfield
III Gruppe, Jagdgeschwader 3 at Verkhnestebliyevskaya airfield
I Gruppe, Jagdgeschwader 52 at Taman airfield
II Gruppe, Jagdgeschwader 52 at Anapa and Taman airfields

II./JG3 Kommandeur Kurt Brändle's Bf109G-2 is typical of the Messerschmitts based in and around the Kuban area during the early months of 1943. Both I./JG3 and II./JG3 were based at Anapa airfield when the Kuban battle ramped up through mid-April. The geschwader's III Gruppe , as well as I./JG52 and II./JG52, were also in the area. Together they comprised the formidable enemy fighter force — with many 'experten' in its ranks — poised opposite the regiments of the 3rd IAK.

An early Ju87G-1. Prior to going into action against Soviet armour for the first time at Kursk, these specialized 'Kannonenvogel' Stukas flew interdiction missions in the Kuban area through the first months of 1943. Here a special unit - Panzerjagdkommando Weiss - employed the machine's powerful 3.7cm cannon against Soviet troop and supply boats and landing craft. During his first months on the Ju87G, Stuka ace Hans-Ulrich Rudel claimed 70 such craft in the Kerch Straits and in the numerous lagoons and rivers near Temryuk and Akhtarsk-Bukht. One of the 812th's tasks was keeping these, as well as the standard Luftwaffe dive-bomber, attack, and bomber types, away from such vulnerable targets. The Stuka's main-wheel fairings were often removed to minimize the risk of nosing over on muddy airfields.

NOT TO SCALE

Here is the recollection of 812th IAP *ace* I. V. Fedorov:

> *An order from 4th Air Fleet to 1st Aviation Corps of 13 April 1943 pointed out that in the event of unfavorable weather conditions for the conduct of operations in the Kuban, aviation units would shift over to bombing oil-refineries in Grozniy, Baku, and Black Sea ports.*
>
> *We were unable to go to sleep for a long time; we conversed in whispers; we tried to imagine what tomorrow would bring. Then tomorrow came. The first encounter with an experienced, cunning enemy. My first aerial engagement. I did not think at the time that for some of my friends it would be their last.*[17]

Savitskiy was worrying for his pilots, knowing full well that his inexperienced and eager young men would be easy prey for

Aleksandr Tishchenko.
"Altitude 5000 meters. Having encountered a group of Bf109s, Tishchenko attacked boldly. The fascists were dispersed, but the 'far easterner' already had selected his victim. The fascist maneuvered. He threw his aircraft into a steep dive; Tishchenko copied his maneuver. The two mortal enemies plummeted like meteors. The green Caucasus mountains loomed. The critical moment arrived, the ground was coming up, they had to pull out. Tishchenko pulled his aircraft out of the dive and the stricken fascist burrowed into the earth. . ."
Regimental staff description of one of Tishchenko's aerial engagements.

the German aces. There was practically no time for familiarization with this sector. And the corps commander understood that this forced measure—"training in battle"—was unavoidable. Those who withstood this trial and did not perish would become genuine professionals of aerial combat. General Savitskiy recalls:

> *Flying to the front, I knew very well that namely the first battles with a powerful enemy would be the most dangerous. Every battle was dangerous, but for my untested pilots, the first battles were three times as dangerous. And though I understood that I was leading the corps the thousand kilometers to this place not for a vacation, just the same I hoped that I would be able to introduce the men into the combat situation gradually, under the leadership of already experienced aerial warriors. Alas, I did not even have the opportunity to report concerning my plans.*[18]

Listening to the stories of the front-line veterans about the aerial battles, young pilots gained an impression about what they would encounter in the air. A. T. Tishchenko recalls a conversation between pilots of the 812th Regiment:

> *"Are you bored with this routine? It will change! It got tougher. The fascists threw us a surprise. Who knows about this "Udet" thing?" the regiment chief of staff Mayor Lepilin asked the pilots. Not receiving a reply, the mayor continued. "'Udet' is a fascist fighter squadron. Sent here from Italy on Goering's order. Many of its pilots have the Knight's Cross. Its commander is Mayor Wilcke. He has several dozens of downed aircraft to his credit."*[19]

The chief of staff was not far off the mark. Concentrated at Anapa airfield were a headquarters detachment along with II and III Gruppen of JG3 "Udet", under the command of Major Wolf-Detrich Wilcke. The I, II, and III Gruppen of JG52, commanded by Major Dieter Hrabak, were stationed not far from them.

Tuesday, 20 April 1943. At approximately 0830, the command to sortie was issued. All the airfields of the 265th Division sprang into action. The first 16 Yak-1s of 812th IAP began to take off at 0850. Taking off first, regiment commander Mayor Aleksey Yeremin led a group of pilots from Kapitan Ivan Batychko's 1st Squadron. Crossing the front line, the aircraft set course for Myskhako. For future Hero of the Soviet Union Aleksandr Tishchenko, this first combat sortie was nearly his last. Over Novorossiysk the attack group began to circle toward the sea, from which enemy bombers were most likely to appear. Attempting to stay in contact with their leaders, the young pilots were barely managing to maneuver.

Black spots appeared on the horizon, which upon closure turned out to be 12 Ju88 bombers escorted by six Bf109s. Two Fw189s were a little farther out. Leytenant Tishchenko, flying in the cover group, was late with his combat turn and suddenly came upon six Ju88s, also on course for Myskhako. Forgetting to inform squadron commander Batychko by radio regarding the appearance of the enemy, Tishchenko and his wingman - Patrakov - raced toward the trailing flight of bombers. Familiar with Soviet fighter attacks, the German bombers increased speed and began to close up into a tighter formation. Rapidly closing on the German group, Tishchenko remembered that he had not warned the rest of his squadron of his maneuver, but all attempts to correct this condition proved futile.

The two Yak-1s, rapidly entering the field of fire of the bomber formation's aerial gunners, experienced for themselves all the discomfort of the situation. Tishchenko laid his sights on the fuselage of the nearest bomber and fired a burst from his cannon. Everything was happening as if in a dream when, it seems that just about... almost... and... the tracers barely missed! Finally, on the third burst the Junkers began to smoke. With the exuberance of young pilots, it is fully understandable that separation in the air flew out of their minds. In an instant the armor plate rattled from blows from the rear. Tishchenko describes his first encounter with the enemy:

Novorossiysk and Myskhako late April, 1943

I turned my head and grew cold when I saw the yellow nose of a Messerschmitt through the shattered armored glass. Quickly - instinctively rather than consciously - I turned to the left and opened the canopy. Then I put the Yak in a dive. I heard whistling and felt sharp pain in my ears from the pressure change. The earth was rushing up to meet me. Carefully I began to bring the wounded aircraft out of the dive. My eyes grew dark and the pressure pushed me back heavily in the seat. Finally I managed to level the aircraft, but my engine had died.[20]

His aircraft was damaged and the pilot was forced to land it at the front line. For Tishchenko the sorties on this day ended relatively fortunately—he survived.

Several minutes after the 1st Squadron, fighters from the 2nd Squadron of Kapitan Timofey Novikov took off. Among the *debutantes* of the 2nd Squadron was the future ace and Hero of the Soviet Union Starshiy Serzhant Ivan Fedorov.

The mechanic reported that everything was ready. I nodded to him and sat down in the cockpit. I quickly checked my instruments and switches. And suddenly some kind of unfamiliar emotion that I had not experienced before swept over me. I felt as though my legs were shaking and somehow applied unusual pressure on the pedals. I relaxed them and looked around in order to distract myself. The blinding disk of the sun already hung above the horizon. The tops of the poplar trees were turning gold; the sky was clear and serene, transparently shading to blue above my head. Various episodes of my childhood and youth danced in my head—a sign of great psychological pressure. I wanted to get up in the air more quickly to stop and change their random flow. Impatiently

I looked down at my watch: soon! And again something pressed on my chest; again I had to relax my legs, stiffly resting on the pedals. One after the other, two green flares arched upward. This is us! Now my main task was to start up the engine, make sure everything was working, and not fall behind. If that happened, I thought, I would not live it down. I pushed on the starter button. Thank God and the mechanic, the propeller rotated.[21]

A pair (Savitskiy and Novikov) from the corps headquarters sortied to observe their pilots. Ye. Ya. Savitskiy recalls the moment.

Yeremin's fighters headed out toward the sea. Papkov's group remained over the bridgehead, and Aleksey Novikov and I decided to await the Germans over the southern portion of Tsemesskaya Bay. Not far from here, in the Anapa area, enemy fighters were forming up, and I was in no hurry to get tangled up with them. The Messerschmitts appeared from the northwest. The morning sun was working for us: we saw the Germans way off and they did not see our fighters against the light of the sun. The two sides closed on each other very quickly—on intersecting courses. The pilots of Papkov's regiment attacked the Germans. I observed the actions of my pilots in the first minutes of the battle as if from the sidelines. Thinking about the effectiveness of their actions, the forms and methods of combat for air superiority, I wanted personally to determine the enemy's most vulnerable spot. I noticed that the pilots of the Germans' best squadrons approached the engagement area at great - almost maximum - speed. I understood that this created an advantage for maneuver. After the first attack our men had to reorganize their combat formations, and in a few more minutes it was already difficult to visualize where we were attacking and where the enemy was. When a group of Junkers appeared, Yeremin's pilots, acting in a tactically appropriate manner, tied up their escort fighters in battle and in their first attack shot down two bombers. The Germans, however, continued their flight toward the bridgehead.[22]

Several minutes later the fighters of Kapitan Fedor Svezhentsev's 3rd Squadron began to take off. By this time the 2nd Squadron was already engaged in combat that was begun by Kapitan Batychko's group. Here is Ivan Fedorov's memory of his first encounter with the enemy.

I felt my spine become wet. The group leader was nervous and everyone felt it, both in his commands and by the motion of his aircraft. The reason was understandable: an air battle was taking place below us, and we heard commands and cursing in our earphones. One after another the remnants of burning aircraft were falling to the earth, and we did not see the enemy. Had we arrived for no good? Suddenly I saw the regiment commander abruptly maneuver in a right turn and increase speed. Aha! There it is—a Ju88! Genuine, not a model.[23]

Three flights of four Ju88s were flying in column at an altitude of 3,000 meters (9,850 feet). One of them, having fallen slightly behind the others, was smoking and making a determined effort not to become separated from the group. It appeared that this was the very bomber that Leytenant Tishchenko had attacked. The regiment commander, Mayor Yeremin, relieved the German group of the burden of the straggling Junkers. He fired a burst from all weapons into it at 100-75 meters (325-250 feet) range.

At this moment, the Myskhako ground vectoring station reported that two groups of Ju87s were approaching Novorossiysk from seaward. The squadron commander, Kapitan T. Novikov, leader of Yeremin's cover group, executed a left turn. After the turn the cover group passed through the haze that had formed at this altitude, and into the sunlight which significantly reduced their horizontal visibility. Only the explosions of antiaircraft shells bursting in front of the Yaks were visible and the black trails from aircraft falling into the sea from various directions. Then Bf109G fighters appeared. Fedorov describes this frightening encounter.

Several Bf109s with outboard cannons flashed like shadows and disappeared in the direction of the blinding sun. Were they attacking or not? We could not tell. I understood that they were firing only when I saw the burning aircraft of Ivan Martynenko, wingman of our flight commander. To the right and slightly above, I caught sight of tongues of flame. I turned my head—pieces of burning Yak, like in a fantastic frightening dream, were flying off in various directions and tumbling toward earth. Not far from me, somersaulting slowly, fell a tail section with a red star on it. Who was the pilot? What happened to him? But after just a moment's glance out into space,

"Let's smoke!" After a combat sortie, April 1943.
"Remember the Kuban, how we flew there, six-eight sorties per day. Everyone was terribly tired there, But we never hid in the shadow."
From a poem by Pavel Vasilyevich Korneyev, former aircraft mechanic of 3rd Squadron, "From Stalingrad to Berlin."

left to right, Kapitan I. Batychko, Mayor A. Yeremin and Mayor D. Nikolayenkov

my lead banked his aircraft and, gritting my teeth, I pushed the throttle forward until my hand grew numb.[24]

Despite these first losses, squadron commander Novikov directed them all into an attack on the group of Ju87s. Suddenly Fedorov saw how one of those same Messerschmitts had gotten on the tail of a Yak and was beginning to close on it. Having completely forgotten the squadron commander's order, Starshiy Serzhant Fedorov, falling off to the side, dove on the Bf109.

Moving the throttle to full stop, I pulled the control stick toward me, tracing the flight trajectory of the Messerschmitt. I was closing on him! I felt a sense of excited belief that I would catch him. I even managed to catch a glance of his cockpit. And then suddenly the blood rushed to my head. I saw that I had failed to switch the fire control switch to cannon fire before firing. I set the switch, confirmed once again that everything was in order, and trained my eyes on the gunsight. I opened fire on the Messerschmitt when the range closed to fifty meters. The cannon barked continuously, creating a wave of delight in my spirit. And only when a long tongue of red flame crawled along the right side of the Messerschmitt did I release the trigger. I closed on him, adjusted my speed and, in order to be completely at ease, took aim and pounded him point-blank with all my weapons. I did not take my finger off the trigger until my weapons went silent. The Messerschmitt burned still brighter, was shrouded in thick black smoke and, falling into a steep spin, fell to the earth.[25]

This was the first Messerschmitt downed by the young pilot. [For unknown reasons, this victory of I. V. Fedorov over the Bf109 was not reflected in the combat actions journal and other regiment documents.] The heat of battle, their first attack, and the subsequent agony of the enemy—for many young pilots this spectacle was also the last that they saw. But on this occasion everything turned out well. Having lost contact with his group, Fedorov attached himself to a group of Il-2s from 230th ShAD of Podpolkovnik S.G. Getman, flew to his airfield, and landed safely. In the evening during the review of the day's battles, he found out whom he had assisted. He had saved Starshina Vasiliy Lugovoy of the 1st Squadron, who had come under *bandit* fire while he was rushing to the assistance of his own commander, Leytenant Tishchenko. A chain of mutual assistance connected Tishchenko, Lugovoy, and Fedorov. In the air it was "all for one and one for all." There was a reason for teaching cadets in the academies:

If in combat of individual fighters all attention is paid to one enemy, then in group combat the basic rule is to assist one's comrade. Despite the fact that occasionally a fighter can defeat an enemy, he often has to break off in order to come to the aid of a comrade who is threatened by danger.[26]

It is interesting to follow the activities of 812th IAP through the eyes of "Dragon," the commander of the 3rd IAK, Savitskiy, who was also in the air on this day.

Our mistake was immediately obvious to me. If the corps' fighters flew over the bridgehead at cruise speed, which would favor an extended loiter time, then the fascist pilots would approach the battle area almost at maximum speed. This placed them in a more favorable position. They attacked and, taking advantage of a speed reserve, departed by executing a climb or combat turn in order to hit us again from above. But we did not lose our heads. We attacked the enemy using head-on intersecting courses, engaged him in combat in turns, and cleverly avoided his blows. However our lack of combat experience was apparent. Some groups dispersed into pairs and even into single aircraft. The pilots lost not only their tactical connection but also fire distribution between them, and sometimes could not even see each other. Many conducted battle, as they say, at their own risk and fear. But no one left the field of battle. The first losses occurred, some with crosses and others with stars. Some, trailing smoke as they dropped, headed toward their own lines. Others fell steeply and dropped like rocks into the bay or struck the earth. After this, a brief explosion or column of erupting water. Some aircraft exploded in midair. And several seconds later there was nothing in the space where a combat aircraft had just passed with a man in the cockpit to remind one of the tragedy that had occurred. There were few parachutes. There is a reason why they say that not all pilots have final resting places on earth.[27]

During the first half of the regiment's flight, Kapitan Svezhentsev and Leytenant Tyugayev each downed a single Bf109 and shared an Fw189. Kapitan Batychko scored two Ju88s, and 1 Ju88 was credited to the group of Leytenant Tishchenko, Mayor Yeremin, and Starshina Patrakov. But the first combat losses of the 812th stunned many. After this battle, eight Yak-1s did not return to their airfield.

At 1050, 11 Yak-1s led by regiment navigator Kapitan Dmitriy Nikolayenkov flew into the same area. Group commander Nikolayenkov, Starshinas Vasiliy Lugovoy and Yuriy Shirokov, and Kapitan Timofey Novikov all opened their records with a single victory over a Bf109. In the Novorossiysk area, squadron commander Novikov also managed to down an He111, however his Yak-1 (bort 61) was damaged in combat. He had to make a forced landing in the Severskaya area. On this same day Kapitan N. K. Naumchik, temporarily assigned to the 812th IAP on order of General-Mayor Savitskiy, flew the regiment's final sortie for the day and downed one more Bf109.

This April 20th baptism of fire for the 3rd IAK showed that the pilots knew how to fight and win. According to preliminary data, the outcome was 11 Bf109, two Ju88 and two Fw189 downed as of 2000. By this time there was an incomplete summary only of the 265th IAD, which on this day flew 102 aircraft sorties, absorbing the main attack. Because not all the pilots had written summaries of their flights, the score of 15 enemy aircraft downed by the corps was later corrected to about 40 claims. The 812th IAP downed 12 aircraft while the 402nd IAP claimed six Bf109 victories. The other regiments also claimed an increase in the number of downed aircraft. However, some 23 aircraft did not return to their airfields in the 3rd IAK and an additional four executed forced landings.

There was considerable grief in the 812th after the fate of pilots who did not return had been confirmed: seven aircraft and five pilots had been lost. In addition to these losses, the following division aircrew also perished: the commander of the 291st IAP, Mayor Vasiliy Semenovich Simonov; and Mladshiy Leytenants Ivan Chernyshov, Pavel Maslennikov, Dmitriy Koloshin, and Vasiliy Pustoshkin. Two more of the division's pilots executed forced landings away from the airfield and another, shot down, parachuted to safety over friendly territory. The group leaders had not yet learned how to lead their subordinates in dispersed combat formations at high speeds, and this frequently led to disastrous consequences. But be that as it may, the 812th Regiment learned how to fight based on their own mistakes and the mistakes of others. The flight crews of 265th IAD possessed excellent piloting skills but, lacking the time to integrate into the unit and be trained for participation in group aerial combat, committed serious errors and suffered great losses.

Another contributing factor was the faulty method of training for aerial gunnery at low closing speeds. The corps and division command were operating by the requirements of NKO [narodny komissariat oborony—people's commissariat of defense] Order No. 074 of 24 January 1943 ("Order concerning the employment of maximum range and duration of flight of an aircraft in combat

Kapitan Fedor Svezhentsev, commander, 3rd Squadron.

"In the Kuban sky to contest with courage, Svezhentsev taught his pilots to fight. He was a straight shooter; he was eager to engage, He was the first in the regiment to be decorated."

From a poem by Pavel Korneyev, 3rd Squadron aircraft mechanic.

Vasiliy Lugovoy

units of the VVS Red Army"), which said the following:

Conduct operational flights, transfer flights, flights for the execution of combat missions (up to encounter with the enemy), patrolling, loitering in zone, cross-country flights in reserve regiments, in zone, and all other flights, except [flights] of higher skill level and practice of the elements of air combat, at the most favorable regimes.

This order was appropriate for flights in the rear area, but totally inappropriate for flights in a zone of continuous enemy aviation activity. Former serzhant and pilot of the 2nd Squadron, Aleksandr Ivanovich Ivanov, speaks about battles in the area of Krymskaya.

On occasion they would give us the mission of covering our own forces at an altitude of 2500 meters (8,200 feet). We attained this altitude and proceeded to the area at this altitude and patrolled, anticipating the enemy, or conducted combat. But later, when we had acquired experience, we did not do this. We proceeded with a deliberately greater altitude—3000-3500 meters (9800–11500 feet), and swept downward into our zone with great speed. Before this we flew at 250-300 kph (155-185 knots), saving fuel. The Germans employed this tactic from the start, and we meanwhile were getting up our speed and seeking position. We did not have communications in the air. Only the flight commander had a receiver/transmitter. And we—wingmen—only had a receiver and could only listen. Useless chatter. The ground vectoring station was screaming, commands were coming in from the neighboring regiments. More noise than useful information. Everyone was on the same frequency. You would hear some things and miss others. Our pairs would get split up. And the Germans lay in wait for stragglers.

Unfortunately, combat experience frequently was gained at the highest cost—the lives of pilots. Both sides amassed forces in this relatively small sector of the front. Having 200 crews assigned to six regiments, the corps represented a powerful fighter force, operationally prepared to fight on any sector from Novorossiysk to Krasnodar. Here is a commentary on the air situation on 20 April 1943 from the memoir of Ye. Ya. Savitskiy.

An engagement by fighters in a typical air combat over Malaya Zemlya or the Kuban in general was like a series of duels between large numbers of aircraft and groups in a small three-dimensional space. Battles in such an engagement might last a long time. Downed aircraft fell out of the sky, others departed for their own airfields to refuel and rearm. New groups arrived to replace them. Pilots might fly four or five sorties over the course of several hours, and participate, in essence, in one and the same battle that had begun that morning. And so it went all day long. Combat in the skies over Novorossiysk, above Tsemesskaya Bay, and over Malaya Zemlya never stopped for a moment. Junkers and Peshkas [Pe-2s], Messerschmitts and Yaks, Fokkers [the Soviet aircrew's moniker for Fw190s] and LaGGs burned, exploded in midair, and fell out of the sky.[28]

Aleksandr Ivanov, a pilot in the 2nd Squadron

Ivan Martynenko, another 2nd Squadron pilot.
"*Three friends, three young pilots in the regiment: Ivanov, Martynenko, and Zenin. They were the most disciplined, most active in party-political work. In the conditions of the Far East, the regiment was engaged in raising the combat readiness by exercises, primarily for the cadre. Fuel supplies were limited and the young pilots were held back. They seldom flew. But they had a burning desire to fly, to improve, that was so great that they filled each of their rare flights with great substance.*"
Regiment staff in "Combat Path."

The great losses that the 265th Division suffered in its first aerial combat could not help but influence the subsequent change in tactics. Later, after being moved to the rear, the division staff reached distressing conclusions regarding its baptism of fire in the Kuban.

The division's first aerial combat, conducted by the group of Mayor Yeremin, showed that coordination in the group and between groups in combat with the bombers under fighter escort had not been practiced. The commander of the covering group made an incorrect decision when the entire flight engaged a pair of Bf109s on the approach to the target, for by doing so the flight failed to support the battle of the strike group. The strike group, lacking cover, also attacked the bombers with its entire component and subjected itself to attack by enemy fighters. Coordination was not practiced between pairs, which led to the case where, after the first attack, the group and pairs were dispersed, and the battle became disorganized. Each pilot was attempting to shoot down the enemy by himself. Mutual assistance was lacking. None of the pilots bothered to search for the enemy, as a result of which they did not spot the enemy fighters that were escorting the bombers from above and behind. During the encounter the pilots failed to select a target for attack, and attacked everything they saw (fighters, bombers, reconnaissance aircraft, and spotter aircraft).

All these errors of the regiment's - indeed, the entire division's - pilots had to be corrected in battle, unfortunately at the cost of great losses. On the next day - Wednesday, 21 April - a pilot of the 812th IAP downed a Bf109 in aerial combat in the Novorossiysk-Myskhako area. In this engagement, JG3 "Udet" lost, as missing in action, the Bf109G-2 of Leutnant Lothar Myrrhe, a 19-victory veteran. Regiment commander Aleksey Yeremin, who shot down another Bf109 near Neberdzhayevsk, gained his first personal victory. No additional victories over the enemy were tallied for this day, but neither were there the terrible losses of the previous day. General Savitskiy recalls:

I could not offer any serious pretense, or excuse anyone, for the misfortune for another reason. Even our seasoned teacher from the division of Polkovnik I. M. Dzusov (9th GIAD) - whom General K. A. Vershinin, like he had promised, had sent to train my inexperienced pilots - did not hide his surprise at the size and ferocity of that day's battles. Hero of the Soviet Union Kapitan N. K. Naumchik, and also experienced aerial warrior and future Hero of the Soviet Union Starshiy Leytenant I. M. Gorbunov, declared straight out: 'Comrade General, that was not the place for training. There was only time to attack or attempt to avoid attack.'[29]

On 22 April the fighters of the neighboring 402nd IAP, which downed nine Bf109s and 1 Fw190 in two group battles, bore the brunt of the battle.

A day later the group of Kapitan Batychko and Kapitan Sveshentsev, comprising 10 Yak-1s covering 27 (3 groups of 9) bombers on a strike mission in the Novorossiysk area, was attacked by two consecutive groups of six Bf109s. Batychko remained with his flight in direct escort of the A-20 Bostons from the 219th BAD while two flights, led by Starshiy Leytenant Svezhentsev and Leytenant Tishchenko, attacked the enemy fighters from various directions. In shooting down a Bf109, Fedor Svezhentsev added to his combat score on that Friday. Aleksandr Tishchenko and Ivan Martynenko also shot down a Bf109 each. This action forced the remaining German fighters to depart the area. The first victory of Starshiy Serzhant Ivan Martynenko is written up thusly in the regimental digest, "Combat Path."

We were flying in a flight of six, covering Bostons that were bombing the enemy's forward edge. Martynenko flew in pair with Tyugayev, guarding his leader, and at the same time attentively looking around. He spotted a pair of Messershmitts diving toward them from the direction of the sun. Knowing that they had been spotted, the Germans thought they could break off with a turn into the

Deputy squadron commander and flight commander Starshiy Leytenant Dmitriy Tyugayev.
"We lost such men of the Far Easterners,
The best pilots are with us no longer.
But in the Kuban sky they held superiority,
Over the aces of the 'Udet' group.
Our men heroically fought,
Very few of them remain in formation.
Many of them did not receive decorations,
The Eagles died in terrible battles."
From a poem by former 3rd Squadron aircraft mechanic Pavel Vasilyevich Korneyev "From Stalingrad to Berlin."

Ivan Fedorov, a pilot of the 2nd Squadron. His unassuming character seems to come through in this early photograph.

sun. With full throttle and left pedal, our dare-devil quickly laid his sight on the German. Already, before he could squeeze the trigger, he glanced back and, having confirmed that enemy aircraft were not creeping up on him, he gave the Bf109 a long burst. Pieces flew off the German aircraft. With more right pedal, Martynenko again took up formation with the lead Boston. He reported to his commander on the ground, "Knocked down one fool."

But not everything went as smoothly. Later Ye. Ya. Savitskiy recalled the deficiencies in the corps' combat effort.

Not all of the pair leaders and group commanders always took into account the peculiarities of the air situation. There were cases when, because of a generally commendable desire to destroy the enemy, the leaders of the covering groups themselves changed the mission and abandoned the attack on the bombers in favor of engaging the escorting fighters in combat. For the same reason, wingmen left their leaders and attacked the enemy. On occasion, therefore, the combat formation of pairs and flights, which I myself can confirm, were broken up into individual aircraft. Pilots lost tactical, fire, and even visual contact among themselves. In a word, possessing good personal preparation, the corps' fighters conducted group combat not always in an organized fashion, and sometimes became victim to their own personal lack of attention. Flying skills are not acquired all at once. It takes time and lots of practice. During the forming up of the corps, during the transition training in the reserve aviation units, our pilots learned well how to fly Yakovlev's aircraft. They learned and developed many tactical methods. But, unfortunately, they did not have enough firing practice. And in the first battles this showed. Many of the pilots' mistakes resulted from their lack of combat experience.

The story of A. I. Ivanov, whose aircraft was shot down by a German *hunter*, serves an example that confirms the words of the corps commander.

We were flying on our combat mission as a group and I flew close up behind the flight commander. Suddenly I looked and I was all alone. What should I do? We had

Zampolit Timofey Pasynok (left) and regiment commander Mayor Yeremin

From left to right, Aleksandr Tishchenko, Dmitriy Nikolayenkov, Ivan Batychko

already been flying for thirty minutes. I made a few circles and saw no one. Off in the distance I saw some aircraft and I flew toward them. They flew off. I continued to circle, and suddenly I felt the pounding of strikes on the back of my seat and the armor plate. Glancing around, there was no one near me. My aircraft was not on fire but the engine began to miss. No more attacks followed. I began to lose altitude and decided to make a forced landing without lowering the gear. I turned off the ignition and began to glide to my selected landing site in a vineyard.

Aleksandr Tumanov and Aleksey Mashenkin

There were more than a few cases like this in the corps. Pairs cf German *hunters* patrolled in assigned sectors, catching and shooting down straggling pilots. Aleksandr Ivanov was lucky that he was not killed, though he woke up after the forced landing of his Yak-1 in a hospital, saved by cavalrymen. He returned to his regiment ten days later. The hardest part for the young serzhant was the fact that many of his friends of the 534th IAP had perished and not returned from their combat sorties.

On the morning of 25 April, conducting battle in a group of six Yak-1s, Starshina Patrakov opened his personal score by downing a Bf109 (a version armed with under-wing cannons). This was the only victory in the entire 4th Air Army on this day. Here is a note from the combat actions journal of 812th IAP, entered on 26 April 1943:

> Yeremin's group consisting of 13 Yak-1s encountered 12 Ju88s and four Bf109s in the Krymskaya area. Yeremin attacked Ju88s and scattered them, but at the same time was himself attacked by a Bf109. The group lost its combat formation and on the whole conducted combat singly.

As was normally the case, the group had been divided into strike and cover elements. However, because of inexperience, all the pilots held close to their leaders, flying in a compact formation. Having attacked a group of Ju88s, and having become entangled with their escorting Bf109s, the pairs broke up. The pilots acted independently, orienting on their commander. In this group the wingman of Georgiy Churakov was Starshiy Serzhant I. V. Fedorov. Here, he reconstructs the details of this combat sortie.

> We rushed up behind him and there I saw tracers coming from the right. I concluded immediately that they were attacking us from behind, from the direction of the sun. To avoid being pierced by the second salvo, I abruptly went down and to the right. It was a Bf109 that flashed past me and with a turning climb departed into the sun. I could not have chased him even had I wanted to—he had speed and maneuver and I had little speed.[30]

In these few words are obvious all the deficiencies of the practices of fighters patrolling at cruise speed in anticipation of contact with the enemy. The advantages of attacking from above, with skillful use of vertical maneuver, are clearly shown. Despite all of this, one Bf109 collided with Kuban soil after a heated fight with Ivan Fedorov. (According to 4th VA summaries for this day, only two enemy aircraft were shot down: 1 Bf109 and 1 Ju88.) The ground vectoring station, having identified the fall of the enemy fighter, asked Fedorov for his callsign.

> I gave him my callsign and only now recall that that I had to be on continuous lookout. I was rotating my head to the right and left. Above and in front of me was a Yak-1. He was alone, like me, and was warily sneaking across the slippery sky, where disaster could strike at any moment. I was overjoyed and formed up on the left of the Yak. I looked at the number—it was my pair leader, Leytenant Churakov. I waved at him and he joyfully replied. Now it was possible to relax.[31]

Suddenly a Bf109 attacked Fedorov's Yak-1 from the rear. A burst covered his fuselage. The engine died and several rounds passed through the cockpit, destroying the instrument panel and wounding him. Practically blinded by fragments that had struck him in the eye, and with blood flowing down his face, he lost altitude. Yet, he was able to set the Yak-1 down quickly, gear up, on a swampy field in the Slavyanskaya area. After being picked up by Kononov (the 3rd IAK navigator) in a U-2, Fedorov was already in the hospital by evening. Surgery was performed to remove a fragment from his eye. Twelve days later, immediately upon the doctor's confirmation that his eye could be saved, he fled the hospital back to his regiment.

Meanwhile, the intensity of the fighting had not subsided. The loss in air combat of Fedorov's Yak-1, along with two others, was a tough outcome for the 3rd IAK on this day. One of these, bort 47 flown by Starshiy Serzhant Yuriy Shirokov, did not return from a combat mission and the other made a forced landing on friendly territory. Just the same, Georgiy Churakov managed to get even with one Messerschmitt for his wingman.

As before, new groups of enemy aircraft appeared over the front line and air battles were conducted without interruption. At 1000 on Tuesday, 27 April, Starshina Kalugin shot down a reconnaissance Hs126 from extremely close range in the Krymskaya area. Later squadron commander Novikov chased to ground yet another *crutch* (Soviet airmen's nickname for the Hs126). Closer to evening the pilots of 402nd IAP also excelled, downing five Bf109s in the same area. The corps lost two aircraft and one pilot: the Yak-1 (bort 28) of Starshiy Leytenant Dmitriy Tyugayev was shot down in air combat while a Yak-7B made a belly landing because of battle damage.

On the ninth day of combat, 28 April 1943, the commander of 2nd Squadron, Kapitan Timofey Novikov, shot up and destroyed a He111 from close range. This was the only victory over an He111 attributed to 4th VA in April. That afternoon he failed to return from a lopsided fight with Messerschmitts. Back in 1939, during air combat with the Japanese, he was awarded the Order of the Red Banner for courage and bravery in the skies of Khalkhin-Gol. The pilots of the squadron doted on him for his fairness and sense of justice.

Sixteen Yak-1s had sortied at 1300 to cover friendly forces in the Krymskaya area. Divided into two groups, the pilots began to patrol in their assigned area. Eight of the Yaks, under Kapitan Novikov's leadership, tangled with 12 Bf109s. In the course of 25 minutes of aerial combat Mayor Yeremin, Starshina Patrakov, and Starshiy Serzhants Tarasov and Kosov each shot down a single Bf109. With losses mounting, an additional six-ship fight came to reinforce the German group. These new arrivals directed their attacks first of all on group commander Novikov's Yak-1, bort 61. The squadron commander handled his aircraft very skillfully, using the maneuver qualities of the Yak to evade entrapment.

The Luftwaffe pilots, just the same, managed not only to disrupt the coordination between flights and pairs but also broke up pairs, breaking the fire coverage of the Yaks with each other. After downing a single Messerschmitt, flight commander V. Shirobokov was shot down. With his airplane on fire he was forced to bail out. The squadron commander's aircraft was also damaged. Abandoning his aircraft at low altitude, Kapitan Novikov managed to deploy his parachute, but not in time. He died.

An additional four Yak-1s of the 3rd IAK failed to return to their airfield. Over nine days of combat, pilots of the 265th IAD had participated in 38 group and seven individual aerial engagements, shooting down 63 enemy aircraft. The corps losses were 32 aircraft and 25 pilots. After factoring in the wounded air crews, the division had been effectively reduced by one regiment. By the beginning of the 56th Army offensive operation (29 April 1943), the 265th IAD had 46 air crews remaining. On the eve of this offensive (28 April), just as in all other units of the division, a meeting took place in the 812th Regiment. It was conducted by Mayor Pasynok, the regimental zampolit. Later, the famed Marshal of Aviation Ye. Ya. Savitskiy recalled this meeting.

I myself called Pasynok and his colleague political workers "winged commissars." Not only because the majority of them were excellent fighter pilots. I knew pilots who went on missions in the "commissar" group of Kapitan Pasynok with great enthusiasm.[32]

With the transition to the offensive in the area of Krymskaya stanitsa on 29 April, German aviation attempted to interfere with the actions of advancing Soviet forces, attacking with large groups of bombers escorted by powerful ranks of Bf109 and Fw190 fighters. Corps commander Ye. Ya. Savitskiy wrote in his memoir, "*Over the battlefield in the outskirts of Krymskaya stanitsa erupted a second aerial conflagration in the Kuban, not less in scale and intensity than the multi-day battle in the skies around Novorossiysk.*"[33] In the sky above Krymskaya, Abinskaya, and Neberdzhayevskaya, aerial battles took on a renewed fierce nature and lasted many hours.

Kosov, a pilot of the 1st Squadron   Starshina Mikhail Patrakov

The pilots from the Far East faithfully covered the advancing forces. Group leaders executed their primary mission, which was to destroy enemy bombers, first and foremost. Squadrons that had sortied to protect ground forces were replaced in the air, not leaving the troops without the cover of the division's fighters for a minute. On this memorable Thursday, 12 Yak-1s under Kapitan Svezhentsev sortied first at 0615. Within minutes, Bf109s arrived in the coverage zone. As a result of this encounter Kapitan Svezhentsev and Starshina Ilya Kukushkin each shot down two Messerschmitts, and flight commander Kostenko and Starshiy Serzhant Martynenko one Bf109 each. The group returned without loss and landed on their airfield at 0732.

An hour later eight Yak-1s took off under Batychko's command. In group battle Kapitan Batychko, Leytenant Kramarenko, and Starshina Ilya Kukushkin shot down one Bf109 while Mladshiy Leytenant Adamchuk destroyed another. The 402ⁿᵈ IAP had also engaged enemy fighters at this time. One of its pilots on this day was now mayor and navigator of 812ᵗʰ IAP, Dmitriy Nikolayenkov. Conducting a series of attacks on Bf109s, he forced them to disperse, but not before downing two of their number. The details of this battle, recorded in 1943, are preserved in the regiment digest.

In a pitched aerial battle Mayor Nikolayenkov remained alone against four enemy fighters. The fierce engagement lasted a long time. Nikolayenkov quickly caught one of the Messerschmitts in a turn and shot him up at almost point-blank range. Several minutes later the Mayor attached himself to the tail of a second Messerschmitt and set it on fire with one burst. But at this moment an enemy shell damaged his aileron and punctured his Yak's right fuel cell. The battle continued. An additional pair of Bf109s came to the assistance of the Germans. There were now four Germans against the mayor. Closing on one of the enemy, Nikolayenkov fired his last burst at the Messerschmitt. His ammunition had been
expended. New enemy tracers hammered the damaged Yak. His engine was smoking and his airplane was on fire. The flames were causing unbearable pain in his right arm and the clothing on his right leg was beginning to smolder, causing sharp pain. Drops of gasoline were burning on his face. Three times the mayor managed to extinguish fire by skidding but three times the fire erupted again. The Germans closed in for the kill and fired long bursts at him, but as before, the Mayor managed to avoid their strikes. During maneuvering he lost altitude and close to the ground found himself in a company of Shturmoviks and their fighter escort. The comrades in arms took the pilot under their care. The Germans broke off their attacks and departed, but Nikolayenkov's Yak caught fire again. The suffocating smoke in the cockpit was mixed with the odor of burning flesh. The mayor sought a landing site. Below him it appeared smooth. Having spotted the water, the pilot landed his wounded aircraft on a lush growth of reeds. The aircraft, burrowed into the mire, stopped burning. Mayor Nikolayenkov lost consciousness. The pilot was soon found by hurriedly approaching infantrymen who rendered him first aid. They took the barely alive pilot from the sinking and broken aircraft and delivered him to the hospital in an unconscious condition.

It is a good thing that a person cannot glance into his future. If Dmitriy Nikolayenkov knew that in five months he would be unlawfully convicted for an absurd accusation and sentenced by the court to 10 years of confinement, the mayor might not have returned alive from this battle.

At 1035 another group of fighters sortied from the regiment with the outcome of Leytenant Grigoriy Kramarenko shooting down an Fw190 southeast of Krymskaya. Kapitan Batychko's

Starshina Sergey Krysov

3ʳᵈ Squadron commander, Fedor Svezhentsev.
"Kapitan Svezhentsev was the first in the regiment to receive the Order of the Patriotic War II Class. He was recommended for the Order of the Red Banner. To the last breath, Fedor Svezhentsev gave his young bright life for a great cause."
Regiment staff in "Combat Path."

Pilots of the 812th IAP who died on 29 April 1943 in the Krymskaya area. Having sortied on a mission at 1315, they did not return. The combat pair of friends: Flight leader Leytenant Grigoriy Kramarenko and his wingman Starshina Ilya Kukushkin, and pilot Leytenant Aleksey Kostenko

group, this time with 10 Yak-1s, took off for their second time that day at 1235. At an altitude of 2500 meters (8200 feet) at 1314 the fighters of 812th IAP spotted two groups of 20 Ju87s, escorted by six Bf109s, approaching the front line. Batychko gave the command to his covering group (four Yaks) to engage the German fighters in combat, and to his strike group (six Yaks) to rapidly attack the group of bombers closest to the front line. From close range he shot down a Ju87. The remainder of the dive bombers began to drop their bombs wherever they fell and flee. But these same Stukas once again began to turn toward Krymskaya, forming an extended semi circle.

It was clear that the leader of the enemy group had not been hit and now the main effort had to be to destroy the commander of the bombers. Leytenant Sergey Krysov, who was closest of all to this aircraft, fired a long burst with all weapons at the enemy. The Ju87 blew up. The remaining aircraft, cutting loose their bombs over their own troops, quickly fled the battlefield. The second group also turned on a reverse course. Patrakov, Balabanov, and Lugovoy each shot down another Ju87. During this aerial engagement, the report came over the radio from the ground: "Beat the German occupiers! They are dropping bombs on their own troops. Way to go!" And they expressed their thanks to Pokryshkin.

But for the pilots of the 812th IAP, who had downed five bombers (increasing the regiment's score to 105 downed aircraft), it was not important whom they were praising. The important thing was that the enemy had suffered significant losses and had not accomplished his mission. Friendly losses were great as well. Three Yak-1s were shot down in air combat. Deputy squadron commander Leytenant Grigoriy Kramarenko, Leytenant Aleksey Kostenko, and Starshina Ilya Kukushkin had died. The hand-written digest "Combat Path," as maintained by the regiment staff during the war, was preserved as a legacy of the 812th IAP. The following description of Grigoriy Kramarenko's character was recorded in this digest.

He flew with the brave Kukushkin, loved his wingman,

and believed that his wingman would sooner die himself, but until the end he would be a faithful shield of the commander. One time the pair did not return. We did not know what had happened to them, but we were sure that both Kramarenko and Kukushkin had fought in their last battle as genuine heroes.

The 402nd Regiment did not lag behind the 812th. Its pilots also fought battles in the areas of Anastasevka and Krymskaya. Having shot down 15 enemy aircraft in a day, the regiment established a unique record in number of destroyed enemy aircraft in a day. Leytenant Aleksey Gorin, who destroyed four aircraft on that day, became a hero of the 402nd Regiment. But the regiment did not accomplish this feat without its own tragic losses. The commander of 402nd IAP, Mayor Vladimir Vasilevich Papkov, after he shot down a Ju87, also died that morning. This left the regiment without a commander practically until its withdrawal from the Kuban. Two of the three regiment commanders in the 265th IAD were lost during 10 days combat.

Pilots of the 4th Air Army flew 1028 aircraft sorties on this day, shooting down 71 enemy aircraft and damaging another eight. Among these were 39 Bf109s and 23 Ju87s. Fifteen Yak-1s did not return to 3rd IAK airfields.

In the last days of April, the intensity of the battles did not weaken. Only in the first days of May did enemy air activity slacken somewhat because of changes in the weather and the great losses in pilots on both sides. On 2 May 1943, the 812th Regiment lost its best young pilot when 19-year-old Starshina Mikhail Patrakov did not return from a combat mission. For displayed courage and bravery, he was awarded the Order of the Patriotic War II Degree. Also on this day Kapitan Batychko shot down a Ju88 in the Nizhne-Bakanskaya area, Kapitan Svezhentsev set a Bf109 on fire, and Leytenant Mashenkin destroyed an Fw189 in the Neberdzhayevskaya area. The 812th IAP lost one other Yak-1 before the end of the day: Starshina Balabanov, whose aircraft was set on fire, force-landed in the Slavyanskaya area.

Kapitan Timofey Novikov, commander 2ⁿᵈ Squadron, was killed in action on 28 April 1943.

"At this time I was at the ground-vectoring station, somewhere in the vicinity of Abinskaya stanitsa, two kilometers from the front line. The fighting was fierce; the sky was full of airplanes. I personally witnessed this battle. The advantage in numbers was to the Germans, but acting resolutely and decisively, Novikov's group shot down several fascists. Novikov himself was hit and he bailed out. He got a full chute and landed 200-300 meters (220-325 yards) from the front line. I hurried to the landing spot and found the pilot (at that time I did not know who it was) receiving artificial respiration from a doctor and nurse. But it was too late. During the deployment of his parachute, one of the straps wrapped around his neck and he suffocated. They gave me his documents, revolver, and Order of the Red Banner, which I returned to the headquarters. We buried T. Novikov there where he fell."

Igor Leonidovich Deryugin.

Monday, 3 May 1943, marked the beginning of what later came to be known as "black week" for the 812ᵗʰ IAP. During this week the regiment lost two squadron and three flight commanders. Three aerial battles were fought on Monday, in which four Bf109s were destroyed. At 0850 in the Krymskaya area, Aleksandr Tumanov shot down a Bf109. When the group returned to its airfield, it was missing the aircraft of Starshiy Serzhant Stepan Tarasov. At 1405 Kapitan Svezhentsev and Starshina Lugovoy each shot down a Bf109. Three hours later the group sortied again. At approximately 1700, covering the damaged Yak-1 of Lugovoy from an attack by Messerschmitts from JG52, Leytenant Tishchenko destroyed one more Bf109. Later he recalled:

> The ground vectoring station was silent. But suddenly out from behind scattered clouds jumped a pair of Messerschmitts. The Germans spotted us and went into a

Clipping from an Army newspaper of 1943

"Take vengeance upon the German scum!

(Letter of a combat friend to the pilots of Unit "N")

The wife of decorated pilot Kapitan Svezhentsev…

'…To be truthful, it was difficult to see Fedya off to the front. But I tried to keep control of myself. After he left, I frequently wrote letters to him. This was my only comfort. In his letters Fedya shared his intimate dreams, was quick to share the news with me of his first downing of a German airplane. In response I told him to hunt down the German scoundrels even more fiercely and take vengeance for our separation, for the suffering of millions of Soviet people, for the darkened childhood of our little children, for our own daughter. She is so much like her father! She reminds me of my friend every day…

…take revenge on the fascists for his death.'

Taisiya Svezhentseva"

deep turn. Lugovoy and I repeated their maneuver, believing that we could delay their maneuver and engage them. But the Germans had no intention of departing. In the turn our aircraft were so close that I could see a blue arrow on the fuselage of the lead Messerschmitt, penetrating a red ball. We turned for several minutes, watching each other and selecting the right moment for an attack. Then the lead Messerschmitt dropped his speed and began to approach me. I surmised his intention was to get on my tail and I pulled up. For some reason Lugovoy delayed, and the lead German immediately took aim at him. Energetically turning my aircraft, I threw it into a dive in order to assist Lugovoy. And at this moment directly in front of me I saw the German wingman. The range was not great, and I gave the Messerschmitt a long burst on the run. He lit up, the pilot popped his canopy, and bailed out.**34**

It can be added that the image of the red heart pierced by an arrow, which is probably what Tishchenko saw, was the unofficial emblem of Geschwader 52's 9ᵗʰ Staffel (9./JG52). Also on this day, a note regarding the fifth enemy aircraft shot down appears in the flight log of Kapitan Ivan Batychko. It was a Bf109.

Flying this Yak-1b, Kapitan Timofey Novikov lost his life in air combat with Luftwaffe Bf109s. Earlier he had also force-landed in a Yak-1b with this same bort number in the Severskaya area after a combat in which he downed an He111.

Yak-1b, bort 32 of the 1st squadron commander, Kapitan Ivan Batychko. The 8 victory ace was killed in action while flying this Yak-1b on his second sortie of the same day that he was awarded the Order of the Red Banner. During the height of the Kuban battle, the 812th lost three squadron commanders and two deputy squadron commanders in air combat. Though in heavy use, Yak-1bs typical of the regiment's Kuban days did not often exhibit a great deal of weathering, due to their relatively short time in service.

Stretching Our Wings and Gaining Strength

Because of the reduced number of flight crews, the command of 265th IAD was forced to curtail the number of aircraft in a coverage group from 10-12 to 4-6 and to assemble them from all the regiment's squadrons. Now the combat instructions gave greater independence to the lead commanders, which increased their combat capability and greatly reduced their combat losses. They no longer contained illogical orders concerning patrol altitude, speed, and time, which were calculated based on economic flight regimes instead of on combat necessities. The 3rd IAK losses for 3 May totalled 13 aircraft; three Yak-7B and a single Yak-1 were confirmed as shot down in aerial combat, while seven Yak-1s and two Yak-7Bs were tallied as not having returned to their airfields.

For reliable coverage of friendly troops, it was decided to engage and attack enemy bombers on their turf. The decision was reinforced by a strict combat instruction No. 8 of the 265th IAD headquarters from 4 May 1943. This order said the following:

> Do not fly east of the line Sementsevskiy-Sheptalskiy. For departing the indicated region, the group leaders and their commander will be subject to the judgment of a military tribunal.

The result of this division staff action was immediate. On Tuesday, 4 May, the 812th IAP destroyed five German aircraft. In the first sortie in the Krymskaya area, Kapitan Svezhentsev and Starshiy Serzhant Nikolay Kosov excelled by downing a Ju87 each. At noon Kapitan Batychko destroyed a single

Serafim Kalugin

Messerschmitt and at 1640 Starshina Mashenkin attacked an Fw189 in the Neberdzhayevskaya area. After first taking out the gunner, he fired at it again with all barrels.[35] This was already the second *frame* [a Soviet aircrew nickname for the Fw189] in the Kuban that was unable to escape from the sights of the talented Aleksey Mashenkin. In this same battle the pair of Tishchenko-Svezhentsev first fired on a Bf109 point blank from 10 meters (32 feet) and later destroyed another enemy fighter. This combat passion and energy did not abandon the pilots for a single minute. Despite all the weight of the combat losses they had suffered and the pain of losing their comrades, their youth won out. There always remained time for the demonstration of their boldness.

> Already when all our aircraft had taxied to the parking area, when the mechanics awaited the last aircraft with anticipation, suddenly Mashenkin's fighter appeared on the horizon. With great skill he executed a slow roll over the airfield, then dropped his landing gear and came in for a landing. His report to the commander was exceptionally terse: "Hunted together with a Cobra. Shot down a 'frame.' Mission accomplished."

Thus this event was recorded in the digest "Combat Path" of the headquarters, 812th IAP. The corps' losses on this day were minimal—one Yak-1 was damaged on landing.

On Wednesday, 5 May, eight Yak-1s, led by the commander of 1st Squadron, Kapitan Ivan Batychko, attacked a large group of German Ju87 dive bombers in the Krymskaya area. The attack was so unexpected that the enemy pilots released their bombs directly over their own forces. The squadron commander burst through the dense barrier fire toward the group leader and shot him down with his first burst. The bombers broke formation and scattered, permitting Leytenants Churakov, Mashenkin, and Kalugin each to shoot down another Ju87. Leytenant Krysov destroyed a Bf109 from the escort group, and three other aircraft were damaged.

In the evening of this same day, Kapitan Svezhentsev and Leytenant Kalugin, in a combined flight with General-Mayor Savitskiy, downed one Bf109 each, while Leytenant Mashenkin chased another pair of *skinnies* (a Soviet aircrew nickname for the Bf109) to ground.[36] All the regiment's aircraft returned to their airfield on this day. But the enemy analyzed every mistake and made adjustments, so the regiment continued to lose pilots. Starshina Sergey Krysov died on 6 May. In an aerial engagement four Yaks of Leytenant Tumanov intercepted a group of Ju87 bombers from 1/StG3. Having shot down two of the enemy, the pilots lost sight of Sergey Krysov for a time, whose aircraft was limping toward friendly lines with a smoking engine. Starshina Krysov did not make it back to his airfield.

In these May days an order came to the regiment concerning the promotion of all pilots currently wearing the rank of starshina or even serzhant to the rank of leytenant. On the morning of 7 May, the regiment's fighters again took flight. In an aerial engagement over the Krymskaya area, three Bf109s were shot down. Leytenants Lugovoy and Kalugin destroyed one each, and Kapitan Batychko shot another one from 10 meters (11 yards). Kapitan Batychko was awarded the Order of the Red Banner on this day. But the second sortie to the

Neberdzhayevskaya area was not so lucky. Taking off in two pairs (Batychko-Lugovoy and Tishchenko-Kosov), the squadron commander ended up going it alone. Lugovoy, his wingman, had damaged his Yak's propeller while taxiing and had to abort. At 1150 they encountering two Bf109s and immediately engaged them in battle. Leytenant Tishchenko shot down one of the enemy fighters. Looking around, Tishchenko's pair failed to spot the Yak-1 (bort 32) of Kapitan Batychko. The pilots returned home with a sense of sadness and, at the same time great hope, that Batychko would soon follow and not force them to await him. But still, on the following day, 1st Squadron commander Kapitan Ivan Batychko, an 8-aerial victory *ace*, did not show up at his airfield.

Kapitan Fedor Svezhentsev, commander of the 3rd Squadron and referred to in combat lists as the "fearless aerial knight," died on Saturday, 8 May. Through two weeks of combat he had flown 28 combat sorties, conducted 28 aerial battles, and personally shot down 10 enemy aircraft. On this day, while in combat with a pair of Bf109s in the Neberdzhayevskaya area, the pilots of the 812th IAP lost sight of their commander. Returning to their airfield and analyzing the aerial engagement, Leytenant Serafim Kalugin reported that he saw two Yak-1s collide during the combat, and that one pilot parachuted over our own territory in the area of the battle. An addendum to the 265th IAD headquarters operational summary for 12 May 1943 reads as follows:

> *Squadron commander of 812th IAP Kapitan Svezhentsev, F. K., having rammed a German aircraft, bailed out at 1030 on 08.05.43. He was shot by German fighters at an altitude of 2000-1500 meters (6500–4900 feet) and was dead upon landing.*

On this same day yet another young pilot went missing. Starshina Vasiliy Lugovoy, who had shot down four enemy aircraft in a relatively brief period of time, failed to return after his second sortie of the day. It was only determined after the war that Vasiliy Ivanovich Lugovoy was not killed in action, but had been taken captive. He was liberated in 1945.

After the loss of Lugovoy only Tishchenko, Mashenkin, Tumanov, Churakov, and Kosov remained combat capable along with the regiment command element. Another four pilots were in the hospital. Leytenant Kosov gained his second victory over a Bf109 in the Kuban sky in the afternoon, adding to his two Ju87s. On the following day (Sunday) Leytenant Fedorov shone. Still in a period of recuperation after being wounded, he was flying in pair with Leytenant Kosov. At approximately 1140 they encountered a German Fw189 reconnaissance plane. Fedorov attacked the *frame* from close range The German aircraft, dropping down, belly landed in the Moldavanskaya area. Later Fedorov recalled:

> *I saw, straight ahead and almost at the same altitude as me, a "frame"—a reconnaissance-spotter Fw189. I immediately came out of my turn, pushed the throttle forward, and began closing on it. I was slightly lower than the spotter plane; there were thin wisps of clouds, through which the rays of the sun were penetrating, making observation more difficult. The Fw189 began to maneuver energetically, apparently having realized that it was under attack. I selected an RPM setting, stabilized my speed, and*

Aleksandr Tumanov

"Having begun combat operations in the Kuban on 20 April 1943, this pilot did not stand out from the other ranks of pilots. He adapted himself, studying the tactics of the enemy and the tactics of his commanders. But already from the very beginning he defended and covered his comrades well while warning of the enemy's tricks. He fought bravely in his pair, never leaving his commander's side. There were intense aerial battles. The pilots flew four or five sorties per day. By the fourth and fifth, each pilot experienced near exhaustion, but Tumanov was calm, quiet, and withstood what seemed like the heaviest loads. He took off on a combat mission hoping to execute a normal flight. Aleksandr Tumanov had 67 combat sorties. He destroyed four enemy aircraft."

Regiment headquarters in "Combat Path."

Starshiy Serzhant Konstantin Mikhaylov's Yak-I of the 628th IAP (126th IAD, PVO) 14 May 1943, returns to terra firma with damage incurred during a ramming incident.

A. Tishchenko's eyewitness account of this aerial battle:

This was in the heat of the famous aerial conflagration in the Kuban. Our air regiment was based 20 kilometers (12 miles) from Krasnodar. In the morning we heard the explosions of antiaircraft shells from the direction of the town—a fascist He111 reconnaissance airplane appeared overhead. He maneuvered energetically, attempting to get out of the zone of fire. It must be said that he succeeded. Then a pair of our fighters went after him. An aerial duel unfolded. The Heinkel's gunner was silent, but the pair leader also turned away—either he was wounded or he had run out of ammunition. His wingman took his place, later revealed to be Starshiy Serzhant K. Mikhaylov. He fired two machine gun bursts from close range, after which it appeared that he also had run out of ammunition. However the Soviet pilot did not abandon his enemy. We determined that Mikhaylov had decided to ram the enemy aircraft. He stopped flying a "snake" maneuver around the Heinkel and began to approach it from above. First there was only five meters (16 feet) separating the two aircraft, then three, but the fighter passed by without cutting off the tail section of the enemy airplane. Our concern grew. Hundreds of people on the ground were watching this duel. We wanted somehow to support this brave fighter pilot, who for good reason did not want to abandon his prey, and continued to fight with him. Mikhaylov again approached his target. Now he came in a little lower, in order not to lose the Heinkel from sight for a single second. The coolness of the pilot as he undertook this considerable risk carried us away. Now he pulled the control stick to himself ever so little. The gap between the airplanes closed. Pieces of the enemy aircraft flew out from under the fighter's propeller. It went into a flat spin and began to fall.

got in behind the "frame." Now it could not get away. Now if only the Messerschmitts that the German could summon for assistance would not interfere. I got closer to the Focke-Wulf. I could see the pilot in his cloth helmet. The thought flashed through my mind, "You have come a long way, you swine, all the way to the Kuban!" I shot him with all my weapons. The Fw189 began to smoke, then burst into flames.[37]

On the pair's next sortie Leytenant Kosov, with his Yak damaged in an engagement with enemy fighters, had to make a forced landing. By Monday morning (10 May) there were only 22 combat-capable air crews in the entire division. This was all that remained of the three regiments of "far easterners." For the 812th IAP the morning and part of the afternoon passed without incident. At approximately 1700 a single Ju88, probably on a photo-reconnaissance mission, passed over the airfield at very low altitude. Coincidentally, regiment aircraft were launching at this time on a mission to clear the airspace of neighboring Abinskaya airfield which was under attack by German fighters. Unable to catch the Ju88, they continued on to Abinskaya, where Leytenant Fedorov managed to set one of the attacking enemy fighters on fire. Coming away from the attack, his own aircraft came under fire from another German fighter, and as a result received damage to the wing and engine. All his attempts to break away from the engagement, or go into the clouds, met with failure. Fedorov recalls:

Suddenly I saw a Messerschmitt with under-wing cannon coming straight at me, attacking me head-on. I made a lightning decision—ram! As long as I had not been shot down, I would fight! But how to execute the ram? My brain was working at the limit of its capabilities, feverishly seeking a feasible variant. Not long ago Spartak Makovskiy had rammed with his wing, the end of it. The German was firing at me, but I already was not paying attention to that. If only I could accomplish what I was contemplating. If only I could succeed! The Messerschmitt, attempting to avoid me, slightly changed course, but too late. I sharply banked the airplane, one wing raised up and the other dropped. There was a terrible shaking. I opened my eyes and I was falling. Without an airplane. Apparently, during the collision I was catapulted from the cockpit. All I saw was sky. I hurriedly pulled the parachute ring. I felt the shock and I was under canopy.[38]

Wounded in the legs and thrown through the canopy as a result of the collision, he regained consciousness, opened his parachute, and descended under the protective cover of 43rd IAP pilots Semen Lebedev and Spartak Makovskiy. The downed Bf109 was the second aircraft destroyed by ramming in the 812th IAP.

On Sunday, 16 May, the division headquarters, along with 291st and 402nd IAPs, was transferred to Novovelichkovskaya. These regiments continued to cover ground forces and the bombers of 223rd BBAD [blizhnyaya bombardirovochnaya aviatsionnaya diviziya (short-range bomber aviation division)] of Polkovnik L. N. Yuzeyev. At this time the 812th IAP was based at Novo-titarovskaya. However, because of the large losses in flight crews, it did not participate in further combat until the end of the month. Several pilots were involved in the retraining and preparation of new arrivals — replacements who had flown the I-16 and I-153 earlier. Six of the regiment's pilots were transferred to 291st IAP, on the basis of which was created a composite group of the division's pilots. The pilots from 812th IAP who joined this group were Kapitan Pavel Tarasov, Starshiy Leytenant Aleksandr Tumanov, Leytenant Aleksandr Ivanov, and Leytenant Serafim Kalugin.

From 17 to 25 May the intensity of combat in the Abinskaya-Krymskaya area fell, and the corps' pilots were able to regain their breath and rest somewhat. The single incident in the corps during this period occurred on Friday, 21 May when, after executing a combat sortie under the control of the 278th IAD, Kapitan Pavel Tarasov, landing in the corps' single La-5, missed his spot and overshot the runway. As a result the fighter suffered broken landing gear and damage to the tail portion of the fuselage. It was quickly repaired and on Monday, 25 May, the corps commander Leytenant General Savitskiy flew it as part of a composite group of corps pilots to escort Pe-2 bombers from the 2nd BAK.

Unexpectedly, rumors were circulating around the division that squadron commander Kapitan Ivan Batychko had been found in a field hospital at Elizavetinskaya stanitsa. With some hope the pilots awaited the results of a search for their commander. But pilots who arrived from the hospital on 23 May reported that this was a mistake. Squadron commander Kapitan Ivan Batychko was still missing in action.

On Wednesday, 26 May, battles on this sector of the front were renewed with an increased ferocity. On this day the 4th Air Army headquarters recorded 1,415 aircraft sorties, in which 87 enemy aircraft were damaged or destroyed. Pilots of the composite group demonstrated their mastery in full measure. Kapitan Pavel Tarasov, from a range of just 10 meters (33 feet), fired up a Bf109 near Krymskaya and a short time later a Fw190A (fuselage number LN-A) from 5./Schl.G1, the pilot of which (Leytenant Walter Schulze) perished along with his airplane.

At 1815 a flight of six took off under the command of Leytenant Lavrenov to escort Pe-2 and Boston bombers in the Kievskaya-Krymskaya area. On the return route at an altitude of 4,500 meters (14,750 feet) the group was forced to accept battle with six Bf109s near Krymskaya. Leytenant Aleksandr Ivanov, flying in the second pair, recalls that incident:

Tumanov, Kalugin, and Tarasov, and I sortied to cover a large group of bombers in a formation of 12 Yak-1s at an altitude of 2,500 meters (8,200 feet). During the approach to the target, we encountered heavy antiaircraft fire and because of that we knew that the German fighters would be waiting for us. The explosion of Oerlikon shells filled the sky, but we did not maneuver because the shell bursts were all around us. We were lucky and made it through. On the return leg, suddenly I saw a Messerschmitt come up behind me. I veered off and to my surprise a pilot from the rear of our formation attacked him. The Messerschmitt was hit, turned, and literally passed tens of meters in front of my airplane. I saw enormous crosses on his wings and immediately fired at him with my cannon and machine guns. He turned over and dropped away. A minute later I felt a heavy strike on my left wing and instantly all the skin of the wing was torn, and oil was running over the top of my canopy. The engine began to miss. I had either been shot at by an airplane or struck by antiaircraft fire Tumanov flew up on my right side, saw that I was damaged, and began to cover my landing. I dropped down, limped across the front line and saw a field near Abinskaya. I lowered my landing gear but the flaps would not deploy. I set it down softly and suddenly through my stained canopy saw a wall in front of my airplane. I was unable to react quickly enough and hit it hard.

The 812th IAP operational summary for 26 May 1943 reads:

"1845. Leytenant Ivanov fell behind in the same battle and as a result was damaged. He made a belly landing south of Abinskaya. The pilot was pulled out of his airplane by ground troops. His condition is unknown."

Leytenant Ivanov's Yak-1, without brakes, had slid into a revetment perimeter ditch that was located, as it turned out, on a dummy airfield. The impact was so heavy that the pilot was thrown from the cockpit and he flew across the ditch. During the fall Aleksandr struck his face heavily and his right foot was rotated 180 degrees. He ended up in hospital with a head injury and broken leg. Leytenants Kalugin, Ivanov, Tumanov, and Vasilev, each of whom shot down a single Bf109, excelled in that battle. One Yak-1 was lost.

Altogether during that day the 3rd IAK conducted 23 group air battles and destroyed 21 Bf109s, three Fw190s, four Ju87s, two Ju88s and two He111s. The corps lost two Yak-7Bs and one Yak-1,

Kapitan Pavel Tarasov

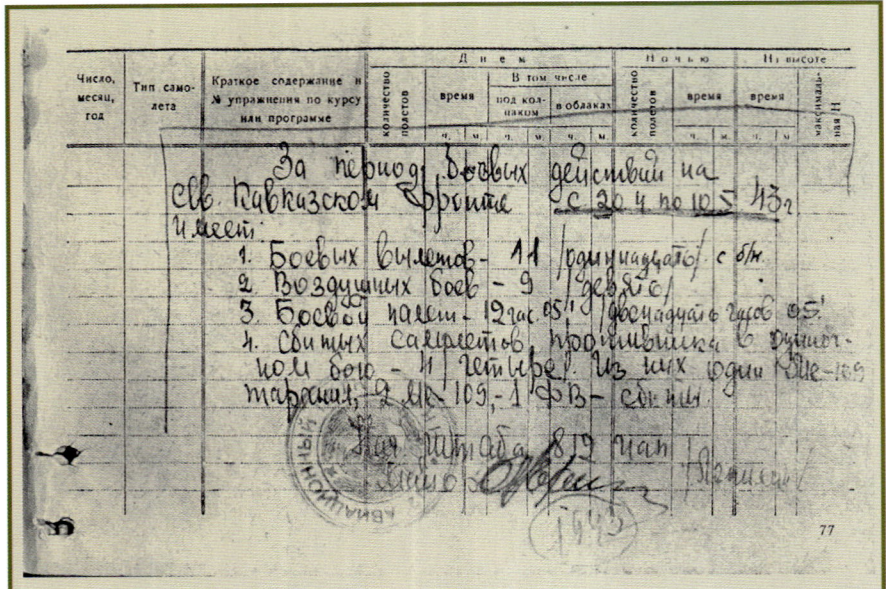

More victories for Leytenant Ivan Fedorov in the Kuban, as witnessed by a page from his logbook for 10 May 1943 — three Bf109s and one Fw189.

"Fedorov flew like everyone there,
he tried to hit the enemy with aimed fire.
He got damn tired,
But fought fiercely with the aces,
He even rammed a fascist,
And lived to tell about it!"
Pavel Vasilyevich Korneyev
"From Stalingrad to Berlin."

Kuban. Stanitsa Novotitarovskaya, end of May 1943. Practically everyone who remained of the regiment: (left to right) A. Tumanov, A. Ivanov, I. Fedorov, I. Martynenko, A. Mashenkin

with another Yak-1 damaged. In air combat on the following day, 27 May, the group lost three Yak-1s that did not return to their airfield. In the Kievskaya area, Leytenant Loginov and Mladshiy Leytenant Georgiy Churakov shot down one Fw190 each and Kapitan Tarasov destroyed a Bf109. One Fw190A-5 (white W) of Leutnant Willi Auster, lost on that day in an engagement with fighters, was registered as a loss by 5./Schl.G 1.

Tumanov's wingman, Leytenant Ivan Martynenko, lost his Yak also. The engine suddenly burst into flames in the air. Maneuvering sharply and thinking there was a Messerschmitt on his tail, Martynenko headed toward Soviet lines. Soon, the fire began to engulf the fuselage and cockpit. Not waiting a second longer, he bailed out and deployed his parachute at approximately 4,000 meters (13,100 feet) altitude. On descent he came into the enemy aviation zone of actions. This jump could end tragically for the young pilot. Luftwaffe *hunters* were reported to have no qualms whatsoever about shooting parachutists under canopy. Realizing the loss of his wingman, Leytenant Tumanov, just as in the case with Ivanov, did not abandon his pilot but flew circles around the him as he descended. Everything worked out all right. When he observed Martynenko touch the earth, Tumanov waggled his wings and flew off to his airfield.

On Friday, 28 May, a group of six Yak-1s sortied at 0725 to clear the airspace in the Kievskaya area. Soon after take-off, they attacked a group of Ju87s, shooting down three of them. Kapitan Pavel Tarasov, Leytenant Serafim Kalugin, and Mladshiy Leytenant Georgiy Churakov each scored. Ten minutes later, the group arrived in the Kievskaya area and encountered a group of Bf109s. The battle turned out fortunate for the Yaks. Tarasov, Tumanov and Kalugin each scored a Bf109. A forth Messerschmitt was scored as a group kill. Tumanov's wingman, Kutsenko, suffered damage in the same engagement and headed for Soviet lines at low altitude. Continuing the flight, Kalugin's Yak-1 was struck by German antiaircraft fire. He too had to leave the formation and return to base. On the way back his aircraft caught fire and he bailed out in the Slavyanskaya area. He was delivered to the airfield by the headquarters U-2 at 2030.

War Prize: Eric Hartmann's Bf109!

At this time a rare event occurred in the corps, one seldom repeated throughout the war. The deputy commander of the 812th IAP, Kapitan Pavel Tarasov, managed to lead a Bf109G-4/R6 (Wr.N 14997) to Soviet lines and force it to land. The operational summary of 4th Air Army on this day notes:

> *"A group of Yak-1 pilots formed a ring around a Bf109*
> *and forced it to land near Mayskiy, south of Slavyanskaya.*
> *The pilot was taken into custody."*

Here is what happened. After accomplishing the mission for covering ground troops, Kapitan Pavel Tarasov noticed that a single Bf109 was below and to the right of his group. Deciding to attack the enemy, Tarasov and a Yak with a black prop spinner quickly came up behind the Messerschmitt. He crowded the German fighter toward the ground, and both fighters led the German toward Soviet territory. Kapitan Tarasov wanted to deliver the captured German fighter to his own airfield, but the Bf109 attempted to escape several times with energetic maneuvers. On the approach to the Kuban River, in the Slavyanskaya area, the Messerschmitt deviated toward the west, ignoring Tarasovs instructions, conveyed by way of machine gun tracers. Carefully approaching the German fighter so that the pilot could see him, Tarasov instructed him where to land with arm and hand signals—to the left and below. For complete clarity he drew his hand across his throat and gave another warning burst. The German ignored him and Tarasov fired one burst at his tail, after which the German force-landed south of Slavyanskaya in the area of Mayskiy village.

As Tarasov observed, a large crowd of people gathered around the grounded Messerschmitt, while the Yak with the black spinner disappeared in the direction of Novotitarovskaya. They never managed to determine whom it belonged to. Because the spinners of the 812th IAP aircraft were white, it was presumed that it belonged to a 278th IAD regiment.

The captured German pilot turned out to be Uffz. Herbert Meissler from 7./JG52. But the most interesting thing was that the aircraft that had fallen into the hands of the 812th pilots had belonged to Leutnant Eric Hartmann, who by the end of the war had become the leading ace among all warring powers. Just two days before this episode, on 25 May, Hartmann made a forced landing in this aircraft — his fifth over a short period of time. His commander sent him on leave and his fighter, after repair, was given to Meissler. He was captured on his first flight in this aircraft! After the war, returning from captivity, Meissler stated that he made his forced landing because of a "navigation error." But, as they say, "after a fist fight, don't mouth off."

The pilots of neighboring 402nd Regiment shot down four Bf109s on this day, three of them credited to Mladshiy Leytenant R. I. Ishkhanov. On Sunday, 30 May, the 265th IAD had 23

Yak-1s and 18 air crews available. Meanwhile, the 278th IAD inspector for flight technique, Mayor A. I. Novikov, shot down an He111 bomber near Troitskaya. The 402nd IAP put a close to the actions of the 265th IAD and the 3rd IAK in the Kuban. On 3 June, Mladshiy Leytenants Gorin and Gradusov shot down two Bf109s each and shared two Ju88s in the Kievskaya area. These were the last of the corps' victories attained in the skies over Southern Russia.

Leaving 46 pilots for all eternity in the soil of the Kuban, the 265th IAD was removed from the 4th Air Army of the North Caucasus Front to the supreme high command reserve. On Friday, 4 June 1943, the 265th IAD turned over its 14 remaining Yak-1s to the 278th IAD. At this time the 3rd IAK consisted solely of the 278th IAD (15th, 43rd and 274th IAP), which were all equipped with Yak-1 and Yak-7B fighters.

Above: Hartmann's Bf109G-4/R6 *Kanonboote*, Wr.N 1499729 on strength with III./JG52 in the Kuban area of operations, and (left) dutifully employed by Soviet propaganda makers only a short time later.

Izvestiya newspaper, No. 230, 29 September 1943
This celebrated "Messer" served as a theme for much speculation in the press at various levels (from informational leaflets to central newspapers), on both the Soviet and the German side.
As in this example, one can often see a striking photo of this aircraft in various published sources of the time with various stories! These texts describe this aircraft as a victory on this or that pilot. The "persuasiveness" of the publications, in the opinion of their originators, was reinforced by the thick smoke surrounding the enemy aircraft which, however, is parked on lowered landing gear with bent propeller blades. This "beauty" was achieved by nothing else but a smoke pot thrown under the aircraft. These methods, utilized as propaganda, nonetheless do not in any way cast a shadow on the heroism of Soviet pilots. All participants in the war, be they political or military, had their duty. And each fulfilled it in their own way.
Courtesy of Izvestiya archive

Лётчик 88 Новороссийского Гвардейского истребительного авиационного полка, Герой Советского Союза, капитан В. А. Князев (справа) сбил 23 немецких самолёта. На снимке слева: горящий немецкий самолёт, сбитый Князевым.
Фото специального военного корреспондента «Известия» Л. Бернштейна.

On 10 June the enlisted personnel from 265th IAD were assembled on Tikhoretsk airfield. Six days later the 3rd IAK commenced rebasing at Lipetsk, simultaneously turning its command element and 278th IAD regiment aircraft over to the 236th IAD. Altogether they transferred 92 serviceable and seven unserviceable fighters, along with two Yak-7[UTI] trainers. An additional 37 aircraft from the corps' strength remained in the repair facilities of the 4th Air Army. The withdrawal of the corps to the rear and transfer of its aircraft permitted pilots of 236th IAD to move up from their old I-16s and I-153s. Thus the 611th IAP (as part of the 236th IAD) surrendered its I-16s and I-153s at Stavropol and received the former 812th IAP Yak-1 fighters at Novotitarovskaya airfield.

The pilots of the 812th IAP trained the new "owners" of their former mounts at this same airfield. Leytenant Aleksey Mashenkin, who has been able to recall his instructor duty, was particularly successful in coaching the pilots of 611th IAP. Soon the remnants of the 812th IAP aircrews, who were loaded into an Li-2 transport, flew away to Lipetsk for reforming. Leytenant Fedorov recalls:

> Our airplane was carrying the aircrews of the 812th Fighter Aviation Regiment, more precisely, those who had survived the terrible battles in the Novorossiysk area. On this airplane were the regiment commander Mayor A. U. Yeremin, zampolit Mayor T. Ye. Pasynok, regiment navigator Mayor D. Ye. Nikolayenkov, recently named squadron commanders Leytenants A. T. Tishchenko and A. M. Mashenkin, deputy squadron commanders Leytenants G. P. Churakov, A. I. Tumanov, and I. V. Fedorov, and also flight commanders Leytenants I. N. Martynenko and S. P. Kalugin. I involuntarily counted— ten altogether. We were missing comrades who had been removed from flight status because of wounds and contusions received in combat.[39]

The last one to leave the Kuban sky was corps commander General Savitskiy. Before he flew to Lipetsk, Savitskiy ordered the corps head doctor to assemble all the pilots who could be found in hospitals. Aleksandr Ivanov remembers:

> I was in Krasnodar hospital, when our doctor arrived from the corps. Having reached agreement with the hospital's head doctor, he came and got me. On the following day, I arrived at the airfield and learned that the aircraft with the 812th IAP crews had just departed for Lipetsk. At the controls of the Li-2 in which we flew was Savitskiy, who had organized the assembly of all of us wounded pilots. At first he flew the airplane at tree-top level, and later, when we had traveled about 150 km (93 mi.) away from the airfield, he went to normal altitude.

The memory of two squadron commanders—Kapitans Fedor Svezhentsev and Ivan Batychko—was preserved in the regiment until the very end of the war. New pilots arrived and zampolit

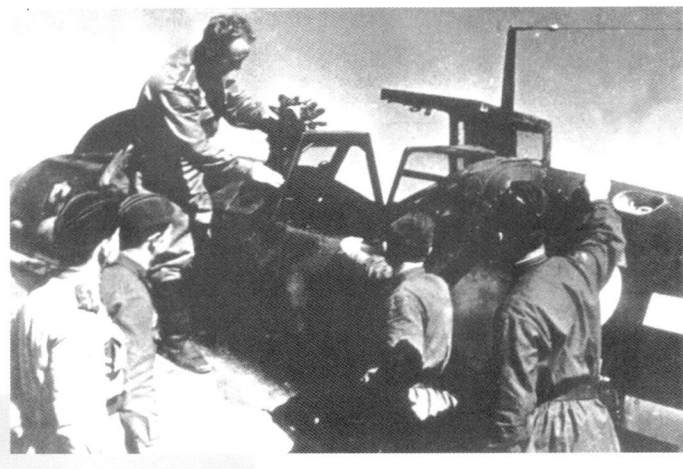

Kapitan Pavel Tarasov and corps commander Yevgeniy Savitskiy visit the trophy together.
"Kapitan Pavel Timofeyevich Tarasov was the oldest warrior in our unit. He fought against the German air forces from the first day of the Great Patriotic War. Kapitan Tarasov marked his glorious combat activity on the North Caucasus Front by escorting and landing a fascist 'carrion' on our territory. This was done with such skill that the enemy pilot was literally stunned."
Regiment headquarters in "Combat Path"
Contrary to the official Soviet account, the pilot of the Bf109 disclaims the fact of a forced landing on a Soviet airfield, insisting on loss of orientation in the air.

The Yak-equipped 3rd IAK had one La-5 in its command unit. Interestingly, it was one of several Lavochkins sporting the factory applied "Eskadrilya Valeriy Chkalov" dedication script. Pilots with experience on the type flew combat sorties in it. On 21 May 1943 Kapitan P. Tarasov damaged it while landing, but it was promptly repaired. On 24 May General-Mayor Savitskiy flew it as controller on a Pe-2 bomber-escort mission. On 30 May HSU Kapitan Novikov, deputy Corps commander for aerial gunnery, shot down an He111 bomber while flying this airplane. After the 3rd IAK left the Kuban area, this airplane was transferred to the 236th IAD (20 June 1943). Its further destiny remains unknown.

Bf109G-4/R6 "Kanonboote" Wr.N 1499729, 7./JG52, May 1943. Not quite the last, but certainly the most famous Kuban-era victory for the 812th IAP. Kapitan Pavel Tarasov, assisted by another Yak from a neighboring unit, forced Uffz. Herbert Meissler to land this former mount of Eric Hartmann behind Soviet lines on 28 May. A Po-2 brought down on 15 May was the German ace's 15th victory — his last in this aircraft. The tail and rear fuselage exhibit what is very likely bullet-hole damage. The refueling point hatch is missing while the prop blades are well and truly bent as a result of a nose-over during landing. Interestingly, the engine cowl panel features mounting holes for the tropical filter installation, although this particular aircraft was not a 'trop'.

Timofey Pasynok always told them about the unit's fallen heroes, by whose example the young men had to be trained. Verses, written in the regiment at that time, though they are not notable for meter or high poetic art, reflect all the pride and pain felt for fallen comrades:

Soon combat decorations, handed to them by the corps commander Savitskiy, adorned the chests of the participants of battles who excelled in the skies of Novorossiysk and above the Kuban. This awarding, which occurred in front of a formation of the 265th IAD, was unique in two ways. It was a small formation of pilots who had survived the combat and the phrase "is awarded posthumously" was often heard that day. The majority of awards in the 812th IAP were distributed in that manner. And for so many pilots who did not receive awards, who heroically perished in their first sortie, only the brief note in the journal of combat losses remained: "Did not return from combat mission."

Altogether in the period from 19 April to 29 June 1943, the 812th IAP conducted 462 combat sorties with a total flight time of 453 hours. 95 enemy aircraft were shot down in aerial engagements: 62 Bf109s, two He111s, two Hs126s, four Ju88s, 16 Ju87s, five Fw189s, and four Fw190s. The regiment's losses were 17 pilots (killed and captured) and 25 aircraft.

At Lipetsk the pilots of the 291st, 402nd, and 812th Aviation Regiments were able to rest, fill out their ranks with new young pilots, receive aircraft, and conduct training of the new crews. The brief two-week rest came to an end. Young pilots -

graduates of flight schools - began to arrive in all three 265th IAD regiments. Massive reinforcements were being added to the nine pilots of 812th IAP who had survived the Kuban battles. From 1 July to 1 August the regiment was supplied with 26 pilots. Altogether 101 rated personnel arrived in the corps.

Flying began and pairs—the basic tactical units in fighter aviation—were formed. Command was in a hurry, as the Kursk battle was just beginning. Nonetheless, the delivery of Yak-1 aircraft from the Saratov plant was delayed. Not long before this, the Luftwaffe had conducted bombing raids on industrial targets in Gorkiy, Yaroslavl, and Saratov. The Saratov aviation plant, which produced the Yak-1, had been damaged heavily enough to noticeably reduce its output. Thus, the division's units received new 37mm cannon-armed Yak-9T fighters from the Novosibirsk production line.

A change of leadership occurred at all levels. Podpolkovnik Aleksandr Aleksandrovich Koryagin was named the commander of 265th IAD, and Podpolkovnik M. A. Lovkov became the division chief of staff. New regiment commanders were also named: Mayor Yakimov in 291st IAP, the former commander of the 812th IAP Mayor Aleksey Yeremin was named commander of 402nd IAP, and Mayor Nikolayenkov, formerly the regiment navigator, was named commander of the 812th IAP. For many of the pilots, the motive and thought behind the transfer of Mayor Yeremin to another regiment was not entirely clear.

Ye. Ya. Savitskiy in the Kuban. A general who frequently flew with his men.

Mayor A. U. Yeremin, regiment commander with Ivan Batychko's Yak-1b in the background.

Incoming - Mayor D. Nikolayenkov (left) - and outgoing - Mayor A. Yeremin - commanders of the 812th IAP. Yerimin would stay in the corps, taking up the helm of the neighboring 402nd IAP.

In their memoirs, the former commander of the 3rd IAK Savitskiy and 812th IAP squadron commander Tishchenko clarified the situation. The circumstances that developed in the 812th IAP forced the commander of 3rd IAK to consider and then take measures. Savitskiy recalls one of the events that occurred on 19 April 1943, during a familiarization flight over the territory of upcoming battles, and the subsequent discussion of that flight.

The commander of the 812th IAP, Mayor A. U. Yeremin, managed to lose his subordinates during the flight, which might have made them easy prey for the Messerschmitts or they could have become lost. Fortunately, everything turned out all right, but the first reaction to this information was to remove Yeremin from command of the regiment. However, after some consideration, I allowed him to remain in command. To remove Yeremin would mean to put someone else in his place, someone I felt was better. But there was no one in the regiment to replace him. His deputy, Kapitan Nikolayenkov, did not yet have the experience of command. And the primary reason was that tomorrow the unit would be in combat, and any new commander, even if he be a Solomon, could not come into this situation and immediately have people recognize him as their "Tsar and God."

I went to the "far easterners," to the 812th Regiment myself. I wanted to visit another, less familiar regiment. But the incident with the 812th IAP command group forced me to attend a party meeting specifically at this regiment. They had assembled right on the airfield. Tishchenko was not afraid to talk about what had happened that day during the familiarization flight. Before the meeting I had

already spoken with the regiment commander, Mayor Yeremin, with the pilots who had participated in this ill-fated flight, and had a complete understanding of what had happened.

Having received the order to overfly the area of flight operations, Mayor Yeremin had decided to take his entire regiment up at one time. In the center flew the 1st Squadron under the leadership of the regiment commander himself. The 2nd Squadron to the right was under the command of Leytenant F. V. Svezhentsev, and the commander of 3rd Squadron, Starshiy Leytenant T. T. Novikov, who had the same last name as my deputy for aerial gunnery training, was leading the squadron on the left.

They reached altitude and set a course for Abinskaya stanitsa. After several minutes of flight, below the regiment formation both Mayor Yeremin and many pilots spotted a two-engine aircraft. Yeremin, having decided that this was a German Heinkel, without even warning his wingman Leytenant Tishchenko, did a wing-over turn and went down. Tishchenko managed to repeat the maneuver of his leader. When they approached the bomber to the range of opening fire, they looked around, fortunately, for it was one of our own Pe-2s. They needed to return to the group.

They climbed back to altitude and looked around. They could not see the regiment's aircraft anywhere. They began to maneuver. Searching for the regiment, they forgot about orientation. They could not locate neither the front line nor Abinskaya. Fuel was inexorably dwindling

A meeting of the 265ᵗʰ IAD leadership. From left to right: Mayor D. Ye. Nikolayenkov, Mayor A. U. Yeremin, General-Mayor Ye. Ya. Savitskiy, Polkovnik P. T. Korobkov. For Pavel Terentyevich Korobkov, this meeting was his farewell with his division. No less talented, commander A. A. Koryagin replaced the division's Kuban-era commander.

away. Finally, Tishchenko managed to look around and then report to the commander that there was some kind of airfield beneath them.

They needed to land, without even confirming by the traffic pattern that this was not an enemy airfield. Again, fortunately, it was ours. It belonged to the air army. They refueled, had the route home explained to them, and took off again. The regiment's remaining aircraft, after the unanticipated "disappearance" of the regiment commander's aircraft, were left without leadership, and without a commander (Yeremin had not even named a deputy in the event his aircraft became disabled) dispersed in all directions. And only good training (the vast territories of the Far East were a good school) in orientation permitted all the pilots to reach their own airfield. Any other group, the more so separate pairs, might have become easy prey for the Messerschmitts that were poking about everywhere. I had to have a rather stern conversation with Mayor Yeremin.[40]

Of the division's three regiments, by the end of the intensive Kuban actions the greatest personnel losses were in the 812ᵗʰ IAP. After the 7 May death of squadron commander Ivan Batychko, the corps commander visited the regiment once again. Tishchenko recalls this visit in his memoirs:

In the evening General Savitskiy arrived in the regiment.

He was tired and dissatisfied. It was no joke that after two weeks, we had lost so many pilots. And what kind of pilots they were! Where would he find replacements? How could the unit keep fighting? It seems that the general also spoke with the regiment commander eyeball-to-eyeball about this in the headquarters dugout. We guessed by the mood of Mayor Yeremin, who accompanied the corps commander, that the conversation was anything but pleasant.[41]

Yeremin himself had mixed feelings. The regiment's enormous losses during a time of heavy combat weighed heavy upon his shoulders. Discussing the newly arriving young pilots with his zampolit, Timofey Pasynok, he said:

"The best training for a pilot is combat. If I had not flown combat as much with Batychko, Svezhentsev, and Novikov, then nothing would have become of the newcomers for a long time."[42]

Having discussed the theme of the young pilots, their capability to conduct aerial combat on a par with the Germans, and having talked about their confidence in the arriving reinforcements, the commander and zampolit did not find common ground. Pasynok was angered by Yeremin's "panic" and lack of confidence in the people whom he was to lead into combat. By mutual agreement, and in a straightforward manner, like true leaders, they decided to report to the corps commander, and inform him of the developing situation.

Having listened to both sides, General Savitskiy gave Yeremin a reprimand and after some consideration made the following decision:

"Leave Pasynok in his present assignment. Transfer Yeremin to another regiment."[43] *The flow of circumstances and the general situation did not permit the corps commander, General Savitskiy, to leave Mayor Yeremin in the 812th IAP. He was appointed to the position of commander of the neighboring 402nd IAP.*[44]

Located in Lipetsk and engaged in planning work, the division and regiment headquarters also conducted analyses of the battle that had been fought in the Kuban. Tactical aviation conferences for the generalization and exchange of battle experience were not uncommon in this period. As a result of these discussions, the 265th IAD developed its plan for the conduct of aerial battle and the basic deficiencies in fighter tactics were exposed.

First is the illogical construction of the combat formations of groups. Squadrons of 10-12 aircraft were in a battle area in a compact combat formation, at low speed, and at an assigned altitude of 2000-5000 meters (6,550–16,400 feet). All this, as the pilots were informed, gave encouragement to the defenders of Malaya Zemlya. The high command liked this, the so-called psychological factor for ground troops. The sky is covered with red-starred fighters. And only at the conclusion of the battles for the Kuban, after the large and unjustified losses, was the "Kuban bookshelf" mastered.

The second substantial deficiency is the striving of pilots to attack the enemy personally, forgetting about their primary obligation—to execute their combat mission as part of a combat formation of a group. Sometimes even pairs were split up, and the German pilots quickly took advantage of this. The majority of our pilots were shot down by enemy fighters without warning. The leader, relying on his wingman, confidently went into the attack, and the wingman, distracted by battle, left the leader without cover. The loss of one of the pilots from a pair gave birth to another problem—the sortie on combat missions of uncoordinated pairs. As a result, they did not always understand each other in combat: the wingman, not knowing the peculiarities of the piloting techniques of his leader, did not always manage to react to the commander's maneuver, and frequently lost sight of him.

It was in this way, at the price of enormous losses, that mastery and experience in the conduct of battles were born. And thanks to such experience, by 1945 some 20 of the division's pilots would achieve the rank of Hero of the Soviet Union. Fully half of those would surpass the of 20 victories threshold.

At the end of August 1943, the 3rd IAK, now equipped with 193 fighters, became part of the 8th Air Army. In this period the headquarters of the 3rd IAK and the 265th IAD, together with the 402nd IAP were based on Lipetsk airfield, while the 291st and 812th Aviation Regiments were located on Trubetchino airfield, which belonged to the airfield network of 15th Air Army of the Steppe Front. 28 August was a long-awaited and celebrated event in the history of the 812th IAP. It may seem strange, but before this day the it had fought without a regimental banner — the primary *sacred object* of any unit. For reasons unknown, this regiment simply did not have one. And now, finally, on this Saturday summer day, the commander of the 265th IAD, Podpolkovnik Koryagin, arrived at the regiment and in front of the formation handed over its own combat banner, in accordance with Order of the Presidium of the Supreme Soviet of the USSR from 23 December 1942. For the regiment, new battles were about to begin—the battles for southern Ukraine.

Stalin christened us with the name "Eagles",
Svezhentsev and Batychko became heroes!
Their hearts glowed with an awesome strength of vengeance,
And they often sortied together!
Fiery tracers burned through the air,
Our aces were downing Messerschmitts.
German cemeteries were quickly growing,
They were beating the Germans often, as Stalin taught them!
It was their habit to help each other in combat,
Here comes Kapitan Batychko from the south.
He forced the black armada to stop,
And shot down five of the cursed enemy.

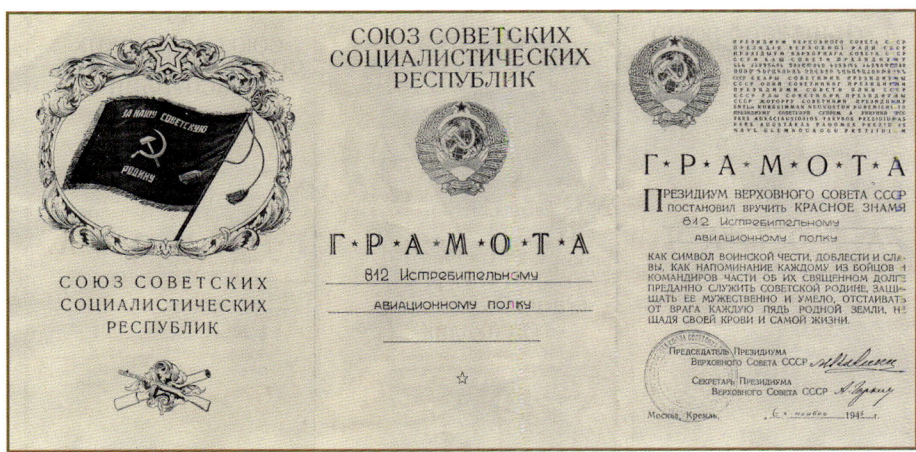

Citation that was awarded to the regiment upon receipt of its own regimental Combat Red Banner, 6 November 1943.

3

Fall and Winter 1943: In the Tavri Sky

Banner of the 812th Sevastopol IAP now preserved in the Central Museum of the Armed Forces of the Russian Federation. Two order streamers show the fact that the regiment was awarded the Order of the Red Banner and the Order of Suvorov III Degree.

An overview of fighter coverage in the Melitopol operation. Winter, 1943.

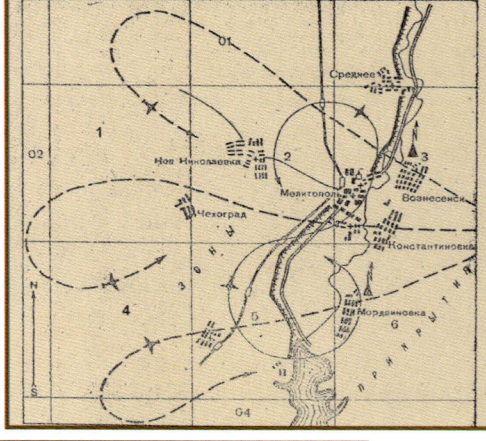

The Molochnaya offensive: September - October 1943

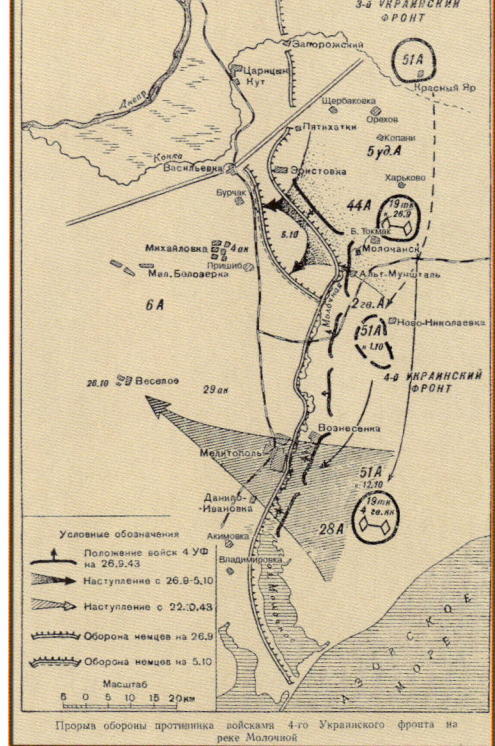

OVERVIEW:
Combat Actions of the 265th IAD in the South Ukraine

Having broken the enemy's stubborn resistance in the Voroshilovgrad-Taganrog sector, by the end of August 1943 the forces of Southern Front were rapidly developing the offensive. With that, the enemy withdrew to a line on the Molochnaya River and held for twenty days. With defenses broken in the last week of October, he successfully withdrew, digging in on the right bank of the Dniepr River.[45] Subsequently the forces of the 4th Ukrainian Front fought battles for Crimea and Sevastopol, overcoming a stubborn enemy resistance that was based on a system of heavily engineered fortifications. German aviation, operating continuously against Soviet forces, was striving to limit the tempo of the Red Army's advance. By the beginning of the offensive some 250-300 enemy bombers, and up to 100 fighters, were operating against the 4th Ukrainian Front. The 265th IAD, as part of 3rd IAK, was subordinated to the 8th VA. At that time the combat composition of the division was 46 Yak-1s and 50 Yak-9Ts. Of its 108 pilots, 20 had just arrived from flight schools. While the basic cadre of pilots already had a fair amount of combat experience against fighters, the young replacements were inadequately prepared. They had to be trained and introduced into the unit structure in the midst of combat operations. The division's mission, as before, was to support the combat operations of ground forces. Missions were also assigned to escort bombers and ground attack aircraft in action against enemy ground forces.

The air situation was characterized by groups of up to 100 Axis He111, Hs129, Ju87, and Ju88 bombers and attack planes massed in strikes against Red Army mobile forces and lines of communication. More often than not these aircraft were escorted by large numbers of fighters. Additionally, the enemy protected his ground forces with *hunting* pairs and four-ship elements of Bf109 and Fw190 fighters. The primary mission of VVS fighter aviation here was to contend with the bomber and attack formations. Enemy fighters were to be secondary in priority. The 265th IAD was assigned the job of preventing the full range of enemy aviation combat operations focussed on Red Army troop concentrations around Bolshoy Tokmak and Voroshilovka.

Soviet aviation was based at airfields a mere 10-15 kilometers (6–10 miles) from the front line. Despite this, fighter sorties were initially delayed, as a rule, because the notification and communication system functioned poorly. This deficiency was alleviated only with the introduction of the RUS-2S *Pegmatit* radar detection system. Using airfields too close to the front line also negatively affected *on call* efforts; pilots were unable to gain sufficient altitude prior to reaching the target when they sortied in response to alarms. Enemy bombers were often engaged from positions unfavorable to fighter effectiveness. The bombers' gunners were thus able to inflict greater losses. Nonetheless, it was necessary to engage as soon as possible, regardless of position, in order to hinder the enemy attacks from getting through to friendly forces on the ground.

Adding to the problem in the Tokmak and Melitopol areas, the enemy escorted his bombers with potent fighter groups. Designated pairs of *hunters*, as well as larger groups of Bf109s,

Pulse "radio-detector" [radar] RUS-2 featured 180° detection, a long wave length of 4 meters and 50 kilowatts of power. Its signal generator was based on IG-8 vacuum tubes while the signal modulator had G-300 tubes. The transmitting/receiving set, with "wave channel" type antennas, was assembled in rotating bodies on the chassis of a GAZ-AA truck. It had a special design that synchronized the rotation. The unit permitted continuous determination of target range, azimuth, and flight speed. Its detection range was up to 95 km (59 miles) for 7,500 m (24,600 ft) altitude targets and 30 km (19 miles) at 500 m (1,650 ft). The information was presented on a small cathode-ray tube with a range accuracy of 2–3 km (1.2–1.8 miles). These sets were produced by plants No. 339 of the People's Commissariat of Aviation Industry and No. 703 of the People's Commissariat of Ship Industry. In 1942-43, the RUS received the VPM-1, -2, and -3 "altitude attachments" — components for determining the target altitude. A single-antenna collapsible variant "Pegmatit" was developed and accepted into the inventory in 1942. Designated RUS-2S, it had better high altitude range — up to 110 km (68 miles) at 8,000 m (26,250 ft) — but no change in low altitude capabilities. Coordinate position accuracy tightened to 1.5 km (.9 miles) and ±7 degrees. Overall, it was equal in effectiveness to the Allies' MRU-105 or SCR-270 sets. The vectoring stations of the 3rd IAK used both the RUS-2 and RUS-2S "Pegmatit".

were tasked to clear VVS fighters from the target-area airspace. The bombers would normally assemble and await their escort over Mikhaylovka village, some 30–40 km (20–25 miles) from the front line. Soviet fighters would take off in time to intercept the enemy 10–15 km (6–10 miles) before he reached the target. Thanks to timely notification, the division downed 10 enemy aircraft on 25 September 1943 and 18 on the following day. Then the enemy changed his tactics again, launching groups of bombers at various altitudes via the shortest route. It was almost impossible to intercept them, so the division resorted to patrolling tactics that were wasteful of aviation engine hours.

With that, the enemy also had to react appropriately, changing his tactics often. At one point they began to arrive over the target before dawn and again at dusk. In response, the division was quick to train night interceptors who successfully engaged in air combat not only in periods of dusk and dawn, but also in the full dark of night. In an additional effort to avoid detection by RUS radar, the enemy began to send out groups of Hs129 assault aircraft at tree-top level. Oddly, there were no similar changes in enemy fighter aviation tactics throughout the Tokmak-Melitopol operation.

Following a swift offensive by Southern Front forces from the Mius line, any remaining enemy forces were dug in on a well-prepared defensive line along the Molochnaya River by October 1943. Initial Red Army attempts to overcome this line from the march were unsuccessful. The front's forces planned a more deliberate breakthrough, regrouping for an *en masse* concentration along the main attack axis. Enemy aviation increased its level of activity in late September, with up to 600 aircraft at its disposal along this front alone. On the whole it focussed its efforts against Soviet concentrations in the Bolshoy Tokmak area.

The commander of the 265th IAD, Aleksandr Koryagin, decided to use airborne patrol groups to effect the destruction of enemy aviation. To be able to pile on forces while any given aerial battle developed, he intended to have *alert* or *duty* groups on the ground at readiness level No. 1 and No. 2, ready to sortie upon receiving data from the RUS-2 assigned to the division.[46] The first days of such missions yielded unsatisfactory results. Having acquired mostly fighter-on-fighter air combat experience in the Kuban, the division's pilots failed to embrace the tactics and techniques needed to combat bomber formations. During the initial sorties they engaged the enemy escort fighters, leaving only an insignificant portion of the force to engage the bombers. Hence, they did not pose a serious threat to the enemy. By fulfilling their secondary mission they left their primary mission—to combat with enemy strike aviation— unattended. In response, the division and regiment commanders reappraised their combat organizations and formed permanent groups headed up by regiment commanders, their deputies, and the more experienced of the squadron commanders.

Strike groups, equipped with the *up-gunned* Yak-9T aircraft, now consisted, on the whole, of pilots who demonstrated the best results in combat against bombers and attack aircraft. Pilots who were well-versed in fighter-versus-fighter combat were assigned to escort groups equipped with the *lightweight* Yak-1. Fully two-thirds of the fighters were assigned to the strike group. The subsequent actions of these groups gave reliable coverage to friendly ground-force concentrations. The basic combat entity (a *pair* or a *four-ship* group) was affirmed and strengthened by the tactics employed. Radio communications between aircraft and with the ground were broadly used. Loudspeakers were installed at fighter airfields to keep everyone up to date on the aerial situation.

The flight crews and technical staff of the regiment prior to the battles in the Crimea.

265th IAD Commander Podpolkovnik Aleksandr Aleksandrovich Koryagin

The First Offensive Step

Soviet forces advanced toward the Sea of Azov, liberating territory as they went. Taganrog was freed from German occupation on 30 August. The transfer of the 812th IAP to the Southern Front was scheduled for Sunday, 5 September. They would stage out by squadron: 1st Squadron at 0900, 2nd at 1000, and 3rd at 1100. The fighters, accompanied by the Li-2 transport carrying maintenance personnel, followed the Trubetchino-Alekseyevka-Urazovo-Opytnoye-Polye-Millerovo-Shakhty route. The transfer was completed by the end of the day, with the corps' regiments (186 aircraft in all) deployed at their new airfields.

The 15th and 812th IAPs settled in at Shakhty airfield alongside the 3rd IAK command element. The 291st and 402nd IAPs occupied the airfield at Novoshakhtinsk beside the command element of the 265th IAD, while the 43rd and 274th IAPs went with the command element of 278th IAD to Novocherkassk airfield. Combat commenced on the following day, with two He111s and three Ju52s destroyed in two group aerial engagements. Two more Heinkels were downed at approximately 0730 the 157th and 158th victories for the 812th.

Mladshiy Leytenant Peskarev and Leytenant Kalugin, of the 812th IAP, marked their presence early on in the Makeyevka area. As part of a formation of four Yak-9Ts and four Yak-1s, they attacked a group of approximately 30 He111 bombers from 1. and 2. Staffeln, I/KG55. Former commander of the 812th, Aleksey Yeremin excelled on Monday, 6 September. His flight of six 402nd IAP Yak-1s attacked a withdrawing German column in the Marinka area, destroying several trucks and more than 10 wagons. During this action they also encountered an airborne group of Ju52s. In the ensuing battle Mayor Yeremin, Kapitan Rubakhin, and Mladshiy Leytenant Yegorovich each downed one of the transports.

The 812th IAP, under the leadership of Mayor Dmitriy Nikolayenkov and chief of aerial gunnery service Kapitan Pavel Tarasov, with 27 combat-capable fighters, was supposed to operate in circumstances that differed significantly from the Kuban. Nonetheless, it changed airfields frequently: on 7 September they moved to Pervomaysk airfield, on the 9th to Mokryy Yelanchuk, on the 14th to a landing strip near Chervonnyy village, and on the 18th to Gulyaypole airfield. For the pilots and maintenance personnel of the regiment, this attractive-to-no-one-airfield era was well remembered because a former resident of a local orphanage, Vasya Ivushkin, was adopted as a "son of the regiment" there, becoming an equal member of the large 812th IAP combat family.

Initially, the weak level of enemy aviation activity permitted young pilots to be paired up with the more experienced ones so as to hasten their combat readiness. If they did not encounter enemy aircraft in the air, they attacked the withdrawing German ground forces. Regimental headquarters issued combat instructions that pointed out, *"During return from a combat mission and not having encountered the enemy, use your remaining ammunition for ground attack of enemy forces."* They were thereby mastering ground attack technique as well.

On 11 September, the corps downed two Fw189s. As a result of this air combat Mladshiy Leytenant Belous had to make a forced landing. On this same day, the famous 9th GIAD of Polkovnik Ibragim Dzusov was operationally subordinated to the corps.[47] Additionally, the 16th GIAP, with 21 P-39s, occupied Obryv airfield while the 100th and 104th GIAP, with 17 aircraft each, were at Bezymenovka airfield. Enemy aviation increased its activity level as well. Ever larger groups of bombers, escorted by fighters, began to appear over the Soviet ground forces. Once again the defending pilots had to sortie several times a day as the intensity of combat mounted.

On 14 September corps aircraft were involved in 28 aerial battles, destroying 14 Ju87s, eight He111s, seven Bf109s, two Fw189s, and a Ju88, while damaging four Ju87s and two He111s. Of these, the pilots of 265th IAD accounted for four He111s and one Bf109. Throughout the following day the intensity of flight operations remained high, with the division contributing five Bf109s and three Ju87s to the overall take.

The absence of suitable airfields on the newly liberated territory, and service for them, did not permit timely transition of the division's air regiments to front-line locations. Temporarily, fighter bases were up to 75-100 kilometers (45–60 miles) distant from the front line. This made the combat work to cover ground forces—especially to fight off enemy bombing raids along the forward edge—extremely difficult. Errors committed by the command elements—such as covering friendly forces with small groups of six-eight fighters—plus errors made by the pilots in battle, led to cases where the division was not performing its primary mission (coverage of ground forces against enemy bombers). As a result they suffered heavy losses in flight crews and aircraft.

On Saturday, 18 September, four 812th IAP Yaks were suddenly attacked by eight Bf109s. The group's combat formation was broken up such that each pilot had to fight on his own. Serzhant Mikhail Belous and Mladshiy Leytenants Petr Kondrakov and Anatoliy Rusakov did not return from this combat. The following day also brought no joy: the deputy commander of the 1st Squadron, Leytenant Georgiy Churakov, was shot down in an aerial engagement. At 1340-1515 his eight Yak-9Ts were escorting Pe-2 dive bombers operating in the Andreyevka area. Having bombed their target, the group had just turned for home when four Bf109s jumped them.

Choosing an opportune moment to attack, the Messerschmitts flew out of the sun at almost the same altitude as the Pe-2s. Churakov reported to the cover group leader, Tishchenko, that he had spotted four Bf109s below and to the left and had decided to attack them. With that, the pair of Leytenant Churakov and Mladshiy Leytenant Stryuk closed on the enemy. Georgiy immediately downed one Bf109, but then the pair split up and fought solo. After downing his second German fighter, Churakov himself fell under a burst from a Messer that struck his engine and left wing. He turned his burning airplane toward friendly territory, attempting to reach the front line. Lacking sufficient altitude, his Yak landed just short of no-man's land on the Germans' forward edge, not far from the village Andreyevka. That evening, while liberating this very area, friendly ground forces found the burnt remains of Leytenant Churakov's Yak-9. They buried the pilot, whose body had been stabbed all over with bayonets. In memory of his friend and for all his comrades who had perished in combat, I. V. Fedorov had "For Georgiy" painted on the fuselage of his Yak.

Corps comander General-Mayor Ye. Ya. Savitskiy inspects the regiment's fighters before combat commences. Savitskiy's "Dragons" became one of the main aviation strike forces of 8th Air Army in the Tokmak-Melitopol operation.

"Savitskiy's corps they sometimes called it,
All the pilots were proud of this.
They fought bravely in their Yaks,
They were always prepared for battle!
They are the 'Dragon's' wingmen,
The fascists cannot get out of their sights!
They always fly from any airfield,
They went in battle from From Stalingrad
to Berlin!"
Korneyev, "From Stalingrad to Berlin."

During return from a combat mission on 20 September 1943, Starshiy Leytenant Ivan Martynenko ran out of fuel, stalling the engine of his Yak-9. In the resulting forced landing, his fighter suffered a damaged right wing, left landing gear, and bent propeller. It was thus not counted among the regiment's 11 Yak-9s and 11 Yak-1s remaining on strength at the end of the day.

Having liberated the Donbas, Southern Front forces had reached the prepared German defensive line along the Molochnaya River by Tuesday, 21 September 1943. That same day, in the area of Bolshoy Tokmak area, the 812th IAP fought one of its most memorable air battles. Mladshiy Leytenant Maksimov set the tone while it was still morning (0800), downing a Ju88 in the Yanchekrak area. Later, at 1230, a group of fighters (three Yak-9Ts and five Yak-1s) under the leadership of Kapitan Ankudinov encountered a group of 12-14 He111s at 4,000 meters (13,100 feet) in the Orekhov area. These Heinkels, of Oberst Lt. Wilhelm Antrup's KG55 "Greif", dropped their bombs, turned westward, closed up their formation, and headed toward their base at Kirovograd.

The first attack by Kapitan Ankudinov (Yak-9 bort 30), from a range of 400-300 meters (435–325 yards), knocked down one of the He111s over Shcherbakovka. It fell west of the village Yakovlevka. A second group of bombers, inbound to the target 100 meters (325 feet) higher than the first, was attacked by Leytenant Fedorov's pair. Before the attack Fedorov (Yak-1 "37"), having selected the lefthand element of this group as his target, gave the command for the lead of the second pair to concentrate on their righthand counterpart. Making a combat turn, Fedorov launched a frontal attack but spotted a pair of Bf109s immediately below. He *had* to attack the Messers. Unsuccessful, he pulled out with a turn into the sun. At an altitude of 5,300 meters (17,390 feet) he came down into the face of the bombers once again.

After his attack, one bomber was set on fire and fell behind the others. The formation hurriedly jettisoned its bombs. Turning around to the right, Fedorov finished off the smoking enemy bomber. He later recalled:

I aimed directly at the center of the aircraft, where the fuselage intersects the wings. I saw the flash of tracer rounds, and then nothing except the rapacious body of the Heinkel, which like a large, gray-green fish was swimming in my crosshairs. I pressed the trigger and with my whole being felt the heavy stream of shells dig into the middle portion of the aircraft. As if striking an invisible barrier, its speed fell off sharply, it hung helplessly, and then its nose dropped and the aircraft plunged toward the earth. I saw a wing break off and then other pieces of metal. The Heinkel disintegrated before my eyes.[48]

Fedorov's wingman, Mladshiy Leytenant Ivan Maksimov (Yak-1 bort 22), saw a single Bf110 behind the bomber group. Apparently its crew was to photograph the results of the bombers' work. Maksimov set the enemy airplane on fire in his first pass. The burning hulk fell in the area of Shcherbakovka village.

Yet a third group of Heinkels was approaching from the west. Leytenant Fedorov turned to attack but saw the canopy of a deployed parachute below and a diving Bf109 above. He then recalled that when he was in the Kuban, descending by parachute after a ram, he was covered against enemy fighter attack. He did the same for this parachutist, fending off the Messerschmitt. Ironically, the parachutist turned out to be a German pilot from a downed He111 of 6./KG55, who was subsequently taken into custody.

— text *continued on page 52*

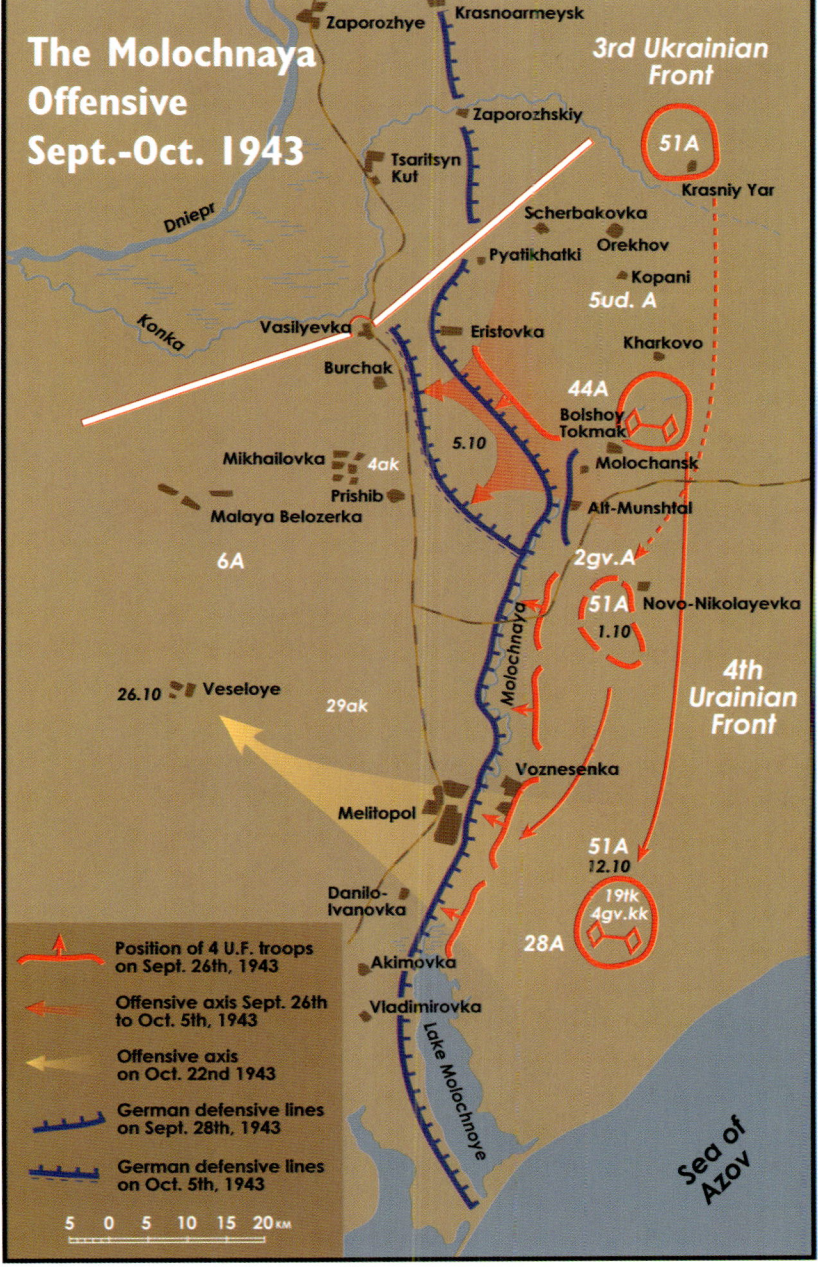

Map: The Molochnaya Offensive Sept.-Oct. 1943

Aircraft of the 812ᵗʰ IAP

The lightweights

Although the number of versions of Yakovlev's fighters may seem overwhelming, in reality there existed just two major families of these aircraft. The first, the Yak-1 and its ultimate development, the Yak-3, represented the line that had started with the state competition for a new fighter in 1939. The slighter later Yak-7/Yak-9 family came into being in a rather haphazard way in the fall of 1941, when the VVS desperately needed aircraft.

The Yak-1 was designed with two major concerns in mind: light weight and the capabilities of the Soviet industry. The airframe was designed around the M-105P engine coupled with the ShVAK 20mm cannon. The main structural element of the fuselage was a steel tubular frame to which a single-piece wing of all-wooden construction was attached. The fuselage featured metal covers around the engine and cockpit, while its rear part was covered with plywood and fabric. The empennage was all-wooden. Control surfaces comprised a metal frame covered with fabric. These features were characteristic of all Yak-1 modifications until it went out of production in July 1944. During this time several versions of Klimov's engines were in use. During 1941 the initial 1150 h.p. M-105P was replaced by the M-105PA, which was better suited to inverted flight. The later M-105PF featured increased performance at lower altitudes. It came into use from June 1942 (in March 1944 Soviet engines received their designers' initials for designations instead of faceless "M" for "motor," so M-105PF became VK-105PF). Other visible changes included a "P-40 style" rear canopy quarter-light glazing incorporated in late 1941.

A major change in appearance came in October 1942, when extensive aerodynamics refinements were introduced together with an all-around visibility canopy. More importantly, the standard pair of 7.62mm ShKAS machine guns mounted over the engine was replaced by a much more powerful single 12.7mm UBS machine gun. This new version is often referred to as Yak-1b, although the official name of the modification was "Yak-1 with improved visibility, protection, and armament". It has to be kept in mind that major design features of the aircraft remained the same: all-wooden wing and empennage, metal forward plus plywood and fabric rear fuselage skinning, and the same landing gear.

Major changes occurred in 1944 with the Yak-3 evolution of the design. The aircraft received a totally new, smaller wing of mixed construction featuring metal structural elements and plywood skin. The armament was complemented by a second 12.7mm UBS. Other changes included two wing-root oil cooler intakes (replacing the chin design), a modified undercarriage, new empennage, a plywood rear fuselage skin (replacing the fabric covering), and a reduced fuel capacity. The resulting aircraft demonstrated outstanding performance at low and medium altitudes, thus culminating the development of the Yak-1/3 family.

The beginning of the heavies

The Yak-7 was born just a few months after the Yak-1, intended as a two-seat trainer to facilitate VVS pilots' transitioning onto the new closed-cockpit, monoplane, inline-engined (i.e. liquid cooled) Yak, LaGG, and MiG fighters. A second cockpit was placed right behind the pilot's office with the glazing extending back accordingly. Only one (port) ShKAS machine gun was retained. While trying to achieve maximum production commonality with his Yak-1 fighter, A.S.Yakovlev had to relax some weight constraints. The new aircraft received a stronger undercarriage plus larger oil and water coolers. To counter the shift in balance caused by the second crew member and the removal of the armament, the wing was moved aft and a totally new, lighter all-metal empennage was introduced. To make the trainer less sensitive and more stable, the elevator area was reduced and the stabilizer area was correspondingly increased. Designated Yak-7UTI, this version was manufactured from April until September 1941.

Catastrophic loss of aircraft in the first days of Barbarossa resulted in a desperate need for fighters. Expediency and logic prevailed in that a cannon and a second ShKAS were reintroduced to the basic airframe while the aft cockpit equipment was removed so that fighters could be delivered instead of trainers. Only 62 of these initial Yak-7 fighters were manufactured (from September until December 1941), marking the birth of a separate, highly successful family of Yakovlev fighters. Streamlined manufacturing processes and some aerodynamic improvements resulted in the interim Yak-7A, which was, in turn, replaced in May 1942 by the more refined Yak-7B – the most mass-produced version of the Yak-7. This new version sported a pair of hard-hitting 12.7mm UBSs instead of the rifle-caliber ShKAS machine guns. It stayed in production until July 1944 with later series progressively introducing the all-around visibility canopy, Yak-9 type exhaust stacks /fairings, as well as both oil and water cooler installations from the later Yak-9. Another version of the Yak-7 that is worth mentioning is the Yak-7-37 armed with a 37mm cannon in place of the standard ShVAK. Only 22 were manufactured, but they did make it to the frontline (for combat trials) in the second half of 1942.

The new wing design

As the Soviet economy and industry recovered from the terrible losses of 1941-42, the opportunity appeared to substitute the all-wooden wing of the Yak-7 with one of mixed construction combining metal structural elements with stressed plywood skin. The decision gave appreciable payoffs in both weight reduction and in the space gained inside the wing. Wooden spars were actually dense, bulky bars of almost square cross section. Metal spars of similar strength were much thinner and lighter. The new wing also featured slightly squared wing tips to enable the installation of slats. This design was first used in May 1942 with the long-range (11 fuel tanks) two-seat reconnaissance Yak-7D development aircraft. But this sub-variant did not enter series production. The wing was

subsequently incorporated in the Yak-7DI long-range fighter.
Here, the number of fuel tanks was reduced to four internal
wing tanks and one fuselage tank with double protection. The
armament was reduced by deletion of the starboard UBS,
while visibility was improved by lowering the rear decking
for an all-around vision canopy. A number of aerodynamic
refinements were also introduced, including revised forward
wing-root and chin air intake shapes and reactive exhaust
pipes.

Mass production of the new fighter began in October 1942
under the new designation "Yak-9". Interestingly, the
number of fuel tanks on production Yak-9s was reduced
down to just two wing cells. In March 1943 this decision was
reversed, and the Yak-9 was replaced in production by the
Yak-9D, featuring four internal wing fuel cells. At the same
time another version of the Yak-9 was introduced sporting the
37mm NS-37 cannon instead of 20mm ShVAK. To
compensate for the increased weight of the armament, the
cockpit was moved 400 mm (15") aft. This version reverted to
the two fuel cell wing.

The Yak-9D and Yak-9T were the most numerous versions
of the Yak-9 (3058 and 2748 manufactured respectively), but
there existed a host of other versions produced in smaller
numbers: The "special reconnaissance" Yak-9Ds mentioned in
the text may in fact be Yak-9R sub-variants (see Scale
Drawings section). The Yak-9B was a fighter bomber (109
manufactured), the Yak-9DD was designed as a long-range
fighter (399 manufactured), the Yak-9K had a 45mm cannon
(53 manufactured). In an effort to streamline production, in
May 1944 the "short-nosed" fuselage of the Yak-9D was
abandoned in favor of the one with the cockpit moved aft.
Some additional refinements were incorporated and the
resulting machine received a designation of Yak-9M. From
that time, this airframe was used as a basis for manufacturing
both lightly (ShVAK) and heavily (NS-37) armed fighters.

Similar to the Yak-1/3 family evolution, a major change to
the Yak-9 design came in April 1944, when the aircraft
received two oil coolers in wing tunnels instead of a single
chin oil cooler. Additionally the armament increased with a
second UBS, the wing was moved 100 mm forward, and –
most importantly – a new, more powerful, although less-
reliable VK-107 engine was installed. This ultimate wartime
version received the designation Yak-9U. Development of the
Yak-9 family continued after the war with the all-metal
Yak-9P, finalizing the history of Yakovlev's piston-engine
fighters.

In conclusion, it is important to note that many of the
models designations used in this sidebar (e.g., Yak-9M, Yak-
9DD) were not in common use during most of the war,
neither at factories, nor at the units. Many were introduced
post factum when production was long under way or even
finished. Therefore, in this volume you may not find those
exact designations in the excerpts from pilots' logbooks.

—Alexander Rusetski

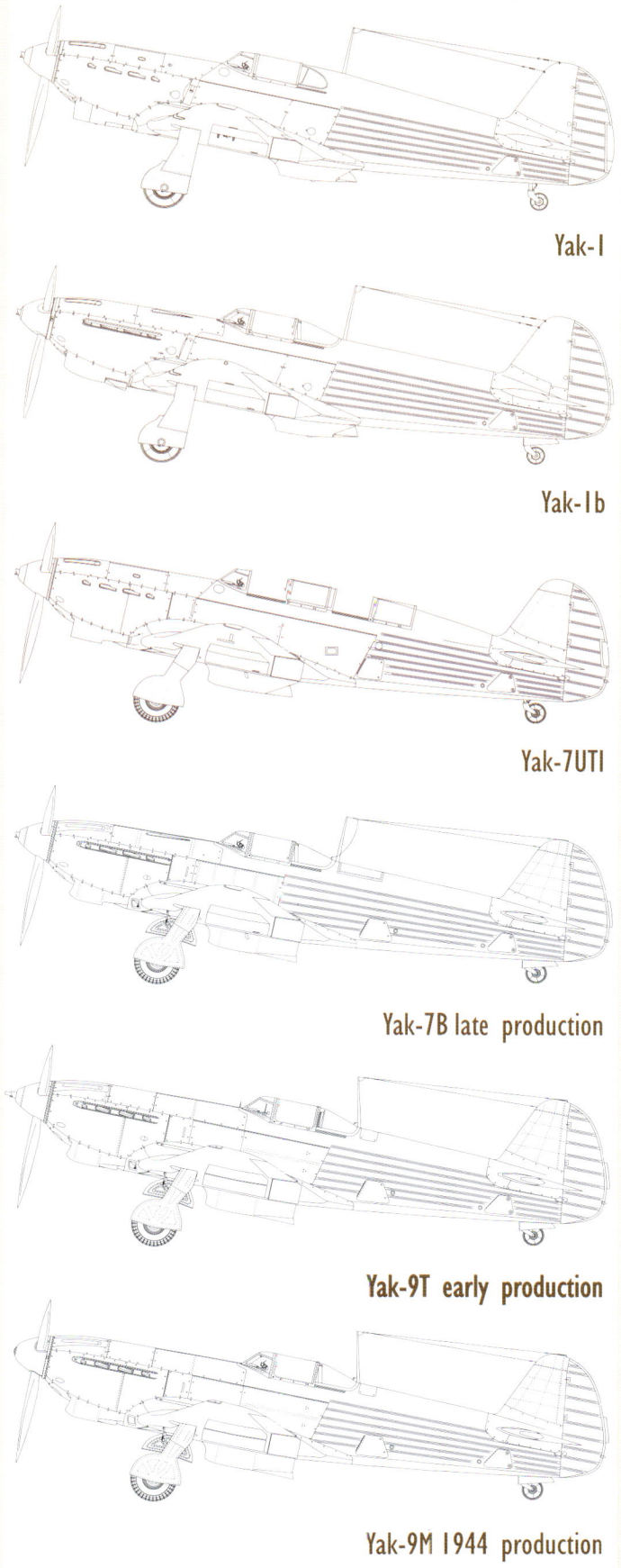

Yak-1

Yak-1b

Yak-7UTI

Yak-7B late production

Yak-9T early production

Yak-9M 1944 production

See the Scale Drawings section (page 134-145) for enlarged, more detailed views
The Yak-3 and later Yak-9 variants will appear in volume 2

Kapitan I. F. Popov, shturman [navigation officer] of the 812ᵗʰ IAP, experienced pilot and instructor, seen here in the cockpit of a Polikarpov I-16. Before assignment to the regiment, he flew the U-2, R-1, R-5, I-3, I-5, I-15, I-16, I-153, MiG-3, Yak-7, Hurricane, and Li-2. He fought his first aerial battles in the 812ᵗʰ IAP on the Southern Front. When the commander in chief of the 8ᵗʰ VA assigned I. V. Fedorov the mission to conduct a demonstration air battle with enemy bombers and demanded he take the regiment's best pilots for this, he responded: *"Comrade commander in chief, permit me to take eight pilots from 2ⁿᵈ Squadron in the strike group. It will include the coordinated pair of regiment navigator Kapitan Popov. We well understand each other in battle…"*

The group fought this air battle well, downing two He111s and one Bf110 without losing any of their number. Forty minutes later the regiment's pilots also *clipped the wings* of five Ju88 bombers. Altogether on this day, the 265ᵗʰ IAD fought eight group aerial engagements, destroying 12 enemy aircraft. Six Ju88s, two He111s, one Bf110 were tallied by the 812ᵗʰ IAP. Mladshiy Leytenant Ivan Maksimov gained his first two victories, a Ju88 and a Bf110. Kapitan Yegor Ankudinov and Leytenant Ivan Fedorov each scored an He111, Fedor Tikhomirov downed two Ju88s, and Leytenant Ivan Martynenko added one Ju88 to his score while Mladshiy Leytenants Mikhail Kashirin and Andrey Kuznetsov downed a Ju88 each. This day, on the whole, was a remarkable victory for the regiment's pilots.

The battles in the air did not die down. On 24 September alone the corps was party to 20 group aerial engagements, downing 14 enemy aircraft (half of which were Hs129 ground-attack planes). Nearing the end of September the enemy occupied a prepared defensive line roughly east of Zaporozhye-Melitopol, extending to the south along the Molochnaya River to the Sea of Azov. Beginning on 25 September, ferocious aerial battles developed with large aviation forces from both sides participating. Luftwaffe bombers, frequently 40 or more at the same time, assembled in coordinated groups (12-16 aircraft each) with raids on the combat formations of Soviet ground forces as their objective.

They assembled over populated areas, typically 20 kilometers (12 miles) from the front, and set course eastward. Arriving from their various assembly points in a coordinated fashion, these small groups effectively became a large mass over the forward edge of Soviet forces, where they conducted serial, or serial-salvo, bombing runs. Lead aircraft would mark the moment of bomb release with time-fuzed smoke pots and depart to the west in a left turn. The bomb-release altitude was on the order of 3,500-3,600 meters (11,480-11,800 feet). Cases were noted when enemy bombers executed simultaneous raids at several locations in order to disperse forces and weaken the counteraction put up by VVS fighters.

If the German bombers encountered Soviet fighters on their side of the front line, they circled deep within their *own* airspace to await fighter escort before heading out on their raid. Soviet battle experience with this scenario showed that it would be necessary to send out the second shift of fighters somewhat early, with the first shift having already expended its fuel engaging the enemy formation.

On 25 September the entire regiment (12 Yak-9s and nine Yak-1s at the time) flew almost to the front line in the Melitopol area. For the 812ᵗʰ IAP this was an event-filled Saturday. To begin with, the 2ⁿᵈ Squadron's usual combat formation was changed. Squadron commander Leytenant Ivan Fedorov doubled as the leader of the strike group while Kapitan Yegor Ankudinov led the cover group. Regiment navigator Kapitan Ivan Feoktistovich Popov also flew in the 2ⁿᵈ Squadron formation. He did not yet have combat experience in the 812ᵗʰ IAP, but Fedorov had this to say about the future regiment commander:

He possessed excellent piloting techniques, was bold and decisive, both on land and in the air. He was older than most of us but was not ashamed to be taught the tactics of combat. He strove to participate in each mission, in order to grasp the experience of the best aerial warriors as quickly as possible. He flew in the strike group as the leader of the second flight.[49]

The fact that Ivan Feoktistovich possessed outstanding piloting abilities is easily explained. From the beginning of the war through to the first half of 1942, he was a squadron commander in the 17ᵗʰ ZAP, which performed the intensive training of fighter pilots for the front. In an evaluation for I. F. Popov for this period, it was noted:

Outstanding pilot. Rated in the following aircraft: I-15, I-16, I-153, Yak-7, MiG-3, Hurricane. The squadron entrusted to him holds first place in the regiment by the basic indicators of training-combat readiness. During the period from 5.8.41 to 25.1.42 this squadron flew 1,377 hours, making 13,224 landings. Despite the high intensity

One of the episodes of aerial combat conducted by the pair Fedorov-Maksimov on 26 September 1943. The handwritten text reads:

"In one of the attacks, the leader Fedorov flew in close and began to shoot up the bomber at point-blank range. At this time two Bf109s attempted to draw off Fedorov. Both of the enemy aircraft came from the external flanks. Maksimov quickly evaluated the situation, maneuvered horizontally, and attracted the Messers' fire to himself, but did not permit them to interfere with Fedorov until the completion of his task."

from "Combat Path"

of work, the aircraft are in excellent condition. Squadron personnel melded and mobilized for execution of the assigned missions. The squadron of Starshiy Leytenant Popov during work period trained two regiment cohorts on the Hurricane aircraft. Altogether they trained 61 aircrews on Hurricane and of variable flight-rated personnel of the squadron trained 98 single air crewmen for the I-16 airplane. During the entire period of this training on the Hurricane aircraft, the squadron did not have a single accident.

Popov managed to acquire a only a modest amount of combat experience on the Karelian Front from July 1942 as a squadron commander in the 835th IAP. This regiment fought in Hurricanes in the Far North [Murmansk area], where Popov flew nine combat sorties.

Back to 25 September, 1943: The first flight of the 2nd Squadron began at approximately 0800. Half an hour later, at an altitude of 3,000 meters (9,850 feet) in the area of Bolshoy Tokmak, Leytenant Fedorov attacked an He111 and sent it plummeting to earth, its right engine burning. The regiment's second sortie was put together at 1500. In attacking a pair of Messers in the Kopan area, Starshiy Leytenant Aleksandr Tishchenko downed one of them. Right behind it appeared a group of Ju87s. Mladshiy Leytenant Sergey Vasilevskiy set one of the bombers on fire with an attack from behind.

Then again at 1600 Leytenant Fedorov led a flight of six 2nd Squadron fighters (two Yak-9Ts and four Yak-1s) aloft. Once in the air, the RUS-2 station reported that a large group of aircraft was coming toward them. On reaching the area of Bolshoy Tokmak, they still did not see anything and so began their normal patrol. Soon they were running low on fuel due to the long duration of their transit flight. A squadron of 402nd IAP Yaks was scheduled to arrive in this area soon to replace them. No doubt, the pilots recalled Starshiy Leytenant Ivan Martynenko's incident of 20 September. His fuel-starved engine had stopped dead while returning from a combat mission. Miraculously he survived the forced landing but his aircraft was a total wreck.

Still in the patrol area because the relief group from the 402nd IAP had not yet arrived, they spotted a large Luftwaffe force: six flights of nine He111 bombers, with their Bf109 escorts slightly above and behind, at an altitude of 4,500 meters (14,750 feet) in the Ognevka area. Low fuel and enemy aircraft in sight, the mission appeared to be getting difficult. In attacking the lead bomber group, attempting to disrupt their bomb drop, the fighters of 812th IAP were soon dragged into a heavy aerial engagement.

They were informed by radio that their replacements from the 402nd Regiment had taken off. The Air Army command post radio broadcast over the net, ordering any fighters in the air to attack the German bombers with all their might. Leytenant Fedorov reported back, *"Our patrol time has expired, our replacement has not arrived, we are attacking the enemy."*

With that, he set up his maneuver for the attack on the lead nine. Behind the strike group Kapitan Ankudinov's flight was providing cover. Several minutes later, the commander of the 402nd IAP group, Starshiy Leytenant Akop Manukyan, reported by radio that his Yak-9s had arrived in the area, whereupon they immediately attacked the second group of nine He111s. Meanwhile, the 812th IAP fighters, their fuel nearing its end, had only sufficient remaining for one more pass. Later Fedorov recalled it in this manner:

We closed. I saw sparkling points reaching out toward us from the bombers' tracers. True, we had already mastered how to evade aimed fire—with small movements of our legs we moved our aircraft to the left or right. Two hundred meters, one hundred fifty, one hundred meters, hit them! Manukyan's squadron had already arrived. It was attacking the second group of nine. The Heinkels dropped their bombs and turned around to the west. I heard Popov's report—'100, this is '85. My wingman and I are out of fuel.' 'Go to the airfield,' I responded. 'Land straight in!' I asked my own wingman about his fuel supply. Maksimov reported that he still had some left. The needle on my fuel gage was near zero. But it was still possible to finish off this Heinkel, the more so in that I was so close.[50]

A discussion of the battle commenced. The regiment commander, Mayor Dmitriy Nikolayenkov, strode quickly toward the group of pilots, who were still discussing the fight. He informed them that the commander of 3ʳᵈ Squadron, everybody's favorite Leytenant Aleksey Mashenkin (Yak-9 "48"), had not returned from aerial combat. While covering friendly forces in the Shcherbakovka area at 1715, Leytenant Mashenkin's group of four fighters had engaged three groups of He111 bombers escorted by four Bf109s. After attacking the closest bomber and shooting it down, Mashenkin himself came under fire from a pair of Bf109s. According to reports by 402ⁿᵈ IAP pilots who were in the area, he bailed out of his damaged aircraft only to be carried by the wind to enemy-held territory.

In this same battle Kapitan Popov, who had refueled and sortied again after the mission described above, shot down his first Bf109 (while in a turn). His victim, going into a dive, exploded on the ground east of Yanchekrak. During this battle Kapitan Ivan Popov and Mashenkin's wingman, Mladshiy Leytenant Petr Peskarev, suffered damage to their aircraft as well. Unlike Leytenant Mashenkin however, they were both able to coax their Yaks along to forced landings at home base.

After the attack, Kapitan Popov (Yak-9 "39") and his wingman, anticipating engine stalls at any second, made it to their airfield on their last drops of fuel. Leytenant Fedorov, ignoring the same possibility, continued to pursue the damaged bomber. Making four passes at the Heinkel, he finally shot it down. It fell near Shcherbakovka in the Bolshoy Tokmak area. Deputy squadron commander Fedorov described the last pass in his report to regiment headquarters:

> I went to the right and down. The gunners were pounding us on all sides, not sparing their ammunition. I hit it point blank with the cannon and part of the bomber's right wing broke. The bomber turned over on the stump of its wing and lay on its back. Then, awkwardly dropping its nose, it began to break apart. Separate pieces of the fuselage and wings were falling.[51]

From the same report:

> I shot down the enemy Heinkel bomber in the area of Bolshoy Tokmak. The Heinkel was smoking and fell west of Bolshoy Tokmak. At 1640 in a turn I attacked a straggler from a formation of He111s, and with cannon fire shot off a half-meter section of the right wing. The aircraft burned and fell in the area of Ognevka.

In addition to this Heinkel, the pilots of Manukyan's 402ⁿᵈ IAP group added another three He111s to their own scores. They then made successful landings with their tanks practically empty.

Once again, the regiment's pilots were shown their deficiencies in combat. Coordination of pairs and the proper actions of wingmen during an attack by enemy fighters were evidently still a problem. What ultimately happened to Mashenkin was discovered at the end of October. Conducting a search for its pilot, after the liberation of this area by ground forces, the regiment command sent the leytenant's wingman to the area where it was believed he had landed. After Peskarev's return from the search area, the results of questioning the local inhabitants were recorded in the regiment's combat actions journal.

> Wingman Mladshiy Leytenant Peskarev, sent to the site of the fall of Leytenant Mashenkin on 24.9.43, reported: Leytenant Mashenkin landed on the square in Neyron and there was immediately surrounded by a large group of

Fedorov's #37 "For Georgi" is believed to be one of the replacement batch of Yak-1bs assigned to the regiment in South Ukraine. Unfortunately we could not find a photo of the other side of this aircraft where the inscription would have been. "Leytenant Ivan Vasilyevich Fedorov was outstanding in that he poured all of his spirit into any task that was assigned to him. He was always driven to fly. When he did not fly for a day or two, he felt out of sorts. He became morose and the sparkle left his eyes. But assign him a flight, and he was renewed. His eyes sparkled and he talked animatedly. The air was his poetry, his romance." Regiment staff in "Combat Path."

Mashenkin's Yak-9T #48. This aircraft appears to be a very early (series 2) example of the 37mm armed Yak-9T, as evidenced by the smaller profile spinner, starter dog around the 37mm muzzle, simple Yak-7 style armour-plate headrest (in place of armoured glass), and the absence of armoured glass behind the windshield. The ace's sixth victory, an HeIII shot down on 25 September 1943, was not recorded in this aircraft's "victory stars" markings. Soon after downing the Heinkel bomber he fell victim to a pair of Bf109s and had to abandon his stricken fighter over the front lines near Shcherbakovka. It would be some months before his comrades learned the details of his fate.

enemy soldiers. He had burn marks on four places of his face. His hands and arms were burned. He was not wearing boots. They grabbed him and took him to the headquarters, from which an hour later he appeared bandaged and under heavy guard. He held himself like a man, bravely. Turning to the assembled populace, he said, 'Are you waiting for us? We will come soon!' After a day in Neyron, he was sent to Vasilevka. He was called in for interrogation several times but said nothing. They put him in with the prisoners. I was unable to learn where they sent him.

A subsequent discussion of the reasons for, and consequences of, what happened with Aleksey Mashenkin was long remembered. This is how Leytenant Fedorov remembered this discussion.

At the discussion I accused Mashenkin's wingman of not carrying out his assignment to the end. No matter how many times we run into them—don't panic; do not overreact when someone gets on your tail; maneuver in such a way as to not lose fire contact with your leader. And sometimes one gets startled and veers off so that later he cannot find his leader. The fascists need only wait: they chase down your now defenseless leader, who suspects nothing. This is what happened with Mashenkin, the commander of the 3rd Squadron. At this memorable discussion there was a big conversation concerning the actions of the wingman in combat. The regiment's best pilots recounted how they execute a counter-aiming

The wingman of 2nd Squadron commander Starshiy Leytenant Ivan Fedorov, Mladshiy Leytenant Ivan Maksimov perished on 29 October 1943. He was 21. Born in the town Pushkino, Moscow oblast. From 6 September to 29 October 1943, he flew 68 combat sorties, conducted 26 aerial battles, and personally shot down five enemy aircraft.

maneuver when they are covering their leader, what they do to accomplish this, how they coordinate with other pilots of the group. Again and again the words are repeated: The combat pair is inseparable![52]

Besides the heavy loss of the squadron commander, over the course of a day the regiment had two accidents. Serzhant Sidorenko, taxiing his Yak-1, collided with the Yak-9T of Kapitan Yegor Ankudinov, who also was taxiing. This collision resulted in damage to the wing of Ankudinov's aircraft and a bent propeller on the Yak-1. A while later, taking off on a mission in his Yak-9, Serzhant Kuznetsov drifted to the right and with his right main gear struck another Yak-9 parked on the periphery of the airfield. As a result of this collision, the gear of Kuznetsov's Yak-9 was broken. During a subsequent rough landing his propeller was bent and his fuselage was deformed. The Yak-9 parked on the airfield suffered a damaged left wing. Altogether for the day, the 812th IAP had seven of its 15 serviceable fighters disabled.

Toward evening, the corps commander Ye. Ya. Savitskiy, accompanied by the commander of the 278th IAD, Polkovnik V. T. Lisin, flew in to the regiment to see what was going on. Having listened to the regiment commander, Savitskiy ordered all of them to pay attention to the coordination of pairs and the study of the tactics of aerial combat. The main thing that distressed Savitskiy was the loss of the squadron commander Leytenant Aleksey Mashenkin. The duties of commander of the 3rd Squadron were handed off to Mashenkin's deputy, Leytenant Tumanov.

Savitskiy also warned Nikolayenkov, the commander of 812th IAP, that the commander of 8th Air Army, T. T. Khryukin, would soon visit. The commander liked the air engagement conducted by the regiment's pilots on 21 September, and he wanted to organize one similar, but this time a demonstration air battle for the intercept of enemy bombers. Savitskiy soon departed, having left the perplexed pilots to discuss the upcoming flight. Here is how one of the future participants in the "demonstration" battle, Fedorov, recalls this assignment.

This was a complicated thing. In peacetime we set up demonstration battles—we agreed who would attack whom, how to get out from under attack, what kind of maneuvers would be employed so that the observers would be able to see that. This time there was no prior arrangement. We decided to fight normally, only more attentively, more precisely, in order not to make any mistakes. The main thing was to hit as many enemy aircraft as possible and not lose any of our own. This was the focus of all tactics. For this demonstration battle we would not come up with something new! We had worked it out and now we had to 'demonstrate' it.

Altogether on 25 September the corps conducted 27 aerial battles, in which 13 He111s, two Ju87s, one Ju88, eight Bf109s, and two Fw189s were shot down. The 265th IAD destroyed six He111s, two Fw189s, one Bf109, and one Ju87.

Among the "Left Behind"

Sunday, 26 September 1943 arrived. On this day, the forces of Southern Front began the Melitopol offensive operation to defeat the German defensive line along the Molochnaya River. Soviet units were to liberate northern Tavriya and advance to the lower Dniepr River. Having renewed the pressure on the enemy, the Southern Front went over to the offensive and the intensity of combat work grew by several times.

The pilots of 812th Regiment destroyed eight enemy aircraft in aerial combat on this day. At approximately 0800 Vasiliy Shishkin downed one He111. In the afternoon, over the course of 15 minutes (between 1250 and 1305), several pilots distinguished themselves in combat and added to their scores: Mikhail Dergunov (Ju87), Ivan Fedorov (Ju88), Serafim Kalugin (Ju88), and Ivan Martynenko (Bf109). Toward evening, Mladshiy Leytenant Dergunov shot down his second Stuka of the day. Twenty minutes later (at 1745), Mladshiy Leytenant Maksimov also scored a Stuka, and five minutes after that Leytenant Shishkin decided the fate of a Bf109, a fitting close to the regiment's successful combat day. At the close of 26 September, the 3rd IAK had downed 38 and damaged 10 enemy aircraft in 32 aerial engagements. The score for 265th IAD was recorded as seven Ju87s, four Ju88s, five Bf109s, one He111, and one Hs129.

It turned out that combat fortune began to smile more often on the pilots, however after Sunday there is always Monday. In the lives of some pilots, by its consequences this particular Monday became "black" without exaggeration. The first half of the day on 27 September did not forewarn misfortune. The pilots of 1st and 2nd Squadrons, 812th IAP had just returned from a mission and were examining their just completed combat sortie. At approximately 1400 Aleksandr Tumanov scored a Ju88; almost simultaneous with him, Kapitan Popov, continuing to specialize in *skinnies*, destroyed a Bf109 in the air. The day did not seem so bad and the pilots already had something to discuss: at 1340, in the Kopan area, a strike group consisting of three Yak-1s and one Yak-9 attacked a flight of Ju88s. They conducted a precise attack: Leytenant Tumanov shot down one Ju88 as it came out of a dive. The enemy aircraft burst into flames and fell 8 kilometers (5 miles) west of Bolshoy Tokmak. Other participants in the flight, Kapitan Popov, Leytenant Fedorov, and Mladshiy Leytenant Maksimov confirmed the fall of the Junkers. Several minutes later, the four fighters encountered the next group of bombers and shot down another Ju88.

Pinning down the enemy escort fighters in battle, at 1340 Kapitan Popov shot down a Bf109 that fell 3 kilometers (2 miles) east of Prishib. Infantry observed the battle and saw where the Messer fell. The 5th Guards Artillery Regiment chief of staff issued a confirmation on their behalf. But here, as was planned, some senior commanders arrived at the regiment: commander of

Leytenant Pavel Serezhenko pauses for the camera. The later version of the 3rd IAK emblem seen on the Yak-9T dates the photo as later in the war

the 8th Air Army, General Leytenant Khryukin, corps commander Savitskiy, and the division commander Podpolkovnik Aleksandr Koryagin.

Greeting the pilots, the air army commander laid out, in general terms, the situation on the ground and in the air. Summing up, he indicated that the division had positive experience in combat with large groups of bombers. He pointed to the successful battle of 25 September, involving the 2nd Squadron, 812th IAP and the squadrons of 402nd IAP, that he had personally observed. Leytenant General Timofey Khryukin was interested in the pilots' success under the command of Leytenant Ivan Fedorov, who on that day had personally shot down two He111s. The secret to defeating large groups of bombers was simple—conduct attacks not in pairs, but in a group of up to eight fighters from various directions. This reduced the density of the bombers gunners' defensive fire, making it easier to penetrate to the range of aimed fire.

Having listened to Leytenant Fedorov talk about the efforts of 2nd Squadron in the fight with the bombers, Khryukin inquired of the regiment commander, Mayor Nikolayenkov, who should sortie on the very next mission. At 1745 a combat sortie was to be launched, by this same 2nd Squadron with Leytenant Fedorov leading. The squadron's pilots, according to the plan of the leadership now at the airfield, were to demonstrate in combat what Fedorov had reported to the army commander. A short time later the pilots were assigned their mission.

The combat formation was established as a group of eight aircraft. Fedorov, as leader of the group, chose Maksimov for his wingman and three other pairs: Martynenko-Kuznetsov, Dergunov-Serezhenko and Tumanov-Popov. If conditions proved favorable, one flight (four Yak-1s) from the covering group would attack the bombers, reinforcing the strike group. Specific goals for each pilot were expressed, since in recent times the Germans did not change their formation and flew in a literally predictable pattern.

Serafim Pavlovich Kalugin (first from right) among his comrades in the 291st IAP. Serafim Kalugin, wingman of Pavel Tarasov while in the 812th IAP, was transferred to the 291st IAP after the Kuban.

Detailed preparation took into account all possible variants of the battle. The exercise concluded with a training "flight walk-through." The army commander was satisfied with the pre-flight preparation so the mechanics arranged the fighters in flights and prepared them for the sortie. But 50 minutes before start time the VNOS posts warned of a group of German bombers following a course toward Bolshoy Tokmak.[54] Several minutes later, Ju88s began to bomb friendly forces with absolutely no opposition from the fighters of 8th Air Army, which was obligated to provide protection to this sector of the front.

Tishchenko, who was at this airfield, recalled:

> At this very moment west of Bolshoy Tokmak the antiaircraft guns began to fire crazily. We looked in that direction and on the reddish horizon we saw a large group of enemy bombers. Soon thereafter we heard the sound of explosions. The Germans were bombing the cavalry corps of General N. Ya. Kirichenko, which we were covering. The army commander lost his great mood. Looking through his binoculars, he did not see a single one of our fighters in the air.[55]

The regiment commander, Mayor Nikolayenkov, who was standing next to Khryukin, suggested to the army commander that he should send his regiment up. But in hopes that someone from the other fighter forces of 8th Air Army would *appear* for the intercept, Khryukin replied in the negative. Distressing minutes passed but there were no airplanes, other than German, in the sky! Nikolayenkov finally received an approval to sortie

from the army commander only after a second appeal. With some delay Fedorov's group sortied. Fedorov recalled the unfolding situation:

> I was nearby and heard the entire conversation. "Ivan— go!" Nikolayenkov gestured to me. I rushed to my airplane and several minutes later we took off. I glanced at my watch—it was 1715. Yes, we were late. Alas, there would be no time to set up the combat formation. We had to attack from the march, for the time being without cover. The last group of enemy bombers is heading for Tokmak. We had to catch it. We had to! We had barely reached altitude and our cover was behind and below.[56]

In the Kopan area the group attempted to overtake the column of Ju88s that were flying in groups of 18-20 aircraft under the escort of eight Bf109s. The situation was further complicated by the fact that, as a rule, an additional group of German bombers bringing up the rear would be accompanied by another large group of covering fighters. Worst fears were realized when, as the regiment's fighters were still climbing out, four Bf109s attacked the cover group from the left and behind. As a result of this attack, the eight Yaks were split up, their effectiveness thus reduced by half, easing the task of the bombers' gunners. Now there was no possibility that the army commander could witness his demonstration air battle.

Because the 812th IAP fighters had taken off with considerable delay, they immediately fell into an unfavorable, and quite dangerous, position. The unfolding situation was far from

Mladshiy Leytenant Nikolay Konovalov was lost in air combat flying Yak-9T #57 on the afternoon of 1 October 1943. In setting up a flanking attack (together with his leader, Shishkin) on a formation of Luftwaffe bombers he was attacked by an escorting Bf109. Soon afterwards, his Yak rammed an He111. Both aircraft fell in the Burchak area. The other bombers dispersed without reaching their target.

Kapitan Popov flew Yak-9T #39 often during the regiment's early tenure in South Ukraine. He was in action twice on the day of Konovolov's loss. Having shot down a Bf109 during the mid-morning sortie, he was up again during the afternoon's bomber intercept mission. He was witness to Konovalov's sad final victory while, at the same time, experiencing air pressure problems in his own Yak. Both of these Yak-9T are early production (#39 – series 2, #57 – series 3) examples similar to Mashenkin's #48 shown on page 55.

demonstrative. Enemy fighters also intercepted the four-ship strike group from above, denying them the possibility of making a precision attack on the withdrawing bombers. A carousel of turning *skinnies* and Yaks ensued, after which the Messers dove down and departed toward their own territory. During this battle Leytenant Martynenko was hit and bailed out in the Bolshoy Tokmak area. What had begun in a great rush ended just as suddenly. The enemy was already behind the front line.

The pair of Dergunov and Serezhenko landed thirty minutes after taking off. Kuznetsov's single fighter landed five minutes later. Popov and Tumanov returned to base at 1800 followed by the last pair - Fedorov and Maksimov - five minutes later.

> *Nearby was only my wingman. The radio was silent, as if all ground and aircraft transmitters had been turned off. It was literally the calm after a storm. My spirit was crushed. I analyzed the aerial combat. There were seemingly no mistakes on our part. From this situation in which we had to fight, we had given it everything. The circumstances were hardly in our favor—we took off too late. I landed and looked around the pad. Kostya Motygin helped me to get out of my parachute. He looked at me anxiously. I wiped the sweat from my face, neck, and the back of my head. I asked, 'Kostya, why the sour look?' He was silent. He looked at me as if I had returned from the battle crippled. 'The leadership has departed. The army commander was unhappy with the battle. Before he left, he said that the regiment and group commander would be tried.' For what! I did not believe my ears. How could they try me? For what?*[57]

Here, in front of his Yak-3 later in the war is Major Timofey Pasynok, a pilot's zampolit. At the "face saving" tribunal orchestrated by army commander Khryukin against some of the 812th's best men, Pasynok goes on the record as standing by their side. His involvement here may have cost him later promotion and awards, but he had the higher moral ground in this event.

Not understanding what was happening, Fedorov went to the regiment commander, around whom the pilots had assembled. Discussing the flight in detail, they arrived at the conclusion: all pilots had fought bravely, displaying courage and mastery in difficult and unequal conditions that arose by the guilt of the leadership. All very much regretted that the army commander did not grant permission to sortie fifteen minutes earlier. If he had, the outcome may have been very different. Altogether on this day the pilots of 265th IAD conducted nine aerial battles, destroying one Ju88, one Bf109, and two Hs129s.

On the following morning, the entire personnel component of 812th IAP was formed up, and a message was read to them from army commander T. T. Khryukin. It contained an analysis of the previous day's battle. The message evoked disbelief from the pilots. The "order" portion of the document informed them that Leytenant Fedorov, commander of the group, was being handed over to a military tribunal "for cowardice," and Mayor D. Ye. Nikolayenkov, the regiment commander "*for poor leadership of the regiment.*" In what manner Fedorov had displayed cowardice the message did not say.

The pilots were simply numbed by such a misinterpreted evaluation of their work and the stunning conclusions of the army commander. Many of them could not conceive who "gave birth" to this gibberish: to accuse of cowardice a combat ace-pilot, who had eight personal victories to his credit, including one ram! Tishchenko later recalled, "*No one expected such a turn of events. To charge people who had not committed any kind of crime? It was unbelievable!*"[58]

The commander of 265th IAD, Podpolkovnik Koryagin, quickly appealed to the corps commander, Savitskiy, with a request to recommend to the army commander Khryukin that he change the formulation of the "order" portion of the message. Several hours later a second message was received, that explained precisely why Leytenant Fedorov was being sent before a military tribunal, and this was "*for poor command and control of an air battle by radio*"(!).

By dinner time an investigative group had arrived in the regiment. They informed Fedorov that a session of the military tribunal would meet at 2100. But the enemy, not knowing what was happening in 265th IAD, did not reduce his level of activity, continuing his air effort against concentrations of Soviet forces. On the ground, meanwhile, the accusatory clerical work continued at a pace that surprised the air crews. After supper they informed the pilots that the session had been put off until morning. However at midnight, as had been contemplated, the accused squadron commander Fedorov was summoned to the chairman of the military tribunal.

The participants of this ill-fated flight, including I. F. Popov who was summoned as a witness, stood like a mountain for Fedorov. Notwithstanding the possible consequences and discomfort from the command, they were unanimous in their depositions: "*It was not our fault that the battle did not turn out like it had been planned on the ground. They authorized our sortie too late.*"[59] [This assertion was not forgotten by the higher leadership and it played a role in the subsequent fate of both Fedorov and Popov.]

Being accustomed to "ruling quickly and without thinking," the chairman of the tribunal ignored the witness statements completely. Hence the sentence: "*Fedorov is sentenced to eight, and Nikolayenkov to 10 years of confinement, with serving of the sentence to occur after the end of the war.*"[60]

The verdict of this hasty and unjust court produced the effect of an "exploding bomb" on the cohort that was present. The "hall" was noisy. Mayor T. Ye. Pasynok jumped up from his seat and, with tears in his eyes, called the representatives of the tribunal "ne'er-do-wells, blind executers of the will of the senior leaders, cowards, who did not have their own personal opinion".

For the true commissar of 812th IAP and combat pilot, this bold pronouncement also did not pass without notice. By the end of the war he also had not become a Podpolkovnik, and many awards avoided him. But Pasynok was not fighting for the sake of awards. For him the best award was the sincere love and respect he experienced from the pilots, technicians, mechanics—all the regiment's personnel. Timofey Yevstafevich concluded his angry speech with the following words: "*We should be beating the fascists and not our own pilots!*"[61]

At this utterance the chairman of the military tribunal replied, "*You should be thankful that we did not impose a more strict measure of punishment—we could have used the highest [death sentence]: remember, this is war time.*"[62]

This is how "*our dear father did us a favor*" and reminded the combat pilots of what they should not forget, no matter what; this was wartime. The following is from the report of the chief of the political section of the 265th IAD, Podpolkovnik Zaytsev, to the deputy commander of the 3rd IAK for political affairs:

> *To your question I report that by my own investigation, the materials provided by the chairman of the military tribunal concerning the conduct of Mayor Pasynok in the court and after the pronouncement of Nikolayenkov's and Fedorov's sentences, on the whole the facts are confirmed. Mayor Pasynok indeed in the court, while a witness, in his testimony in essence took the side of the accused, and after the imposition of sentence in the presence of the accused stated that 'the sentence is unjust, the facts speak out against you.' Such conduct of Mayor Pasynok cannot be interpreted in any way other than that he was defending the accused. Pasynok will be subjected to party discipline through party processes and he will receive a 'reprimand with annotation in his personnel file.'*[63]

Here is how the corps commander General Ye. Ya. Savitskiy described this episode:

> *Koryagin [division commander], in short, did not hold back his opinion of the sentence. 'Squadron commander Fedorov—a coward! Regiment commander Nikolayenkov—did not tend to his flight duties! And what do they know about our people, these investigators?!' the division commander indignantly shouted. 'Did they see the time when that same Fedorov recently fought as one of six against forty Junkers? How he shot down a Messer from the escort? How on that occasion his group did in five fascist bombers? And who will fly, who will*

defeat the Germans? Will it be these investigators?' I understood very well that Koryagin was waiting for intervention from me. However, I myself considered that what had happened to Nikolayenkov and Fedorov was drastically undeserved.[64] *[This "indignant shouting" of the commander, 265th IAD also was not forgotten by the higher command.]*

Hero of the Soviet Union, pilot from the 1st Squadron A. T. Tishchenko recalls these events:

> *However the tribunal members had not taken account of the opinion of the collective. The intervention of Mayor Pasynok and Polkovnik Koryagin did not help. Soon Nikolayenkov was sentenced to twelve and Fedorov to eight years of confinement, with the imposition of sentence delayed until after the war. It was decided to remove them from flight duties and send them to a rifle unit. But General Savitskiy arranged for the accused to remain in the corps. Although, Nikolayenkov was relieved of his position and sent to another regiment.*[65]

Starshiy Leytenant Aleksandr Tishchenko distinguished himself on this same Tuesday, 28 September. Taking off at 1715 in an eight-ship group (two Yak-9s and six Yak-1s) under the command of Kapitan Popov, they intercepted two groups of 18-20 Ju87s in the Neydorf area. This time the *laptezhniki* ("boots", as

Eventual Outcomes of the Tribunal

D. Ye. Nikolayenkov was subsequently adjudged "not guilty" by the Supreme Court of the USSR, so the 8th Air Army military tribunal sentence was nulified. Mayor Nikolayenkov remained in the 3rd IAK but was transferred to the 278th IAD, where he became the 43rd IAP navigator. He was then made navigator in 274th IAP of the same division in mid-August 1944, and later commanded a squadron. Mayor D. Ye. Nikolayenkov finished the war in Berlin, like his comrades in the 812th IAP. By this time he had 98 combat sorties and 8 personal victories in the air to his credit. After the war he continued service in various command positions in the VVS and PVO. He retired at the rank of Polkovnik. No doubt, his service history deserves a separate treatment that is outside the scope of this work.(Unfortunately, at the time of writing, the authors were unable to locate D. Ye. Nikolayenkov.)

Things turned out somewhat differently for Fedorov. Corps commander Ye. Ya. Savitskiy appealed to Khryukin with a request not to remove the pilot from combat flight status and offered that for each subsequent downed aircraft, one year of Fedorov's future sentence should be *written off*. Everyone has the right to draw their own conclusion as to why all this was necessary. How this tribunal, initiated by the army commander, turned into a farce. How it *raised* the combat capability of the 812th IAP, in which two regiment commanders had already been replaced. Mayor Nikolay Kornilov, temporarily transferred over from 15th IAP, was appointed as the regiment's third commander.

Soviet airmen called the Ju87 *Stuka*) of St.G 2, based at Pervomaysk airfield, were subjected to attack. As a result, the enemy dropped his bombs before reaching the target, and Tishchenko destroyed a Ju87D-5 bomber belonging to 5./StG2.

Often in this period it was possible to hear the call sign - "Dragon" - of the corps commander, General-Mayor Yevgeniy Savitskiy in the air. Despite his high rank and heavy workload at headquarters, he often flew on missions with the pilots of 265th IAD and occasionally shot down enemy aircraft. On 29 September, flying in pair with Leytenant Merkulov, the commander shot down a Ju88 in the area of Vishnevskiy.

By 30 September the command of the Southern Front (from 20 October renamed the 4th Ukrainian Front) concluded that the offensive it had begun was not achieving the necessary results. In order to avoid unnecessary losses, they brought it to a temporary halt. Aerial activity then began to subside somewhat. On this day the entire corps participated in only eight aerial battles, shooting down five Ju87s, two Bf109s and one Ju88.

The month of September 1943 had not been an easy one for the pilots of the 8th VA. Over the course of the entire operation for the liberation of the Donbas and Azov region, its formations were constantly immersed in intense combat. Flying 16,230 combat sorties (13,400 in daylight and 2,830 at night), they fought 453 air engagements. Continuous fighter group patrols over the battlefield were routine during the autumn battles on the line southwest of Zaporozhye. Sorties in response to data from ground vectoring stations were also broadly employed. This facilitated the early detection of enemy bomber formations, monitoring of their movement, and timely dispatch of fighters.

The presence of these ground vectoring stations at the forward line of troops made it possible to accomplish re-direction of fighters, in direct response to enemy bombers changing their course. However this method of coverage justified itself only if enemy aircraft were operating at high and medium altitudes. For enemy aircraft operating at lower levels *hunter-fighters* were employed, with varying degrees of success, to *hunt for them*. To ensure the free actions of friendly ground forces, the predominant air cover method remained continuous fighter patrols over the battlefield at 4,500 meters (14,750 feet) and lower.

Two groups of 6-8 fighters operating simultaneously, together with a ground vectoring station and functional radio communications, could cover an area of 10 x 20 kilometers (6.2 x 12.4 miles) up to an altitude of 4,500 meters (14,750 feet). The fighter groups were echeloned by altitude. Each was responsible for a specific tier, within which it *locked out* enemy bombers. In the case of two-tiered coverage, the group of the first tier were positioned within an altitude range of 600-700 to 2,500 meters (2,000 to 8,200 feet), while the second-tier group patrolled from 2,500 to 4,500 meters (8,200 to 14,750 feet).

The tactic of patrolling in groups within altitude limits was based on the *combing* principle. The strike group arranged its flight for vertical maneuver with the mission to watch over the entire assigned area. The cover subgroups flew back and forth at the altitude limit, each in their own tier, maintaining reliable communications (visual and radio) with the strike group of their tier. In the event of the appearance of enemy bombers in the first tier, the commander of the patrolling group immediately radioed a report to his neighbor above and launched his attack. In this case, the commander of the second tier would then be responsible for supporting the engaged lower-tier group by keeping a lookout for, and warding off, any enemy fighters that might attempt to enter the area.

Upon the appearance of enemy bombers in the second tier, the group commander would attack the enemy aircraft with the required cover of his own strike group, independent of whether the enemy bombers had fighter escort or not. The commander of the lower group, when necessary, was required to assist his *neighbor* by entering the battle with any portion (up to all) of his forces. Depending on conditions, the composition of the covering group could vary in number. However, it was not recommended to have it comprise more than eight fighters, as it complicated maneuver and made the command and control of

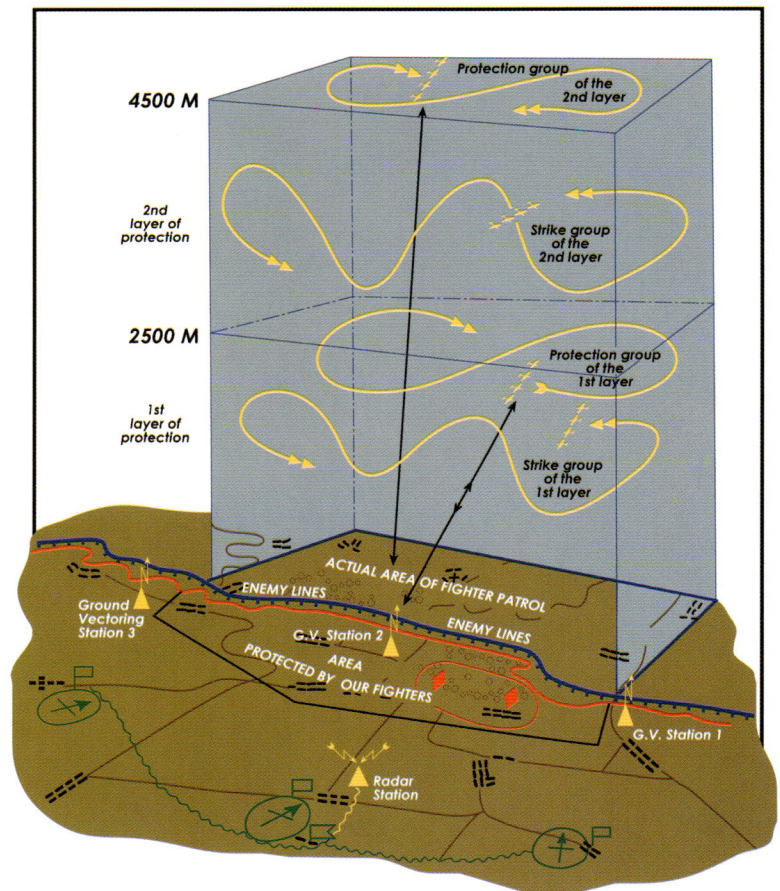

A schematic showing VVS fighter coverage "tiers" and their associated ground vectoring stations. Fall-Winter, 1943.

Based on an original diagram sketched out in Bulletin of the Air Fleet for 1944

pairs and four-ship elements more difficult. It should be said that this continuous patrol method required great expenditure of fighter forces and their various support infrastructure. So much so, that it could only be employed over a relatively modest sector of the front at critical stages of the operation.

By Friday, 1 October 1943, the 291st IAP (11 Yak-9s and eight Yak-1s) and the 402nd IAP (10 Yak-9s and six Yak-1s) had been repositioned on airfields at both the Karl Libknekht sovkhoz [state farm] and Hill 93.0. The division headquarters and the 812th IAP (five Yak-9s and five Yak-1s) were at Kharkovo airfield. On this day the 265th IAD conducted six air battles in which the pilots of 812th IAP shot down two Bf109s and an He111. At 1053 eight fighters (four Yak-1s and four Yak-9s) of the 2nd Squadron sortied to intercept an enemy bomber formation spotted in the area west of Bolshoy Tokmak and to cover the area of Pokaznyy-Rovnoye. Here is a staff summary for one of the resulting engagements:

The assigned area was covered from 1100-1150 at an altitude of 3,000–1,000 meters (9,850–3,280 feet). At 1125, from an altitude of 2500 meters (8,200 feet), Kapitan Popov shot down one Bf109 from behind and above at a range of 50-40 meters (54-43 yards). Dropping down, a second Bf109 avoided attack. The Bf109 fell in to a farmstead located between Mikhaylovka and Orekhovskiy. All crews that observed the fall confirmed it.

This was the third personal victory for Ivan Popov. The destruction of this Messer also was recorded by the chief of staff of the 217th Guards Artillery Regiment, Mayor Rubtsov.

Another sortie launched at 1307. Leytenant Fedorov (Yak-1, bort 37) shot down another Bf109 two kilometers (1.2 miles) southeast of Burchak. The Yak-9T of Leytenant Maksimov was set on fire in this fight. Reaching home base, he managed to land and escape from the damaged fighter before it burned up on the airfield. Mladshiy Leytenant Nikolay Konovalov (Yak-9 bort 57) did not return from combat over the Burchak area. From the regiment journal of combat actions:

The time in the coverage area (east of Mikhaylovka) was from 1314 to 1410. At 1445, west of Voroshilovka, at an altitude of 4000 meters (13,125 feet), 12 Ju88s appeared escorted by four Bf109s. The strike group of six attacked the Ju88s from below and behind. They were not able to gain altitude. The Ju88s were driven off in two attacks and, not having dropped their bombs, departed to the west. The fighters attempted to engage the Yaks in combat. At 1457 the group of Junkers came in again, but again fled to the west without dropping their bombs. The second group came under escort of 6-10 Bf109s. In the air battle that unfolded, Leytenant Fedorov shot down one Bf109, which fell 2 km (1.2 miles) southeast of Burchak. Konovalov did not return from the mission. Aircraft Yak-9 (0362). Damaged in air combat, Ml. Lt. Maksimov's aircraft caught fire during landing.

Incidents: Gun failure on Leytenant Fedorov's aircraft — ruptured cartridge cases; Kapitan Popov (Yak-9 bort 39) loss of air pressure, Leytenant Shishkin (Yak-9 bort 63) ShVAK stoppage.

These sparse annotations in the regimental journal of combat actions cannot convey all the dynamics and everything that happened in the battle. According to analysis of regiment and division-level documents, this air battle took shape in the following manner. At 1450 Leytenant Fedorov's group encountered approximately 20 enemy Ju88 and He111 bombers in the Voroshilovka area. Attempting to prevent the bombers from reaching friendly forces, the 812th IAP pilots each selected a bomber and closed on them all at one time. At this time a report arrived from the command post that nine trailing He111s were heading toward the target absolutely unhindered.

The command post demanded that these inbound enemy aircraft be attacked but there were no fighters available. They were all already engaged in combat. Unexpectedly, the pair of Shishkin and Konovalov, which had initially separated and then come back together, headed toward these bombers and attacked them in a coordinated fashion from separate flanks with their cannons. Mladshiy Leytenant Konovalov closed on an He111, but a Messer rocketed down from above, attacking him from behind. In an instant the radio echoed a question from Kapitan Popov: "Who rammed a bomber?" None of the pilots were able to respond clearly to this question. From the operational summary of the 812th IAP for 1 October 1943: "*Kapitan Popov observed two falling aircraft northwest of Burchak.*" There were questions in the air during the battle—'Who rammed?' A participant in this battle, I. Fedorov, recalled:

Later we learned that Nikolay Andreyevich Konovalov executed the ram. The Heinkels, failing to reach their target, were turning around and hurriedly departing to the west in disorder. I do not know what Nikolay was thinking about before his death, but I believe that he was not experiencing fear. Cowards do not execute ramming maneuvers.[66]

A day later Kapitan Pavel Tarasov achieved his next victory in the air.

I bring to your attention that at 1140, in air combat with two Bf109s, one enemy airplane was shot down at an altitude of 1,600 meters (5,250 feet). After a deliberate attack it fell in the area of Nizhnaya Andreyevka, 25 km (15.5 miles) northwest of Bolshoy Tokmak. I fired with my OKB-16 (37mm). The attack was from behind and above at a range of 120–100 meters (130–110 yards). It was observed that, typically, the cannon rounds almost completely destroyed the tail section of the Bf109. Mayor Pasynok and Leytenant Tikhomirov witnessed the downing.

The constant pressure and the death of their comrades weighed heavily on the regiment's pilots. Fatigue that had accumulated over the last two weeks began to tell on them. During takeoff, Kapitan Popov's Yak-9 collided with another airplane parked on the ramp. As a result, both Yaks were damaged. On Tuesday, 5 October, only three Yak-1s and three Yak-9s were considered combat capable in the 812th Air Regiment. As if in mercy, a change in the weather brought heavy overcast. A relative calm settled over the zone of actions of the 3rd IAK until 15 October.

The broken remains of a Romanian Henschel Hs129 brought down in the Melitopol area during the battles of late 1943. Under local Luftwaffe control, the three Romanian Hs129 squadrons operated their aircraft in the close support role, while those of the neighboring German units flew both general close support missions and specific anti-tank close support missions.

Dmitri Karlenko

Meeting the Henschel

Within the two days before this the 812th IAP was repositioned to Astrakhanka airfield. Air battles shifted from the Bolshoy Tokmak area to the Danilo-Ivanovka, Akimovka, Vladimirovka, Melitopol area. The corps command learned that Hs129 ground-attack aircraft were very active in this sector. Unlike some of its fellow 3rd IAK regiments, the 812th's pilots had not yet encountered this aircraft in the air. In the first combat sortie after the forced layoff, Mladshiy Leytenant Ivan Sosegov from 15th IAP (278th IAD) shot down the first Hs129 ground-attack airplane that appeared in the area of Bolshoy Utlyug.

Yet another 812th IAP Yak-9T was damaged on this day. Leytenant Fedorov did not control his aircraft properly during rollout and put it on its nose. This accident was compensated for in the afternoon when replacement aircraft - 10 Yak-7Bs - were flown into the regiment. On 18 October, with seven Yak-7Bs, four Yak-1s, and three Yak-9Ts assigned, the regiment continued to fly combat sorties, covering ground forces in the Novo-Danilovka area. On the following day the group of Leytenant Fedorov took off with three Yak-1s and one Yak-9. On their return, one Yak-1 and one Yak-9 were missing. The pair of Mladshiy Leytenant Kuznetsov and Mladshiy Leytenant Serezhenko, flying low-level, fell behind the others and got lost. All night the pilots of 2nd Squadron held out hope that the young pilots had not become easy prey for German fighters. On the following day, Wednesday, the "missing pair" landed smartly, rolled out on the landing strip and taxied to their parking spots like old pros. On this occasion everything turned out all right. Having become lost and unable to contact the group leader, they stuck together and landed at another airfield for the night.

In the most critical period during the recapture of Melitopol, and during the breakthrough against the enemy's defensive line along the Molochnaya River, a low layer of clouds appeared that interfered with aviation operations on both sides. Enemy bombers transitioned to actions in small groups and even individual aircraft. In such conditions the ground vectoring station was unable to get fighters into action in a timely fashion. The time expended in taking off plus the transit time to their assigned area was sufficient for the enemy to get in, accomplish his mission, and depart the area unhindered. To counter this situation, to make more effective use of the fighters, to allow for the timely redirection of fighters during flight, and to facilitate the rapid response of units to mission orders coming in from stations, the entire Melitopol area was divided into zones and sectors. These were memorized by crews and headquarters alike.

A portion of the fighters covered the ground forces by continuously patrolling specific zones in flights of four. Meanwhile, other fighters, in pairs, flew deep into enemy territory to hunt for bombers. These *free hunters*, though having the primary mission to search out and destroy enemy aviation, would also conduct attacks on enemy ground forces, selecting their targets independently as they patrolled. Thus, on Thursday, 21 October, fighters of the 812th IAP destroyed eight trucks (with ammunition loads) and two wagons. They also set one Bf109 on fire on the ground, blew up an ammunition dump, suppressed the fire of three antiaircraft positions, and put five field guns out of action. As a rule, flights by the regiment's fighters in this time were conducted at altitudes from 200 down to 50 meters (650 to 165 feet).

On this same day, 21 October, the neighboring 402nd IAP shot down its first Hs129 ground-attack airplane. Taking off at 1038 for reconnaissance in the Udachnoye—Novo-Nikolayevka area, Leytenant Pavlushkin, passing near the village Akimovka at an altitude of 200 meters (650 feet), spotted a lone Hs129. Approaching the enemy aircraft undetected, he delivered two long bursts from his Yak-1's cannon. After the attack the Henschel began to drop, belly landing 5 kilometers (3 miles) from the village. Having returned to the airfield, Pavlushkin reported the damaged aircraft to regiment headquarters and the fact that the enemy plane had made a belly landing. Having received this report, the headquarters of 265th IAD decided to become more familiar with the specifications of this type of aircraft.

Led by Leytenant Savin, two fighters (Yak-1 and Yak-7B) from the 291st IAP took off at 1415 to photograph this airplane. Having made several passes, the pilots photographed the damaged aircraft and then made three attacks on it, severing the engines from their mounts and holing the fuselage. According to German records, one Hs129B-2 was lost on this day. It was from 12.(Pz)/SchlG9 [12th Staffel (Panzer) of Schlactgeschwader 9].

Meanwhile, the 812th Regiment busied itself with combinations of combat reconnaissance sorties and free hunts. The first, at 0845, comprised the pair of Starshiy Leytenant Tishchenko in Yak-9 (bort 59) and Serzhant Stryuk in Yak-9 (bort 67). Here is an excerpt from their post-flight report:

> We conducted a free hunt in the area southwest of Melitopol-Akimovka-Goreloye. In the Goreloye area we attacked a column of up to 50 men on horses, then attacked two trucks. Soldiers piled out of the trucks. [We attacked] a large concentration of infantry in the forest south of Radionovka. Up to a platoon of soldiers was destroyed. One battalion of infantry was moving from the Akimovka area to Radionovka.

The pair of Kapitan Popov (Yak-7 bort 11) and Leytenant Tumanov (Yak-7 bort 20) left at 1020 to hunt in this same area.

> Over the target from 1025 to 1110. In the area of Gutental and on its eastern outskirts they were fired upon by two batteries of antiaircraft machine guns. Two fires burning near Akimovka. Some 12-13 flatcars loaded with trucks were parked at Utlyug station. We attacked them from an altitude of 150 meters. The results could not be observed.

The next pair, which had departed on a free hunt to this same area at 1144, was Leytenant Fedorov (Yak-7 bort 14) and his irreplaceable wingman Mladshiy Leytenant Maksimov (Yak-7 bort 12).

> We were flying on free hunt southwest of Melitopol. In the Akimovka area we spotted 20 self-propelled guns on the road moving west. We made five gun runs from an altitude of 100-40 meters(325–130 feet), destroying three and damaging two self-propelled guns. In the area of Utlyug station we were attacked by a battery of small-caliber antiaircraft artillery. We suppressed the battery. On the road from Davydovka to Goreloye, we destroyed a covered truck.

The consecutive actions of hunters flying in three coordinated pairs was the tactically correct decision. For during the flight of one pair, those remaining *unengaged* had the ability to rest and restore their energy. Pilots could thus keep a vigilant look-out for the enemy, uncovered his firing positions throughout the day.

The pair of Tishchenko-Stryuk sortied on its second hunting mission at 1311, this time destroying two cars and three wagons. Thirty minutes later, Popov and Tumanov took off and suppressed an antiaircraft battery. Fedorov's pair sortied at 1425, destroying a Bf109 attempting to take off from a forward airfield and shooting up a lone truck. The last hunting sortie of the day, the third time up for Fedorov's pair, destroyed a cargo truck and an antiaircraft gun.

On the following day, all of the regiment's flights were committed to escorting Pe-2 bombers from the 6th GBAD. Not a single bomber was lost to enemy action. But Kapitan Ankudinov's escort group (three Yak-1s, two Yak-7s, and one Yak-9), that took off at 1442, clenched their teeth as they witnessed a tragedy unfold before their very eyes.

> We were escorting nine Pe-2s to the area north of Mikhaylovka. The Pe-2s were bombing enemy forces in the area of Shevchenko. Two flights dropped their ordnance through the clouds, one flight from under the overcast. The bombs of the first flight fell in a field and the bombs of the two remaining flights on enemy troops.

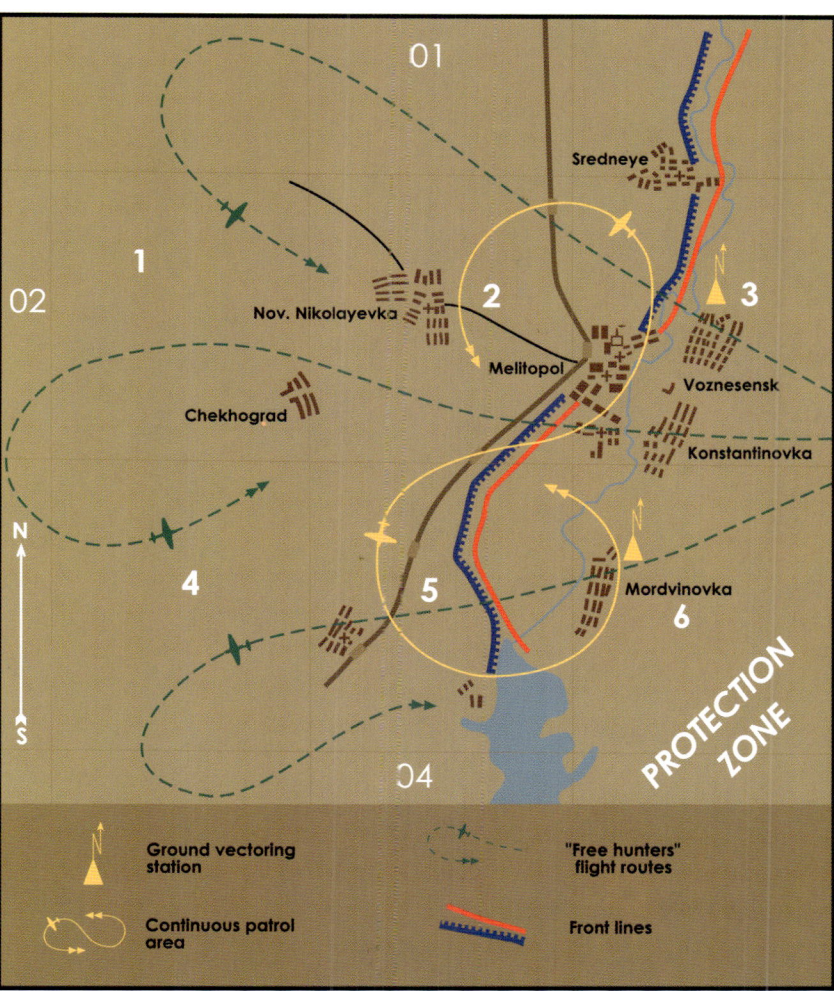

An overview of fighter coverage in the Melitopol operation, Winter, 1943, illustrating the patrol zones and free hunter elements more clearly than the "3-D" representation on page 62.

Based on an original diagram from Bulletin of the Air Fleet for 1944

The initial Romanian Hs129B-2s, as used by the 8th Air Assault Group in and around the Melitopol area, were all from existing Luftwaffe stocks. These did not employ the underslung heavy cannon usually associated with the type's anti-armour role. Instead they were fitted with the standard under-fuselage 4-bomb carrier. Though it may have encountered 3rd IAK Yaks at some point in its brief operational history, this particular machine was brought down by Soviet AA fire in the Tavri area of southern Ukraine.

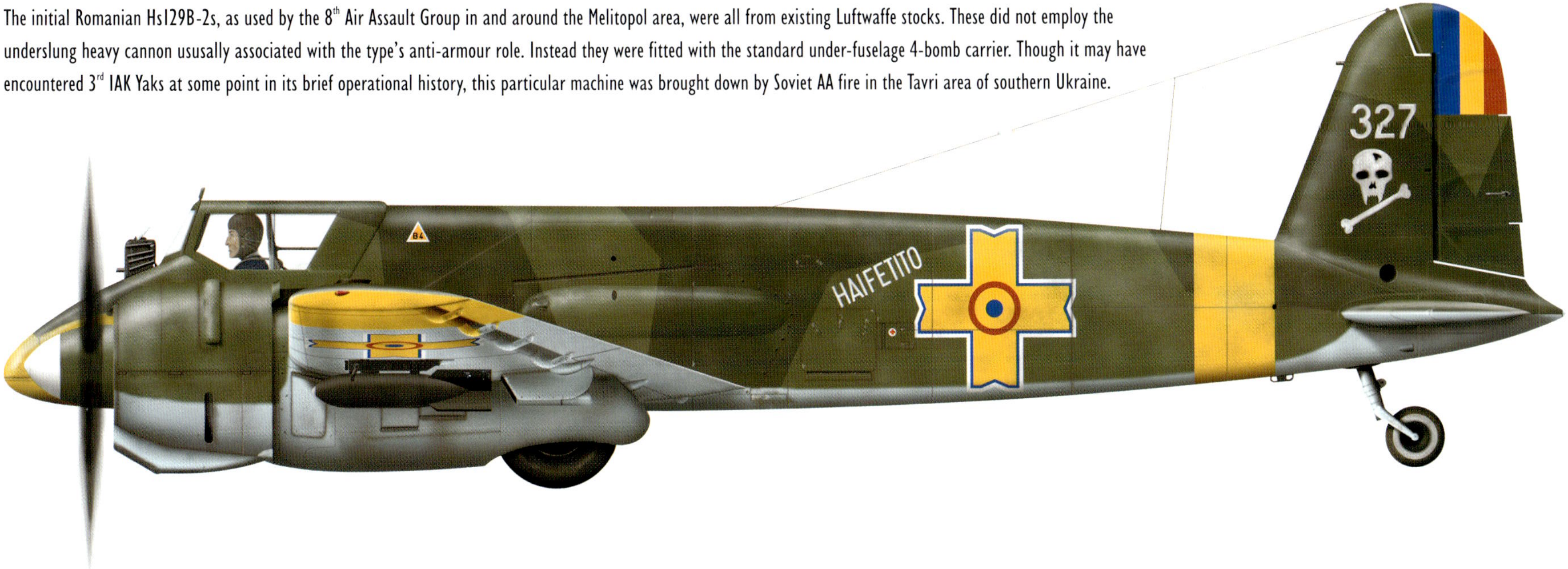

Mladshiy Leytenant Ivan Fedorov downed the 812th's first Henschel twin in Yak-7B #14 on 23 October 1943. Ten of these series-47 Yak-7Bs came into the regiment's inventory as replacement aircraft at the beginning of October. Though outwardly similar in appearance to the earliest Yak-9s, it retained early 'razorback' Yak-7 features such as the two machine guns above the engine and the round-tipped wing. The oil cooler, radiator and carburetor air intakes, as well as the exhaust fairings, cockpit armour, empennage, and canopy components are identical to those on Yak-9s of the same production 'vintage'. By the end of October, only five of this replacement batch remained. During this time — 28 October — Fedorov became a division-level scout flying Yak-7B #04 (series unknown).

During the turnaround after the bomb drop, two Pe-2 aircraft collided. Leytenant Shishkin observed the fall of two Pe-2s to the ground; after the fall of one Pe-2 it burst into flames. The aircraft fell 2-3 kilometers (1.2–1.8 miles) north of Shevchenko.

Altogether 21 sorties were flown in escort of the Pe-2s.

For the pilots of 812th IAP, the first familiarization with the Hs129 occurred on 23 October over Danilo-Ivanovka. At 0935 the transmitter at General Mayor Savitskiy's command post vectored Leytenant Fedorov's group (two Yak-1s and two Yak-7Bs) onto German ground-attack aircraft in the Udachnoye-Danilo-Ivanovka area. Observing a flight of eight Hs129s flying at 100 meters (325 feet) near Vladimirovka, Fedorov attacked first. After a brief burst from the group leader's Yak-7B (bort 14) cannon, one Henschel went down without any particular difficulty. It fell in the Akimovka area.

Continuing to pursue the German aircraft, the Yaks developed a frontal attack some ten minutes later. Despite their powerful forward-firing weapons, the German Henschels did not risk a cannon duel, but rather dumped their bombs and turned around to the west. In the brief and fast-moving running battle Leytenant Shishkin destroyed one additional Hs129, which fell near Vladimirovka. Fedorov was less lucky this time; having expended all of his cannon ammo, only his machine gun remained with which to attack another Henschel. Although he couldn't set this next target afire, he inflicted enough damage so that the enemy aircraft had to belly land after limping back across the front line.

At the same time, a mixed group from the 291st IAP (two Yak-7Bs, one Yak-1, and one Yak-9) intercepted 10 Hs129s in the area of Danilovka. In the ensuing attack Starshiy Leytenant Loginov shot up one Henschel at 150-100 meters (165–110 feet) range. Trailing smoke, yet another ground attacker had to force land on its belly. On pulling out of that attack, Loginov shot up a Bf109 with a long burst, driving it out of the fight as well. They claimed the ground-attack plane plus a Bf109 fighter shot down in this action.

Having sortied at 1119, the three Yak-7Bs and one Yak-1 under Kapitan Ankudinov's leadership observed two Hs129s lying on their bellies southwest of Akimovka. It appeared that the Germans had not yet recovered them after the combat with Fedorov's group. After making several passes at the downed aircraft they returned to their airfield. Altogether the 3rd IAK had destroyed three Hs129s, one He111, one Ju87, and one Bf109 in eight separate aerial engagements. All of the downed ground-attack aircraft were credited to 265th IAD pilots, who marked, in this manner, the granting of the honorary title "Melitopolskaya" to their unit. [that is to say, they became the 265th "Melitopol" Fighter Aviation Division–ed.]

This autumn Saturday, 23 October 1943, which concluded with the liberation of Melitopol, became a holiday for the 265th IAD. During the Melitopol offensive operation, in providing immediate aviation support to the front's ground forces, formations and units of 8th Air Army conducted 12,380 combat sorties (7,487 during the day and 4,893 at night). They destroyed, or otherwise put out of action, 130 enemy tanks, 770 wheeled vehicles, and up to 100 field artillery batteries. 186 aircraft were shot down in 268 air battles and another 57 set on fire on the ground. Fully 132 of October's air combat victories were by fighters under the direct assistance of radio vectoring. By order of the Supreme High Commander, the 265th Fighter and 206th Ground Attack Divisions, 76th Guards Ground Attack and 8th Separate Reconnaissance Regiments were awarded the honorary title "Melitopolskiy." Moscow saluted them with 20 artillery salvoes from 224 guns.

On the following day four fighters flying in the Melitopol area intercepted two Bf109s. The pair of Mayor Pasynok and Leytenant Tumanov encountered two Bf109s at 1730 and, without hesitation, attacked them. Out of surprise, the German pilots flew this way and that. After several passes both were shot down. Based in immediate proximity to the front line, the 812th IAP covered the attacking ground forces for another three days. This distance, all of 8–10 kilometers (5–6 miles), permitted the pilots on the ground to observe the approach of enemy aircraft.

In later analyzing the lessons of the battles during October, the headquarters of 8th Air Army noted:

In flights along the front, as were noted before, the He111, Ju88, and Ju87 aircraft constituted more than 70 percent [of all aircraft]. In the second half of the month we noted the simultaneous actions of from 10 to 35 Hs129 aircraft, that according to interrogation data belonged to a Romanian aviation corps and the German groups "Schwartz" and "Steinkopf."

It should be noted that the army intelligence department almost exactly indicated all groups that were flying the Hs129B. The Royal Romanian Air Force (FARR—Fortele Aeriane Regale ale Romana) 8th Ground Attack Group (Grupul 8 Asalt), under the command of Kapitan Ioana Khara [replaced by Lt. cdor. av. Dutu Vasiliu since early August – ed.], with the 41st, 42nd, and 60th Squadrons, was operating in the interests of the Luftwaffe's Luftflotte IV (4th Air Fleet). The "Steinkopf" group, in all likelihood, comprised the IV.(Pz)/SG9 with its constituent 10th, 11th, 12th, 13th, and 14th Staffeln. This group was formed on 18 October in Kirovograd under the leadership of Major Bruno Meyer. Its 11(Pz)/SG9 was commanded by Oberleutnant Hans-Hermann Steinkamp. We unfortunately are unable to identify the group under the name "Schwartz."

Continuing successfully to hunt for Hs129 ground-attack aircraft, the pilots of the 265th and 278th IAD's destroyed another five of them, together with an equal number of Ju87s, four Bf109s, and one Fw189 in 28 aerial engagements on 25 October. The division staff noted the following:

Enemy aviation over the course of 25.10.43 significantly increased its activity level. Hs129 ground-attack aircraft attacked our forces in groups of 8-12 aircraft flying at ground level, 10-50 meters (30–165 feet) altitude. The bombers conducted raids in groups of up to 12 aircraft against our mobile advancing groups. Enemy Bf109 fighters, in pairs and four-ship flights, covered their forces withdrawing to the west and counteracted our own fighters. Over the course of the day our aircraft conducted nine group and one individual aerial engagement, resulting in seven destroyed and one damaged enemy aircraft. We had no losses. All our aircraft returned to their airfields. The enemy conducted raids by groups of Hs129 at treetop level. Bomber aviation continues to bomb our forces from medium and high altitude, from 2,000 to 4,500 meters (6,550–14,750 feet). It is necessary for our covering aircraft to execute their coverage echeloned by altitude and to pay special attention to the actions of the ground-attack aircraft.

On this day the 812th IAP, which now comprised two Yak-1s and six Yak-7Bs, conducted its first aerial engagement at 1308. The group of Leytenant Fedorov (four Yak-7Bs and two Yak-1s) encountered two Hs129s on an opposite heading, but at treetop height, in the Akimovka area. The four Yak-7Bs conducted attacks from two different directions, damaging both enemy aircraft. After dropping their bombs they withdrew to the west. Leytenant Maksimov, pursuing one of the retreating Henschels, shot it down from a range of 100 meters (109 yards). It fell 10 kilometers (6.2 miles) west of Akimovka. On this occasion the Hs129B-2 of Feldwebel Joachim Bannier, 10.(Pz)/SchlG9, was reported as missing in action.

At this time two Bf109s approached in an attempt to drive off Fedorov's four-ship from intercepting the Henschels. Kapitan Pavel Tarasov's group then engaged these two enemy fighters at an altitude of approximately 100 meters (325 feet). An additional group of Bf109s showed up several minutes later. What made this encounter unusual, in the recollections of Fedorov, was the additional fact that...

> "A strange Yak painted in a mousy color kept interfering with Tarasov and us. Because of this we did not shoot down a single airplane. The Messers departed with a steep dive. I think that the pilot in this gray Yak was not ours. To this day this remains for me an unresolved riddle."[68]

From the account of 812th IAP for 25.10.43:

20 aircraft sorties were flown. one Bf109, one Hs126, four Ju87 shot down. At 1325 west of Danilo-

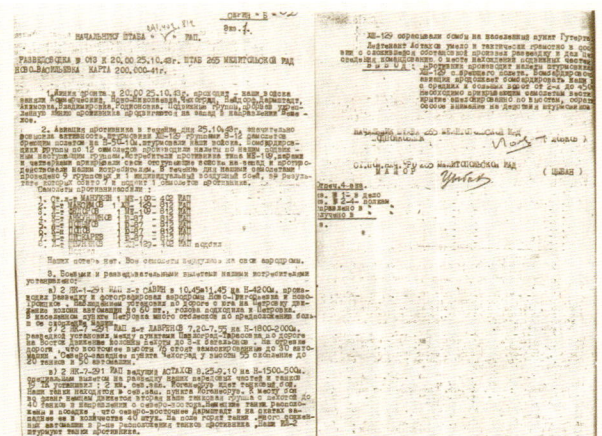

Intelligence report #013 K20.00 25 October 1943 HQ of 265 Melitopolskiy IAD. Map 200.000-41, Novo-Vasilyevka.

1. Front line by 2000 25.10.1943: our troops occupied Kommercheskiy, Novo-Nikolayevka, Chekhograd, Neydorf, Darmshtadt, Akimovka, Vladimirovka, Radionovka. Mobile groups penetrated enemy's fortified line and move towards the West in the direction of Veseloye.

2. During the day of 25.10.43, enemy aviation significantly increased its activity. Hs129 ground-attack planes in groups of 8-12 strafed our troops at tree-top level (altitude 50 -10m); bombers in groups of 12 planes attacked our mobile advancing groups. Enemy Bf109 fighters acting in pairs and fours covered their own retreating forces and opposed our fighters. During the day our planes conducted 9 group and 1 individual aerial engagements. As a result 7 enemy planes were shot down and 1 damaged.

Enemy planes were shot down by:

1. St. Leyt. Manukyan – 1 Bf109 – 402 IAP
2. Leyt. Maksimov – 1 Hs129 – 812 IAP
3. Leyt. Fedorov – 1 Bf109 – 812 IAP
4. Kapt. Ankudinov – 1 Ju87 – 812 IAP
5. Leyt. Podymov – 1 Ju87 – 812 IAP
6. Kapt. Popov – 1 Ju87 – 812 IAP
7. Leyt. Peskarev – 1 Ju87 – 812 IAP
8. Leyt. Shpunyakov – 1 Hs129 (damaged) – 402 IAP

No losses on our side. All airplanes returned to their airfields.

3. By combat and reconnaissance sorties of our fighters it has been determined:

a) 2 Yak-1 of 291 IAP, Leyt. Savin, at 1045 and 1145 at altitude 4200m conducted reconnaissance and photographed Novo-Grigoryevka and Novo-Troitskoye airfields. By observation he determined movement of a column of up to 60 trucks on the road to Petrovka from the south. The head of the column approached Petrovka. In Petrovka there was much glare, probably large concentration of vehicles.

b) 2 Yak-7 of 291 IAP, Leyt. Lavrenov, at 0720-0755 at altitude 1800-2000m determined by reconnaissance that between Pavlograd and Tarasovka on the road leading east is movement of an infantry column, up to 3 battalions. On the section of the road to the east of Height 76 are up to 30 camouflaged trucks. To the northwest of Chekhograd at Height 55 is a concentration of up to 20 tanks and 50 trucks.

c) 2 Yak-7 of 291 IAP leader Astakhov, 0825- 0910 at altitude 1500 – 500m performing dedicated reconnaissance sortie of our advanced units and tanks of 19th Tank Corps determined: there is a tank battle 2 km northwest of Ioganesrue. Our tanks are to the northwest of Ioganesrue. Our second armor group—up to 40 tanks with infantry—is moving northeast toward the German flank in the combat area. Forty German tanks are located in the wooded area northeast of Darmshtadt and on the slopes west of it. Tanks are burning in the field; there are many burned trucks in the area of enemy tank locations. Our Il-2s are strafing the enemy tanks.

d) Hs129 were bombing Gutertal.

Leytenant Astakhov skillfully and tactically correctly performed reconnaissance and brought our commanders valuable information about the location of mobile units.

Conclusions: The enemy performs attacks by Hs129 ground-attackers from tree-top level. Bomber aviation continues to bomb our troops from medium and high altitudes of 2000 – 4500m.

It is necessary for our cover aircraft to perform their mission in an echeloned manner at different altitudes, paying special attention to the actions of the enemy's ground-attackers.

Chief of Staff, 265 Melitopolskaya IAD
Podpolkovnik Lovkov

Senior Assistant to the Chief of Intelligence, 265 Melitopolskaya IAD
Mayor Tsiban

Ivanovka, six fighters conducted battle with four Bf109s at 1,500 meters (4,900 feet) altitude. Leytenant Fedorov and wingman Mladshiy Leytenant Maksimov attacked two Bf109 without result. Second pair of Bf109 attacked Maksimov. Maksimov and Fedorov fought individual air combat with Bf109 without result. Bf109 withdrew from engagement with steep dive and departed to west at high speed. In the process of aerial engagement, a gray-colored Yak continuously interfered with Fedorov's and Tarasov's attack of enemy. During our fighters' attack, the Hs129 maneuvered sharply, presenting frontal aspect, and fired its cannons. During withdrawal from attack conducted covering fire at fighter.

The possession by the enemy of a Yak aircraft, which not only interfered with but also shot down Soviet airplanes, was first noted in the Kuban. Here is an account from 402nd IAP for 28 April 1943:

In the period 1900-1910, in the area southwest of Kievskaya, at an altitude of 3,000 meters (9,850 feet), Starshiy Leytenant Rubakhin was attacked by one Bf109, behind which were two Yak-1s with red spinners, white lettering on the fuselage, red stars, and lacking numerical markings. The right wing had striped paint and the left wing green paint. The Yak-1 aircraft were in immediate proximity to the Bf109 and did not fire at Rubakhin. Starshiy Leytenant Rubakhin reported that the two Yak-1s indicated above pursued a Pe-2 to our territory and fired on it. After the Pe-2 fended off the attack of the Bf109 and two Yak-1s, the two Yak-1s and Bf109 departed to the west. Starshiy Leytenant Rubakhin believes that the aircraft of Mladshiy Leytenant Ishkhanov, which did not return from the mission, was shot down by the Yak-1s mentioned above. [Mladshiy Leytenant Ishkhanov, who returned on 10.5.43, reported that he was shot down by two Yak-1s on 28.4.43 and parachuted to the area of Troitskaya.]

Sometimes, the observations of pilots and their subsequent accounts appear to be very convincing.

Kapitan Mikhail Vlasov [15th IAP/278th IAD, who in 1945 became the commander of 812th IAP] on 27.10.43 during a flight to the coverage area at 1530 and altitude of 150-70 meters (490–230 feet) saw two blue-gray Yak-1s, which were flying an eastward heading. When they passed below him, a minute later, glancing back, he spotted a Yak that fell burning approximately in the Pushkino area. At this time the second Yak was heading westward at treetop level and high speed, and disappeared into the haze.

Not less mysterious is the description of the attack of such a Yak by Mladshiy Leytenant Viktor Kuznetsov from 43rd IAP/278th IAD.

On 21.11.43, during the period 1617 to 1702, four Yak-1s of 43rd IAP, led by Leytenant Osadchiy, during the execution of a combat mission to cover ground forces in the area of Novo-Petrovka, Veseloye, Ponevka, at 1645 noticed a Yak-1 without number come out of the overcast. He began to turn in behind our group, masked by the

overcast. Mladshiy Leytenant Kuznetsov noticed how the unidentified Yak attacked Leytenant Koshman from behind. It fired a single burst at him, and then immediately departed into the overcast. Mladshiy Leytenant Kuznetsov began a pursuit. The unidentified Yak-1 came out of the overcast west of Verkhniy Rogachik and turned toward Nikopol. North of Verkhniy Rogachik enemy antiaircraft fire opened up on it; the numberless Yak gave a signal by lowering his nose several times. The antiaircraft fire stopped. Mladshiy Leytenant Kuznetsov gave the same signals. The antiaircraft artillery did not fire any more. In the area 5 kilometers south of Bolshaya Znamenka, the numberless Yak came out of the overcast and Mladshiy Leytenant Kuznetsov immediately attacked it and fired one burst. The numberless Yak was set on fire and fell in a field 5 kilometers (8.2 miles) south of Bolshaya Znamenka. Mladshiy Leytenant Kuznetsov arrived at his Chekhograd airfield at dusk, where he made a forced landing because of the onset of darkness. On 22.11 he refueled and returned to his unit.

For pilots of the 812th IAP, yet another encounter with this unidentified Yak occurred on 27 October.

We were providing cover in the area of Fedorovka, Veseloye, Novo-Nikolayevka. At 1130, at an altitude of 2,500 meters (4,850 feet), a mouse-colored Yak attempted to take up position behind Tarasov. Tarasov turned around to face it head-on. The mouse-colored Yak departed to the west and took cover in the overcast.

Mayor Pavel Tarasov was a Kapitan during the winter fighting of 1943. He was the first in the regiment to be awarded the highest honor — Gold Star of Hero of the Soviet Union. His score rose to 30 personal victories.

This is a fragment of the regimental journal (Operational Record Book) with activities on 28 October 1943.

On the left page are the aircraft type and bort number (e.g., 7-12 = Yak-7 Bort number 12) while the corresponding pilots' names are given with time of take-off and landing plus the total time for the sortie. It is obvious that the listings were arrayed into groups as they were formed for a sortie.

On the right page we can see assignments for each sortie, expenditure of ammunition for machine guns and cannons, and notes on aerial engagements.

This kind of document is a valuable "primary source" for many researchers as it provides day-by day description of the unit's actual combat work.

One would hope that the mysterious presence of this hostile mouse-colored Yak would eventually be cleared up. [possibly operated by JG52 — ed.]

Observation of the enemy revealed an increase in ground-attack aviation numbers. The Ju87s of SchlG 77, reorganized as SG77 (on 18 October under the command of Mayor Helmut Bruck) were rushed into this area in mid-October. On Monday, 25 October, pilots of the 812th IAP conducted another three aerial engagements from 1625 to 1735. At 1630 two Yak-1s and four Yak-7Bs under the command of Kapitan Ankudinov spotted a group of up to 40 Ju87s at an altitude of 3000 meters (9,850 feet) in the Danilo-Ivanovka area. Having reported the sighting to the vectoring station command post, six fighters of the 812th went into the attack. Not waiting until the fighters closed to striking range, the Stukas began to release their bombs in dives. Kapitan Yegor Ankudinov caught up to one as it was pulling out, while Mladshiy Leytenant Nikolay Podymov attacked another. Both bombers, not having regained altitude, fell in the battle area. Here is the report written by Nikolay Podymov.

At 1645-1650, at an altitude of 3,500 meters (11,480 feet), I spotted three groups of Ju87s flying on a heading of 120 degrees south of Chekhograd. Gaining altitude I, along with Kapitan Ankudinov, attacked the first group from the front with an angle of approach of 1/4. The group dispersed and randomly dropped their bombs. Having caught up to the Junkers with a turn, I attacked one without result. Banking my aircraft to the right, I spotted another Ju87 above me and began to close with it and fire. He saw me and turned left, but there was another aircraft there and so he resumed his original heading. I fired at him again from a range of 100-20 meters (109–22 yards). The gunner did not shoot back. I watched as the Junkers came apart. Pieces were flying off in every direction.

Barely avoiding collision with it, I made a combat turn. The airplane lost altitude and exploded into the ground at 1655. I saw dust from it in the area of Marienfeld. I chased after a second [target] to the west, fired at it, but it flew away. To my left I saw Ankudinov's attack; the airplane went down and blew up at 1658. Having completed the pursuit east of Ivanovka, we paired up and went home.

A short time later, at 1710, Kapitan Ivan Popov and his wingman Mladshiy Leytenant Peskarev also encountered a large group of Ju87s, north of Akimovka at an altitude of 1,100 meters (3,600 feet). The Luftwaffe pilots, having dropped their bombs, attempted to get away in a dive. Popov chased a Junkers that had fallen out of the formation and shot it down with two bursts from behind and above at a range of 50 meters (55 yards). Peskarev also destroyed a Ju87, as it came out of its dive. At this time Fedorov's flight spotted six Ju88s escorted by two Bf109s. Unable to penetrate to the bombers, the flight fell under the attack of the pair of Messers. Gaining altitude, Leytenant Fedorov noticed that Kapitan Ankudinov was attempting to attack another two Bf109s. Diving on a Messer that had not spotted him, Fedorov shot it down on his first pass from above and behind. The pilots of 402nd IAP put the finish on the division's combat sorties for the day. Starshiy Leytenant Akop Manukyan destroyed a Bf109 at 1815 in the Chekhograd area. I. V. Fedorov, recalled the end of this day.

At the end of this memorable day, the regiment received several telegrams from the commanders of ground units. They thanked the pilots and confirmed the number of downed aircraft. These telegrams normally were read in front of the formation, and there was not a better award for a pilot than a warm testimonial of combat comrades fighting the Germans on the ground.[68]

Leutnant Walter Krause's Hs129B-2 "K" of 10.(Pz)/SG9, spring 1944. As the 812th worked its way south from the Nikopol-Melitopol area toward the Crimean Peninsula in late 1943, the Luftwaffe's main Hs129 unit in the area worked its way northwest through Uman and Vinnitsa, ultimately ending up at Proskurov by March of 1944. Here they recieved replacement aircraft, one of which was the MKI03 cannon-armed "K". Preliminary research suggests that this aircraft left the factory very early in 1944 as Wk.N 141586 (remnants of the radio code SS-LF can still be seen). By mid-April they were "reunited" with the 812th, flying anti-tank missions in support of the final German effort on the southweast tip of the Crimean Peninsula. It is possible that the month-old winter-camouflaged "K" may have made the trip with Lt. Krause.

"Mouse-coloured" or "blue-grey" Yak? A former 3rd IAK Yak-Ib captured and reconditioned for operations by JG52 (?) in the Kuban area of operations during the spring / summer of 1943. Close examination of reference photos leads to this possible interpretation. The original VVS upper camo colours seem to have been sprayed over with Luftwaffe fighter paints RLM74 and RLM75 following the Yak's factory pattern closely, leaving only the upper half of the aerial mast untouched. The nose area, port landing gear covers, inboard wing leading edge, canopy framing, and part of the radiator fairing may have received RLM76. Close-up photos also suggest that the 3rd IAK emblem was somewhat modified.

Nikopol Bridgehead

Unable to withstand the Soviet onslaught, the enemy was forced to begin a general withdrawal on Tuesday, 26 October 1943. Mobile formations of the 4th Ukrainian Front flowed into the breach. Thus they began a speedy advance with aviation support. The 3rd IAK destroyed 10 Ju87s, six Bf109s, five Hs129s, and one Fw190 in 15 separate aerial battles on 26 October. Fighter pilots of the 265th IAD contributed four Hs129s, three Ju87s, and two Bf109s to these totals.

On the following day the air regiments, as well as the command and control elements, of the 265th IAD moved to Chekhograd airfield southwest of Melitopol. Nonetheless, they were included in combat patrolling "from the march." During the day the corps conducted four aerial battles. Two pilots distinguished themselves: 15th IAP squadron commander Kapitan Leontiy Slizen, who downed two Ju87s, and General-Mayor Ye. Ya. Savitskiy himself, who destroyed a Ju88 bomber in the Novo-Rubanovka area.

On Thursday, 28 October, the division chief of staff Podpolkovnik Mikhail Lovkov arrived in the 812th IAP and assigned Ivan Fedorov an individual mission—to continuously observe for the advance of Red Army tank and cavalry formations as an air scout and to fly in reconnaissance of German positions in the Perekop area and Ochakov Port not less than twice daily. The former defendant [Fedorov] was to become a marvelous master of aerial reconnaissance, and during the war flew 180 combat reconnaissance sorties against enemy forces, ports, and airfields. If there ever was a flyer talented in this work, he stood above all the rest. Fedorov later recalled this time.

Thus on 28 October 1943 I became a scout. It was responsible, complicated, and dangerous work. At first I could not even imagine what it was. I jumped right in but quickly realized that I didn't know anything about it. In order to figure out what they were cooking up on the ground, *I had to go back and study the tactics of ground units and formations, equipment, armaments, speed of movement of various types of forces, the peculiarities of the employment of motorized and cavalry groups, infantry regiments, divisions, and so on. Plus types of defensive fortifications, port activities, and the movement of trains. All this I had not only to know but also be able to analyze, draw conclusions, and report to higher headquarters.*

Between flights I devoured the science of reconnaissance, ignoring sleep and rest. I wanted to acquire information sufficient to compensate for my lack of participation in combat. And something else worried me: try to report something non-objectively, imprecisely. It was daunting to think about the consequences, especially with this damned "load" in my personnel file. Decisions would be made, based on data I provided, on which depended the lives of hundreds, even thousands of men, the success or failure of divisions, corps, the front! I had no time to consider the danger of flights over the territory occupied by the enemy, where at any moment I could be shot down by antiaircraft guns or fighters. I feared more something else—to commit a blunder in my work or to report something in error to the command.[69]

It can only be added that all the intelligence data that resulted from the flights of I. V. Fedorov were practically always correct, and the reconnaissance flights themselves were outstanding in the professionalism of their execution. Based on them, headquarters made decisions that would ensure the success of both ground and air operations. The lives of many hundreds and thousands of soldiers and officers were saved.

In addition to the first of these reconnaissance flights, the 265th IAD conducted four air battles on this day. Pilots of the 812th IAP shot down two Bf109s, one Fw189, two Ju87s, and an Hs129. Mladshiy Leytenant Tikhomirov was the first to distinguish himself in the regiment. Taking off at 0815, he downed a Bf109 in the Nizhniye Seragozy area at 0925. Pavel Tarasov took off a short time later (0847) with a group of six Yak-7s and destroyed an Hs129 — the 20th personal victory for this outstanding ace.

About an hour later, the commander of a four-ship flight, Kapitan Ankudinov, shot down a Bf109. Simultaneously with him at 1040 Ivan Fedorov sent a *rama* [*frame* in Russian - a nickname for the Fw189] to the ground while Leytenant Maksimov shot down a Ju87. After dinner Tumanov took up a group of three Yak-7Bs and one Yak-1. At 1540 at an altitude of 1,500 meters (4,900 feet) in the Danilovka area, they encountered two groups of Ju87s, each with about 20 aircraft, escorted by four Bf109s. Having shot down one of the bombers, Mladshiy Leytenant Mikhail Kashirin himself came under attack from the escorting Messers. Wounded in both legs, the pilot made a forced landing of his Yak-7B near the village Reshtaki, and was sent to a hospital at the BAO (*batalon aerodromnogo obsluzhivaniya* [airfield service battalion]). Two Ju87D crews from I/SchlG2 were lost in combat on 28 October.

At 0754 on Friday morning, Leytenant Fedorov and Mladshiy Leytenant Maksimov took off in a pair of Yak-7s (bort 4 and bort 3 respectively) to reconnoiter forces in the Seragoza area. Flying toward the front line they established communications with the 3rd IAK command radio station. It defined the mission further, requiring them to transmit reconnaissance data quickly in open text. The flight was conducted at altitudes not to exceed 250 meters (800 feet). However, because of inadequacies in the radio equipment, they had to fly higher in order to transmit reports and then drop back down almost to tree-top level to resume their mission. The altitude profile of the flight resembled a wave. At 0815, at the moment of observation of the enemy in the Nizhnyaya Torgayevka area, Leytenant Maksimov was suddenly attacked by a pair of Bf109s. Turning around to fend off the Messers, Fedorov lost sight of his wingman. According to Mayor Pasynok's report, Maksimov was shot down in aerial combat and buried near Kolcha.

Leytenant Maksimov was noted as the best wingman in the regiment from the cohort that had arrived at Lipetsk. Subsequently he became Fedorov's wingman. From 6 September through 28 October 1943 the pair flew 68 combat sorties, conducting 26 aerial battles in which Ivan Maksimov shot down five enemy aircraft.

Parallel with this pair of scouts, a six-ship flight of fighters (5 Yak-7s and one Yak-9) took off and headed for this same area. Of these, the landing gear did not retract on Shishkin's Yak-9, so he and his leader, Tumanov, were forced to turn back. The remaining four aircraft, flown by Mayor Pasynok, Kapitan Tarasov, Starshiy Leytenant Tishchenko, and Leytenant Tikhomirov, spotted a group of Ju87s and attacked them. Kapitan Pavel Tarasov was the first to shoot down one of the German dive bombers. A minute later he also destroyed another Ju87, while Mayor Timofey Pasynok shot down two more in subsequent attacks. During one of these, the zampolit's aircraft was damaged by a rear gunner's burst. Here is how Aleksandr Tishchenko, a participant in this battle, remembers it.

'My engine is hit, I'm going home,' Pasynok's voice suddenly filled the earphones. As it later was revealed, during the third pass one burst, fired by the Junkers' rear gunner, had struck his aircraft. And not only the engine was damaged. The instrument panel was also hit. The aircraft began to respond poorly to the control column. 'Go low. We will cover you,' I hurriedly shouted and began to break away from the Messerschmitts. They continued to press forward. One of them raced toward Pasynok's aircraft and began to fire short bursts at him. While Tarasov hurried to his aid, the German pilot managed to riddle the Yak with holes. Somehow it managed to stay in the air. 'I'm making a forced landing,'

Leytenant Fedor Tikhomirov. He had 8 personal victories.

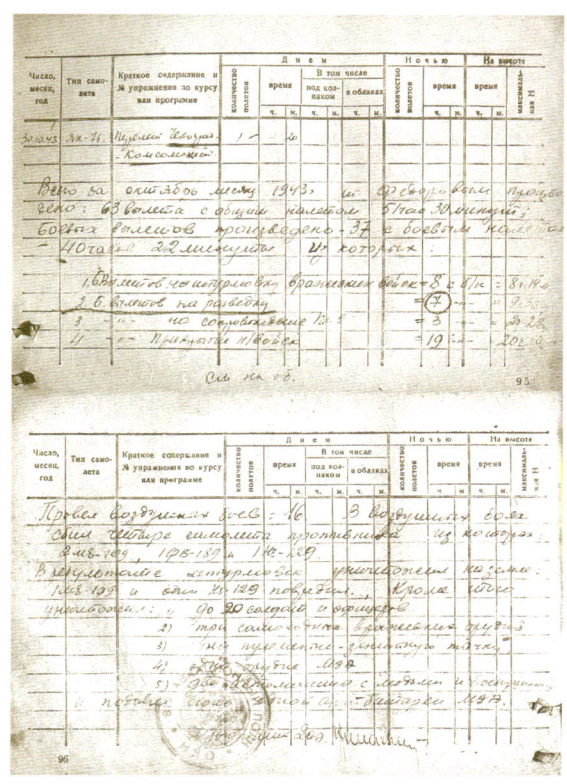

Excerpt from the pilot log of HSU I. V. Fedorov, that reflects the outcome of combat for October 1943.

Pasynok's tired voice was heard, while we were fending off the Messerschmitts' attacks.[70]

Here is how this incident was recorded in the combat actions journal of the 812th IAP for 29 October 1943:

0810-0815, altitude 1,000 meters (3,280 feet), northeast portion of Nizhniye Seragozy, concentration of our trucks and tanks. In a gully north of Nizhnyaya Torgayevka on the Nizhniye Seragozy River, a large concentration of troops. Dropped down and gave recognition signal. Wingman was attacked by two Bf109s, beat off attack, but too late. Lost wingman after brief aerial engagement. Maksimov did not return from mission. Aircraft Yak-7 No. 5103. At 0810 in area of Nizhnyaya Torgayevka, conducted aerial engagement with four Bf109s. At 0820 saw 30 Ju87s escorted by up to 10 Bf109s coming from west from direction of Nizhniye Seragozy River. Tarasov with his four-ship flight cut into the bomber formation and engaged in aerial combat. As a result, Kapitan Tarasov shot down one Ju87, which fell in the area of Malaya Blagoveshchenka. At 0830 up to 11 Ju87s were dispersed, dropping their bombs in a field. At this time we spotted one Yak with black smoke, but it was attempting to attack one Bf109. The Bf109 fired one burst from range of 300-200 meters (325-220 yards). Tarasov cut him off. At this time Tarasov was engaged by a second Bf109. The damaged Yak landed in the Nizhnyaya Torgayevka area.

That evening a note appeared in the division account that explained the fate of Maksimov:

Mladshiy Leytenant Maksimov was downed in the Kolcha area. He was buried by the deputy regiment commander for political affairs, Mayor T. Ye. Pasynok, who was damaged in aerial combat and forced to land near the place of death of Maksimov.

Fedorov conducted one more sortie in reconnaissance of Ochakov port on a Yak-9D at 1625. Returning to the airfield and reporting to the headquarters, Fedorov learned that a tribunal had arrived at the airfield and after supper a session would be convened. In the evening all of the pilots assembled in the regiment headquarters, where division commander Koryagin and the representatives of the military tribunal were already present. The chairman of the tribunal announced the decision to remove the judgment against Leytenant Fedorov. Further, he emphasized that the function of the military tribunal included not only the punishment of the guilty but also their rehabilitation, and this was affirmed by this example. Thus he had just granted Leytenant Fedorov a reprieve.

With these words, Mayor Timofey Pasynok attempted to stand up and respond to the tribunal chairman. But Division commander Podpolkovnik Aleksandr Koryagin, who was sitting nearby, extinguished the outburst of emotion by the 812th IAP zampolit, holding him by the arm. I. V. Fedorov recalls this moment with bitterness.

I thanked the military tribunal and the division command for its high evaluation of my humble combat service. I reiterated that henceforward I would continue to be faithful to my military duty, oath, to my combat comrades. The division commander, knowing my attitude toward the tribunal, smiled imperceptibly. I did not have the strength to completely forget what had happened to me. Many years after the war, when I had to fill out various forms, personnel paperwork, and other documents associated with my personal history, these unpleasant recollections, literally like a stab in the heart, came back to me.[71]

The complicated relationships with the SMERSH [*smert shpionam* (literally "death to spies," the name of the military counterintelligence organization)] officers, who were in every regiment looking after discipline and carrying out their work, were felt by practically everyone. Pavel Vasilevich Korneyev, formerly the mechanic on Aleksey Mashenkin's aircraft, recalls this:

One time they suggested to me that I join SMERSH. But that which they suggested that I do was very foul and low. The first mission was to be the following—observe a mechanic who was working next to me and later report about this. This was a low thing. The man is working, he is fighting the enemy, and we should "study" him. I refused to do this. Later, already in Poland, we, as an example, were advancing with such speed that the regiment itself was divided into three groups. One group was already at a new airfield, one was en route, and the third was still at the old airfield. In such conditions they again suggested to me that I observe to determine who among the mechanics and pilots were picking up German leaflets. I right there pulled a German leaflet out of my pocket and showed it to the leytenant. "You!" he cried. I responded, "And what is the big deal? We are grownups. You understand everything. Who now will go over to their side, the more so at this time, when we are advancing?

Aviation mechanic, and future regimental poet, Pavel Vasilyevich Korneyev

Even if someone would try it, he would not be able to reach them! And in general, this paper is good for cigarettes; almost everyone has it!" There were many injustices and we suffered much from this.

From 30 October the regiments of the 265th IAD commenced rebasing at Komsomolskiy airfield. And still, on this day, the division's pilots downed two Ju87s and one Bf109. Also for the first time, German He115 amphibians were encountered in the air over the Sivash area. For the 812th IAP the day passed with relative quiet; there were no encounters with the enemy in the 28 sorties they conducted. Ironically they did lose one Yak-7B (bort 30) as a result of a "friendly" Airacobra attack.

Having taken off at 1502, the group led by Leytenant Tumanov (four Yak-7Bs, one Yak-1 and one Yak-9) headed for the area of Verkhnyaya Torgayevka—Novo-Aleksandrovka with the mission to cover a troop advance. Not encountering the enemy, the pilots turned back. Mladshiy Leytenant Pavel Serezhenko, flying trail, became separated from the group and was suddenly attacked by an Airacobra. A round from the cannon of the attacking fighter burst on his left wing. The damaged Yak's control response was so poor that the young pilot had no choice but to make a forced landing in the area of Pushkino hamlet. A few hours later, Serezhenko was back at his airfield.

Now comprised of only five Yak-7Bs, one Yak-9, and one Yak-1, on 2 November the regiment was positioned at a new airfield in Krestovskiy. In this period, developing the offensive in a southward direction, Red Army forces had broken into the Perekop peninsula, reached the Sivash, and forced it. As a result of this successful 4th Ukrainian Front offensive, by 5 November they had liberated all of northern Tavriya and practically locked the German XVII Army in Crimea. The left bank of the Dniepr River's lower course was finally cleared of the enemy. However, they still held a bridgehead in the Nikopol area from which their command was planning to launch an attack to hold the entire Crimea for itself.

On Saturday, 6 November, Fedor Tikhomirov managed to catch a Bf109 in his sights, gaining his fourth personal victory against the enemy in the air. The next day, the regiments of the 265th IAD were rebased to Novopetrovka and Uspenskoye. On 8 and 9 November the command elements of division, along with the 402nd and 812th IAPs, flew to Nizhnyaya Torgayevka airfield closer to the the Nikopol bridgehead. Meanwhile, the 291st IAP remained at Novopetrovka to conduct combat operations in the interests of the 5th Shock Army. At this time the 812th IAP employed two Yak-9Ds on long-range reconnaissance for the air army. Aleksandr Tishchenko became the regiment's second reconnaissance pilot. Together with Fedorov he carried out reconnaissance flights at a rate of 2—3 sorties per day.

These reconnaissance pilots were assigned the mission to control the movement of vessels and transports in the Dniepr and Bug River estuaries, the ports Nikolayev and Ochakov, and the Dniepr River crossings in the area of Bolshaya and Malaya Lepetikha. The weather began to worsen; autumn was approaching with its full sovereignty. Continuous cloud cover with low ceilings ranging from 100-200 meters (325–650 feet) in the morning to 200-500 meters (650–1650 feet) during the day permeated the area. Accompanied by poor visibility down to 1-3 kilometers (.6–1.8 miles) in the morning, further restricted to just one kilometer in fog, the conditions brought flight operations to a standstill. Good flying weather finally resumed on 30 November.

In this period - more precisely on Sunday, 14 November - the regiment personnel celebrated a festive and memorable event. And it had nothing to do with war, blood, and death. It was quite the opposite a wedding. Deputy squadron commander Ivan Fedorov, in deciding to join his fate forever with nineteen-year-old nurse Valya (from the airfield service battalion), had proposed to her. He reported this event to Pasynok without delay.

The zampolit thought about the necessity of this serious move for some time and, in the end, gave his approval and also became best man. Well, of course, as it should be in such circumstances, on 14 November, a rainy autumn day, a celebratory dinner was held at Nizhnyaya Torgayevka airfield. Efficient cavalrymen, who brought in an entire barrel of wine for the occasion, helped the pilots to organize the holiday. But certainly it happens in life that *"the joy of others stirs up worse than one's misfortune."* On this occasion the division political section became agitated. The following is from a report from the chief of the political section of 265th IAD, Podpolkovnik Zaytsev, to the chief of the political section of 3rd IAK:

Kapitan A. Tishchenko
*"Sasha Tishchenko was a modest pilot,
He shot down many aerial carrion!
The commander was attentive and careful,
He received the rank of Hero in the regiment!"*
Korneyev, "From Stalingrad to Berlin."

The deputy commander of 812ᵗʰ Regiment, Mayor Pasynok, on 14 November 1943 organized a party in the regiment on the occasion of the marriage of Leytenant Fedorov, a pilot of this regiment. Fedorov married one of the workers of the BAO [airfield service battalion]. Pasynok gave this occasion an official character, failing to inform the division command about it. [The division command was not only informed, but was invited to the wedding! — Authors' comment] Measures taken: for organizing the wedding, which in no way facilitated an increase in combat readiness, neither of Fedorov himself nor of the regiment as a whole, Mayor Pasynok received a party reprimand.⁷²

It can only be added that though some never believed in this kind of marriage, to the surprise of especially zealous *upholders of morality*, this front-line marriage joined these two people together for their remaining lifetime. In any event, Podpolkovnik I. S. Zaytsev was soon relieved from his position, and in his place arrived Podpolkovnik Dmitriy Ivanovich Zakharov, who remained with the division until May 1945.

Heavy rains poured buckets of water, so that it was impossible not only to fly, but sometimes simply to taxi. Fog, slush, and mud made work from the soggy airfields practically impossible. Just the same, whenever the weather improved even a little (especially in the mornings), the division's best pilots flew reconnaissance sorties with a ceiling of 50-150 meters (165–490 feet) and visibility of 2-3 kilometers (1.2–1.8 miles). In the 32 aircraft sorties logged by the regiment on 20 November, the four-ship flight led by Kapitan Popov was most outstanding. They destroyed an ammunition dump and shot up five cargo trucks located nearby. Before returning to base, they also destroyed four wagons in attacking an enemy column on the road from Volnyy to Gorodishche.

The next Bf109 was shot down by Kapitan Popov on Monday, 22 November, in the area east of Novo-Znamenka, marking his fifth personal victory. The regiment navigator wrote the following in his claim for the victory:

I report that on 22.11.43, on a mission assigned by the regiment command, a group of four Yak-1b aircraft, was flying to the area of Verkhniy Rogachik to provide cover for our own forces. Our pairs were conducting a hunt beneath the overcast for the destruction of enemy aircraft. Northeast of the outskirts of Verkhniy Rogachik, I spotted two Bf109Fs [likely early Bf109Gs — ed.] on a meeting course, at an engagement angle of 3/4 with subsequent approach to their rear. I fired two long bursts and shot down one Bf109F with a pale-blue spinner (time of shootdown 1545-1547), which fell in an area 2-3 kilometers (1.2–1.8 miles) north of Novo-Znamenka. This report can be confirmed by my wingman, Mladshiy Leytenant Peskarev, and Starshiy Leytenant Tumanov.

On the following day, flights were limited by bad weather. But even in these conditions, data came in concerning the basing airfields of enemy aviation.

At 1525, altitude 700 meters (2,300 feet), southwest of Pervomayskiy was observed an airfield. Four Hs129s executed landings. Nothing noted on airfield. At 1530, Bolshaya Kostromka, no airfield. At 1540, Vysokopolye, two kilometers (1.2 miles) south of the point Dolina was an airfield. . . No ground equipment at this time. 1550, Novo-Vosorino, no airfield.

By 28 November, the command element of the 265ᵗʰ IAD, together with the air regiments, were rebased on Agayman airfield. On this day the regiment's pilots shot down five enemy aircraft. The main intensity of the aerial engagements occurred on Sunday in the the second half of the day. Four fighters (three Yak-1s and one Yak-7) led by Kapitan Ankudinov took off at 1430. Mladshiy Leytenant Aleksandr Razumovich shot down one He111 at 1510 in the area of Belozerka, while Leytenant Shishkin shot down a Bf109 from the bomber formation's cover group. They returned to the airfield without losses.

A group of fighters (four Yak-1s and two Yak-7s) was designated to sortie at 1505 to cover forces in the Tsvetkov-Bolshaya Belozerka-Krasnyy Mayak area. After 10-15 minutes of flight, six were reduced to four. One of the Yak-1 pairs - Starshiy Leytenant Tishchenko (bort 31) and Mladshiy Leytenant Serezhenko (bort 21) - had to return because the wingman's landing gear would not retract. The remaining four pilots - Tarasov, Obukhov, Tikhomirov and Kashirin - carried on to the patrol area.

In the Ukrainka area at 1520, altitude 3,000 meters (9,850 feet), we encountered four Bf109s. We engaged in aerial combat, in the course of which one Yak was shot down (believed Kashirin). The burning aircraft exploded on the ground in the Ukrainka area. At this time the pair of Kapitan Tarasov was fighting with a second pair of Bf109s. As a result of this combat, Kapitan Tarasov shot down one Bf109, which struck the ground north of Verkhniy Rogachik. Tarasov's wingman, Mladshiy Leytenant Obukhov, conducting aerial combat with another pair, after several attacks from below shot down one Bf109. The airplane fell east of Ukrainka. In the course of an aerial battle Leytenant Tikhomirov lost contact with Tarasov's pair and returned independently to his airfield. Obukhov landed later. He landed at another airfield.

The young pilot Mladshiy Leytenant Mikhail Kashirin perished in this battle. A chance at "rehabilitation," for the previous sortie's forced return to base, presented itself to Mladshiy Leytenant Pavel Serezhenko within the hour. Two pairs took off at 1610 and headed for the Bolshaya Belozerka area: A. Tishchenko (Yak-1 bort 31)-P. Serezhenko (Yak-7 bort 30) and I. Fedorov (Yak-9 bort 63)-P. Peskarev (Yak-1 bort-45). The regiment headquarters reported the following:

They encountered two pairs of Ju88s in the Belozerka area. Tishchenko with his wingman attacked the first pair of Ju88s. As a result of the attack, Serezhenko shot down one Ju88, which fell north of Bolshaya Belozerka. Fedorov attacked the second pair; after the first attack the Ju88s departed into the overcast and did not appear again. They then encountered an Fw190, which did not accept battle and departed to the north.

On 30 November the regiment flew eight sorties. In the first, the reconnaissance pair of Leytenant Fedorov and Starshiy Leytenant Tishchenko took off at 1022. Fedorov's mission was reconnaissance of the port and area of Ochakov-Kherson. Tishchenko was to reconnoiter the Apostolovo railroad station, Vysokopolye, and the positioning of enemy aircraft on airfields. From the report of Leytenant Fedorov:

> *From an altitude of 500 meters (1,640 feet) in the Ochakov area I observed six cutters, three empty barges, seven boats, and four motorboats. A cutter and two motorboats were moving from Pokrovskiye settlement to Ochakov along the estuary. There were four boats and up to 30 personnel along the shore at Pokrovskiye settlement. [I saw] the movement of one transport in the Dniepr estuary south of Dmitrievka toward Ochakov; no German steamships and transports were observed in Berkskiy estuary. Two Hs129s were parked on the landing strip south of Chernobayevka; I was fired on by antiaircraft artillery from the east side of the landing field.*

In his turn, Starshiy Leytenant Tishchenko reported:

> *Area of Apostolovo, Chkalovo covered by fog. Hospital train moving toward Vysokopolye. Four trains at Vysokopolye station. Up to 30 aircraft at airfield northwest of Bolshaya Kostromka on southern and southwestern boundary of airfield: 15 fighters and 15 Ju87s, and 15 Hs129s. From Novo-Vorontsovka to Dushino—movement of up to 50 covered trucks. An accumulation of up to 40 trucks at Zolotoy gully. Two Bf109s patrolling over Bolshaya Lepetikha.*

Judging from the reconnaissance data received, the regiment commander decided to launch a strike against the Bolshaya Kostromka airfield. A group of four Yak-1s and two Yak-7Bs, led by Starshiy Leytenant Tishchenko himself, took off at 1545 to carry out this mission. After about an hour's flight, this group could not find the enemy airfield so they attacked their secondary target instead. The regiment headquarters noted:

> *Mission not accomplished, reason: airfield not found. Deviated to the right (west), to the Shirokov area. They attacked the reserve target— accumulation of trucks in a tree-planted area east of Shersternya and train on the Vysokopolye sector. Conducted two attacks. Fires and explosions not observed. Attacks conducted with shallow dive from altitude 200-100 meters (650–325 feet).*

This misfortune was fully compensated in a second, more successful, strike on this same airfield exactly one month later (see page80).

December came, but it did not bring a noticeable improvement in the weather. The rains were replaced by frequent snow showers, worsening visibility to less than one kilometer (1100 yards). There were only three good flying days in all of December, four days of limited flying, and fully 24 non-flying days. The division covered friendly ground forces in small groups at a ceiling of 100-200 meters (325-650 feet)

over the battlefield in the face of heavy enemy antiaircraft fire. It continued to provide tactical reconnaissance, both over the battlefield and against the enemy's airfield network, and long-range reconnaissance.

There were frequent occasions when flight crews, carrying out their combat mission, were forced to land at reserve airfields, or off the airfield, because the weather would suddenly worsen at their own airfield. On attempting to return to home base in haste, pilots frequently took off without sufficiently evaluating the meteorological situation. The result was sometimes catastrophe. Such losses occurred in the 291st and 402nd Fighter Regiments. The persistent overcast often compounded the problem, forcing returning pilots to fly at low altitudes where some fell to enemy antiaircraft artillery. The 812th IAP passed this cup, suffering no such losses in December.

German bombers also remained grounded because of the poor flying weather. Taking advantage of the relative quiet, 8th Air Army headquarters held a conference of fighter pilots - hunters - from 11 through 14 December 1943. At the conclusion of the discussions, the pilots worked out "Tactical Rules of Actions for Fighter Pilots—Hunters." The most talented pilots of the Air Army were invited to the conference, among whom were Heroes of the Soviet Union Mayors D.B. Glinka (100th GIAP) and A.I. Pokryshkin (16th GIAP), Kapitans N.Ye. Lavitskiy and B.B. Glinka (100th GIAP), Amet-Khan Sultan and V.D. Lavrinenkov (9th GIAP), A.M. Reshetov (31st GIAP) and other pilots of the 6th and 9th GIAD. A large group of pilots from 3rd IAK was also invited to the conference, led by the corps commander General-Mayor Ye. Ya. Savitskiy, the commanders of 265th Aviation Division Podpolkovnik A. A. Koryagin and 278th Aviation Division Polkovnik V. T. Lisin.

An excerpt from the 3rd IAK's "Instructions Concerning Actions of Hunter-Fighter Pilots"

The free hunt for the enemy is one of the forms of combat work of aviation. It gives the pilot freedom of action, broad initiative in the selection of target, the moment and method of attack on the enemy. By its method of action, the free hunt is most inherently distinctive to the nature and character of fighter aviation and clearly involves an offensive spirit, initiative, daring, and suddenness of attack on the enemy. The combat actions of the hunters—this is a measure of operational-tactical procedure, and therefore should be planned by the air army in areas of greatest activity of enemy aviation and in sectors of the main attack of ground forces. Hunters are not organized into any limited groups; they are in the table of organization of any aviation regiment. They are selected on the principle of volunteerism and their level of preparedness to be hunters. The basic tactical unit will be the well-coordinated and working pair. There can be one or two pairs of hunters in each aviation regiment. Hunters are personally monitored by headquarters of large formations and cannot be moved from unit to unit without an order of the Air Army commander. The hunter should have the best aircraft, which will guarantee his flight over enemy territory. Gun cameras are installed on the aircraft of a hunter for control of his combat work and errors.

The birth and rapid development of new methods of aerial combat had a positive impact on the efficiency of the fighter pilots and on the big picture of winning air superiority. The principle of training the *hunter* differed substantially from the routine training of the ordinary pilot. The 3rd IAK, which developed the "Instructions Concerning Actions of Hunter-Fighter Pilots," was an innovator in the increase in the number of such pilots.

In a follow-up exchange regarding the free hunt experience, presentations from certain representatives of the 3rd IAK deserve attention. One of the speakers was the commander of 278th IAD, Polkovnik Vladimir Timofeyevich Lisin. He expressed his opinion in a straightforward and succinct manner:

> *Speaking about the hunter-fighters, we finally have talked in detail about the nature of the fighter pilot. I have divided fighter pilots into three categories. Hunter fighter pilots are in the first category, average fighter pilots are in the second category, and pilots who just fly fighter airplanes are in the third category. The pilots sitting in front of us are the brains of our fighter aviation. Why have we clogged up fighter aviation with pilots who just fly fighter aircraft? This clogging was begun with the system itself of selection of fighter pilots for fighter aviation. In the past, upon completion of school, they selected out the best pilots for fighter aviation. Then they began to send the best pilots to DBA (long-range bomber aviation), and the rest to fighter aviation. And now they are making the same selection of pilots to fighter aviation, which is why these laggards are dragging us backward. Thanks to this, we are losing our best pilots. The good pilots want to prove that they want to work, but the laggards do not let them do this. Here are assembled the best hunter pilots and our mission, as for the best pilots, is to declare here that the Bf109 has superiority only when they fight in a tactically coherent way and when they have superiority in altitude. What should a hunter look like? A hunter should destroy the enemy with a single burst. We did not engage in hunting in the Kuban. We began to engage in hunting for ground targets on the Southern Front. We gave the hunter a section of the railroad where he was supposed to destroy ground targets that he observed. We did not achieve great results from hunting for aerial targets. Nonetheless, we now are having some successes in the hunt. Pilots have begun to move about more skillfully, even when alone. Frequently they are using our hunters in other forms of combat work. In the future we have to use hunters only for their designated purpose, assigning them to separate groups and using those groups only for hunting. I consider it necessary for hunters to have two aircraft, one heavy and the other light. Depending on the situation and the target, this group will provide the needed effect using these aircraft. We need to do away with the words "coverage of ground forces." With the words "coverage of ground forces," we do not give the ground forces the capability of employing sufficient measures of maskirovka [camouflage and concealment], thanks to which they concentrate 300-500 horses in a*

> *ravine, and the same around wells for watering. As a result, they suffer great losses, and all this is attributed to the fighters for providing poor coverage. In the future the mission should be formulated as "conduct battle with the aerial enemy in a specific area, and not to cover the area." The ground forces often do not see the combat work of fighter aviation. There have been cases when the enemy bombers have assembled in the area of Mikhaylovka and our fighter aviation drove off these groups, but the ground troops did not know about it. But the division, corps, and army commanders did know. Often they assign to us a specific altitude; we fly at great altitude and the enemy bombs at a low altitude. We transition to a low altitude and the enemy begins to bomb from a high altitude. In neither case do we have any encounters with the enemy. As a result, the ground forces declare that the fighters are covering them poorly, but often it does not depend on the fighters, because in such conditions they are incapable of destroying the enemy bombers.*

Kapitan Pavel Tarasov shared his own observations in speaking for the 812th IAP at the conference.

> *In the first days of the war we had to engage the enemy at 3:00 o'clock in the morning. I had a group of 12 MiG-3s, and lacking the experience of the conduct of aerial battle, I decided to attack a group of Heinkels with my entire group of MiGs. As a result of the attack the entire group became dispersed, and I lost command and control. After the aerial battle, each aircraft returned to its airfield singly. The three Heinkels were shot down. After this the question arose at a discussion concerning control of the group in aerial combat. It was decided to create two groups, one called the strike group that broke up the enemy bomber formation, and the other the group for destruction of the bombers. It must be acknowledged that we, as fighter pilots, are destroying few bombers. In my understanding, a fighter pilot should be brazen and bold. If he spots a target, he should rush to its destruction. But we are not yet at that point. It often occurred that upon our arrival in the coverage area, we were ordered by radio from one ground vectoring station to go to another area, while another radio ordered us to remain in place, and we did not know what to do. I will tell you about mutual assistance in an aerial engagement. I had an occasion when Twice Hero of the Soviet Union Mayor Pokryshkin assisted me in a difficult situation during the conduct of an aerial engagement. He cut off the enemy aircraft that was on my tail. But sometimes other pilots listen to a request for help over the radio and pay it no attention. We must instill in pilots the sense of mutual assistance. Now a few words about hunters. Before one sends hunters to a given area, it is necessary to carefully develop their actions. Especially to become familiar with operational documentation that could paint a picture of the concentration of enemy troops and aviation in a given area. In this case, a pair of hunters with good preparation will provide greater success. I consider it necessary to note at this conference that the pair of hunters also should be*

Lt. Walter Wolfrum's Bf109G-6 W.Nr 411777 of 5./JG52, March 1944. As the conclusion of the Crimean retaking approached, Walter Wolfrum was one of the JG52 "experten" still remaining on the peninsula's airfields in the Luftwaffe's futile attempt to regain superiority. Having been with 5./JG52 since the year before at Rostov-on-Don, he gained three of his first five victories over Yak fighters. It is possible that he had tangled with 812th IAP pilots from time to time throughout the year, prior to meeting them again above the Crimea (see page 103). This aircraft was written off after the crash-landing that followed an aerial engagement on 11 April, 1944. The red spinner spiral, unusual for a Luftwaffe fighter of this era, was effected with VVS paint left behind on one of the airfields.

#63 was one of the initial series 2 Yak-9Ts still remaining in the 812th as it followed the Red Army's southward drive towards the end of 1943. Newer production Yak-9Ts would come on strength within the coming months. This aircraft was flown by future HSU Ivan Fedorov during an afternoon sortie on 28 November, though his "standard" mount at the time appears to have been one of the two special reconnaissance Yak-9Ds [Yak-9Rs?] operated by the regiment.

well coordinated; the pair should have a high sense of officer honor and veracity in regards to the report concerning their activities and the damage they inflicted on enemy supplies and equipment.

All the conclusions reached by the pilots would be taken into consideration in the future, and many of the pilots who attended this conference surpassed the 20-victory barrier by the end of the war.

Taking advantage of the foul weather, the pilots of 812th Regiment switched over to ground-attack actions against enemy airfields, not waiting for the enemy aircraft to take off in improved weather. They launched 16 combat sorties throughout the day on 20 December. Four Yak-1s, one Yak-7B, and one Yak-9 took off at 1110 led by Kapitan Popov. Flying cover for friendly troops in the Dneprovka area ended up with an attack on an enemy truck column. Tumanov and Peskarev each set one truck ablaze. A four-ship flight, led by A. Tishchenko, arrived in the same area at 1306.

Coverage was executed at an altitude of 190-200 meters (625–650 feet). There was no enemy in the air. We observed artillery firing 2-3 kilometers (1.2–1.8 miles) south of Dneprovka. We spotted the movement of five Tiger tanks from Kamenka toward Dneprovka, but some Il-2s were working on them. Antiaircraft fire got one of the Il-2s.

Kapitan Ankudinov's four-ship flight, sent out to replace Popov's group, also covered the Il-2 attack. A single Fw190 was attempting to attack the *shturmovik* group. Making several passes at the Luftwaffe fighter, Kapitan Ankudinov shot it down. This was the pilot's fifth personal victory. Two days later the pair of Tumanov-Prikhodko, flying on free hunt, shot up a string of wagons moving along the road in the Dneprovka area. They were stopped and scattered as a result of the attacks. Four were set on fire.

On 30 December, 3rd IAK command decided to attack the airfield at Bolshaya Kostromka. Although it was a dangerous and risky venture, they pulled it off. But not right away. A. T. Tishchenko, 1st Squadron commander, led the group of eight Yaks. They took off and set course for the enemy airfield at 2,000 meters (6,600 feet) altitude, passing through scattered clouds along the way. On the other side of the Dniepr River the weather worsened. The group was forced to drop down to 150-200 meters (500–650 feet); visibility did not exceed 1-1.5

kilometers (.6–.9 miles) and continued to worsen as they sped forward. The group, as a whole, veered off to the right of their assigned objective, while some pairs reported they had lost contact with the group. Pressing on became more dangerous with each passing moment. The leader made the decision to attack the secondary target before returning to base.

Regimental headquarters developed a new plan for a strike against the Bolshaya Kostromka airfield. Not wanting to put off its visit for too long, they were successful on Friday, 31 December 1943. The pilots joked that they had hurried *to congratulate* the enemy on a Happy New Year. They took off at 1520 and reached the bottom of the cloud cover at a mere 200-250 meters (650–800 feet) AGL. With a horizontal visibility of up to 2 kilometers (1.2 miles) they forged ahead with confidence. Ten Yaks reached the enemy airfield, where the pilots saw before them long rows of Heinkels. They executed the attack in a right echelon with two passes. As a result of this skillful, well-calculated *shturmovka*, the pilots of 812th IAP destroyed five and damaged five enemy aircraft. They also hit the airfield structures, auxiliary equipment and antiaircraft assets. The 3rd IAK journal of combat actions noted:

A group of six Yak-1s, two Yak-9s, and two Yak-7s conducted a ground attack on Bolshaya Kostromka airfield. The group leader was Kapitan Ankudinov. Four He111s were destroyed on the ground and up to five Hs129 aircraft were damaged as a result of the raid. Kapitan Ankudinov shot down one Hs129 (during the Hs129's landing approach).

The group did not suffer any losses on this sortie. In addition to the single Hs129 shot down by Yegor Ankudinov, three He111s and one Hs129 were officially credited to the 812th IAP score as being destroyed by fire on the ground.

The chief of logistics of the Air Army arrived in the regiment that evening to hand out valuable New Year presents to the pilots for their successful action in the last hours of the difficult wartime year of 1943. The final tally of the combat work of 812th Aviation Regiment on the Southern (4th Ukrainian) Front from 1 September to 31 December 1943 included 1,156 combat sorties with over 1,241 flight hours. They shot down or destroyed on the ground not less than 68 enemy aircraft, including 21 Bf109, 15 Ju87, 10 Ju88, 10 He111, five Hs129, one Fw189, one Bf110 and one Fw190 in aerial combat and three He111 and one Hs129 were destroyed on the ground.

January to May 1944:
On the Southern Flank

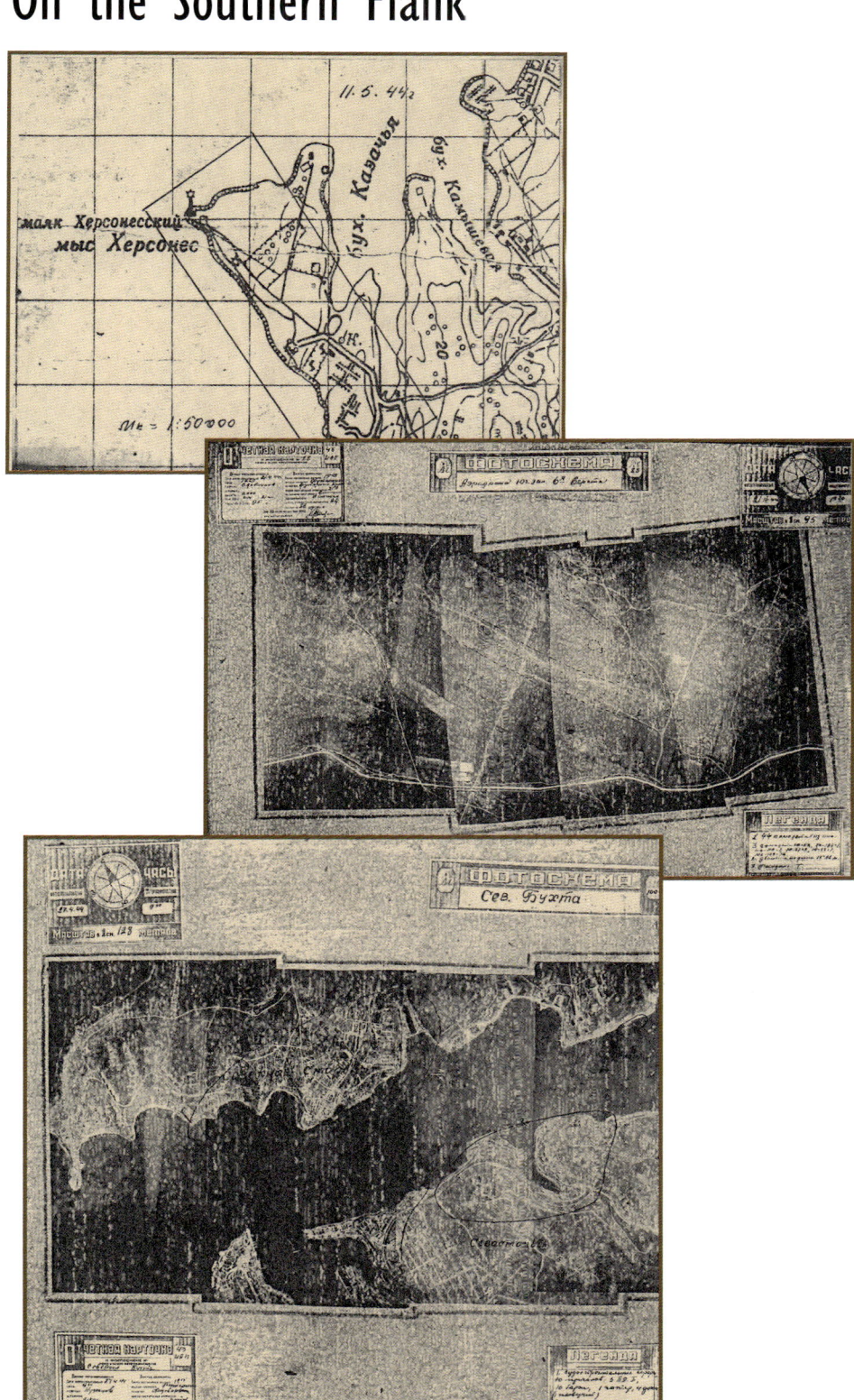

3rd IAK recconaissance photographs (lower 2 items) and the resulting detailed maps (top item). Regiments of the corps often carried out this type of work on behalf of the air army.

OVERVIEW:
Combat Actions of the 265th "Melitopol" IAD during the liberation of the Crimea

Having broken through the enemy's defensive lines near Melitopol, Soviet forces rushed toward the Dniepr River and onward to the Crimea. Red Army units reached the Turetskiy swell and created a bridgehead on the southern shore of the Sivash. The enemy dug in on the left bank of the Dniepr in the area of Bolshaya Belozerka, Verkhniy Rogachik, and Bolshaya Lepetikha, creating the Nikopol bridgehead. This became an arena of great air battles, largely because the enemy was determined to defend their hold on the Crimea and regain Melitopol at any price.

With a crossing over the Sivash in place, Red Army command transferred ammunition, provisions, equipment, and reserves to the southern shore. The concentration of both combatants' forces at the crossings attracted aviation like magnets, generating aerial conflict on a large scale. The Germans attempted to bomb the crossings every day, sending in groups of 30 to 50 Ju87s escorted by four to 12 Fw190s and Bf109s. The bombers did not employ any special tactics, with the exception that groups of Fw190s flew above the bomber formations to protect them. Some also dropped bombs as fighter bombers. Above this entire group flew a third layer of Bf109s unencumbered with bomb loads.

VVS fighters opposed these German tactics with the proven RUS-2 radar-assisted intercept. Thanks to well-organized command, control, and warning, the Germans were unable to destroy the bridge toward Sevastopol—the Sivash crossing. Alerted by RUS-2 stations, fighters took off from the closest airfields in a timely manner to intercept enemy aviation on the approaches to the target. Individual pairs of hunters patrolled at altitudes of 5,000-6,000 meters (16,400–19,700 feet) with the mission to engage enemy hunters. Eight-ship formations, sortied by the alerts, were echeloned by altitude. Usually, half of these flew in the cover group. However, it was pointed out in the mission statement that, in the absence of enemy fighters, only one pair would maintain the cover position while the remainder attacked the bombers. Combat orders specifically directed who should attack and open fire from what range. In the event that the attack on the enemy aircraft was unsuccessful, the fighters were instructed to ram enemy bombers in full view of all groups. The mission - to protect the Sivash crossing site at any price - demanded this measure. "Do whatever has to be done to disrupt the bombers"— this was not simply an order but an essential requirement.

Simultaneous with the actions on the Sivash to the south, Soviet fighters were engaged over the Nikopol bridgehead to the north, where the Germans were also attempting to block the advance of our ground forces. In order to gain unchallenged air superiority over the Sivash and Nikopol bridgeheads, VVS fighter aviation employed active blockading of enemy airfields on a broad scale. Luftwaffe bases at Apostolovo and Bolshaya Kostromka were subjected to systematic fighter ground attacks. Enemy aviation was thus driven from the frontal area and forced to shift to airfields in the immediate rear.

After several ground attacks on Apostolovo and Bolshaya Kostromka airfields, the Germans moved to Voroshilovka airfield. Here, they were again detected and subjected to several successive fighter attacks. With the enemy fighters forced farther to the rear and under constant pressure, Soviet aviation gained the capability to work over the battlefield uninterrupted. This also occurred in the Crimea proper. Enemy airfields at Veseloye,

Liberation of the Crimean Peninsula April-May 1944

Just-liberated Nikopol — where these Cossack guards escort captured German combatants along a road — is situated some 250 kilometers directly north of the Crimean Peninsula's land bridge at Perekop. By Order of the Supreme High Commander, J. Stalin, the 3rd IAK was awarded the honorific title "Nikopolskiy" for excellence in combat during the liberation of this city. *Dmitri Karlenko*

Ichki and Dzhankoy were subjected to systematic fighter raids to the extent that they were effectively eliminated from further meaningful operations over the Sivash. The units forced to vacate Veseloye airfield relocated on a primitive field at Sarabuz. But long-range fighters found them there as well, following up with several successive raids on the same day. These attacks almost completely paralyzed enemy fighter activity, giving the VVS complete mastery of the air. Air superiority was gained not only numerically, but also by active battles in the area of the Sivash, Perekop, and Sevastopol, wherein Soviet pilots made skilful use of vertical maneuver, competent attacks from out of the sun, and from cloud cover.

Additionally, setting up the RUS-2 coverage justified itself fully — pilots had encounters with the enemy on every sortie. The *free hunt* method was broadly employed and in countering enemy airfields, fighters made frequent use of small AO-25 fragmentation bombs.

The *free hunt* method of supporting ground forces, with no specified limits on the altitude and speed of separate pairs, was used here for the first time. This justified itself particularly during operations in the Crimea. Luftwaffe command left twelve JG52 *experten* based on the peninsula. These pilots, operating as pairs of *hunters* against larger groups of Soviet fighters, inflicted significant losses. To counter, 3rd IAK command created a group of *hunters* from among the division that, in a brief period of fierce aerial battles, was able to demonstrate its mastery to the enemy. The enemy was soon driven from Crimea completely.

Return to the Crimea

1944 arrived. Having been resupplied with new aircraft in the first days of January, the 812th IAP, consisting of 19 Yak-1s, 12 Yak-9s, and eight Yak-7Bs, began flying combat sorties. On Monday, 3 January, after receiving information about enemy aircraft based at Bolshaya Kostromka and Apostolovo airfields, the division staff decided to launch an attack. Although it was initially planned to employ all three regiments of the 265th IAD, the command later decided to use only the 402nd and 291st IAPs. The 812th would provide cover for the division's own airfields.

A combined group of eight Yak-1s and Yak-9s from 402nd IAP flew the strike against Bolshaya Kostromka airfield while 10 Yak-1s of 291st went against Apostolovo airfield. The 812th IAP launched missions to cover its own airfield and to escort the 402nd IAP's fighters enroute to the target. Strikes on the two airfields resulted in seven aircraft destroyed on the ground plus one Ju87, one Hs129, and four fighters in aerial engagements above the airfields. The events of this Monday once again showed the importance of the continuous close coordination between the groups in these actions, and what just 10 minutes of delay could mean in the conduct of the strikes. We will examine in greater detail this operation against three enemy airfields in the areas of Apostolovo and Bolshaya Kostromka.

Preceding the attacks, careful reconnaissance was conducted by the same fighters that would later fly the strikes. These missions were executed systematically, photographing the enemy airfields and reporting details by radio to the 265th IAD command posts.

Data thus obtained was used to maximum effect by the pilots assigned to the attacks. Before launching, they studied the most suitable approaches to the airfields as well as the locations of aircraft and antiaircraft defenses.

On 3 January a reconnaissance pair confirmed the presence of a large number of enemy aircraft on Apostolovo airfield and on the two primitive airstrips near Bolshaya Kostromka. At this time the 265th IAD was assigned the mission of suppressing enemy aviation on the ground. Its commander, Aleksandr Koryagin, decided to conduct simultaneous concentrated strikes on all three airfields at 1400. Two squadrons of the 402nd Regiment (comprised of a combination of eight Yak-1s and Yak-9s each) were to conduct a strike on the airstrips in the Bolshaya Kostromka area while a single squadron of the 291st IAP (10 Yak-1s) was ordered to attack Apostolovo airfield.

In accordance with this plan, the 402nd IAP contingent sortied at 1330, crossing the front line at 4000 meters (13,100 feet) as they proceeded northwest into the target area. This relatively high altitude was chosen to achieve tactical surprise. To further confuse the enemy, the entire formation flew a general heading slightly to the north of their actual objective. The 1st Squadron encountered four enemy fighters soon after turning back toward the target. In the battle that ensued, the squadron's cover flight shot down two German aircraft. The attack flight, led by the squadron commander, took advantage of the fact that the enemy fighters were engaged in battle, and attacked the aircraft on the airfield, destroying three of them in the first pass with cannon and machine gun fire.

After completing their engagement with the enemy fighters, one pair from the cover flight attacked observed antiaircraft positions while the second pair engaged a group of enemy attack aircraft that had appeared in the area at this time. They shot down one Ju87 and one Hs129.

In conducting its strike on the second makeshift airstrip, the 2nd Squadron did not encounter any enemy opposition in the air. The strike flight made three passes at the target. Then it supported the subsequent actions of the cover flight which, on the squadron commander's order, kept up the fire on revetted enemy aircraft. Three Bf109s and one Fw189 were destroyed while a fuel truck was set on fire. An antiaircraft artillery battery was also silenced.

The 291st IAP squadron did not take off until some 10 minutes after the designated launch time. Thus the strikes on all three enemy airfields could not be put in simultaneously. In fact, the squadron encountered two six-ship flights of Bf109s while still on the far approaches to Apostolovo airfield. After the inevitable dogfight it was forced to return to home base. Nonetheless, they claimed several enemy fighters in this battle.

Thanks to the proper coordination between the two tactical groups within the squadrons of 402nd IAP, the enemy based in and around the smaller airfields suffered significant losses. However, as a direct result of its late takeoff, the 291st IAP squadron was not as successful against Apostolovo airfield. It was forced to engage a superior enemy force enroute.

From this point on, the division command often made any additional attacks on enemy airfields using these same three regiments, augmenting the strike force and the sortie count according to target size. Through these experiences the division developed the tactics to employ the Yak-9 as a fighter bomber, evolving a methodology that later became classic.

On the following day, during return from a combat mission, an emergency situation developed on the aircraft of Mladshiy Leytenant Yuriy Obukhov: the engine of his Yak-9T (bort 0238) began to smoke. The regiment headquarters noted:

At 0950 a pair of fighters, lead Kapitan Tarasov, wingman Ml. Leytenant Obukhov, on Yak-9T aircraft each flew two attacks on ground targets. After breaking up for landing, Ml. Leytenant Obukhov lowered his gear and set up a 30° approach for landing. As a result, the exhaust pipe of his number six cylinder cracked, and the exhaust gases filled the cockpit. The pilot inhaled the poisonous gases and at the same time gained the impression that the engine was on fire. He made the decision to bail out, using his parachute. He deployed his parachute too early, causing his abdomen to impact against the vertical stabilizer.

Mladshiy Leytenant Obukhov died in the hospital four days later.

On 10 January, Starshiy Leytenant Ivan Fedorov, while on a reconnaissance flight to Apostolovo in a Yak-1, spotted and shot down a German Ju52 transport. Although this victory was not officially counted, it was important in that he spotted a new enemy airfield not far from Voroshilovka settlement. A strike using the the corps' fighter forces was planned immediately, but worsening weather prevented an en masse launch. Nonetheless, Ivan Fedorov still managed to destroy a Bf109 in the Lepetikha area later that afternoon.

The combat actions of the 265th IAD fighters in strikes against the Luftwaffe airbase at Apostolovo and the two forward airfields in the Bolshaya Kostromka area. 3 January, 1944.

This Yak-1b appears to have been the regular mount of Starshiy Leytenant Tishchenko within the last two months of 1943 and into the beginning of 1944 as the Crimean operation picked up pace. From a mid / late 1943 manufactured series, it may have been from the earliest batch of Yaks delivered to the corps in the new grey-on-grey fighter camouflage; a scheme which became more commonplace through 1944. Like Fedorov, Tishchenko also became a reconnaissance specialist flying either his regular Yak-1b or a Yak-9D.

Flight commander Fedor Tikhomirov was shot down by Bf109s on April 9, 1944 while flying Yak-9T #28. Although less than a year in the regiment, he was already the veteran of 144 missions wherein he engaged the enemy 37 times. He was a budding ace with 8 aerial victories accredited. The aircraft is a series 10 example, likely part of the new batch delivered to the regiment in early January 1944. Note the spring-operated wing-root intake covers not present on earlier series. Like Tishchenko's Yak-1b, it is adorned with the "Crimean era" version of the 3rd IAK winged star emblem.

Apparatus for viewing aerial reconnaissance film in field conditions. *the intelligence department, 3ʳᵈ IAK*

In the evening exchanges of personnel occurred in the regiment. The former regiment navigator, Mayor I. F. Popov, was named as the new commander of 812ᵗʰ IAP. Kapitan Yegor Ankudinov took his place in the navigator position while Starshiy Leytenant Ivan Fedorov inherited the 2ⁿᵈ Squadron. The information about the reconnoitered airfield was not ignored at corps headquarters. On Tuesday, 11 January, fighters of the 43ʳᵈ and 274ᵗʰ IAP of 278ᵗʰ IAD (3ʳᵈ IAK) sortied. Since he had originally spotted the airfield, Starshiy Leytenant Fedorov flew at the head of the group. Here are his words:

> *'Attention, this is '100', right turn, drop beneath the cloud.' This moment was no less important than the attack itself. To lead such a large cluster to the target while maintaining combat formation, using breaks in the overcast, is complicated. Finally we got there. Seeing the airfield directly in front of us, I breathed easier—I had done my job. And suddenly, before our group began its dive, directly ahead on course, from right to left, were two groups of He111 and Ju88 bombers. Slightly above them were six fighters. I made the decision and gave the command: 'This is '100.' The enemy is above and in front of us. Cover group—attack the bombers. Borodin's group—do not ground attack, engage the enemy fighters. Strike group—follow me. We are attacking the target!' I increased my angle, and an He111 quickly grew in size on the sight crosshairs until it reached the required mil value. Fire! I gave the enemy aircraft a long burst. The He111 burst into flames.*[73]

Squadron commander of the 43ʳᵈ IAP Starshiy Leytenant Semen Lebedev, who participated in the attack on the airfield, later recalled this successful flight:

> *Fedorov, who 1.5-2 hours before the takeoff for this attack had conducted a pre-reconnaissance on Lepetikha airfield with a pair of Yak-9s, led the group to the target. Before launch on this combat mission, Fedorov instructed the pilots in detail about the layout of Lepetikha airfield, the location of the enemy aircraft stands and about the approaches for the attack on the target. At 1408 the aircraft sortied for the combat mission. Mayor Klimov's strike group reached Lepetikha airfield at an altitude of 2000 meters (6,500 feet) and, with a dive angle of 30-35° conducted an attack on enemy aircraft, destroying three*

> *Hs129s. The strike was so unexpected by the enemy that his antiaircraft artillery opened fire only during our fighters' second pass on the target. During the approach to Lepetikha airfield, we saw above us a group of enemy bombers and accompanying Bf109s. By radio I signalled Mayor Klimov not to rely on my cover, because we were about to attack the enemy bombers. I ordered the single pair of Leytenant Dydygin to attack the fighters. We shot down three Ju88s in our first attack. After this the enemy became totally confused. The bombers dispersed and began to dive, dropping their bombs, which fell almost on their own airfield. Leytenant Dydygin's pair boldly attacked the German fighters, which also got tangled up. Good radio communications permitted me to hold the group together in a fist and make a fighting withdrawal to our own territory. But eight Bf109s, still in the air, attacked Mayor Klimov's group during withdrawal from the target. As a result of the aerial engagement that ensued, two enemy fighters were shot down. Our aircraft returned to their airfield.*[74]

As a result of the attack on the airfield, nine enemy aircraft were destroyed; one of them, the He111 destroyed at the airfield, was credited to Starshiy Leytenant Fedorov.

At 1207 on 14 January, a group of Yak-1s led by the new regiment commander, Mayor Popov, conducted two more attacks within four hours on the German airfield. All told, they destroyed seven Bf109s in the air and six Hs129s plus an He111 on the ground. The new commander distinguished himself in shooting down two of the Bf109s on this Friday. The net result of these two attacks, including the aerial engagements, was the destruction of 10 Bf109s, six Hs129s, three Ju88s, and one He111.

On 14 January 1944, the regiment headquarters recorded the first attack:

> *Strike on Lepetikha airfield. Combat formation was comprised as follows: commander of entire attack group—commander 812ᵗʰ IAP, Kapitan Popov. He also led the cover group, consisting of Leytenants Tumanov and Peskarev, Ml. Lt. Zuyev, Kapitan Ankudinov, and Leytenant Prikhodko (he was to photograph the results of the attack).*

Strike group no. 1: Kapitan Tarasov group commander, wingmen Leytenants Tikhomirov, Shishkin, Razumovich.

Strike group no. 2: Starshiy Leytenant Tishchenko group commander, wingmen Leytenants Serezhenko, Podymov, Sukhorukov.

In addition, a group of six aircraft from the 291st IAP was designated for suppression of antiaircraft fire from the enemy airfield. Regiment navigator Ovchinnikov led the strike group from 291st IAP. The combined group of 14 fighters launched at 1207. During formation assembly, Kapitan Tarasov's engine quit and he, accompanied by his wingman Leytenant Tikhomirov, made a forced landing back at their airfield. Group leader Kapitan Popov, together with the entire group, reached the target airfield exactly at 1245. On approach to the airfield, Bf109 type fighters took off from the airfield, apparently alerted. Kapitan Popov gave the command 'Target in sight, attack at will.' In order to draw antiaircraft fire upon himself, he headed for the center of the airfield without changing course. The strike group of six aircraft, along with the flak suppression group from 291st IAP, attacked from the north and northwest perimeters of the airfield. Enemy antiaircraft guns opened fire, primarily at Kapitan Popov's group. AA shell bursts were in two distinct layers – the first at an altitude of 2,000 meters (6,500 feet) and the second at 2,500 meters (8,200 feet). The cover group was quick to engage the Bf109s that were taking off. In the resulting aerial battle four Bf109s were shot down. Meanwhile, the attack group set three Hs129s on fire on the ground. There were no friendly losses. Leytenant Prikhodko photographed the results of the strike.

On 15 January, reconnaissance flights established that eight Hs129s were on Bolshaya Kostromka airfield, and that 10 Bf109s and five Do217s were on the airfield near Voroshilovka settlement. The 265th IAD divided its regiments to conduct operations along two axes on 20 January: toward Nikopol and toward Crimea proper. The 812th IAP flew to the airfield at Veseloye farmstead. And once again attacks continued on the detected enemy airfields. On 25 January 1944, during a solo flight to photograph the results of an attack on Rayzendorf airfield, the Yak-9D of flight commander Mladshiy Leytenant Aleksandr Prikhodko disappeared. The young pilot had flown 58 combat sorties and conducted seven air battles during his time in the regiment (since July 1943). Altogether in January, the division destroyed 18 Bf109s, eight Ju87s, two Fw189s, and one each Fw190, He111, and Hs129. Of the total number of Bf109s destroyed in combat, pilots of the 812th IAP were credited with seven. In addition, the 812th set 10 enemy aircraft on fire during airfield attacks.

Sorties on Sunday, 6 February, began with an attack on a Luftwaffe makeshift airstrip in the area of Bolshaya Lepetikha. A four-ship flight of fighters under the command of Kapitan Tishchenko attacked this airfield first at 1130. A round from a rapid-fire antiaircraft cannon struck the engine of Mladshiy Leytenant Ivan Sidorenko's Yak-9T over the airfield. The group had to depart from the airfield and accompany the damaged fighter to friendly territory, whereupon he made a belly landing in the area of Novo-Petrovka airfield. But the most significant

event occurred in the afternoon. Here is an excerpt from the 265th IAD operations summary:

The commander of the 3rd Squadron, Starshiy Leytenant Aleksandr Ivanovich Tumanov, aircraft no. 0298, did not return from the mission in the area of Bolshaya Lepetikha crossing. During the attack on troops, Starshiy Leytenant A. I. Tumanov dove into a column of enemy trucks and perished. The other aircrews observed a powerful explosion in the crossing area, with many trucks burning.

Starshiy Leytenant Aleksandr Tumanov executed a fiery ram, directing his damaged Yak-9 (No. 0298) into a group of German vehicles. This was truly a courageous act. Until the day of his death, Aleksandr had managed to complete 164 combat sorties and in 65 aerial battles destroyed six enemy aircraft.

Two days later, as a result of stubborn combat, Soviet forces liberated the town of Nikopol. In honor of distinguishing itself in this battle, the 3rd IAK was awarded the honorific title "Nikopolskiy." An encoded telegram of the Military Council of 5 February 1944, addressed to the commanders of all combat and logistic units of the 8th Air Army, noted:

Despite the difficult weather conditions and limited suitability of our airfields, the units Glitserin, Georgin, Klad, Oksilit, and Buer executed in an outstanding manner their assigned combat missions to destroy the retreating enemy forces and combat equipment on the Nikopol bridgehead and the enemy's Dniepr River crossing sites.[75] A large quantity of equipment, bridging

Entrance to a dugout, the normal accommodations and conditions for the air crews of both sides at rudimentary airfields, such as many of those in the Crimea.

assets, and personnel were destroyed. Crossing assets were destroyed near Bolshaya Lepetikha and Bozhanovka, and over the course of the day this destruction continued. The personnel of the listed units displayed courage and heroism in battles, and the commanders of units and formations personally led their groups in combat. For outstanding combat actions in the destruction of the enemy crossing sites, combat equipment, and personnel on the Nikopol bridgehead, I DECLARE MY GRATITUDE to the outstanding pilots and technical personnel of the units Klad, Georgin, Glitserin, Oksilit, and Buer, and their supporting logistic units. I call upon you to undertake the complete destruction of the retreating enemy forces across the Dniepr River to the west.

Among the units listed in this telegram signed by the commander in chief of forces, Obukhov, and member of the military council, Subbotin, was the 3rd IAK whose two divisions made a substantial contribution to the accomplishment of the mission.

During the period from 3 to 8 February 1944, the 812th IAP flew 241 combat sorties in attacking enemy ground forces along the Dniepr left bank, resulting in the destruction of three aircraft, 254 wheeled vehicles, 84 wagons, and other combat equipment. Later, after shifting its fighters from this sector, the entire 265th IAD began to work on the Crimean axis. Yaks of the 812th IAP covered the crossing site over the Sivash.

On Saturday, 12 February, Mladshiy Leytenant Sergey Zuyev was shot down during aerial combat in the area. At 1420, a Yak-1 four-ship, led by Leytenant Shishkin, sortied to cover the crossings after an alert was raised by the ground vectoring station. Twenty minutes later the group encountered about 30 Ju87 bombers escorted by 12 Bf109s at an altitude of 4,000 meters (13,100 feet) near Russkiy Island. An additional four-ship, plus three pairs, of Yak-1 fighters were sent up to bolster the forces in the air. The pair of Leytenant Shishkin and Mladshiy Leytenant Razumovich made the first attack.

Everyone heard group commander Shishkin in their earphones: *"I am attacking, Sukhorukov cover me."* But the second pair, Mladshiy Leytenant Sukhorukov and his wingman Mladshiy Leytenant Zuyev, was already committed to combat with six Bf109s. In his second attack, Zuyev engaged a '109 that was twisting into his sights. The German fighter began to smoke. Simultaneously, the wingman of the smoking "Messer" fired a cannon burst, after which Zuyev's Yak-1 (No. 22147) started burning. No one could fend off the attack on Zuyev; everyone was engaged in combat. He promptly bailed out and deployed his parachute at about only 200 meters (650 feet) altitude. Not having enough altitude for his chute to fill, he was killed when he hit the ground. From the day of his arrival in the regiment in August 1943, Mladshiy Leytenant Sergey Zuyev had flown 20 combat sorties. Division headquarters,

Mladshiy Leytenant Sergey Zuyev became one of the regiment's first losses after the unit shifted its focus from the Nikopol to the Crimean axis.

in analyzing this sortie and the attack launched against the bombers, noted:

Rather than the massed fires of four aircraft in the attack, "pin pricks" were inflicted by individual aircraft. The pilots rushed to destroy the flank aircraft and failed to resolve the main mission—to break up the bombers' combat formation and force them to turn away from their assigned mission. The fire coordination in the enemy's formation was not disrupted and, therefore, the fighters suffered losses from the gunners' fire. Fire and maneuver of the group was not worked out, and in fact they gave it no significance. Had a massed fire attack been launched against the bombers, they couldn't have taken it and would not have been able to reach the target.

On Monday, 21 February 1944, everyone's favorite, squadron commander Starshiy Leytenant Aleksey Mashenkin, returned to the regiment from having been captured in the fall of 1943. Here is how Mayor N. F. Isayenko, the navigator of 236th IAD (subsequently commander of the 611th "Peremyshl" IAP) recalled this event.

When they reported reported Mashenkin's return from captivity to Savitskiy, the general said 'Is it Mashenkin? Aleksey? Squadron commander from the 812th Regiment? He is an outstanding pilot and excellent commander! Prepare a request addressed to the commander in chief of the 8th Air Army concerning the assignment of Mashenkin to his previous duty position![76]

Arriving back at his regiment, Aleksey Mashenkin recounted to his comrades his complicated story. Having fallen into captivity, he made friends with Leytenant Arkadiy Lodvikov, a squadron commander from the 611th IAP (236th IAD) who was also captured on 18 September 1943, along with Yuriy Osipov, a Pe-2 navigator, and Vladimir Panazhchenko, a fighter pilot. They were all in the same camp and made two escape attempts—the second of which was successful. They fell in with the partisans and fought with them for a while. The group was guided through the front line on 15 January 1944.

But bad luck led us to a penal battalion and they told us we would exculpate our guilt before the Motherland with our blood. Here is what happened next. We did not have anything against being sent to the infantry, but none of us felt any guilt before the Motherland for our conduct. Each of us had done everything in our power to be useful to the Motherland, both in captivity and with the partisans. Indignant at this injustice, I went to the headquarters and asked a podpolkovnik to listen to me. He believed me and promised to help me return to aviation. He understood that I could inflict greater losses on the enemy there than in the infantry.

Soon after that, they handed me an assignment instruction and I was sent to the

Not long after joining the Gruppe's 5. Staffel in the summer of 1943, Heinz Ewald became the wingman of II./JG52 Gruppenkommandeur Gerhard Barkhorn. This Stab-marked Bf109G-6 was his aircraft at the time. The pilot's personal "E-Sau" emblem is believed to have been on the port side only. This variant of the big-engined Messerschmitt was typical of the fighters remaining in the hands of the final cohort of JG52 experten in the Crimea. By the time it was all over in the late spring of 1944, many remained as mere scrap metal on Sevastopol and Cape Khersones area airfields. (see page 112)

Yak-9T, #01. Flying this aircraft, former POW Starshiy Leytenant Mashenkin scored the 812th IAP's last confirmed air-to-air victory of the Crimean campaign, shooting down a Bf110 on 12 May, 1944. Like Tikhomirov's ill-fated #28 illustrated on page 85, this machine is a late '43 / early '44 production Yak-9T featuring the series' more rounded prop spinner, modified 37mm cannon muzzle fairing (no starter dog present), armoured glass front and back in the cockpit, spring-operated wing-root intake covers (aerodynamically opened, so not vivible in this illustration), and grey-on-grey upper camouflage colours.

headquarters of the Air Army. The commander in chief received me. He greeted me, invited me to sit down, and asked me several questions. But for some reason he talked circumspectly. This greatly surprised me. He knew me, even if only vaguely. At the end of the conversation, the general unexpectedly declared that he did not have the right to send me to my unit. He did not say say it outright, but it seems I already understood his intention: let those, he was thinking, who had the responsibility to review my case do so. Almost crying from such unfair treatment, I asked him to report about me to our corps commander. The general finally agreed to do that. Three days later, Yevgeniy Yakovlevich Savitskiy flew to the army headquarters. After talking with the commander in chief, he took me back with him. His personal guarantee returned my honor and wings. I will not forget this faith.[77]

Only the interference of General Savitskiy, who was in desperate need of every combat pilot, permitted Mashenkin to avoid a faceless death in a penal battalion and to return to his *home* regiment. Aleksey Mashenkin, the *artist of flight*, came close to never returning to combat aviation. Fedorov recalled:

I couldn't sit down out of worry. But then, Alesha finally opened the door and stopped on the porch. In an instant we suddenly looked at one another and then rushed to embrace. We stood there a long time—both of us at a loss for words. I looked at the burns on Aleksey's hands and face and, trying to conceal the concern that swept over me, pronounced: 'So this is how they rejuvenated you. Well, that's all right. We will pay them back.'

We wanted to know as quickly as possible what had happened to him, but Aleksey was interested in regimental news. I briefly told him how the fighting was going, who had died and in what circumstances, told him about Mayor Popov, the new regiment commander, about how he was well liked in our collective, how he flew, how he fought, how he led groups. Aleksey was glad that he had fallen in with such an experienced and courageous commander, that he had survived, how he would move forward. He believed that he had to start all over from the beginning, that he had to justify himself, that he was guilty before all of us, that his captivity was some kind of crime.

I calmed him as much as I could, but he was in such a condition that it was difficult to convince him and put him on an optimistic footing. 'You know how they checked me,' he said pensively, literally with pain in his voice. 'How terrible it is when they don't believe in you!'

'It's nothing, Alesha, everything will settle down, it will find its place, and the case will be closed. You know they have to check those who returned from there, just in case.'

'I understand all of it in my head,' Mashenkin said, 'but my heart does not accept it when they interrogate me with the cross-examination method, trying to determine if I was recruited by German intelligence.'

We did not sleep until near morning. At noon the regiment commander and zampolit dropped by. They congratulated us on Red Army and Red Navy Day [February 23—trans.], wished us health, happiness, and success in future air battles. 'And when will I be able to fly?' Aleksey asked? 'Don't worry.' said Ivan Feoktistovich, 'Get your strength back, rest a week, there is still war left for you.'

After dinner the pilots, technicians, and mechanics filled our room. They greeted Aleksey upon his return to the regiment, shook his hand, and expressed their delight that he was alive and healthy. Mashenkin joined them in their delight. He saw they had not forgotten him and that he had not lost respect among his friends, and this gave him strength and courage.[78]

Soon the other pilots who had been in captivity and with the partisans were flown out to their own regiments.

A flying accident occurred in the regiment on 24 February—a Yak-1 was damaged during a belly landing. The deputy commander for aerial gunnery service, Mayor Pavel Tarasov, forgot to lower his main gear after buzzing the field, despite the fact that he was given a flare signal to go around for a second try. Maintenance technicians repaired the aircraft in three hours.

In fending off air raids against the crossing on 25 February, the 265th IAD pilots shot down 15 and damaged four German aircraft. Leytenant Vasiliy Shishkin added the fifth enemy aircraft to his score that day, sending a Ju87 dive bomber into the ground. Eleven of the victories were counted for the 402nd IAP. On that same evening, the headquarters of 291st, 402nd, and 812th Regiments received an encrypted message which the division commander, Polkovnik Koryagin, recommended be read to all flying and technical staff of the regiments.

Maintenance personnel: First row: A. Lipkin, M. Novikov, K. Motygin.
Second row: Goryashchenko, Lomovtsev, P. Korneyev, Grigoryev.

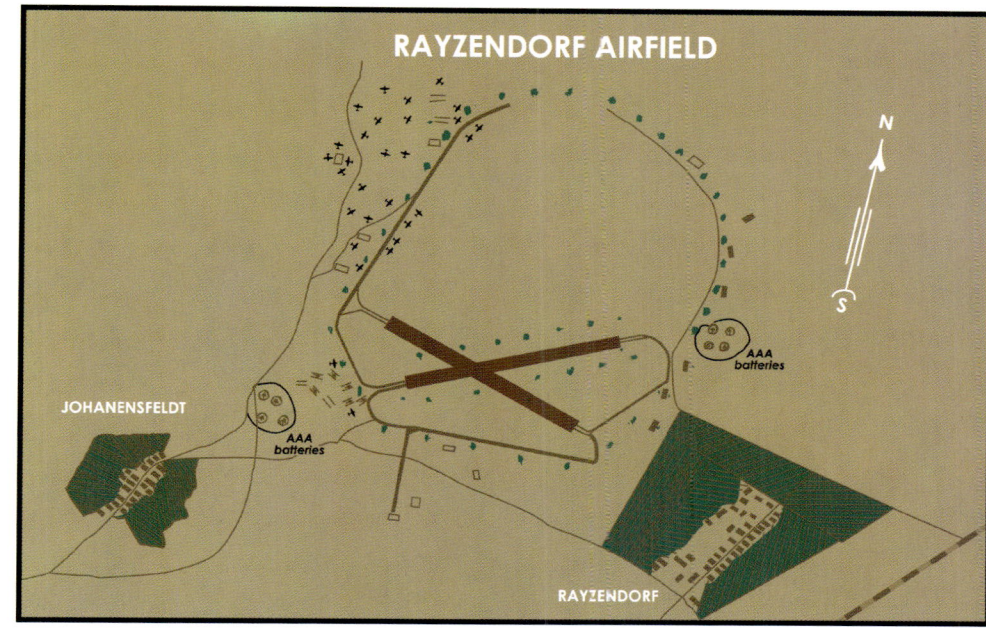

RAYZENDORF AIRFIELD

JOHANENSFELDT

AAA batteries

AAA batteries

RAYZENDORF

A schematic of Rayzendorf airfield (configured for night flights) with indication of location of aircraft stands, AA batteries, searchlights, and landing strips.
based on original sketches from the intelligence department, 3rd IAK

Over the course of 25 February, the enemy conducted three massed raids in order to destroy the crossings. All three of his bomber groups, totalling 85 aircraft, flew with powerful fighter cover. As a result of the sixteen group battles fought by the division's fighters on the approaches to the crossing and over the crossing itself, 15 enemy aircraft were destroyed and four were damaged in a day. Of these, 402nd IAP shot down 11, the 291st IAP—3, and the 812th—1 aircraft. Positioned at the ground vectoring station, I personally observed the fall of eight enemy aircraft in my field of view. I give a high evaluation to the actions of the pilots who participated in these air battles. As a whole, all acted skillfully, courageously, and persistently, and boldly pursued the enemy to his total destruction. As a result of their skillful actions that resulted in the destruction of 15 enemy aircraft, the enemy was unable to carry out precision bombardment. Only a single bomb fell some 15 meters (50 feet) from the crossing; its shock wave was carried to the planking of the crossing, halting the movement of vehicles for three hours. Our losses were four damaged aircraft, of which three safely landed on their own airfields and one at the forward edge. One aircraft was shot down and the pilot bailed out. Two pilots were wounded and two aircraft did not return to their base for unknown reasons. Pilots Lavrenov, Shpunyakov, Kulikov, Manukyan, Novikov, and Shishkin were fighting especially skillfully, bravely, and boldly. The 402nd IAP conducted its combat work best of all and most organized, the 812th IAP not as well because of a great number of maintenance failures. Deficiencies were noted in the course of the battles: individual pairs departed far to the north from the crossing; some pilots were lured into pursuing enemy aircraft, forgetting about the presence of powerful cover. It was only good fortune that they were not shot down. The enemy made his passes at the crossing out of the sun, and the side of the sun also had the most fighter escort. He executed his departure to his own territory in the direction of Chuchak, the shortest distance

to his forward edge. I offer my thanks to the entire flight component of 402nd IAP for good effort in the conduct of aerial battles and personally to the commander of the 402nd IAP, Mayor Yeremin for the regiment's well-organized combat work. In subsequent battles, we must avoid repeating the deficiencies noted above.

On Sunday, 27 February, Mladshiy Leytenant Vasiliy Makarchuk perished in battle over the crossing site. The outcome of the combat actions in February 1944 were 33 enemy aircraft downed in aerial engagements and four destroyed on the ground. During this period, the pilots of 812th IAP shot down two Ju87s and one Bf109, damaged a Ju87, and set three aircraft (He111, Hs129, and Fi156) on fire on the ground.

On 2 March 1944, 23 of the division's aircraft, consisting of 16 Yak-1s, two Yak-7s, and five Yak-9s led by 812th IAP commander Mayor Popov, conducted an attack on Rayzendorf airfield from 1110 to 1200. The 402nd IAP, led by Mayor Anatoliy Rubakhin, covered the strike group. Corps commander General Yevgeniy Savitskiy and deputy division commander Podpolkovnik Sergey Preobrazhenskiy flew in the cover group for this operation. Six Yak-9T aircraft, led by Leytenant Abdrashitov, were designated to suppress antiaircraft artillery. The group carried out its flight toward the target at an altitude of 2,500 meters (8,200 feet), dropping down to 1,500 meters (4,900 feet) in the target area. At this time a transport aircraft was taxiing on the landing strip, and just beyond it, two Bf109s from II/JG52 had just left the ground at the end of their takeoff roll.

On 2 March, by decision of the commander of 3rd Aviation Corps, General Savitskiy, two whole regiments—an armada of Yaks—lifted up into the sky! Mayor Popov was appointed commander of the group. We flew toward the target at an altitude of 2,500 meters (8,200 feet), above the thin scattered layer of clouds, leaving Dzhankoy to the left. Later we slipped under the clouds. 'Target dead ahead and below,' we heard Popov's voice. I was flying close to him and saw how confidently the mayor led the group to the enemy airfield. "Attack!" Popov commanded, and put his aircraft into a dive. Many aircraft lined the field. An enormous transport had taxied onto the runway and directly ahead two Messerschmitts were taking off. The wingman had not yet even raised his undercarriage. 'You're going to get it now!' I thought, and just at that moment heard Popov's command: "100,' attack the pair of Messers taking off!' We were thinking, one could say, the same thoughts. I gave it full throttle. My wingman, Sukhorukov, is a reliable partner and I could maneuver any way I wanted; and in just several seconds our pair came up behind the Messerschmitts. I had the enemy wingman in my sight. He has his main gear still lowered. I aimed and squeezed the trigger. The Messer turned over on its back and careened into the ground. I reduced my engine RPMs in order not to rocket past the second Bf109, but I had such an excess of speed that I had to make a right turn. And suddenly I saw the Messer execute a hard left zoom upward—either he had spotted me or they had warned him from the ground by radio. I pulled my machine around into a left bank. I had sufficient reserves of speed. I might be able to catch him. The German understood that it would not end well for him and placed his aircraft in a left turn. The enemy turned out to be a tough nut. I came up behind him, however it was difficult to get a sight picture—he was continuously changing his speed, turn radius, and altitude. We flew around in circles for a minute. I did not fire because I did not want to waste my rounds and he, rapidly changing flight regimes like a loach, flickered before my eyes. I felt myself getting fidgety. Here was a target, but I could not get it in my sight. I began to calm myself. That helped. And then I could still hear the voice of Aleksey Mashenkin, when he flew for the first time after returning from captivity. He was happy—I could hear it in his voice! However in front of me was an enemy aircraft, and there was no way I could destroy it. I stubbornly hung onto the German's tail, waiting for his littlest mistake. I fired a short burst and watched him. He panicked and when he tried to come out of his turn by dropping down, he dove toward the ground. This was sufficient for me to hold him in my sight for several seconds. I fired a long burst from all guns. The Messerschmitt lit up like a match box, and as it rolled over it exploded, crashing into the earth. "Dragon,' this is '75'. Mission complete, request permission to move to assembly point.' This was Popov reporting to Savitskiy. I looked down at the airfield, which was engulfed in heavy flames. We had done well![79]

This description of the situation above the airfield is from I. V. Fedorov, who shot down two Bf109s during the same raid. It was his second sortie of the day. According to pilot reports and post-strike reconnaissance, 11 enemy aircraft were destroyed on the ground and four were shot down in air combat. The entire group returned without losses. Pilots of the 812th scored all four of the air victories and nine of the 11 destroyed on the ground. Mayor I. F. Popov, the group leader, was outstanding in this raid. He shot up a Ju87 that was taking off and set another Ju87 and an He111 on fire in a strafing attack. Here is the citation from Mayor

Popov's award recommendation:

During the approach to the airfield, up to 60 enemy aircraft of various types were counted, of which only four Bf109s and six Ju87s were just taking off. Popov spotted the final run of a "Savoia" on the landing strip and gave the command to attack the airfield. He set the Savoia on fire in his first pass [In this situation the division headquarters received imprecise information. Actually an He111 was set on fire.] and shot down a Ju87 during his pullout. The pilots under the command of Comrade Popov, acting boldly and expertly in the air and over the ground, destroyed eight [more precisely, nine] enemy aircraft without any losses. Popov's aircraft was struck by intense antiaircraft fire. Applying all of his strength, Comrade Popov safely guided the airplane to his airfield.

Altogether during the period from 31 December 1943 to 2 March 1944, the regiments of 265th IAD conducted 13 strafing attacks on enemy airfields. These raids resulted in the destruction of 54 enemy aircraft on the ground: 15 Ju52, 13 Ju87, 12 Hs129, seven He111, five Bf109, a Ju88, and an Fw189. Two Hs126 and five Hs129 were damaged. Fully 25 airborne enemy aircraft were shot down during airfield attack missions: 18 Bf109, two Hs129, two Ju88, a Ju87, an He111, and an Fw189. In this same period, the pilots of the 265th IAD conducted night sorties, intercepting individual enemy bombers that were working against rear area Soviet forces. After several attempts to intercept enemy bombers during nocturnal raids, Kapitan Ankudinov managed to achieve victory over an He111 on 2 March. This was the first night victory in the regiment. On 3 March, having sortied at 2305, at 2330 the pair of General-Mayor Savitskiy and Mayor Tarasov attacked Rayzendorf airfield, where Savitskiy set an He111 on fire. Ten minutes later, arriving at their next patrol zone, the pair discovered an He111 flying at an altitude of 3,500 meters (11,500 feet). Savitskiy attacked the bomber from the rear and below but did not observe the results of the attack. After ten more minutes of patrolling they spotted the He111 again, and this time attacked it from above. Again, the pilots did not observe the results of the attack. The pair of Yaks landed at 0015.

Reconnaissance flights conducted by 265th IAD fighters showed that the basic strike forces of enemy aviation were concentrated on Rayzendorf airfield on 10 March 1944. They established that 17 Bf109s and 27 Ju87s were present there. A generalized summary of the itelligence department noted the presence, in front of the corps, of JG3 and JG52, units of KG3, KG27, and KG55, StG1 (at least its component I/StG1), Seeaufklarungsgruppe 126, and Wekusta 76. Hungarian and Romanian aviation subunits were also operating on the German side: reconnaissance noted the 4th Hungarian Detachment and 122rd Group.

Saturday, 11 March 1944, was particularly event filled. The notes in the corps combat journal began with a recollection of the first aerial battle conducted by the pilots of 812th IAP.

At 1030 in the Tomashevka-Tarkhan area, the leader Podymov encountered four Fw190s and engaged them in combat at an altitude of 5000 meters. Mladshiy Leytenant Vinogradov shot down one Fw190; the aircraft fell in the

Tauk area. Podymov chased the second Fw190 beyond Ishun. During his return he heard the signal, 'bombers departing.' In zone number 1 they encountered two groups of 10-12 Ju87s. Podymov attacked a Ju87 from above and behind at a range of 50 meters. It fell sharply and departed to the south, smoking. During his pullout from this attack he became tangled up with four Bf109s. As a result of this battle Leytenant Sukhorukov shot down one Bf109, which fell in the Chirik area.

Podymov and Vinogradov did not return from their next battle. Eight Yak-1s led by Starshiy Leytenant Fedorov took off at 1305. The sortie that began successfully for 812th IAP concluded with the loss of two pilots. Fifteen minutes after takeoff, at an altitude of 5000 meters (16,400 feet), the group, which by then had divided into two four-ship flights (strike and cover), encountered two groups of 10-12 Ju87 dive bombers which were on course to the crossing site. The encounter occurred in the Tyuy-Tyube— Koranki area. The dive bombers were escorted by two groups of enemy fighters (four Fw190s and six Bf109s). Six fighters raced toward the Junkers in an effort to prevent the bombing of friendly ground forces, leaving only two fighters for cover. They attacked the bombers head-on from above, with a subsequent attack from above and behind. Squadron commander Fedorov and Leytenant Shishkin each shot down one Ju87 – Shishkin's victory was the regiment's 250th. Right behind them, Mladshiy Leytenant Tikhomirov sent a third dive bomber to the ground after two attacks from close range. The remaining Junkers jettisoning their bombs hurriedly and in a disorderly manner before withdrawing. Defense of the crossing site was successful.

However, at the same time Podymov and his wingman Vinogradov became engaged with enemy fighters. Despite the clear enemy superiority, Nikolay Podymov managed to down one Fw190. Then, in fending off the attacks of the superior enemy, they lost their fire coordination and became separated, as it turned out, forever. The three Ivans—Fedorov, Sidorenko, and Stryuk—shot down an additional three fighters (two Bf109s and one Fw190) upon arriving at the scene of the lopsided fight. Petr Peskarev also increased his score in this engagement by shooting down a single Messer.

The Statement of Combat Loss noted:

The group was conducting aerial combat with a four-fold advantage on the side of the enemy. It was unable to take up a suitable position for the attack. The pilots were drawn into the attack, forgetting about mutual assistance. The leader insufficiently directed the aerial combat of his subordinates. During the approach to the bombers he gave

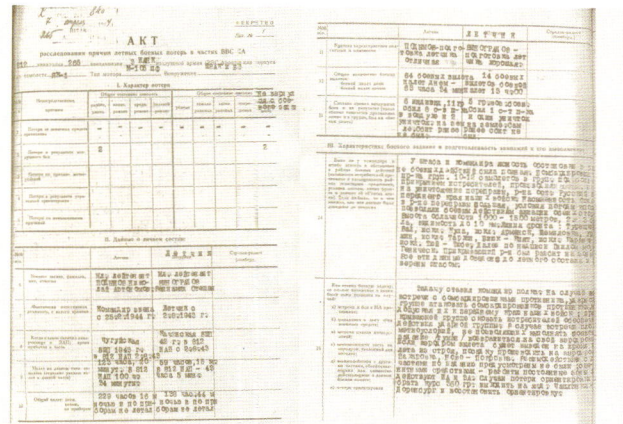

Above: The combat loss report document of Podymov and Vinogradov.

Below: the English translation.

Secret
Copy No. _____

DOCUMENT
Of investigating the causes of aerial combat losses in units of the *VVS KA*
812 Air Regiment 265 Air Division 3 *IANK* air army (*VSS Front*) or corps
Type aircraft Yak-1 Type engine M-105pf Armament ShVAK and BS

1. Nature of losses

No	Immediate cause	Severely damaged, destroyed	Major repair	Moderate repair	Field repair	Killed	Seriously wounded	Lightly wounded	Unharmed	Did not return from combat mission [typed over printed: "parachuted]
1	Enemy air defense	-	-	-	-		-	-	-	
2	Aerial combat	2								2
3	Weather-related causes									
4	Loss of orientation									
5	Unknown causes									

2. Data on personnel

No		Pilot	Navigator [crossed out] Pilot [typed in]	Radio operator/gunner (bomber)
6	Military rank, last name, first name, patronymic	Ml. Lt. PODYMOV, Nikolay Avtonomov[ich].	Ml. Lt. VINOGRADOV, Veniamin Stepan[ovich]	
7	Actual duty position, since what date	Flight commander since 25.2.1944	Pilot since 2.8.1943	
8	When and which flight school and ZAP, time in unit	Chuguyskaya VShP 1943 812 IAP 2.8.43	Kachinskaya VShP 1942 812 IAP 2.8.43	
9	Hours in aircraft type (separately indicate hours in given unit)	123 hr. 20 min. In 812 IAP 100 hr. 34 minutes	59 hr. 15 min. In 812 IAP 43 hr. 5 minutes	
10	Total hours: day, night, instruments	229 hr. 16 minutes. Did not fly at night or on instruments	138 hr. 44 minutes. Did not fly at night or on instruments	
11	Brief description of training and experience	Pilot's training was excellent	Pilot's training was good	

12	Total number of combat sorties: day combat sorties night combat sorties	64 combat sorties, 63 hr. 24 minutes time, day	14 combat sorties, 13 hours 00 minutes time, day	
13	How many air engagements conducted and results (number of downed enemy aircraft personally and in group, was he shot down himself earlier)	6 individual, 11 group engagements; shot down 5 enemy aircraft in air and destroyed 2 on ground not previously shot down	5 group engagements; shot down 1 enemy aircraft in air and destroyed one on ground; not previously shot down	

III. Description of combat mission and preparation of crew for its accomplishment

14	Did the commander and staff have clarity on the situation in the area of combat actions (activeness of enemy fighters and coverage density of anti-aircraft assets, weather conditions, front line, and data on attack targets). If not, then what specifically? What was passed to crew regarding these subjects?	Commander and staff had full clarity on situation in area of combat actions. Group of 10-12 enemy bombers under heavy fighter escort were executing systematic attacks to destroy crossing site at Russkiy Ostrov and forward edge of our forces. Density of [anti-aircraft] fire in crossing area was great. Weather conditions fully permitted air activities of both sides: overcast at 1000-1500 meters, force 2-3, visibility up-to 10 km. Front-line trace: Turetskiy Val (excluding Kula, excl. Armyansk)-Shemilovka-Urzhin excl.Tarkhan) –Biyuk-Kiyat (excl.Karan, excl. Tyuy-Tyube) and beyond by inscription Gniloye Morye, Genichesk. Covered area divided into zones. All data and information passed to flight crew and verified by staff.
15	Who assigned combat mission; its full expression and what were instructions in the event of: a) encounter and battle with enemy fighters; b) coming into zone of fire of antiaircraft means; c) encounter bad weather; d) impossible to land at designated airfield; e) coordination with other units that are supporting or cooperating in this combat mission; f) loss of orientation;	Regiment commander assigned mission. In event of encounter with enemy bombers, strike group attacks enemy bombers to deny them access to forward edge of our troops. Cover group should engage enemy fighters in order to provide for activities of the strike group. In event of bad weather /fog/ that prevents execution of combat mission, return to base. If airfield goes out of service during flight, land at Zakharovka-Novo Porovka airfield. Coordination with other units not envisioned; with antiaircraft assets: permanent zones of fighter activity and antiaircraft artillery activity have been designated. In event of loss of orientation, take heading 360° to Chaplinka-Dorenburg railroad line and re-establish orientation.

An Fw190F-8 from one of the Schlact units based at Khersones airfield, Cape Khersones in the spring of 1944. The formidable Focke Wulf could tote this impressive bombload over the short distances required of Crimean operations and then fight its way back to home base if necessary (and fuel permitting). This particular aircraft remained on the airfield after the Luftwaffe had departed. Reference photos suggest that it was put out of action either by Soviet aircraft or artillery fire, or by intentional demolition charges set by the departing Germans.

Mladshiy Leytenant Davydov's Yak-Ib. He was one of many young pilots whose lives were part of the price of regaining the Crimea from German occupation. Though this aircraft was lost in mid-March 1944, its serial number (39132) indicates that it was from an earlier mid-1943 batch, delivered when black-on-green was still the standard fighter camouflage.

the command 'Attack the bombers,' became engaged in aerial combat himself, and did not lead in the subsequent fight. It is necessary to increase the responsibility of the air crews for coordination in aerial combat. The air crews are given instructions during a battle with a large group to increase their vigilance and to bear responsibility for supporting each other. The group commander leads the battle not only until the moment when the first attack is initiated but also for the entire duration of the fight.

Both pilots had arrived in the regiment in early August 1943. Nikolay Podymov was able to fly 64 combat sorties before his death. He had destroyed eight enemy aircraft (six shot down and two on the ground) in six individual and 11 group aerial engagements. During this same time, Veniamin Vinogradov had executed 14 combat sorties and shot down one enemy aircraft in five group battles. This was the last battle for both of them.

The next aerial battle on this day occurred at 1620. Attacking a group of Ju87s, Mladshiy Leytenant Kureyev damaged one at 1,800 meters (6,000 feet) over the Adzhi-Bulat area. An eight-ship flight (Yak-1s and Yak-9s) from 402ⁿᵈ IAP arrived in the area at 1630. The pilots of the 402ⁿᵈ extracted a price for the death of their comrades, shooting down two enemy aircraft. Mayor Anatoliy Rubakhin destroyed a Ju87 as his second victory of the day, while Starshiy Leytenant Varlygin shot down a Bf109. A single Yak-1 was downed in combat with a Bf109 at about 1800 in the evening. The regiment lost yet another young pilot, Mladshiy Leytenant Pavel Sharapov. He had arrived in the regiment in early October 1943 and engaged the enemy three times in the course of 11 combat sorties . Regiment commander Popov wrote the following in the Statement of Investigation of the Causes of Combat Loss.

South of Russkiy Island, at an altitude of 4,000 meters (13,100 feet), a group of our fighters comprising four aircraft encountered four Fw190s, which were attempting to drop their bombs on the crossing site, and engaged them. The battle ended without losses to either side. After the fight, a group of up to 15 Ju87 bombers was encountered, escorted by fighters (the number of fighters was not established). The weather was clear, with visibility out to 15 kilometers (9.3 miles). Our fighters attacked out of the sun. The strike group conducted the attack on the bombers while the cover group engaged the fighters. After the first attack, the pair of which Mladshiy Leytenant Sharapov was a member was also attacked by enemy fighters. Sharapov was lost from view during this aerial engagement with the fighters. It is believed he was shot down by the enemy fighters. The possibility cannot be excluded that he was lost to fire from the bombers.

In the analysis that was conducted of the loss of the pilot, the following was also noted:

The number of air crews in the group was small and did not correspond to the aerial situation on this day. The aerial situation required that not less than eight aircraft be sent out, with four aircraft in the cover group. Poor command and control on the ground. The covering group was tied down in combat and as a consequence of its small size was unable to support the actions of the strike group.

The strike group (Sharapov) displayed weak vigilance during the conduct of the attack on the Ju87s.

The defense of the crossing site over the Sivash continued to cost the lives of young mladshiy leytenants. The *experten* of JG52 in their Bf109s kept them under constant pressure. Mladshiy Leytenant Mikhail Karasev died 2 days later. He and his wingman sortied in a pair of Yak-9s on Monday, 13 March at 0815. They spotted a group of 20 Ju87s escorted by eight Bf109s approaching at their patrol altitude of 3,000 meters (9,800 feet). In attempting to disrupt the dive bomber formation and interrupt its mission, they closed on them rapidly. Flying literally inside the enemy formation, they broke it up with bursts of cannon and machine gun fire. One of the escorting Bf109s damaged Karasev's aircraft, after which the pair withdrew from the fight to return to their airfield. The engine on Karasev's Yak quit. He lowered the gear and attempted to reach home base in a glide, but lost altitude too quickly. On force-landing in the Zakharovka village area, the aircraft nosed over, caught fire, and pinned the pilot.

Such a death of combat friends placed a heavy burden on the hearts of their comrades. In the course of combat missions, the living would often exact personal revenge on the enemy with all their efforts. On this day, squadron commander Ivan Fedorov shot down his 20ᵗʰ enemy aircraft, an Fw190 fighter bomber in the crossing area.

Aerial engagements in the crossing area did not slacken through the following day. At noon, Mayor Tarasov and Starshiy Leytenant Fedorov shot down an Fw190 each, almost simultaneously. Two and one-half hours later, Pavel Tarasov reduced the fighter aviation strength of the Luftwaffe by yet another Bf109, while Kapitan Tishchenko and Mladshiy Leytenant Tikhomirov each destroyed a Ju87.

On Thursday, 16 March, Starshiy Leytenant Ivan Fedorov shot down two Bf109s in aerial combat within several minutes of each other. In the last dogfight of the day, however, he almost lost his wingman, Mladshiy Leytenant Nikolay Sukhorukov. At 1610 the pair had engaged a pair of Bf109s in the Chuchak area. Fedorov shot down one of the Messers from short range, while at this very same time Sukhorukov's Yak-1, which had received a burst into its engine, began to smoke. Pair leader Fedorov managed to cry out *"Sukhorukhov! Bf109 on your tail,"* and shot down one of the Bf109s in fending off the attack. Both pilots withdrew from the fight. Fedorov watched the sky as he accompanied Sukhorukhov's damaged Yak back to friendly territory. The regiment headquarters recorded it this way:

At 1550, four Yak-1s, led by Starshiy Leytenant Fedorov, conducted battle with two Bf109s at 5,000 meters (16,500) in the Biyuk-Kiyat area. At 1604 they fought an aerial engagement with two Bf109s in the Tarkhan area, one of which was shot down. At 1610, at an altitude of 5,200 meters (17,000 feet) in the Chuchak area, two Bf109s attacked Mladshiy Leytenant Sukhorukhov. The group's combat formation was four ships in trail. Upon encountering the enemy fighters, the group attacked the enemy first. Conducting air battle with two Bf109s in turning maneuvers, Sukhorukhov's aircraft was struck. The pilot made a forced belly landing 800 meters (2,600 feet)

Photographic control of the place of fall of enemy aircraft. Bf-109 (Black 2 + -) II Gruppe, unknown Staffel (possibly 5./JG52). Though the original photogrph is severely damaged, reproducing it at this size does show some of the markings detail, as well as the delapidated state of the aircraft proper.

north of Ashkadak. The pilot received a light injury to his nose and hand. The aircraft was destroyed by German artillery. The pilot is back at his unit.

Having made it out of his aircraft, Sukhorukov was taken to a nearby rifle division command post and, later, to his regiment. Having observed the Soviet fighter landing, a nearby German artillery unit fired a heavy barrage at the landing site until the downed Yak was destroyed. This was the second time in a week for this graduate of the Chuguyev Military Pilot School, Nikolay Sukhorukov, to be shot down in combat. During his entire time in the regiment (from August 1943 to 16 March 1944), he flew 54 combat sorties and fought 16 aerial engagements, shooting down a single Bf109.

On the following day, 17 March, a pair of Messers (from 5./JG52) shot down two Yak-1s in the crossing-site area with a surprise attack out of the sun. Mladshiy Leytenant Yuriy Davydov, a graduate of Stalingrad Military Pilot School, and Mladshiy Leytenant Aleksandr Razumovich perished. Here is an annotation from the 265th IAD journal of combat actions:

17.03.44, at an altitude of 4,000 meters (13,100 feet), Leytenant Tikhomirov spotted two Bf109s that attacked his pair. After the first attack the pair leader, Mladshiy Leytenant Davydov on aircraft Yak-1 No. 39132 went into a dive, then a spin, and fell 300 meters (325 yards) northwest of the crossing site. Tikhomirov continued to engage the two Messerschmitts. At a moment in Tikhomirov's fight, the group commander Shishkin gave Razumovich the command, 'We're going to help him,' but at this time two Bf109s attacked Shishkin's pair out of the sun. His wingman, Razumovich, went into a spiral and without recovering from it fell into the Sivash.

The regiment staff summary recorded the losses thus:

At 0755, at an altitude of 4,000 meters (13,100 feet), southeast of Russkiy Island, four fighters, led by Leytenant Shishkin, were attacked out of the sun by two Bf109s. Weather: high cloud layer, force 8-9, haze, visibility 5-6 km. Combat formation – four aircraft in trail. The pair of

Bf.109s was in the sun with an altitude advantage of 600-800 meters (2,000–2,600 feet). They conducted their attack on Ml. Leytenant Davydov's aircraft at speed. After the attack, Davydov's aircraft went over into a dive, then while spinning struck the ground southeast of Russkiy Island. The pair leader, seeing the two Bf109s above him coming out of the sun, gave the command, 'look out, I see two Messers in the sun.' After the attack he asked Shishkin's pair to assist Davydov.

Like many graduates of flight school, Yuriy Davydov had all of 20 hours of flight time when he arrived in the regiment in October 1943. During his time in the 812th IAP, he flew 12 combat sorties and fought three aerial engagements. His friend, Aleksandr Razumovich, arrived in the regiment earlier (August 1943). In 86 combat sorties he engaged the enemy 26 times, shooting down one aircraft and damaging two on the ground.

The regiment commander, Mayor Popov, sternly reminded the pilots to pay attention that they did not fly directly into or away from the sun, and to scan the altitude when coming out of the sun. Some three hours after the loss, squadron commander Fedorov evened the score destroying a Bf109 in air combat with all barrels blazing. In the afternoon deputy squadron commander Leytenant Vasiliy Shishkin took off for a second time with Starshiy Leytenant Ivan Fedorov. Regiment commander Popov had assigned them a combat mission:

Destroy enemy bombers on the approach to zone Number 1. Mayor Tarasov will lead the strike group of four aircraft and Starshiy Leytenant Fedorov the containment group. Upon encountering enemy fighters, the containment group will engage the escort fighters in battle and the strike group will destroy the bombers. If you come into a zone of antiaircraft fire, get out of the zone of fire using counter-fire maneuver. Pilots who are executing this mission—pay attention to changes in the weather conditions. If you encounter fog, return to your airfield. The reserve airfield will be landing strips at Zakharovka and Pokrovka. Upon loss of orientation, return to our territory on a heading of 360° and re-establish orientation.

Attempting to avoid the mistakes committed in the first sortie, the pilots were extremely attentive. In the area of the covered Sivash crossing site, they spotted German bombers and raced toward them. But again, suddenly, six Bf109s fell upon the pair from out of the overcast. After the second attack, Shishkin's Yak-9T had to make a forced landing in the Chigora area. The regiment headquarters noted:

> At 1500, 8 Yak-1 and Yak-9 fighters comprising a strike group of four—Major Tarasov leader, and a containment group of four—St. Leytenant Fedorov leader, took off on alert to cover the Sivash crossing site. At 1537 at an altitude of 2,000 meters (6,500 feet), a pair of fighters from the containment group—Leytenant Shishkin, pursuing the enemy bombers in the Chigora area, attacked two Bf109s in a right turn. An additional four Bf109s appeared out of the haze, and a second pair attacked Fedorov's pair from the left and behind. Pursuing a Ju87, having spotted the pair of Bf109s, St. Leytenant Fedorov gave the command, 'Shishkin, Bf109 from the right, attack.' Having seen the second pair of Bf109s headed for the crossing site, he gave the command, 'Bf109s from the left,' and turned left. The second pair from the containment group remained behind in the crossing area. Fending off the attack, Fedorov's pair engaged in combat in a left turn. The third pair of Bf109s attacked Leytenant Shishkin and damaged his aircraft. Having given the report, 'I am damaged,' Shishkin began to withdraw from the battle. At this time a pair of Bf109s attempted to attack Leytenant Shishkin. Starshiy Leytenant Fedorov drove off this attack. Leytenant Shishkin was wounded by shrapnel in both legs during the attack of the second pair of Bf109s. The pilot made a belly landing. The pilot was taken to the hospital at Gromovka. His aircraft had the following damage: fuselage damage near the third frame, broken wing, and damaged engine. It was beyond repair.

A graduate of Stalingrad Military Pilot School, Vasiliy Shishkin had arrived in the regiment with a cohort of young replacements in June 1943. He completed 132 combat sorties, and in 34 aerial battles he had destroyed six enemy aircraft and set fire to another four on the ground. His Yak was written off due to the damage it incurred during the belly landing.

That evening corps commander Savitskiy arrived in the regiment. He was interested in the cause of such great losses in the division and in 812th IAP in particular. All the pilots pointed out the sudden appearance of pairs of *hunters* that would just as suddenly disappear in the cloud cover after making their attacks.

> I stood up and told how, on 15 March, a single Bf109 with bright snakes painted on the fuselage suddenly attacked our pair. The corps commander listened to all of this attentively and then said, 'Think in detail about how to fight with these German hunters and report your suggestions by telephone by the end of the day. Fedorov is right—it is more difficult for a pair to defeat a single hunter. And in the second place, it is better to prepare your new personnel for battle. Preserve them, we do not need any more pointless losses!'[80]

This was how Ivan Fedorov recalled this conversation. With his victory over the Messer on this day, once again he proved that it was possible to defeat an experienced enemy. At 1125 on the following day, he attained his 25th personal victory in the air. This time his victim was an Fw190. Elsewhere in the sky at the same time, Mladshiy Leytenant Tikhomirov destroyed his 8th enemy aircraft, sending an Fw190 into the waters of the Sivash. This was Saturday, 18 March.

The headquarters of the 3rd IAK also noted the presence of a powerful enemy in the air. On 31 March it sent the 265th IAD headquarters a brief of the principal enemy units operating in the corps tactical areas. This document noted, in particular, the

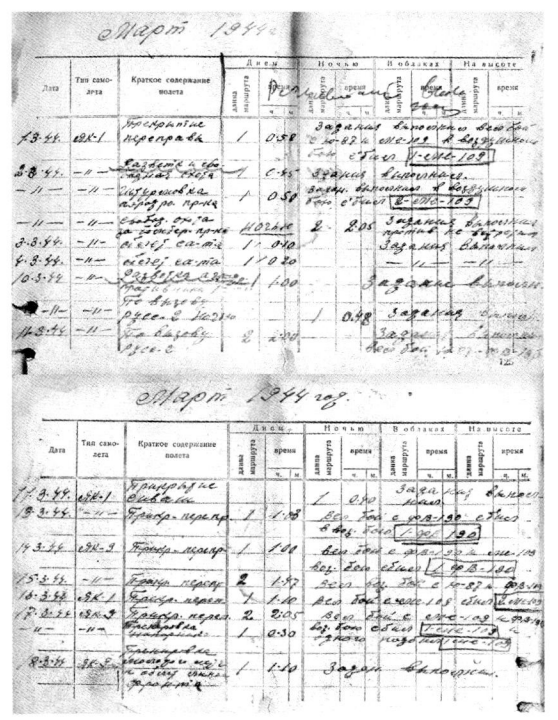

(Left) Pages from I.V. Fedorov's flight logbook (March 1944) showing the types of downed enemy airplanes (circled).

(Right) A document from 30.03.1944 — instructions from the Chief of Staff of the 265th IAD to the Chief of Staff of the 812th IAP requiring more thorough documenting pilots' claims.

presence of JG3 and JG52. Here is the brief's description of JG3 'Udet' operating in Crimea:

The best detachment of all the aircraft is the 9th (9./JG3 'Udet'). The air crews are 20-25 years old, the majority have up to 200 combat sorties in England, France, and Russia. The detachment is credited with 100 downed Russian aircraft in the period from September through October 1943. Our reconnaissance has noted the actions of various detachments of III/JG3 in the area of Kakhovka, Melitopol, from November through February there are no reports of actions, and in March, according to the statements of a prisoner, one detachment of the 'Udet' Geshwader is based in Crimea.

Here is the brief's description of JG52 operating in Crimea:

The JG52 is considered one of the best fighter geshwaders in the German Luftwaffe. The geshwader commodore in February 1943 was Major Hrabak. The geshwader has three combat and one reserve gruppen, equipped with the Bf109G-2 aircraft. The air crews are distinguished by their good combat training and have great combat experience. The pilots have on average up to 100 or more combat sorties. In connection with the losses suffered at the end of 1942, the detachments of JG52 have up to 3-4 young pilots who have 20-30 combat sorties. The best pilot in the 52nd Geshwader is Oberst Graf, who has shot down more than 100 Russian aircraft, and who began the war at the rank of lutnant (he does not fly at the present time). The geshwader is credited with more than 500 aircraft shot down (French, English, Russian). During the time of its combat operations on the Eastern front, JG52 has suffered significant losses, having cycled through its aircraft 2-3 times. Overall losses suffered by its separate gruppen comprise more than 300 percent. During the recent time communications intelligence has noted actions of units of JG52 in the Crimea area.

Having compiled the results of combat actions for March 1944, the 265th IAD headquarters reported incomplete data concerning the destruction of 32 Bf109s, 19 Ju87s, nine Fw190s, and one He111. Eleven enemy aircraft were destroyed in airfield attacks. The pilots of the 812th IAP claimed 30 of the total: 12 Bf109s, nine Ju87s, an He111, and eight Fw190s. They were also responsible for nine of the 11 enemy aircraft destroyed on their airfields.

Leytenant Aleksandr Ivanov, one of the regiment's Far East veterans, was serving in the 2nd Squadron of the 812th at this time. He had been shot down and seriously wounded in the Kuban battles in May 1943. After hospitalization he was evaluated by a routine medical board in Moscow, which banned him from flight duty in fighters. Aleksandr, just the same, managed to prevail upon the doctor to leave him in aviation and not to designate him an invalid. At the end of September 1943, barely recovered, he arrived back in the 3rd IAK and returned to his regiment. It was particularly difficult for the young, former Yak pilot to stay behind on the ground to stand by and watch airplanes take off and land. But all in all it wasn't so bad; at the very least he had the pilots of 2nd Squadron nearby while he performed various staff duties. In March 1944 the regiment commander, Mayor Popov, concerned by the uncertainty of Ivanov's fate, suggested that he become the squadron adjutant. Aleksandr Ivanovich Ivanov recalled this conversation:

'You can't go on like this. You are unable to fly combat missions. In accordance with the condition of your health, we cannot expect from you what we get from a fully healthy fighter pilot. I cannot permit you to fly. Thus I suggest you transition to adjutant work.'

Luftwaffe aircraft brought down by 3rd IAK fighters in the Crimea. Above, a Bf109 (coded "+12") and a Bf110 (coded "S9 + C") dumped near the edge of a city apartment complex. Right, a Ju87 dive-bomber that looks as though it burnt out from an engine-area fire.

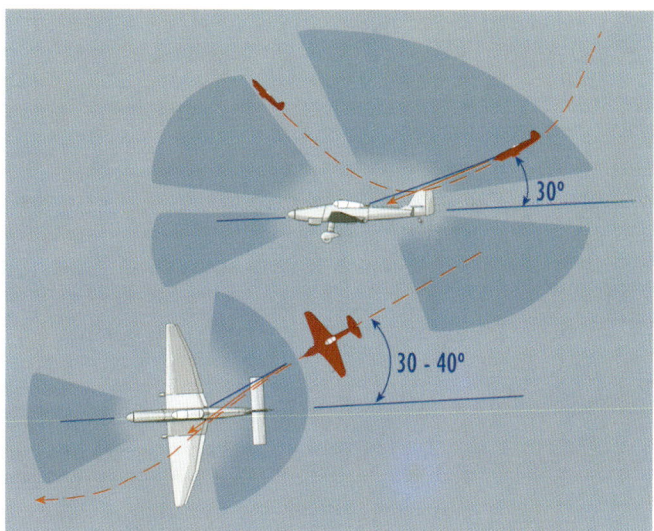

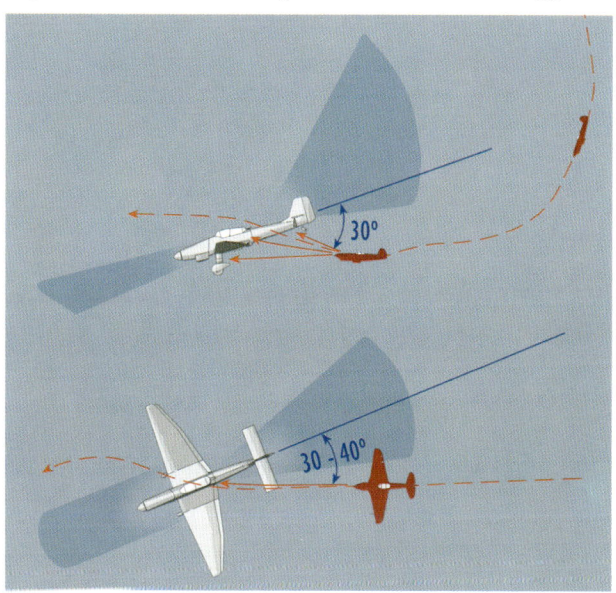

Based on wartime illustrations, these schematics show the optimum set-up for successfully engaging and disengaging the Ju87 while, at the same time, minimizing the risk of entering the field-of-fire of its defensive guns. *A.Rusetski and T.Higgins*

I did not agree to become the adjutant because I did have permission to fly the U-2. But our squadron did not have this liaison aircraft. Popov thought about it and promised to talk with the higher command. I don't know whom he talked with, but soon the order arrived concerning my transfer out of 812ᵗʰ IAP and appointment as a pilot in the 408ᵗʰ OAES [Separate Aviation Liaison Squadron].

Thus, thanks to the regiment commander, Leytenant Ivanov once again returned to flight duty. He had frequent occasion to visit the 812ᵗʰ Regiment in the capacity of a U-2 liaison pilot carrying out the taskings of the 3ʳᵈ IAK headquarters. As it turned out, he became the primary pilot for "Dragon," piloting General-Mayor Savitskiy's U-2. The peculiarity of this easily recognized aircraft was its fully enclosed cabin, and almost always, when the corps' pilots spotted this aircraft at their airfield, they knew that General Savitskiy himself had flown in to see them.

Combating the Ju87 "laptezhnik" and others

On Friday, 7 April, Leytenant Petr Peskarev achieved a victory over a Bf109 at 1027; a note about this seventh victory in battle over an enemy appeared in his logbook. That afternoon, the 265ᵗʰ IAD conducted an air strike on Ichki airfield, where the dive bombers of Oberst Leutnant Hans-Karl Stepp (commander, SG2 "Immelmann") were based. Here, the 812ᵗʰ achieved complete surprise: enemy AA gunners missed their first opportunity to open fire and after that were prevented from doing so. The approach to target was flown low level, over the sea, along the Arabat spit. They left four Ju87s burning and damaged five Fw190s on the ground. I. Popov, P. Tarasov, A. Mashenkin, I. Fedorov, P. Peskarev, Yu. Kureyev, I. Stryuk, and A. Kuznetsov distinguished themselves in this ground attack mission.

Young pilots who had only recently arrived in the regiment participated in this raid. Our regiment returned from the mission without losses. We looked at these young pilots, whose eyes glowed with excitement, and were pleased with the replacements that had been sent to us. On that same day, Savitskiy called. Mayor Popov reported that the young pilots conducted themselves admirably, and in the corps commander's voice we heard happy incantations.[81]

Altogether during the period from 1 January through 8 April 1944, the 265ᵗʰ IAD flew 2,007 combat sorties. Its pilots fought 193 air battles above the Sivash, shooting down 85 enemy aircraft. An additional 72 were destroyed as a result of their frequent raids on enemy airfields.

On 8 April, between 1800 and 1917, a group of 12 aircraft from the 812ᵗʰ IAP commanded by Mayor Popov, plus 14 aircraft of the 402ⁿᵈ IAP commanded by Mayor Rubakhin flew a repeat raid on Ichki airfield. On this occasion 12 Ju87s were destroyed and Fedorov shot down a single Fw190 in air combat above the airfield.

The 812ᵗʰ lost flight commander Leytenant Fedor Mikhaylovich Tikhomirov (Yak-9T No. 1028) in air combat on the following day. He was one of the group of young pilots who arrived in the regiment in early August 1943. Before his death he had flown 144 combat sorties. In 37 aerial engagements he shot down eight enemy aircraft and destroyed another two on the ground. That morning, before the flight to the crossing area, Mayor Popov conducted a short briefing with a group of pilots.

Use the method of free hunt for attacks in the cumulus cloud layer to destroy enemy aviation in the Karanka-Tomashevka area. Attack the enemy fighters suddenly, and if you cannot achieve surprise, withdraw into the overcast to attain a suitable position for an attack. Do not enter the zone of enemy antiaircraft fire. Three pairs of our fighter-hunters will be operating in the crossing site zone. Listen to the ground vectoring station concerning the direction of the enemy's approach.

But the situation and circumstances did not always permit the hunting sorties to be successful. Here is an excerpt from the report of the 812ᵗʰ IAP to the division.

The pair of Leytenant Tikhomirov and Mladshiy Leytenant Serezhenko was conducting free hunt from 1725 to 1800 for enemy aviation in the Karanka area. There were three other pairs of our fighter-hunters in this area. At 1742, at an altitude of 1,500 meters (4,900 feet), Leytenant Tikhomirov spotted up to seven Ju87s, which were flying toward the crossing site. Positioned 400 meters (1,300 feet) above them, he decided to use his altitude superiority and attack the Ju87s. During the attack he was himself suddenly attacked through a "window" in the scattered clouds by a pair of Bf109s. His aircraft was set on fire in their first pass and, burning all the way down, it impacted in the Karanka area. The enemy used the overcast, attacked suddenly at speed, and departed from the attack back into the clouds.

Later, the regiment commander, with grief in his spirit, signed the standard Statement of Death of a Pilot, noting:

The pair of Leytenant Tikhomirov did not maintain the security of its flight and was spotted by the Bf109s before they observed the enemy. The wingman spotted the Bf109 attack on his leader too late, and was unable to ward off the strike.

These sparse words of the commander suggests several thoughts: the pain of the loss, a summons to vigilance, and a routine request to his young men not to "expose themselves" so that they might live to fight again, to learn on the ground and in battle.

The fighter-hunter should use the overcast and the sun for flight security. Having spotted the enemy, attack him suddenly and depart from the attack into the clouds or toward the sun. Wingmen, during your leader's attack on the enemy aircraft, guard his tail vigilantly against sudden attacks by enemy fighters.

These were not empty exhortations; the regiment commander showed by his personal example how one could and should successfully fight with an experienced enemy. , Ivan Popov shot down a Ju87 on this same day in the Tomashevka area, while Petr Peskarev destroyed a Messer a bit farther to the south.

On the following day, the commander of the 812th showed, yet again, that his words did not deviate from his deeds. Here is text from the summary for Monday, 10 April 1944:

At 1609, eight Yak-9s and two Yak-1s, the group led by commander Mayor Popov, took off to attack Rayzendorf airfield. During the approach to the airfield, Popov's group encountered six Ju87s at 3,000 meters (9,850 feet) escorted by Fw190s and engaged them. After several attacks conducted by Popov's group, the bombers dropped their bombs on the run, before they reached their target, and began to withdraw hurriedly to their own territory. Popov's group shot down three Fw190s and one Ju87 as a result of this engagement. Our group suffered no losses.

At the same time, 12 Yak-9s of the 291st IAP sortied to blockade Rayzendorf airfield. Having begun the battle, Mayor Popov set up an altitude advantage from which he attacked the Fw190 escort group, enabling Ovchinnikov's group (from the 291st) to concentrate on the dive-bombers. Group commander Mayor Popov distinguished himself once again; shooting down an Fw190 in the Dzhankoy area (his 10th personal victory) and destroying one of the Stukas. Meanwhile, the pilots of the 291st Regiment shot down four Ju87s.

The group fended off two separate enemy fighter attacks, on its return leg, against homeward-bound bombers and *shturmoviks*. Mayor Tarasov, Mladshiy Leytenant Kureyev, and Kapitan Tishchenko shot down one Fw190 each on this day . Experience dictated that the most favorable attack, on either a dive bomber (Ju87) or fighter aircraft, was one executed from above and behind on *rakurs* 1/4 to 2/4 and disengaged with an immediate pull out upward and to the side while turning back into the course of the enemy aircraft.

Such an attack ensured the greatest probability of scoring hits in a vital, vulnerable place (engine, fuel cell, gunner), because the target was well presented at a lesser deflection angle. This method, with its dive-induced speed reserve and greater deflection angle working in the attacking fighter's favor, complicated the enemy gunner's conduct of fire. Additionally, the speed permitted rapid movement out of the effective range of the enemy aircraft's guns, while at the same time ensuring a favorable distance and altitude for transition to a follow-on attack. This immediate altitude gain was especially important when engaging an enemy fighter, since it did not significantly reduce the rate of climb.

An attack from directly astern (i.e., at small approach angles) was rarely used as a variation on the "from above and behind" attack. On the plus side, it provided for surprise since the

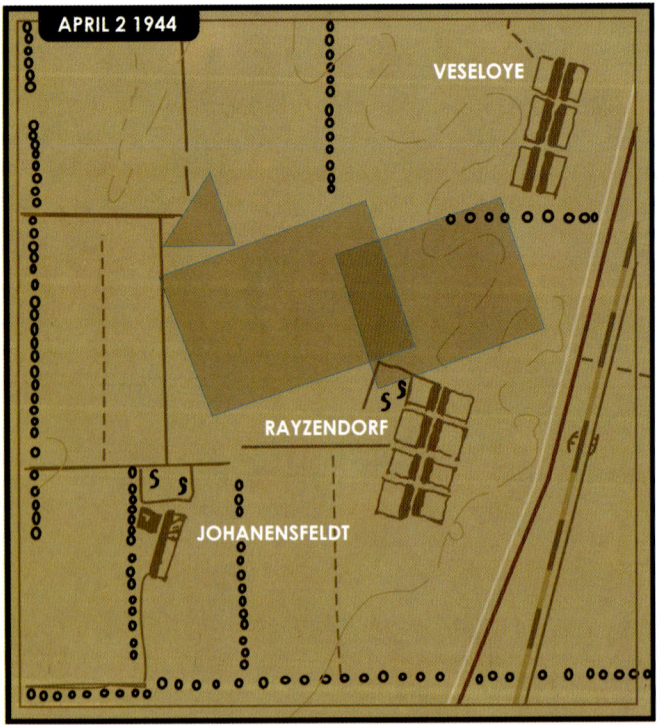

APRIL 2 1944

VESELOYE

RAYZENDORF

JOHANENSFELDT

This illustration is based on a black-inked wartime schematic used as a pilots' quick reference for the Rayzendorf airfield attack. Such drawings were usually derived from a portion of an aerial reconnaissance photograph. The shaded triangular wedge (upper left of center) is likely the "north" indicator.

In describing their aerial encounters, Soviet pilots often refer to the 'rakurs' they approached and fired at their target from. The word itself translates literally as "aspect" or "foreshortening." Based on the original Soviet wartime illustration (below), this schematic explains the relationship between the target's aspect angle and its corresponding 'rakurs' designator. Anything other than the 0/4 aspect, where the target is on the same or fully opposite heading, would be described as a 'deflection shot' by then contemporary American and British fighter pilots. *A. Rusetski and T. Higgins*

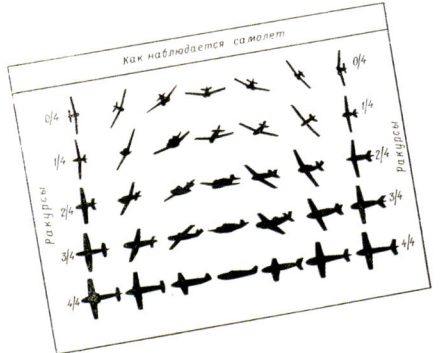

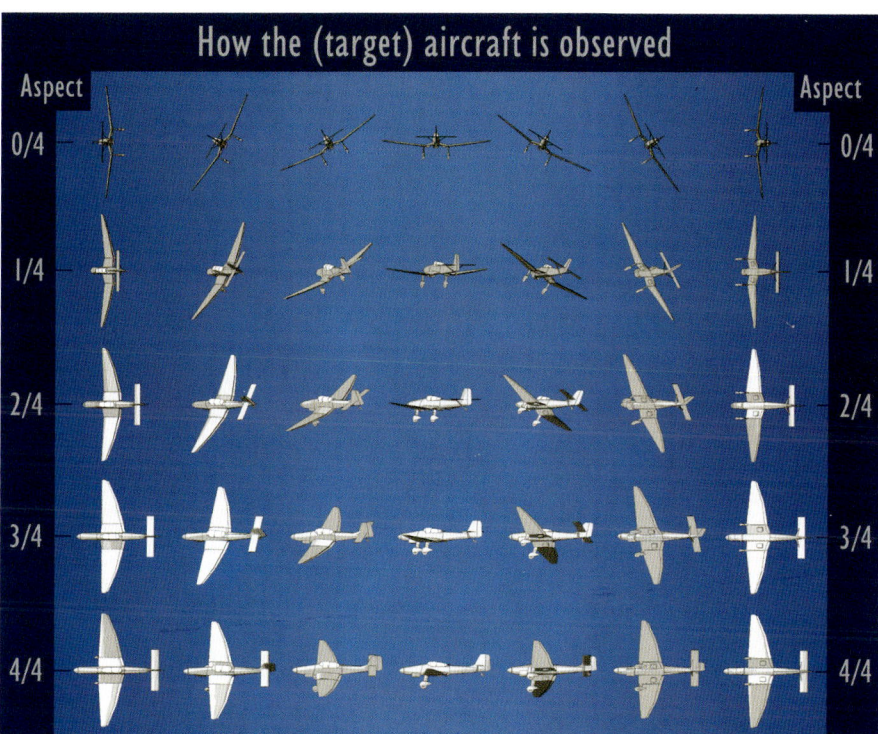

How the (target) aircraft is observed

Aspect 0/4 · 1/4 · 2/4 · 3/4 · 4/4

attacking fighter was usually undetected right up to the moment of commencing fire, and it increased the hit probability if the pilot opted to fire at minimal range. With such an attack on a Ju87 or fighter, the attacking fighter remained completely in dead space (i.e., outside the cone of fire of the enemy aircraft's guns). However, on the negative side, this approach put the fighter directly in the prop wash of the enemy aircraft, the turbulence of which complicated the execution of aimed fire. It demanded outstanding piloting technique during the actual attack, and no less during the pullout.

Attacking dive bombers head on, as a rule, was less successful and more dangerous for the attacker himself. To begin with, aiming was difficult, as the visual projection of the target was relatively small. Then, the attacking fighter usually had to cease fire at the most favorable range, in order to avoid collision. If a forward hemisphere attack on bombers was initiated, it was more effective to attack from the front and side at a relative course angle of 1/4 to 2/4. This significantly raised the probability of a hit in vulnerable places on the enemy aircraft, as the visual projection for this was much better.

From the other side, it was difficult for the enemy's defensive gunner to conduct aimed fire, given the fact that the entire attack occurred mostly in his *dead space*. Nonetheless, the one substantial deficiency of this attack was that the fighter exited the engagement to the rear at a minimal altitude above the bomber, thereby separating from the bomber at a greater speed and complicating the set-up of a follow-on attack. If, to compensate for this, a fighter pilot were to pull up from the attack in the direction of flight of the bomber, he would place himself under aimed fire of the Junkers' rear gunner.

When appropriate, an attack from behind and below could also be employed against Ju87 bombers and Bf110 fighters. Since these types did not have a lower gunner, this method was

relatively safe. Not only was the attack initiated outside of the enemy's zone of fire, but the exit path was also through *dead space*. It allowed for aimed fire into the enemy aircraft's vulnerable places because the target's visual projection was sufficiently complete. In addition, thanks to the attacking fighter's pull-out upward onto the target's flightpath, this method allowed for a relatively quick second attack. The fighter did not become greatly separated, visually or spatially, from the target aircraft. Nonetheless, this profile also had a shortcoming: since it reduced the speed of the attacking fighter; he was in a vulnerable position in the event of a sudden attack from the enemy's fighter escort.

During the set-up of a maneuver for an attack, all these nuances had to be calculated literally in an instant. The position of the sun and the cloud condition had to be simultaneously and reflexively considered. One had to check location on the terrain outside and on the map inside. The location and displacement of friendlies had to be fixed relative to these. One had to keep track of elapsed time, fuel remaining, and constantly rotate one's head, examining the surrounding air space. The smallest distant dot in the sky could turn into an attacking enemy fighter within an instant. All of these habits and subtleties were acquired and internalized only with experience. The enemy, in his own turn, always attempted to interfere with the acquisition of this experience.

The successful approach to an attack was only half the battle. The second (and not less important for one's life) was a correct, or at least competent, departure. Here, an upward arch or steep climb was most often employed. This was true in all regimes—solo, pairs, or as part of a coordinated group. The pullout gave one the altitude superiority favorable to a follow-on attack. It was also good in that it permitted one to observe the target, which usually remained in front and below.

Fine portrait of a VVS fighter pilot: Mladshiy Leytenant Semen Belkin, seen here later in the war in the cockpit of a Yak-3.

As a rule, after the attack on a single bomber (He111, Ju88, etc.), the pullout was made forward and upward, with a combat turn or steep climb. A variation included the same initial pullout, followed smartly by a surge forward and somewhat to the side. A further altitude-gaining climb could then be made later on course.

When attacking a formation of bombers, the pullout was executed away from the formation. It was extremely undesirable to pass above the formation because of the great risk presented by the concentration of fire from the entire formation's upper defensive guns. If the fighter suddenly found itself inside the formation, then it should break away with a steep dive, tracing a path downward and forward. This would be followed by an altitude-recovery pullout, and steep climb or combat turn. On exiting the formation, the rapid angle rate change complicated aimed fire for the bombers' lower gunners and nose gunners.

It was also permitted to depart via a sharp turn to the outside, away from the bomber formation through the *dead space*. The turn could then be continued back toward the formation, at a range of 600-700 meters (650–760 yards) while adding a climb component to gain altitude. This variation was considered to be a viable method to gain the enemy gunners' *dead space*, but justified only if an accurate assessment of the enemy bomber's forward speed could be made.

Irrespective of the means of departure from an engagement, the Yak pilot should not, under any circumstances, permit his airspeed to fall below 300-350 kph (160–190 knots). He should also be aware that enemy hunters most often attacked fighters from the rear at small approach angles.

Soviet fighter pilots most often used three basic methods to disengage from enemy fighter attacks, wherein the enemy was some 150-200 meters (160-220 yards) distant:

1. Sharp climbing pullout. In this case it was often difficult for the enemy fighter to mimic the Yak's maneuver. While the danger existed that a Messer could somehow mimic the Yak's maneuver, the combination of

close range and great speeds gave a high probability that the enemy would end up ahead and below. A sharp upward pullout, combined with *cranking in* a large bank while climbing, ensured a sudden departure from enemy fire while, at the same time, permitting the pilot to observe the Messer's reactive maneuver. Thus the tables could be turned: The hunted could exploit his newly gained altitude superiority, by pouncing from above on an enemy who was now in the undesirable forward, downward position.

2. Sharp slipping with a dive. Using this departure profile, the aircraft could build up sufficient velocity for transition into an altitude-regaining steep climb, or into a combat turn. The maneuver itself was reliable enough to get out from under enemy fire. Then, as the aircraft's velocity increased to a more favorable state, the pilot gained the opportunity to observe enemy's the subsequent maneuver. He could subsequently select for himself the moment for counterattack.

3. Sharp turn toward the attacker, sometimes with a drop beneath him and subsequent transition to gaining altitude by steep climb. This method permitted one to better observe the reactive maneuver of the enemy. It gave the greatest altitude gain in comparison to other methods. The deficiency of this method was the fact that, at the moment of sharp turn the Yak was, for some period of time, in the sights of the attacker. More experienced pilots used this risky method (and more often in especially critical situations). We note that this *cat's lunge* method, competently applied, saved the life of I. V. Fedorov on more than one occasion.

But there was no time to contemplate all of this during air combat. Everything should be well thought out, mastered, and reinforced while still on the ground and in training, so that it could be executed reflexively during rapidly unfolding battle. The real examiner in the air was an experienced and powerful enemy, who did not forgive mistakes and blunders.

In the Ground Attack Role Again

Despite the fact that the enemy was slinking away to the south, aerial engagements still occurred constantly. The town Dzhankoy was liberated from the Germans on 10 April, 1944.

Future Hero of the Soviet Union Aleksandr Tishchenko showed himself once again to be a talented leader in performing fighter ground-attack missions. The modest text of the summary for 11 April speaks eloquently to this:

At 1430-1530, six Yak-9s of 812th IAP and four Yak-9s of 291st IAP, together with four Yak-9s of 278th IAD, the group commanded by Kapitan Tishchenko, a squadron commander from 812th IAP, attacked the enemy airfield at Sarabuz. They executed a single attack on the aircraft located in revetments. As a result, the pilots of 291st IAP set on fire two Ju52s, and the pilots of 812th IAP set on fire three Ju52s. Five Ju52s were set on fire altogether in the raid.

At 1737-1850, four Yak-9s of 812th IAP, four Yak-9s of 291st IAP, and four Yak-9s of 278th IAD, the group commanded by Kapitan Tishchenko, a squadron commander from 812th IAP, attacked the enemy airfield at Sarabuz. The group executed two attacks on the aircraft located in revetments. As a result of this, the pilots of 291st IAP set on fire three He111s. The pilots of 812th IAP, in the cover group, supported the strafing actions of the strike group and photographed the results of the raid. The group did not suffer any losses.

Earlier, in the first half of the day, regiment commander Ivan Popov shot down an Fw190 west of Dzhankoy. Then, at noon, Mladshiy Leytenant Semen Belkin and Kapitan Yegor Ankudinov each shot down a Bf109 in the area of the Sivash crossing site.

On Wednesday, 12 April, the division's regiments were repositioned, ironically enough, to Rayzendorf airfield. The regiment lost two pilots and their aircraft in air combat on this day: flight commander Leytenant Petr Peskarev in a Yak-9T and Mladshiy Leytenant Yuriy Kureyev in a Yak-1 (No. 45138). These were heavy losses for the 812th IAP. The deputy regiment commander for VSS [*vozdushno-strelkovaya sluzhba* – aerial gunnery], Mayor Tarasov, briefed them on the combat mission:

Four fighters will cover the ground forces in the area of Biyuk-Onlar, Kiyabok. The flight altitude will be 4,000–4,500 meters (13,100–14,750 feet). Upon encountering enemy fighters, use surprise in the first attack. Do not engage in combat with an enemy superior in numbers. Upon coming into the zone of antiaircraft fire, get out of the zone of fire using the appropriate maneuver. The primary landing field will be Kirk-Ishun, alternate - Veseloye.

Mladshiy Leytenant Yuriy Mikhaylovich Kureyev, a graduate of Armavir Military Pilot School, came to the regiment in October 1943 from the 13th ZIAP. During his 812th IAP service he flew 44 combat sorties and conducted 12 aerial engagements in which he shot down one aircraft in the air and destroyed two enemy aircraft on the ground. He died at the age of 21.

Leytenant Petr Georgiyevich Peskarev, a graduate of Novosibirsk Military Pilot School, arrived in the regiment in July 1943. He had flown 128 combat sorties, engaging the enemy 27 times in the air. He shot down eight enemy aircraft and destroyed a further two on the ground. The fate of this pilot unfolded in an unusual manner. He arrived in the regiment as the pilot of the U-2, but dreamt to fly in Yaks. He accomplished his dream. Petr transitioned to fighters and in the fall of 1943 began to fly in the squadron of Aleksey Mashenkin. He fought his first aerial combat during at that time in the skies of the Donbas. Petr did not manage to celebrate his 23rd birthday; he died a fighter pilot.

At the end of the day, the regiment headquarters wrote:

The four fighters, led by Mayor Tarasov, was covering ground forces in the area of Biyuk-Onlar. At 1750 at an altitude of 4,200 meters (13,750 feet), they were suddenly attacked out of the sun by two Bf109s, cutting off the flight wingman, Leytenant Peskarev. The pilot was wounded in the first pass and his aircraft was damaged. When the pilot bailed out, his parachute canopy became entangled in the static lines and he was killed. His aircraft burned near Tashly Konrat. The flight now entered the battle dispersed, and in the second pass the two Bf109s shot up the aircraft of Mladshiy Leytenant Kureyev from above and behind, wounding the pilot. Kureyev began to evade pursuit with a glide. Then he pulled up sharply. His damaged control cables broke. The aircraft fell in the area of Tashly Konrat and burned. The pilot was critically wounded and died two hours later. He was buried in Tashly Konrat.

The pilots of the 812th were fighting against the enemy's most potent *experten*. Leutnant Walter Wolfrum of 5./JG52 gained his 65th and 66th victories at this time, having shot down two of the regiment's fighters (which he identified as Yak 7s).

But as they say, "war is war," wherein the misfortunes of loss go right along with the joys of victory. In war, as in ordinary life, outwardly insignificant events can become nonetheless memorable events. For just a single day (Thursday, 13 April) the regiment was based on the just-liberated Sarabuz airfield. Such movements of a whole regiment were something to remember indeed. Though this day is remembered more by the regiment's veterans because of a funny event that occurred on the airfield. Regiment personnel would whisper about this to each other with a smile until Victory Day itself. Podpolkovnik (retired) Nikolay Pavlovich Pechenin, a veteran of the 812th IAP, told this tragic-comic story to the authors:

In the spring of 1944, at Sarabuz airfield (now the settlement of Gvardeyskoye), a mechanic was warming an engine and, it seems, felt the need to relieve himself. One cannot think of anything more stupid than to leave the cockpit of a fighter plane with the engine running at low rpm. But he got out of the cockpit and found a secluded spot nearby where he could answer nature's call. The throttle lever, that is the fuel control lever, began to incline forward under the influence of vibration, and the propeller revolutions began to increase. Finally, at some speed of propeller rotation the brake shoes [wheel chocks–ed.] were deformed (they let go in the dirt), and the aircraft, having now been set free, began independent movement. The mechanic, seeing this, with his pants around his ankles, was chasing after the airplane, shouting, 'Hey, where are you going? Come back here!' The aircraft ignored his cries and began to career about the airfield, but not for long. One of its main gear fell into a hole and the airplane began rotating around that spot. How could it be stopped? Wait until it ran out of fuel? We did not have a 'mindless daredevil' in the regiment who was prepared to risk being struck by the spinning propeller.

Then a young girl showed up, the regiment mail carrier. Before this she had completed ShMAS [shkola mladshikh aviaspetsialistov—school for junior aviation specialists] and had the qualification of an engine mechanic. Choosing the right moment, she jumped onto the rear edge of the right portion of the wing, climbed into the open cockpit, and pulled the ignition switch back to the 'O' position. The engine went silent. Everything was saved. The young girl was awarded the medal 'For Courage.' And the mechanic was punished. He was reminded of this episode for a long time, when they said to him, 'You're the one who had a runaway airplane while taking a 'dump'!'

On the following day, the division's regiments were relocated to the Sevastopol area. The division command and control element together with the 812th IAP displaced to Adzhi-Bulat airfield (now Uglovoye), the 402nd IAP went to the famous Kacha airfield, while the 291st IAP was based at Alma-Tamak airfield. In pushing the enemy from the Crimean peninsula, Soviet ground forces, in concert with the VVS, forced the enemy to concentrate practically his entire remaining aviation assets at a single airfield located on Cape Khersones. Since the corps' primary opponent (II/JG52) was part of this contingent, the division headquarters decided to

conduct a powerful strike the following morning, drawing on two of its regiments. At 1600, the entire personnel component of the 812th IAP was assembled. In the presence of the chief of staff of the 265th IAD and the leadership of the 402nd IAP, Mayor Popov presented the mission to his pilots:

Tomorrow, 15 April, we will fly a strike on Khersones airfield with two regiments. Takeoff is at 0700. The sequence of takeoff is 3rd, 1st, 2nd Squadrons. The flight to the target will be in squadron columns. 402nd Regiment, led by its commander, will be at the distance of sight. The division commander, Polkovnik Koryagin, is leading the overall column. He will be flying in our regiment's 3d Squadron combat formation. Fedorov's squadron will suppress antiaircraft assets.[82]

The command element of 265th IAD also planned to participate in the strike. On Saturday, 15 April, 812th Regiment aircraft began to take off before 0700. Forming up and departure on course to the target were conducted in complete radio silence. Several minutes later, the 402nd Regiment lifted off from Kacha airfield and took its position in the column to the rear of the 2nd Squadron of the 812th IAP. The flight went out over the sea along the coast. With Sevastopol falling behind on the left, passing between Sevastopol and Kamyshevaya, the two regiments of Soviet fighters arrived on a proper heading to attack the enemy aircraft revetments. Meanwhile, Starshiy Leytenant Fedorov's 2nd Squadron set about to accomplish its flak suppression mission. Here is how this attack progressed as recalled by the squadron commander:

The squadron fanned out in pairs and began to dive on the antiaircraft crews. Nikolay Sukhorukov and I attacked a battery located on the opposite side of the airfield. Its crew was firing at us. A duel began. I dove on the gun that was firing on me. The fiery tracers of the shells came

Female armorers of the 812th Fighter Regiment.

Left: M. S. Shcheglova and an unidentified friend.
Right: P. Tishko with an unidentified friend.

812th IAP armorers from left to right: Aleksandra Demidova, Klavdiya Vasilyeva, Nina Kudryasheva, and Klavdiya Yashina. In the war the women's labor was on a par with the men's. But even in such a difficult time, the young girls remained sweet and charming.

M. S. Shcheglova recalls:

"The armorers worked a great deal. When combat duty came along, we got up at 0400 and went to the airfield. There were times when we did not get breakfast. Later they delivered breakfast right to the revetments. We accompanied and met the airplanes, loaded the weapons, and charged the belts. We drove the cartridges in with a small machine and seated them with a small wooden mallet. We hung bombs under the fighters, and only the engineer handled the fuses."

up to meet me. While I was aiming I was unable to maneuver, and the antiaircraft gun could hit me head on. Then the long-awaited moment arrived—I could see the gun clearly in the crosshairs of my sight. I was now sure that I would not miss. I fired a long burst from my 37mm cannon and, as the range closed, from all my weapons. I made a left combat turn out of the dive and watched the explosions of shells in the battery position. This was Kolya Sukhorukov letting go. The battery was silent. We went out over the sea and then back to our own airfield. All the crews of both regiments returned home. That same day the corps commander, General Savitskiy, expressed his thanks to all the air crews who participated in the raid on Khersones airfield.[83]

A bit later, at 1230-1310, eight Yak-9s from the 291st IAD (led by Mayor Petr Ovchinnikov), together with four Yak-9s from the 812th IAP (led by Starshiy Leytenant Aleksey Mashenkin) flew a second strike on the airfield. At 1340, Mashenkin shot down an Fw190 in air combat directly over Sevastopol. Two hours later, Mayor Pavel Tarasov and Mladshiy Leytenant Ivan Stryuk distinguished themselves by destroying a Bf109 and an Fw190 (respectively) over the scenic outskirts of the city. The next day, 17 April, Mayor Ivan Popov successfully attacked a Bf110 in the area of 6th Versta airstrip, shooting it down with his Yak's 37mm cannon at 1710.

On Wednesday, 19 April, the Yaks of the 812th launched their next strafing attack, this time against the Luftwaffe base at 6th Versta. The raid, which played out over Cape Fiolent at 1630, preceded an aerial engagement witnessed by friendlies on the ground. The Guardsmen of the 6th Tank Brigade watched with delight. First, at 1635 a burning Bf109 shot down by regiment commander Popov splashed into the sea. It was followed five minutes later by an out-of-control Fw190, the victim of Leytenant Sergey

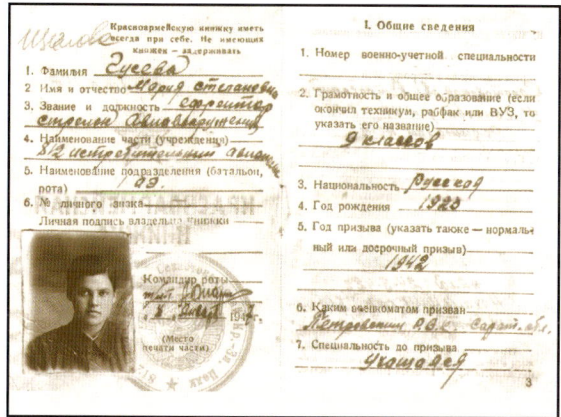

Red Army service booklet of armorer Private M. S. Shcheglova (nee Guseva). The document states that she was in the Army from 1942. Her duty position was gunner-aviation armorer of 2nd Squadron, 812th IAP.

Armorer of the 2nd Squadron, 812th IAP. Mariya Stepanovna Shcheglova

Always and everywhere are hypocrites who see in every person a criminal, or everywhere "moral breakdown with undermining of discipline" caused by the presence in the forces of females. These people judge others against their own personal world view which, as a rule, is not particularly well grounded. Thousands and thousands of young women voluntarily went to the front and many of them died. And it never occurred to some of the "fighters for a moral foundation" what motivated them. War for the front-line soldier was first of all hellish daily labor, frequently in the most difficult conditions. War is tough on everyone, but it was many times more difficult for young girls, since they tried not to fall behind the men in this completely un-feminine endeavor. Indeed, war did not have a feminine side, but the "soldiers in skirts" did not want to be inferior to the men, having voluntarily hoisted onto their delicate shoulders the burden of this very war. Mariya Stepanovna Shcheglov (nee Guseva), who passed through the difficult combat path from the Kuban to Berlin with the 812th IAP remembers:

"I was born on 6 November 1923, but, since our Komsomol group was sent as volunteers to the front, they wrote down my birth month as July to "advance" my age just a little bit. I went to the front from my native town, Petrovsk of Saratov oblast. By the time the war began I had completed 9th grade, and in 1942 they sent me with my friend to the Volga School for junior aviation specialists (ShMAS). There we studied for approximately three months and were turned out with the "aerial gunnery" specialty. I generally fired well—I had two "Voroshilov sharpshooter" badges. In school we flew on the U-2 aircraft, and at the front were supposed to fly in Shturmoviks. After completing ShMAS in the summer of 1942, they sent me to the Southwest Front. But we got only to the area of Staryy Oskol, where there was heavy fighting. Our train was bombed and many died. The rest were formed in a group and sent to North Caucasus. There I entered fighter aviation, and in the Kuban the 812th IAP. I became an armaments technician. I had to master the ShVAK cannon and the Berezin synchronized machine gun, and in school we had studied the ShKAS machine gun. There were 12 of us girls in the regiment. It was my duty to clean, prepare, and load the machine gun; prepare the ammunition, load it into the cartridge boxes, and attach them to the cannon and machine gun. Since I was a young girl and lacked the physical strength, the entire ground crew helped me to remove the weapons from the aircraft: the senior mechanic, engine mechanic, and instrument repairman. The mechanic charged the weapon and test-fired it. If the synchronizer functioned improperly and the propeller was damaged—the mechanic changed it. Immediately before the aircraft was released for a combat sortie, the squadron engineer was with us. The engineer also made the decision to remove weapons from the aircraft. If the aircraft made several sorties in a day and the weapons were used all the time, then by all means we had to remove the weapons for inspection. If one or two sorties were flown and the weapons were not fired– the decision to remove them from the aircraft was up to an engineer. After combat sorties we first set up a shelter in the revetment, then cleaned, wiped with gasoline, and blindly assembled the weapons, since we did not have any battery-powered lamps, and it was forbidden to use a fire."

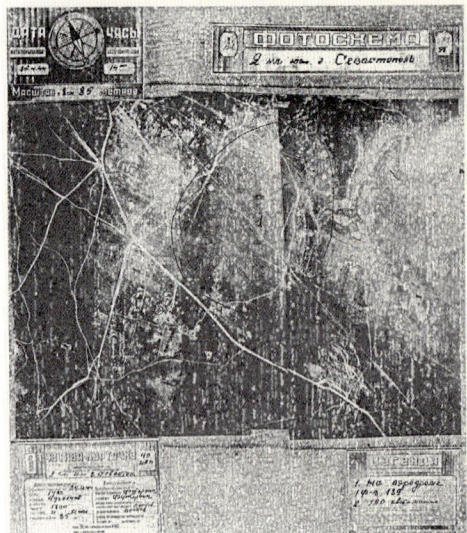

15 April 1944 airfield 2 km south of Sevastopol.

Original scale: 1 cm = 85 m.

Altitude: 1800 m

Legend:
1. 1 Fw189 on airfield

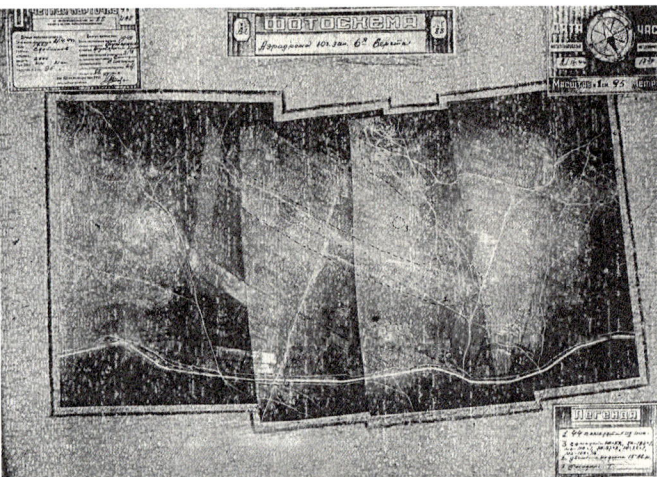

1720, 21 April 1944 over the airfield southwest of 6th Versta.
Original scale: 1 cm = 95 meters. Altitude: 2000 m
Legend:
1. 44 aircraft (3 Ju52, 1 Hs126, 1 Bf110, 2 Ju87, 1 Ju88, 36 Bf109)
2. Movement of 15 trucks on road
3. Landing T.

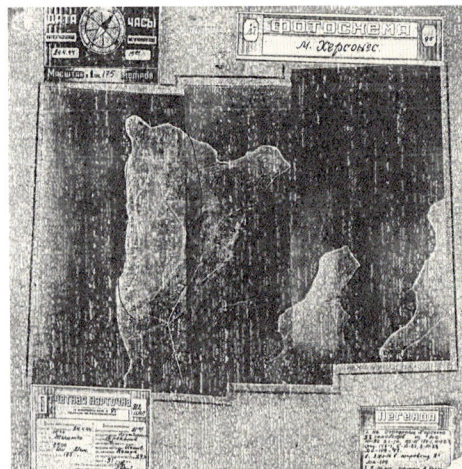

Original scale: 1 cm = 175 m

Altitude: 3500 m

Legend:
1. 58 aircraft on Khersones airfield (2 Ju90, 1 Fw189, 3 Ju52, 1 Fi156, 6 Ju87, 3 Ju88 and 42 Bf109)
2. 2 He111 escorted by 2 Bf109;
3. 2 self-propelled barges.

Kapitan A. Tishchenko, 812th IAP at 1500, 24 April 1944 over Cape Khersones airfield.

Vasilevskiy's guns. The result of the strafing attack itself, which was executed between 1830 and 1930, was five enemy aircraft burning on the ground: Ivan Fedorov (two Ju87s), Ivan Popov, Pavel Tarasov, and Ivan Stryuk (one Ju52 each).

In response to these attacks on their airfields at Khersones and 6th Versta, the Germans also attacked the airfields of the 265th IAD's regiments. The losses, although minimal militarily, had a powerful impact on regiment personnel.

On Thursday, 20 April, an Fw190's bomb detonated right where technicians were working at a fighter revetment on Adzhi-Bulat airfield. It took the lives of 12-year-old Vasya Ivushkin and his mentor, engine mechanic Starshiy Serzhant Ivan Grebnev.

Many warm words were spoken about this pair. Picked up on Gulyay Polye airfield, this former orphanage resident helped everyone, pilots and mechanics alike, warming everyone's heart with his childish openness and reminders of peacetime life. He was the *son of the regiment*, everyone's favorite.

Under constant pressure from the fighters of General Ye. Ya. Savitskiy's 3rd IAK and Polkovnik B.A. Sidnev's 6th GIAD, the Luftwaffe strengthened its patrolling over its two remaining Crimean airfields. But, in spite of this, the attacks on Khersones continued. Nonetheless, the Focke-Wulfs from the ground-attack staffeln, escorted by the Bf109s of JG52, continued to delay the advancing Red Army forces with unrelenting ferocity. P. V. Korneyev, a veteran of the 812th, recalls:

> *The bombing of the airfields in the Crimea was very heavy. First the bombers appeared and dropped their*

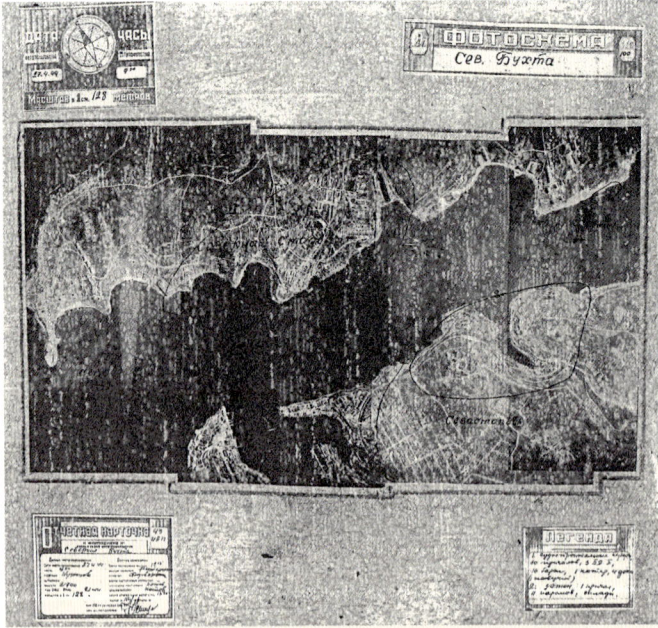

0930, 27 April 1944 over the North Bay in the Sevastopol area.
Original scale: 1 cm = 128 m. Altitude: 2700 m
Legend:
1. Shipyards, 30 berths, 16 barges, 1 cutter, 4 docks (1 floating)
2. Sunk: 1 berth, 11 ferries, warehouse.

bombs, and right behind them came the Focke-Wulfs, strafing our airfield. It was a powerful aircraft with potent armaments. The strafing of an airfield is more frightening than bombing, because the bomber releases his bombs and where they fall - who knows. But during a strafing attack, the pilot is shooting at you. It is a very unpleasant feeling. It continues along these lines: a pair strafes you and then pulls out. Another pair or even four of them come right behind the first, and this merry-go-round continues. First they shoot up the antiaircraft positions. The revetments are your only protection. Frequently their ships at sea shelled us. They approached close in to shore, put out a smoke screen, and then opened up on us. Perhaps they did not know where they were shooting, but the main thing was that they were shooting. They fired quickly and then departed.

Although greatly reduced in number, Luftwaffe aircraft in this area continued to keep the entire fighter aviation force of the 8th Air Army under pressure. Nonetheless, RKKA ground forces still witnessed, and felt, the air cover. The commander of the 30th Guards Mortar Brigade, Guards Polkovnik Chernyak, in his "Testimonial concerning the cover by fighters of the 812th Fighter Aviation Regiment for combat formations from 1 through 20 April 1944," wrote:

The fighter pilots of the 812th Fighter Aviation Regiment, covering our firing positions, have demonstrated courage, valor, and mastery in aerial engagements with enemy aviation. They have fought skillfully, readily accepting aerial combat, even when the enemy has been superior in strength. We consider the pilots of the 812th Fighter Aviation Regiment to be full masters of the Crimean skies, who support our work against enemy forces from the air.

The 812th IAP exchanged blows with the Luftwaffe again on 21 April. Enemy fighter patrols shot down the Yak-9 (No. 1066) of Mladshiy Leytenant Ivan Stryuk. Mayor Popov, in full view of the artillerymen of 14th Tank Destroyer Regiment, shot down an Fw190 in the area east of Khersones, his 15th personal victory. Mladshiy Leytenant Nikolay Sukhorukov, along with Mayor Pavel Tarasov also downed an Fw190 each at 1450, practically simultaneously with the regiment commander's victory. This was Tarasov's 29th personal victory.

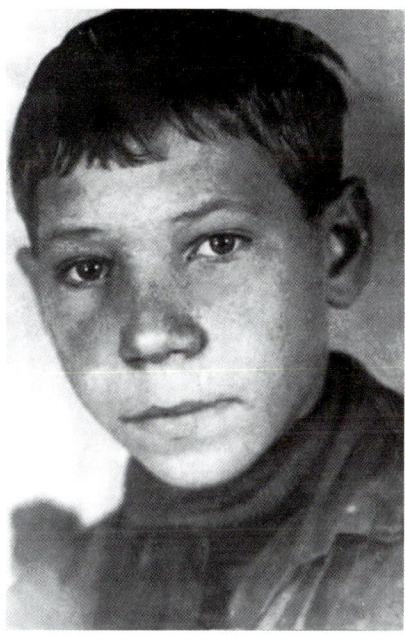

812th IAP ward and "son of the regiment", Vasya Ivushkin. He was killed in Crimea during a strafing attack on Adzhi-Bulat airfield by a single Fw190.

Tablet with the names of fallen soldiers, buried in the village of Adzhi-Bulat (memorial complex). Among the names is Vasya Ivushkin, a 12-year-old soldier of the 812th IAP.

Through the following day, Saturday the 22nd of April, the pilots of the 812th Regiment also shot down three Fw190s and damaged another. Kapitan Yegor Ankudinov gained his 10th personal victory at 1030, shooting down a Focke-Wulf over Sevastopol. One of the other victories of the day belonged to Fedorov. His logbook carries a routine laconic, but eloquent, entry about the victory:

"Mission accomplished. Drove one Fw190 into the sea. Aircraft and pilot perished."

Squadron commander Aleksey Mashenkin, after an enforced break, continued to regain his form. An Fw190 fell to his cannon fire at 1930 in the Khersones area. Kapitan Tishchenko managed to down a Focke-Wulf as well.

The next morning, Sunday, was not a happy occasion for the enemy at 6th Versta airfield. Before 0700 the 812th made a *friendly visit*, strafing four Ju52s to destruction. I. Fedorov, N. Sukhorukov, A. Mashenkin and L. Sivko were the outstanding pilots in this effort.

Monday, 24 April arrived, and once again the strafing of an airfield was the business of the day. This time it would be Khersones' turn. A group of fighters from the 402nd and 812th regiments, under the overall command of division commander Polkovnik Koryagin, reached the target area. A participant in this attack, Aleksandr Tishchenko, recalls:

When the enemy airfield appeared, Mayor Popov commanded, 'Mashenkin—southern revetment, Tishchenko—western. I will attack the northern.' One after the other, eight fighters surged downward, dropping their ordnance. Scores of explosions erupted over the airfield and fires broke out in several places.[84]

Once again regiment commander Popov showed his pilots, by his example, how to beat the enemy. Here he shot down two Fw190s, as witnessed by the infantrymen of the 30th Mortar Regiment, and claimed as destroyed an Fw200 *Kondor* at the airfield. According to archival documents of the regiments and divisions of the 8th Air Army, it is stated that the Luftwaffe used Fw200 in the Crimea. Losses of these planes are actually recorded therein. However, known Luftwaffe data contradict this information. Whereas other heavy cargo aircraft, such as the Me323 and the Italian-built four-engined Piaggio P.108B, were in

Luftwaffe use here. For example, on 17 April 1944 O. Fw. Helm, the pilot of P.108 (J4+AH) reported about his flight: "On the way back from Sevastopol to Galati we were carrying 85 heavily-wounded soldiers". It is thus possible that it was a P.108, mistakenly identified as an Fw200, that was attacked at Khersones.

Mayor Tarasov shot down a Messer over the Novyye Shuli area on this same day. His Yak-9 was damaged and he received a superficial wound during the battle. However, in shooting down this Bf109, he became the first in the corps to attain 30 victories.

Personnel changes took place throughout the 3rd IAK at the beginning of May 1944. Hero of the Soviet Union Mayor Pavel Tarasov, deputy regiment commander for aerial gunnery service, was appointed interim commander of the 274th IAP of the 278th IAD. In the ranks of this regiment he shot down an Fw190 south of Bartenyevka. This was his 31st and final victory of the front lines of the Great Patriotic War.

Sometime before 1000 on 24 April, Kapitan Aleksandr Tishchenko shot down a Bf109, thus reaching the 10 personal victories plateau. Later, at 1815, he added another Messer to his tally. That evening, Kapitan Yegor Ankudinov, not one to lag behind his combat comrades, shot down a Messer as well. This was the 812th Regiment navigator's 11th personal victory.

On the following day, while escorting an Il-2 artillery spotter, Mladshiy Leytenant Konstantin Veselov's Yak-9 was damaged in a group engagement with two Bf109s and four Fw190s. During the subsequent emergency landing at the airfield, with only one main landing gear fully deployed, the aircraft somersaulted and caught fire. The pilot received burns to his face and hands and was taken to the hospital. He died from his wounds on 7 May.

The Red Army kept up the pressure to evict the German forces from the Crimean peninsula. Summaries received from the division's reconnaissance and combat sorties indicated diminishing numbers of German aircraft on Khersones airfield.

At the end of April, the 265th IAD headquarters reported to the corps headquarters about the destruction of 52 Bf109s, 31 Fw190s, 20 Ju87s, and two Bf110s. Of these, the 812th IAP claimed 17 Fw190s, nine Bf109s, two Ju87s, and one Bf110. An additional eight Ju87s, 10 Ju52s, and one Fw200 [discussed above] were set on fire in airfield attacks, while eight Fw190s and two Ju87s were damaged. The bulk of these enemy aircraft destroyed on the ground was also credited to the 812th IAP.

The 402nd IAP lost Leytenant Shamil Abdrashitov on Thursday, 4 May 1944. Returning from an airfield strafing run, four Yaks were attacked by a single Fw190. Abdrashitov's aircraft was damaged, went into a spin, and fell into the sea. Although he managed to bail out and land in the sea, searches for the pilot came up empty. In fact a U-2 [Po-2—ed.] aircraft, with two 402nd Regiment pilots (Anatoliy Filonov and Semen Denisov) onboard, was sent out to search for Abdrashitov on 6 May. It was attacked and shot down by a fighter that sortied from Khersones airfield. This aircraft marked the 114th victory for Oberleutnant Helmut Lipfert, the *experte* commander of 6./JG52. Both pilots in this U-2 perished in the encounter. They were the division's last pilot losses in the course of the liberation of Crimea.

Mayor Popov achieved his 18th victory at noon on 5 May in the Cape Khersones area. The victim this time was a Bf109. The 168th Artillery Regiment, the headquarters of which gave its confirmation, observed the aerial battle. Here is an excerpt from the operational summary:

Ten Yak-9s, two Yak-1s, and two nine-ship formations B-3s [lend-lease Boston bombers—ed.] were operating along the southern shore of Northern Bay at the following altitudes: nine bombers at 4,500 meters; nine more at 3,200 meters (14,750 and 10,500 feet respectively).[85] At 1228, at an altitude of 3,200 meters, on the return leg, two Fw190s and a Bf109 attempted to attack the B-3s. Fending off the attack of the enemy fighters in a turn, Mayor Popov shot down one Bf109. With lowered main gear, the enemy aircraft fell near the shore in the area of Khersones. At 1232, two Fw190s attacked a B-3 from long range. Mayor Popov and Fedorov drove the Fw190s away. An Fw190 and a Bf109 repeatedly attempted to attack, but all the attacks were repulsed in time. Heavy antiaircraft fires came up from the port area. Ammunition expended: OKB-16—18 [37mm cannon], ShVAK—120 [20 mm cannon], UBS—215 [.50 caliber].

Kapitan Yegor Ankudinov and Mladshiy Leytenant Semen Belkin also distinguished themselves; each downed a single Fw190 some four hours later.

At this time, regiment headquarters received a dispatch from Mayor Tsiban, the 265th IAD chief of reconnaissance, about the actions of enemy aviation during 2, 3, and 4 May. It confirmed the continued activity of the Luftwaffe in the general area of Cape Khersones and Sevastopol:

According to the data from aerial reconnaissance in the period 1700 to 1900, over the course of 4 May 1944 the enemy has intensively undertaken the loading of infantry on steamers and barges in Kazachya Bay and Kamyshevaya Bay. Enemy fighters have operated actively to cover the bays and lines of movement of the ships with troops and equipment. Over the course of 4 May 1944, the fighters of the 402nd IAP shot down three Fw190s in aerial combat. As is normal, our ground forces brought confirmation to us regarding two downed Fw190s. Over the course of the last period, Fw190 fighters are continuing to be employed by the enemy as light bombers and strafers against our ground forces and basing airfields. Conclusions: the enemy continues to evacuate his troops and equipment from Sevastopol. The remaining portion of the best fighters continue actively to cover their forces and facilities, to counter our aviation.

On the following day Ivan Fedorov, in a Yak-9, downed the Bf109G of Feldwebel Hermann Evers (7./JG52) in aerial combat over the Kacha village area.[86] The German aircraft exploded in midair. This victory had some unique qualities as Fedorov recalls:

I recall the takeoff on the 6th of May. On this day, the command post very successfully vectored Sukhorukov and me to a pair of Messers, but during the attack something unexpected happened. I already had the wingman steady in my sight when suddenly—this had not happened before—oil was pouring over my forward armored glass. The target almost disappeared from the crosshairs and I almost pulled out of the attack to avoid accidental collision with the enemy aircraft. But the Messer was so close! And though I could barely see the Messerschmitt I did not turn away from the target. I squeezed the firing trigger and immediately pulled sharply left to avoid a collision (the range to the target was about 20 meters). The Messer began burning and several seconds later blew up, falling in pieces. Parts of this airplane fell near the central portion of Kacha Aviation School. If you had told me something like this would happen four years earlier, when I was a cadet at this school, would I have believed it?[87]

The war was being fought not only in the air, but also on the ground. An aircraft mechanic in the 2nd Squadron, Starshina Kuzma Petrovich Aleshin, recalls how on Sunday, 7 May, his friend Mladshiy Military Technician Fedor Alekseyevich Sapozhnikov died at the airfield:

This was in Crimea. We were conducting preventive maintenance on our aircraft. I shouted to my comrade Fedor Sapozhnikov, 'Break time!' We went out of our revetment. Since our revetments were close, we were standing not too far away and smoking cigarettes. We were standing and talking, when suddenly, out of nowhere, we heard the whistling of a falling bomb. We immediately ran to our revetments, where there were shelters, but did not make it before the explosion came. If Fedya Sapozhnikov had not run, but remained in place, the bomb would not have caught him. This was the first heavy loss I experienced.

On this same Sunday, after a 90-minute artillery barrage, the storming of the fortified Sevastopol region commenced. By the end of the day, portions of the 51st Army had driven the Germans from Sapun Heights (Sapun Gora) just above the city proper.

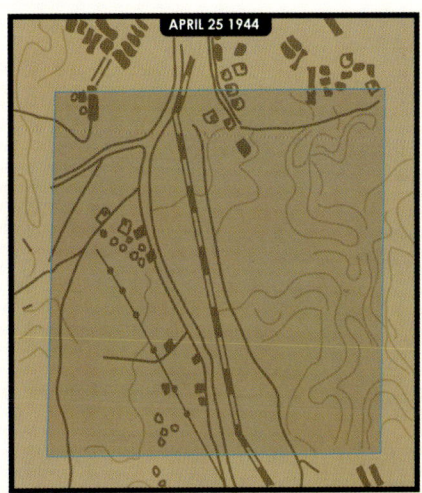

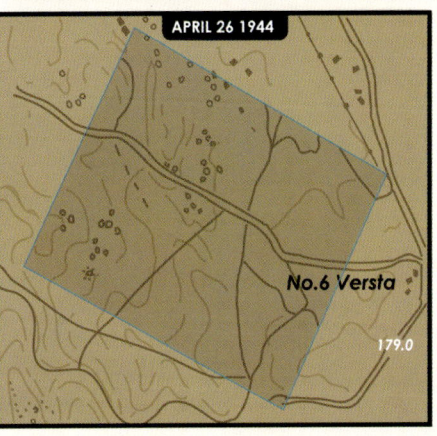

Illustrations based on wartime black and white sketches. Such schematics, derived from the detailed examiniation and overlay of tactical aerial reconnaissance photographs (see page 106), were used extensively as "pilot quick identification" aids in the planning and execution of attacks on enemy airfields and other assets.

Top, the airfield 2 km south of Sevastopol; immediately above, 6th Versta airfield; and below, two separate views on Cape Khersones showing its various airfields, bays, and ports. This was the "last stand" for the Luftwaffe and Wehrmacht on the Crimean Peninsula.

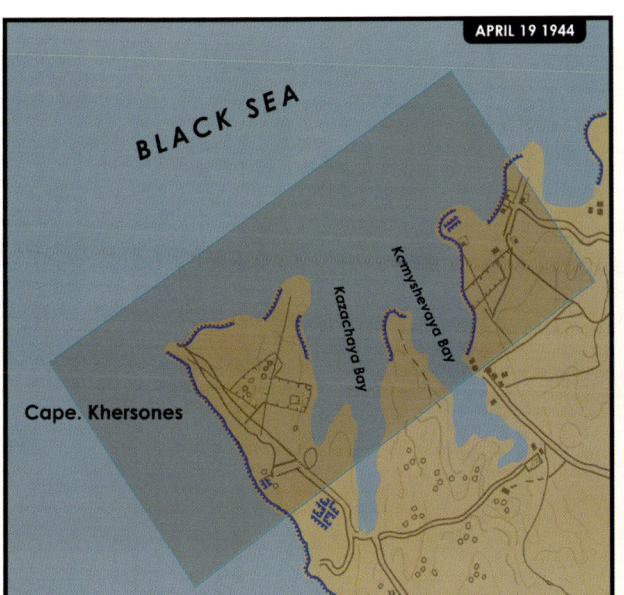

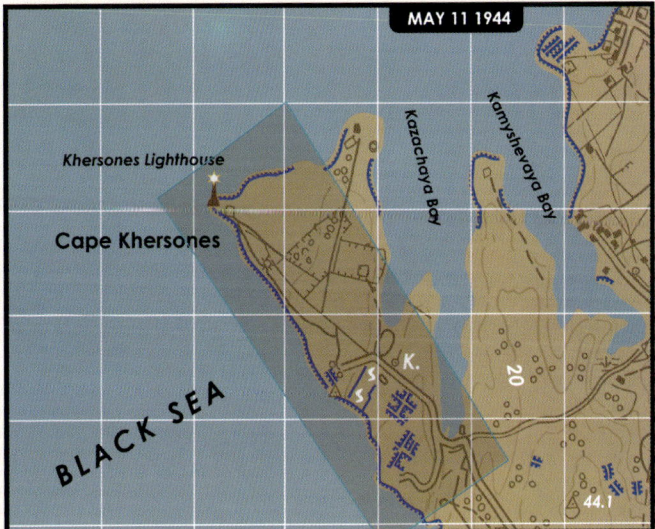

Soviet Army movements during the liberation of Sevastopol: May 1944

Troop positions on May 5, 1944

Troop positions on May 10th, 1944

Axis of Attacks from May 5th to May 9th, 1944

Axis of Fast Attacks from May 9th to May 10th, 1944

Forces in the northern bay

Enemy aviation and naval (incl. transports) forces routes

Liquidated enemy pockets

Tactical movement and landing of Soviet troops

A day later, on Tuesday, 9 May 1944, after fierce fighting, the city of Sevastopol itself was liberated. The remnant German forces, pressed to the sea, withdrew to a small piece of land—Cape Khersones. Only the single Khersones airfield, from which the German evacuation was continuing, remained in their hands. Reconnaissance flights reported that various aircraft were constantly taking off and heading in the direction of Romania.

The pilots of the 812th did not force themselves to wait long; they set out to strafe the enemy airfield on that same day. Conducting cannon fire on parked aircraft with little to no resistance, they returned to base unscathed. As a result of the flight, Mayor Popov set one Ju52 and one Fw200 on fire. Nikolay Sukhorukov and Aleksey Mashenkin each scored an Fw190. Another Fw190, from 6./SG2 "Immelmann," attempting to take off, flew at full speed into a bomb crater and, somersaulting, ended up on its nose. The final blow in the battles for Khersones airfield was its strafing by the pilots of 812th Regiment on 11 May. On this Thursday they turned eight Ju52s to dust. The outstanding pilots were Aleksey Mashenkin, Vladimir Kablukov, Yegor Ankudinov, Nikolay Sukhorukov, Semen Belkin, and Leytenant Morozov.

On Friday, 12 May, Soviet troops reached the seashore, having cleared Cape Khersones of German forces. Early in the morning, a pair of Yak-9s led by Aleksey Mashenkin sortied to reconnoiter enemy naval assets in the Sevastopol area. At 0815, 40-45 kilometers (25–28 miles) southeast of Khersones, the pilots spotted a moving vessel escorted by four Bf110s from II/ZG1 "Wespen". Starshiy Leytenant Mashenkin attacked the twin-

engine fighters, shooting one down into the sea. At the same time, three B-3 Bostons reached the vessel and bombed it. The outcome would, no doubt, have been very different if the Bf110s had not been tied up in battle with Mashenkin's pair only minutes before. Here is an excerpt from the combat report:

Reconnaissance of forces. Mashenkin Yak-9 (bort 1), Shcheglov Yak-9 (bort 3), 0805-0845 at altitude 2,000 meters (6,500 feet). 0810 – Steamer burning in Kazachya Bay, second one is standing not far from burning vessel. At 0815, at altitude 3,000-2,500 meters (9,800–8,200 feet) observed a flight of B-3s [A-20 Bostons] heading southwest. Followed them hoping that they were heading toward a target. 60-80 km (37–50 mi.) from the coast, below me to the right at 2,000 meters (6,500 feet) altitude encountered four Bf110s on intersecting course. Initially took them to be Pe-2s, but confirmed enemy, attacked out of sun. Bf110s took up defensive circle. Attacked trail Bf110 with machine gun-cannon fire from a range of 50-20 meters (55–22 yards), all remaining fired at Mashenkin. Bf110 began to drop and, burning, headed in direction of two vessels moving under escort of three guard vessels and under the protection of their antiaircraft weapons. Attacking the Bf110, ordered by radio – 'Bostons, turn around and return home.' Bostons dropped bombs on vessels and executed turn in flights. One B-3 fell behind and was attacked by Bf110, which after the attack departed. The Boston showed white streamer, began to fall behind, and took up a course to the east. Conducted

Ye. Ya. Savitskiy (left) at the corps observation post. Crimea, spring 1944.

0840, having flown 20–70 km (12–40 mi.), encountered three Bf110s flying at altitude 4,000 meters (13,100 feet). Having attained altitude of 4,500 meters (14,800 feet), commenced attack. Bf110s formed defensive circle above transport under cover of antiaircraft artillery. At this time B-3s arrived, which turned around, dropping their bombs. Ankudinov did not observe the results of Bf110 being shot down. Ammunition expenditure: ShVAK – 120, BS – 250.

I. F. Popov, leader by example and 812th Regiment commander during the Crimean campaign.

another attack on damaged Bf110. Ammunition expenditure: OKB – 14, BS – 120.

Meantime, at 0835 the Yak-9 pair of Kapitan Ankudinov (bort 31) and Mladshiy Leytenant Belkin (bort 83) took off as reinforcements for Mashenkin's pair. Here is an excerpt from their report:

On this same day, a group of 812th IAP pilots gained permission from the division commander to visit the recently liberated Khersones airfield. The main attraction for the pilots was the fact that they were able to see and evaluate their work on the ground. Here is the recollection of Fedorov, one of the visitors to this airfield:

> We drove to the airfield. Heinkels, Junkers, Messerschmitts, Focke-Wulfs, and several Ju52 transports were burned up or standing in their revetments, or lying on their sides. In every direction, soldiers and flight officers were coming out of shelters with their hands in the air. Not far from the shore, we saw scores of makeshift rafts, loaded to the limit with Germans. One after the other they were drifting toward the shore. The former soldiers of the 'invincible army,' not waiting for docking, jumped into the water with arms upraised, climbed up on shore, and surrendered. We went around to look at the airplanes that remained in the revetments. It was interesting why they had not taken off. When we saw that the majority of these aircraft had holes made from above, we understood that this was the work of our pilots. [88]

Suddenly they saw a lone Fw190 pass over the airfield, maneuvering for a landing approach. Everyone froze, wondering what would happen next. The aircraft began to drop down and lowered its main gear. Then suddenly, from the direction of the bay, antiaircraft gunners who perhaps had not yet stood down from the just-finished battle opened up on the German fighter. Receiving several hits, the aircraft banked and, diving, fell into the bay.

Altogether the 265th IAD had destroyed 19 Fw190s, four Bf109s, one Bf110, one Ju52, and damaged four He111s in the air (at night) during the period from 1 through 21 May 1944. The pilots of the 812th IAP set on fire nine Ju52s, two Fw200s, and two Fw190s on airfields.

A stroll around Khersones airfield, circa early summer 1944.

Top row: Destroyed and burned out Ju52 transport aircraft.

Second row, left to right: a Ju52 fuselage hulk next to a destroyed armored SPG, a trio of Ju52 fuselage hulks, and a SM.82 Kangaroo (probably from the Savoiastaffel of Tr.Sta.4)

Above left: destroyed He111s, and above: a row of Ju87s.

Left: a relatively intact Bf109G-6.

Below: abandoned flatbeds with Bf110 heavy fighters.

Although these photos look as though they were processed in less than ideal field conditions, they do illustrate well the finale of the Luftwaffe's presence in the Crimea.

A group of flight and maintenance personnel of the 812th IAP visited the battle sites in just-liberated Sevastopol, 10 May 1944.

Here, they are standing on the dock in Sevastopol near the monument to sunken vessels, a memorial to the "other" Crimean War of nearly one century before (1854-55). This was then, as is now, a Sevastopol "tourist spot."

Pilots' helpers—the aviation mechanics.

They often did their work without sleep and rest, in any weather. The examination, repair, and readiness of the aircraft was their responsibility. Its flight and safe return was their reward.

From left to right:

Lower row—M. I. Pavlenko, M. M. Belokhvost, F. Kryukov, F. P. Sitnikov.

Upper row—F. F. Kurenkov, P. V. Korneyev, Kommissarchik

Yelizarov, Khantemirov, and Legostayev perform technical services on a Yak-3 later in the war.

"They advanced across the entire Ukraine, they passed so many sleepless nights.
They moved the blocks from the carriage under the tarp,
And only laid down for an hour in the morning."
Korneyev, "From Stalingrad to Berlin."

Technicians and mechanics from the 2nd Squadron. From right to left: Ageykin, G. F. Klichko, Legostayev, K. P. Aleshin, Khantemirov, N. P. Popov, Kuzin, Smirnov.

"We carried compressed air bottles on our own backs for the entire war,
We changed engines until our knees buckled.
For five minutes in the cockpit we dreamt,
This is why our back and our hands hurt."
Korneyev, "From Stalingrad to Berlin."

The command element of 265th IAD.

In the center (with the Alsatian dog), division commander Podpolkovnik Aleksandr Aleksandrovich Koryagin. To his left is the division chief of the political department, Podpolkovnik Dmitriy Ivanovich Zakharov.

Beyond the Crimea

On 15 May, an application was prepared and sent to command suggesting to award the "Guards" rank to the 265ᵗʰ IAMD [*Istrebitelnaya Aviatsionnaya Melitopolskaya Diviziya*]. However the division did not become a Guards unit. The underlying reasons for this are unknown to this day. The document itself deserves publication in full text.

To the Commander in chief, 4ᵗʰ Ukrainian Front

General of the Army Comrade Tolbukhin

Copy: To the Commander in chief, 8ᵗʰ VA, General-polkovnik of aviation Comrade Khryukin

The 265ᵗʰ Fighter Aviation Melitopolskaya Division (division commander – Polkovnik A.A. Koryagin, division chief of staff Podpolkovnik Lovkov, and chief of political department Podpolkovnik Zakharov), operating together with the forces of 51ˢᵗ Army, by its reliable cover from the air facilitated the success of the forces in the breakthrough of German defenses on the Molochnaya River and the liberation of the town Melitopol, and then in the pursuit of the enemy to Perekop. With the arrival of the forces of 51ˢᵗ Army at the Sivash, the division's pilots supported the forcing of the Sivash and the seizure of a beachhead by the army's forces on the northern portion of the Crimean peninsula. Despite fierce enemy counterattacks, supported by massed bomber aviation strikes, the troops that were forcing the Sivash stubbornly held onto the positions seized from the enemy, and the fighter pilots of 265ᵗʰ IAMD maintained total air superiority.

In the period of the concentration of our forces in the Sivash area and their preparation for decisive offensive actions for the liberation of Crimea from the German occupiers, the 265ᵗʰ IAMD conducted continuous combat work, both day and night, reliably covering the Sivash crossing sites and positions of our forces, destroying enemy aviation in aerial battles and by systematic strafing of his airfields.

Altogether during this period (from 1 January to 8 April 1944), the 265ᵗʰ IAMD flew 2,007 combat sorties with a flight time of 1,628 hours. The division's pilots conducted 193 aerial engagements above the Sivash, destroying 85 enemy aircraft. In addition, another 72 aircraft were destroyed as a result of frequent strafing attacks on airfields.

In the period of the storming of the enemy's defensive positions in the Sivash area by the forces of 51ˢᵗ Army and the introduction into the breach of the 19ᵗʰ Tank Corps, and as well in the period of rapid movement of the army deep into Crimea, the 265ᵗʰ IAMD, by active support of the ground units from the air, facilitated the development of success in the defeat of his defensive nodes, simultaneously destroying enemy aviation and reliably maintaining air superiority for itself.

In the period of the offensive battles from 8 through 20

April 1944, the 265ᵗʰ IAMD, coordinating with the attached [to 51ˢᵗ Army] 19ᵗʰ Tank Corps, on several occasions displaced to territory just liberated from the enemy, reliably covered vanguard ground forces from the air, supporting their combat actions for the capture of the most important railroad junction in Crimea—Dzhankoy, and the capital of the Crimean ASSR – the town Simferopol, and beyond to the defensive line of Sevastopol, for which it was twice mentioned in the orders of the Supreme Commander in Chief, Marshal of the Soviet Union Comrade Stalin.

During this period, the 265ᵗʰ IAMD flew 1,155 combat sorties with a flight time of 1,084 hours. In the 93 aerial engagements that were conducted, 74 enemy aircraft were shot down. In addition, 33 aircraft were destroyed by strafing actions on airfields.

In the period of the preparation and conduct of the operation for the liquidation of the Sevastopol bridgehead and the final liberation of Crimea from the German occupiers, the 265ᵗʰ IAMD, based on the most forward airfields—Kacha and Adzhi-Bulat, which were under systematic enemy air and artillery attack, conducted continuous intensive combat work in support of the combat actions of 51ˢᵗ Army, destroying enemy aviation both in aerial engagements and on his airfields—Cape Khersones, 6ᵗʰ Versta, and the Central Airfield in the Sevastopol area, simultaneously strafing enemy troops on the battlefield and sea-going vessels, preventing the evacuation of enemy forces from Crimea.

Altogether during the period of offensive battles for the final defeat of the enemy in the Sevastopol bridgehead, the 265ᵗʰ IAMD conducted 1,327 combat sorties with a total flight time of 923 hours. 58 enemy aircraft were shot down in the 86 aerial engagements conducted, and an additional 13 aircraft were destroyed on the airfield.

In the final outcome of the combat actions for the liberation of Crimea, the 265ᵗʰ IAMD, directly cooperating with the forces of the 51ˢᵗ Army, carried out:

Combat sorties: day – 4,309; night – 180. Flight hours: day – 3,484; night – 146.

The division's pilots conducted 358 day aerial engagements and 14 at night, as a result of which 212 aircraft were shot down, including 11 at night. Of these: one Ju88, six He111, 66 Ju87, two Hs129, two Fw189, eight Bf110, 60 Bf109, 62 Fw190, three Ju52, and two Fiesler Storch.

In addition, 148 aircraft were destroyed in strafing actions on airfields. All downed and destroyed aircraft have been confirmed by ground forces, reconnaissance photography, or data plates of downed aircraft.

The division's own losses during this period were 31 aircraft and 24 pilots.

Along with the accomplishment of an intensive combat mission for the support of the combat of the 51ˢᵗ Army, the division covered its own airfields with its own forces and means, preventing any intrusion by enemy aviation.

During the period from 1 January through 12 May 1944, the 812th IAP executed 1,710 combat sorties, of which 1,194 were in coverage of ground forces, 185 for strafing enemy troops, 152 in escorting bombers, 93 to intercept enemy aircraft, 55 for reconnaissance, and 31 to strafe and bomb enemy airfields. The regiment's pilots conducted 92 aerial engagements, resulting in the downing of 76 enemy aircraft in the air, with 54 destroyed and 10 damaged on the ground. The regiment's losses totalled 18 aircraft and 16 pilots. For participation in the liberation of Crimea, the 265th IAD was awarded the Order of the Red Banner, and the 402nd and 812th IAPs received the honorific title "Sevastopolskiy." Corps commander Ye. Ya. Savitskiy became a Hero of the Soviet Union. Many aviators of the 812th IAP received state awards. Many technicians, mechanics, and aviation specialists were also decorated.

On 24 April, Mayor Popov had compiled, signed, and sent to the command a recommendation for the rank Hero of the Soviet Union for Starshiy Leytenant Ivan Vasilyevich Fedorov, born in 1920. The recommendation noted that squadron commander Fedorov had personally shot down 24 enemy aircraft in aerial battles – this significantly exceeded the effective "Hero norms" of this period (15 personally downed aircraft). It seemed that there should not be any obstacle to the granting of this highest state award. Several days later, Fedorov learned that the regiment and division had acknowledged his military effort:

In secret they gave me the welcome news: they had submitted a recommendation on me for the rank Hero of the Soviet Union. What did I feel when I heard this? It was unbelievable that the recommendation would pass through all the approving authorities. To that moment this was only a division recommendation. What would higher authorities say? Savitskiy would sign it . . . Above that it was totally unclear. . . If I responded honestly, after this exciting news I had no hope that the "file" would reach Moscow. But for some reason in the first weeks I expected something to happen—why should I lie? And then later my expectation was diminished. Time passed and I had to accommodate myself to the idea that the "Hero" rank was not for people such as myself.[89]

Skipping ahead, we note the fact that this "total lack of clarity" continued for more than six months. It was 17 November 1944, when the pilot was finally handed his Hero Star. However, it must be clearly stated that by this time, Ivan Fedorov had already also exceeded the "Twice Hero norm." He was not made a Twice Hero, just as Ivan Popov, commander of the 812th IAP did not become a Hero of the Soviet Union.

With Popov, it was simpler yet. On 12 May 1944, Polkovnik Koryagin, the commander of the 265th Fighter Aviation Melitopol Division, signed and sent forward to a higher command a recommendation on Mayor Ivan Feoktistovich Popov, born in 1911, for the rank Hero of the Soviet Union. The division commander drew the following conclusion in his recommendation:

For courage and heroism displayed in battles with the German occupiers, for personally downing 19 enemy aircraft and destroying seven on the ground, skillful leadership of the regiment, and the successes gained by the regiment, he has earned this highest state award—the awarding of the rank Hero of the Soviet Union.

Two days later, on 15 May, General-Mayor Savitskiy placed his signature in the box "Conclusion of corps commander" with the resolution, "Has earned the Highest State Award, granting of the rank Hero of the Soviet Union." Next in the recommend-ation chain was the Conclusion of the Army Military Council, signed by the Commander in chief, 8th Air Army General-Polkovnik Khryukin. Instead of affirming, he "put the brakes on" with the use of a time-tested bureaucratic method: in place of the Conclusion there appeared an anonymous written-in-pencil "Patr. War I. Deg."[Order of Patriotic War, 1st Degree]. Though there was a place for a signature, and the last name of the person who was to sign the Conclusion had already been typed in the space provided, it went up the chain without any signature at all. And no one ever would sign it.

Whether this was an echo of the "demonstration" air battle of 27 September 1943 being "not forgotten" by the army commander or not, it "replaced" the Hero Star for Popov with the Order of the Patriotic War 1st Degree. Was it coincidental that "irregularities" occurred in the Recommendations for the rank Hero of the Soviet Union for I. Fedorov and I. Popov? Hardly. In connection with this, we offer the timely citing of the words of Twice Hero of the Soviet Union, pilot and cosmonaut of the USSR, General-Leytenant of Aviation G. T. Beregovoy, written by him in the foreword of I. V. Fedorov's book *V nebe ostavili sled* [They left a trail in the sky]:

A very unpleasant incident occurred involving Leytenant Fedorov during the war: out of a misunderstanding he was sent before a military tribunal. Perhaps, therefore . . . yes, if you please, namely therefore! – he did not become a Twice Hero of the Soviet Union: this best pilot in the corps shot down 36 fascist aircraft in the air and destroyed another nine on the ground! This combat score far exceeded the statutory norm by which pilots were recommended for a second award of the 'Gold Star'. [30 personal victories – trans.]. However, despite the clear injustice that occurred, Fedorov harbors neither anger nor resentment. . .[90]

Of course, I. V. Fedorov was not the kind of person to harbor anger and resentment, but always permitted himself to have an opinion. And as a rule, his opinion was uncompromising: *"The incorrect decision of General Khryukin—not to send up Fedorov's group—negatively affected the outcome of the battle."* As he wrote in his last book.[91]

The chapter from which these words are cited has a clear and understandable title: "Guilty without guilt." Kirchenko's cavalry corps suffered heavy losses from the unpunished enemy bombing on 27 September 1943. Either the celebrated *little men* or the army commander himself should have answered for this. The pilots of the 812th openly displayed their disagreement with the role of *little men* handed to them. They permitted themselves also to disagree with the decision of T. T. Khryukin. We recall that I. F. Popov was an immediate participant in this sortie and official witness who did not agree with the decision of the tribunal (and that meant, as well, with the decision of army commander Khryukin). Resentment, most likely, could be hidden in the initiator of the legal proceedings, when in April 1944 the Supreme Court of the USSR did not uphold the verdict of the military tribunal of the 8th Air Army in regards to Fedorov and Nikolayenkov. They were adjudged not guilty (a clear blow to Khryukin's authority and pride – they became "guilty" namely with his "light hand"). If one recalls also the "public indignation" of division commander Koryagin with the tribunal's decision, it is appropriate to ask the question, "Was it circumstantial that the petition about awarding his division guards rank was 'buried'?"We do not know the answer to this. It is only known that the memory of army commander Khryukin was excellent, and all three above listed recommendations had to pass through him. They did not gain his approval.

At the end of May 1944, the 265th IAD was sent to the rear due to a shortage of pilots and materiel losses. The 812th IAP's flight back from the front went along the route Adzhi-Bulat – Zaporozhye – Kharkov – Kursk – Orel. Arriving at its new base without incident, the division (and the 812th IAP within it) began training exercises with young replacement pilots, whose flight time totaled all of 20-24 hours. During this training (from 5 to 19 June) the division suffered two catastrophes [major incidents involving death or write-offs in Russian terms–ed.] and two accidents [incidents without death in Russian terms–ed.] in which seven aircraft were damaged.

On 13 June a tragedy occurred within the neighboring 402nd Regiment. During a mock dogfight, the Yak-9T of Leytenant Vasiliy Muravyev collided in midair with the Yak-1 of Mladshiy Leytenant Semen Malimanenko. Division commander Koryagin was personally involved in the analysis of the accident. He was hard in his conclusions: in connection with the violation of flight discipline and oversight, the commander of the 402nd IAP (former commander of the 812th IAP), Mayor A. U. Yeremin was relieved of his command. The talented pilot and aerial warrior Mayor Anatoliy Rubakhin took his place.

But, notwithstanding these incidents, the training was concluded already by 16 June. On Wednesday, 21 June, the transfer of the regiments from Orel to a new basing area had begun. The division command and control elements, along with the 812th and 291st IAPs, were stationed at Yakubovshina airfield, whereas the 402nd IAP flew to Mikulino airfield (Vitebsk axis). The division, with 130 combat-ready air crews and still assigned to the 3rd IAK, was thus removed from the 8th VA and placed in operational subordination to the 1st Air Army of the 3rd Belorussian Front. In a twist of fate, this reassignment did not separate the 265th IAD from their former air army commander. For after the conclusion of the Crimean operation, General-Polkovnik T. T. Khryukin was appointed as commander in chief of that very same 1st Air Army. They were together once again.

Former 812th IAP ace, General-Mayor I.V. Fedorov (right) with his mechanic (a.k.a. crew chief) K.G. Motygin. From joining the 812th onwards, Motygin remained as Fedorov's crew chief throughout the Great Patriotic War portion of the General's career.

A close-up of the pin presented to 812th IAP veterans at a 25th anniversary gathering in 1969.

Veterans of the the regiment selected Adzhi-Bulat (now Uglovoye) as the place for their postwar gatherings not by mere accident. This place, one their wartime airfields, features a monument which commemorates what had occurred there and then.

Regiment veteran A.M. Mashenkin (left) and former 812th IAP chief of staff S.V. Lepilin have a lot to remember as they look out over the landscape — and no doubt back over time itself — at Adzhi-Bulat airfield.

Above: A closeup of the memorial inscription on Malakhov Kurgan, where the numerical designations of the most outstanding aviation formations in the liberation of Sevastopol are carved in stone. The 3rd IAK, its divisions, and their regiments are named in the top portion of the instription. It is poignant, perhaps, that the bomber and ground attack units named on the same plaque are "Guards" units.

Opposite: A memorial to the fighting men and women of the 8th Air Army, established after the war on Malakhov Kurgan in Sevastopol. Although the 8th VA was equipped with different types of combat aircraft—fighters, bombers, and ground attack, only a Yak fighter is represented, in replica form, atop the memorial. Additional commentary on the role of fighters in the liberation of Sevastopol and Crimea is superfluous.

Notes

1 The 283rd "Kamyshin" *IAD* was commanded by Polkovnik V. A. Kitayev in 1942. From 5 July to 8 August 1942, the division command element was formed at Borki airfield, Kimry *rayon*, Kalinin oblast. The first division commander was Polkovnik V. A. Kitayev. On 24 August 1942 the division command element was sent to the Stalingrad Front, to Kamyshin airfield, and assigned to the 16th Air Army. On 4 September 1942, the 431st, 520th, and 563rd *IAP* were assigned to the division, each regiment formed on the two-squadron TOE. The 812th *IAP* was assigned to the division on 24 September. On 1 December 1942, the 431st and 812th *IAP* stood down for reconstitution. The aircrews and equipment of these regiments were assigned to the 520th and 563rd *IAP*, reorganized in a three-squadron TOE. Conducting flight operations on the Stalingrad-Don Front, from 4 September 1942 to 5 February 1943 the division shot down 250 and damaged 25 enemy aircraft in air combat. It also destroyed 17 aircraft, 52 vehicles, 8 buses, 23 wagons, six antiaircraft guns, and up to 450 soldiers and officers in ground attack. Its own losses were 98 aircraft and 60 pilots. During these battles, in connection with combat losses, the division received 48 pilots and 133 aircraft. On 4 May 1943, by People's Commissariat of Defense Order No. 207, the 283rd *IAD* was awarded the honorific title "Kamyshin" for combat merit.

2 The text at this point is non-specific in regard to type of ground-attack aircraft. In most cases *"Shturmovik"* implies the Il-2. This translation will always convey the specific aircraft type if it was used in the original Russian. JG

3 While English-language readers are well familiar with the name "Stuka" for the Ju87, this name is rarely used in Russian text. The Russian nickname for this aircraft was *"laptezhnik,"* a reference to the aircraft's prominent wheel fairings. They reminded the Russians of the *lapti*, a peasant shoe woven from straw. One who wears *lapti* is a *laptezhnik*. JG

4 The *bort* [board] number was painted on the fuselage side, frequently behind the cockpit. It was used as a tactical identification number for the aircraft.

5 The 520th *IAP*, when later it received guards designation, was renumbered to the *56th GIAP*. JG

6 The commander of the 3rd "Nikopol" *IAK RVGK* from 1943 to 1945 was General-Mayor (from November 1944 General-Leytenant) Yevgeniy Yakovlevich Savitskiy. The honorific title "Nikopol" was awarded to the corps by order of the Supreme High Command Number 029 on 13 February 1944. The corps was awarded the Order of Suvorov II Degree for combat actions on the fronts of the Great Patriotic War by order of the Presidium of the Supreme Soviet of the USSR on 25 April 1945. The corps was awarded the Order of Kutuzov II Degree for combat actions in the Berlin operation by order of the Supreme Soviet of the SSR on 11 June 1945.

7 Tishchenko, A.T. *Vedomyye 'Drakona'* [Wingman to 'Dragon'] (Moscow: Voyenizdat, 1966), 13-4.

8 Fedorov, I.V. *V nebe Ukrainy vedomyye 'Drakona'* [Wingman of 'Dragon' in the skies of Ukraine] (Cherkassy: Siyach, 1997), 9-10.

9 This is a not-so-subtle reference to their previous assignment in the Far East patrolling the Amur River, for a long stretch the border between China and the USSR. JG

10 While the original text here does not permit certitude, quite possibly the mechanic was "riding" the wing, fuselage, or tail assembly. This is not the first incident of this nature I have read about in Soviet/Russian accounts. JG

11 Savitskiy, Ye.Ya. *Ya – 'Drakon'. Atakuyu!* [This is Dragon – I am attacking!] (Moscow: Molodaya gvardiya, 1988), 146.

12 Tishchenko A.T., *Vedomyye 'Drakona'*, 16.

13 A *stanitsa* is a large Cossack village, typical of this region. JG

14 Many Western analysts would disagree with this assertion. It has long been an established fact that the Airacobra, lacking turbo-supercharging of its Allison engine, performed best below 12,000-13,000 feet. JG

15 Savitskiy, Ye.Ya. *V nebe nad Maloy zemley* [In the skies above Malaya Zemlya] (Krasnodar: Krasnodarskoye knizhnoye izdatelstvo, 1980), 49-50.

16 Ibid., 51-2.

17 Fedorov, I.V. *V nebe ostavili sled* [They left a trail in the sky] (Kiev: Politizdat Ukrainy, 1990), 19.

18 Savitskiy, Ye.Ya. *V nebe nad Maloy zemley*, 53.

19 Tishchenko, A.T., *Vedomyye 'Drakona'*, 21-2.

20 Ibid., 26.

21 Fedorov, I.V. *V nebe ostavili sled*, 20; *V nebe Ukrainy vedomyye 'Drakona'*, 18.

22 Savitskiy, Ye.Ya. *Ya – 'Drakon'. Atakuyu!*, 157.

23 Fedorov, I.V. *V nebe ostavili sled*, 21.

24 Ibid., 22.

25 Ibid., 24.

26 Cited from *Taktika aviatsii* [Aviation tactics]. *Instructional manual for aviation academies and schools of VVS of the Red Army* (Moscow: Voyenizdat, 1940), 167.

27 Savitskiy, Ye.Ya. *V nebe nad Maloy zemley*, 68-9.

28 Ibid., 87-8.

29 Ibid., 89-90.

30 Fedorov, I.V. *V nebe ostavili sled*, 25-6.

31 Ibid., 27.

32 Savitskiy, Ye.Ya. *V nebe nad Maloy zemley*, 115-6.

33 Savitskiy, Ye.Ya. *Polveka s nebom* [A half century in the sky] (Moscow: Voyenizdat, 1988), 98.

34 Tishchenko, A.T., *Vedomyye 'Drakona'*, 31.

35 The Soviet nickname for this aircraft came from the "frame" (*rama*) shape formed by its tail booms. JG

36 The nickname for the Bf109 in Russian is *khudoy*, which translates to "skinny," a reference to the aircraft's slender fuselage.

37 Fedorov, I.V. *V nebe ostavili sled*, 26.

38 Ibid., 42-3.

39 Ibid., 5; *V nebe Ukrainy vedomyye 'Drakona'*, 50.

40 Savitskiy, Ye.Ya. *V nebe nad Maloy zemley*, 54-7.

41 Tishchenko, A.T., *Vedomyye 'Drakona'*, 46.

42 Ibid., 54.

43 Ibid.

44 The authors do not attach any value judgment to the actions and behavior of this courageous combat pilot, Mayor Yeremin, who finished the war a Hero of the Soviet Union, commander of the 355th *IAP*, 118th "Chenstokhovskaya" *IAD*, with 18 personal victories to his credit. The events are fully presented based on Savitskiy's and Tishchenko's memoirs. The reader has the right to draw his own conclusions from the material that is presented.

45 "Right" and "left" banks are designated by standing with one's back toward the river's source and facing with the direction of current flow. In the case of the Dniepr River, the "right" bank is on the west side of the river. JG

46 At readiness levels 1 and 2, an aircraft was fully fueled and armed, oxygen tanks topped off, and all systems and instruments tested and checked. At readiness level No. 1, the aircraft was parked in a revetment or under camouflage. The pilot was sitting in the aircraft with parachute on. The engine was kept warm by periodic starting, the radio was turned on, and during hot weather the canopy was kept open for ventilation. The aircraft's crew chief was nearby, prepared to assist the pilot as required. The aircraft was expected to take off within two to three minutes of a launch order, normally indicated by a flare fired from the control tower and confirmed by telephone from the tower to the aircraft parking area. At readiness level No. 2, the pilot waited with other pilots in a dugout, ready shack, or tent. The crew chief remained close to the aircraft with other maintenance personnel. Upon signal to launch or to come up to readiness level No. 1, the pilot took his seat in the aircraft, turned on the radios, and put on his parachute. As soon as the readiness level No. 1 aircraft launched for a combat mission, readiness level No. 2 aircraft were redesignated as readiness level No. 1 and another group of aircraft assumed readiness level No. 2. Dmitriy Loza, *Attack of the Airacobras: Soviet Aces, American P-39s, & the Air War Against Germany* (Lawrence, KS. University Press of Kansas, 2002), note 10 on page 345.

47 This division was later commanded by Polkovnik Aleksandr Pokryshkin. Its three regiments had transitioned to the P-39 Airacobra in the early spring of 1943 and were veterans of the Kuban air campaign. JG

48 Fedorov, I.V. *V nebe ostavili sled*, 68.

49 Ibid., 72.

50 Ibid., 74.

51 Ibid.

52 Ibid., 75-6.

53 Ibid., 79.

54 *Vozdushnoye nablyudeniye, opoveshcheniye i svyaz* [air observation, warning, and communication], basically a forward observation and warning post. These posts were manned by soldiers trained in the required duties. JG

55 Tishchenko, A.T., *Vedomyye 'Drakona'*, 64-5.

56 Fedorov, I.V. *V nebe ostavili sled*, 83.

57 Ibid., 84-5.

58 Tishchenko, A.T., *Vedomyye 'Drakona'*, 65.

59 Fedorov, I.V. *V nebe ostavili sled*, 86.

60 Fedorov, I.V. *V nebe Ukrainy vedomyye 'Drakona'*, 91.

61 Fedorov, I.V. *V nebe ostavili sled*, 87.

62 Ibid., 88.

63 Fedorov, I.V. *V nebe Ukrainy vedomyye 'Drakona'*, 92.

64 Savitskiy, Ye.Ya. *Polveka s nebom*, 115.

65 Tishchenko, A.T., *Vedomyye 'Drakona'*, 66.

66 Fedorov, I.V. *V nebe ostavili sled*, 93.

67 Ibid., 96.

68 Ibid., 97.

69 Ibid., 99-100.

70 Tishchenko, A.T., *Vedomyye 'Drakona'*, 69.

71 Fedorov, I.V. *V nebe ostavili sled*, 118-9.

72 Fedorov, A.G. *V nebe Ukrainy vedomyye 'Drakona'*, 126.

73 Ibid., 136.

74 *Sto stalinskikh sokolov v boyakh za rodinu.*

75 These are code names for specific units, not just official or nicknames. JG

76 Isayenko, N.F. *Vizhu protivnika!*

77 Fedorov, I.V. *V nebe Ukrainy vedomyye 'Drakona'*, 161-2.

78 Fedorov, I.V. *V nebe ostavili sled*, 160, 172.

79 Ibid., 174-5.

80 Fedorov, I.V. *V nebe Ukrainy vedomyye 'Drakona'*, 172-3.

81 Fedorov, I.V. *V nebe ostavili sled*, 195-6.

82 Fedorov, I.V. *V nebe Ukrainy vedomyye 'Drakona'*, 178.

83 Ibid., 179.

84 Tishchenko, A.T., *Vedomyye 'Drakona'*, 109.

85 The B-3 was a Douglas A-20B or C-model twin-engine bomber [JG]

86 Kacha Military Flight School was the oldest and most prestigious flight school in the Soviet Union. It is considered the "forge of Soviet aces"[JG]

87 Fedorov, I.V. *V nebe ostavili sled*, 209.

88 Ibid., 210.

89 Ibid., 264.

90 Ibid., 4.

91 Fedorov, I.V. *V nebe Ukrainy vedomyye 'Drakona'*, 86.

Bibliography and Sources

Archival materials:

Central Military Archive of the Defense Ministry of Russian Federation (TsAMO). Collection 16th VA, index 6476, file 477, various correspondence. 1945

3rd IAK

Collection 3rd IAK, index 1, file 1. Historical record.
Collection 3rd IAK, index 1, file 10. Operational summaries of 3rd IAK. 5.9.43 – 31.10.43
Collection 3d IAK, index 1, file 50(1). Operational summaries of 3rd IAK. 31.12.43 – 9.3.44
Collection 3rd IAK, index 1, file 50(2). Operational summaries of 3rd IAK. 9.3.44 – 21.4.44
Collection 3rd IAK, index 1, file 50(3). Operational summaries of 3d IAK. 22.4.44 – 29.5.44
Collection 3rd IAK, index 1, file 53. Operational summaries of 3rd IAK. 9.1.44 – 14.8.44
Collection 3rd IAK, index 1, file 72. Description of corps combat actions.
Collection 3rd IAK, index 1, file 123. Reports on the corps' and formations' personnel rosters, on the combat work of formation and regiment commanders, on air crew members who shot down 10 or more enemy aircraft. Lists of Heroes of the Soviet Union. 1944.
Collection 3rd IAK, index 1, file 134. Corps and formation reports on aerial photographic service. 1944.
Collection 3rd IAK, index 1, file 135. Corps and formation reports on aerial photographic service. 1945.
Collection 3rd IAK, index 1, file 23. Lists of formation personnel who flew combat sorties and who personally shot down enemy aircraft. 1944-45

265th IAD

Collection 265th IAD, index 1, file 1. Division historical record. 1942-45.
Collection 265th IAD, index 1, file 20. Account of the combat work of 3rd IAK during combat actions in the Kuban. 19.4.43-20.6.43.
Collection 265th IAD, index 1, file 21. Award list. 1.1.44 – 23.5.44
Collection 265th IAD, index 1, file 24. Combat reports of 812th IAP. 25.9.43-16.11.43
Collection 265th IAD, index 1, file 29. Journal of enemy aircraft downed by division unit pilots. 6.9.43-31.12.43
Collection 265th IAD, index 1, file 47. Confirmations of enemy aircraft downed by air crews of 812th IAP. 1943-44
Collection 265th IAD, index 1, file 77. Operational summaries of 812th IAP.1.44-20.6.44
Collection 265th IAD, index 1, file 80. Brief overview of enemy VVS activities and summaries concerning enemy ground force groupings. 11.1.1944-9.12.44
Collection 265th IAD, index 1, file 83. Journal of enemy aircraft downed by division unit pilots. 4.1.1944-12.5.44
Collection 265th IAD, index 1, file 87. Various documents. 11.1.44 – 31.12.44
Collection 265th IAD, index 1, file 8. Journal of enemy aircraft downed by division unit pilots.. 14.4.1943-3.6.43
Collection 265th IAD, index 1, file 15. Statements of investigations into combat losses and accidents. 25.3.44 – 28.12.44
Collection 265th IAD, index 1, file 102. Materials on the generalization of war experience. 22.1.45 – 15.9.45

812th IAP

812th IAP collection, index 663354, file 1. Historic record.
812th IAP collection, index 205534 file 2. Record of unrecoverable losses of command and enlisted personnel. 25.9.42 – 25.2.47
812th IAP collection, index 209058s file 3. Journal of combat actions of the 812th IAP on the Kalinin Front. 26.7.42 – 14.10.42
812th IAP collection, index 209057s file 1. Journal of combat actions of the 812th IAP. Kuban.1943.
812th IAP collection, index 209057 s file 2. Operational summaries of the 812th IAP. 1.9.43 – 28.11.43
812th IAP collection, index 209057s file 3. Journal of combat actions of the 812th IAP. 1.10.43 – 30.12.43
812th IAP collection, index 204132s file 1. Journal of combat actions of the 812th IAP. 20.2.44 – 13.5.44
812th IAP collection, index 204132s file 5. Journal of combat actions of the 812th IAP. 19.6.44 – 31.8.44
812th IAP collection, index 205535s file 4. Journal of combat actions of the 812th IAP. 30.8.44 – 12.2.45
812th IAP collection, index 205535s file 3. Operational summaries of the 812th IAP. 8.1.45 – 6.5.45

Literature:

1. Isayenko, N.F. *Vizhu protivnika!* [I see you enemy!]. Kiev: Politizdat Ukrainy, 1981.
2. Kozhedub, N.N. *Vernost otchizne* [Faithfulness to the fatherland]. Moscow: Detskaya literatura, 1969.
3. Kramarenko, S.M. *V nebe dvukh voyn* [In the skies of two wars]. Moscow: NPP Delta, 2003.
4. Kumanichkin, A.S. *Chtoby zhit . . .* [In order to live . . .]. Moscow: Molodaya gvardiya, 1987.
5. Lobanov, M.M. *Nachalo sovetskoy radiolokatsii* [The beginning of soviet radar]. Moscow: "Sovetskoye radio", 1975.
6. Lobanov, M.M. *Nachalo sovetskoy radiolokatsonnoy tekhniki* [The beginning of soviet radar technology]. Moscow: Voyenizdat, 1982.
7. Mikhaylik, Ya.D. *Sokolinaya semeya* [Falcon family]. Moscow: Voyenizdat, 1971.
8. Savitskiy, Ye.Ya. *V nebe nad Maloy zemley* [In the skies above Malaya Zemlya]. Krasnodar: Krasnodarskoye knizhnoye izdatelstvo, 1980.
9. Savitskiy, Ye.Ya. *Polveka s nebom* [A half century in the sky]. Moscow: Voyenizdat, 1988.
10. Savitskiy, Ye.Ya. *Ya – 'Drakon'. Atakuyu!* [This is Dragon – I am attacking!]. Moscow: Molodaya gvardiya, 1988.
11. Tishchenko, A.T. *Vedomyye 'Drakona'* [Wingman to 'Dragon']. Moscow: Voyenizdat, 1966.
12. Tishchenko, A.T. *'Drakon' idet na tsel* ['Dragon' is headed for the target]. Krasnodar: Krasnodarskoye knizhnoye izdatel'stvo, 1969.
13. Fedorov, A.G. *V nebe – pikirovshchiki!* [In the sky – dive bombers!]. Moscow: Izdatel'stvo DOSAAF, 1986.
14. Fedorov, I.V. *V nebe ostavili sled* [They left a trail in the sky]. Kiev: Politizdat Ukrainy, 1990.
15. Fedorov, I.V. *V nebe Ukrainy vedomyye 'Drakona'* [Wingmen of 'Dragon' in the skies of Ukraine]. Cherkassy: Siyach, 1997.
16. *Shla voyna narodnaya. Sbornik* [It was a peoples' war. Collection]. Samara: Samarskoye knizhnoye izdatel'stvo, 1991.
17. *Russkiy Arkhiv. Velikaya Otechestvennaya* [Russian Archive. Great Patriotic]. Vol. 15 (4-5). Moscow: Terra, 1996.

18. Shipilov, I.F., compiler. *Aviatsiya nashey Rodiny* [Aviation of our Motherland]. Moscow: Voyenizdat, 1955.

19. *Krylya Rodiny* [Wings of the Motherland]. Newspaper of the Gagarin Military Air Academy. No. 8, 23 February 1973.

20. *Yakutiya* regional newspaper, 16 March 2000.

21. *Gazeta* [Newspaper]. 9 May 2003.

22. *Vestnik vozdushnogo flota* [Herald of the air fleet]. No. 6, 7, 8, 9. Moscow: Voyenizdat, 1944.

23. *Sto stalinskikh sokolov v boyakh za rodinu*. Sbornik [100 of Stalin's eagles in battles for the motherland. Collection]. Monino: 1947.

24. *Boyevoy put. Sbornik Shtaba 812 IAP 1943-45* [Combat path. Collection of headquarters, 812th IAP 1943-45].

25. Materials of the 265th IAD:
    - *Praktika vozdushnykh boyev* [The practice of aerial engagements]. 1945.
    - *Boyevyye deystviya divisii v VOV* [Combat actions of the division in the GPW]. 1945
    - *Effektivnost deystviy istrebitelnoy aviatsii s pulemetno-pushechnym vooruzheniyem* [Effectiveness of the actions of fighter aviation with machine gun-cannon armaments]. 1945.

26. *Materialy konferentsii letchikov 16 VA po voprosu borby so skorostnymi samoletami nemetskikh vozdushnykh sil* [Materials of the 16th Air Army pilots' conference on the issue of the struggle against the high-speed aircraft of the german air forces]. 1945.

27. Aders G., Held W. *Jagdgeschwader 51 "Molders"*. Stuttgart: Motorbuch Verlag, 1999.

28. Rosch Barry *Luftwaffe Codes, Markings and Units 1939-1945*. Atglen, PA: Schiffer Publishing, 1995.

29. Forsyth R. *MISTEL German Composite Aircraft and Operations 1942-1945*. Hersham, Surrey: Midland Publishing, 2001.

30. Smith, Jack H. *Mustangs and Unicorns. History of the 359th Fighter Group*. Missoula, MT: Pictorial Histories Publishing, 1997.

31. Stachura P., Bernad D., Haladej D. *Henschel Hs 129*. Prague: MBI, 1996.

32. Ledwoch J. *Henschel Hs129*. Warsaw: Wydawnictwo Militaria, 1996.

33. Bernad D. *Henschel Hs129 in action*. Carrollton, TX: Squadron/signal publications, 2001.

34. Prien J., Stemmer G. –
    Messerschmitt Bf109 im Einsatz bei der II./Jagdgeschwader 3
    Messerschmitt Bf109 im Einsatz bei der III./Jagdgeschwader 3

35. *Air Fan International*, Vol.1 No.1, October 1995

36. *The Army Air Forces in World War II* - Vol.3. Washington, DC: Office of Air Force History, 1983.

Internet sites:

Aviatsionno-istoricheskiy forum (AIF) [Aviation historical forum (AIF)] - www.airforce.ru
LES AS DE LA LUFTWAFFE - http://perso.club-internet.fr
Hermann Graf and Alfred Grislawski - www.graf-grislawski.elknet.pl
Traditionsgemeinschaft Jagdgeschwader52 - www.jg52.de

Appendices

Appendix 1
The 812th IAP within the 3rd IAK

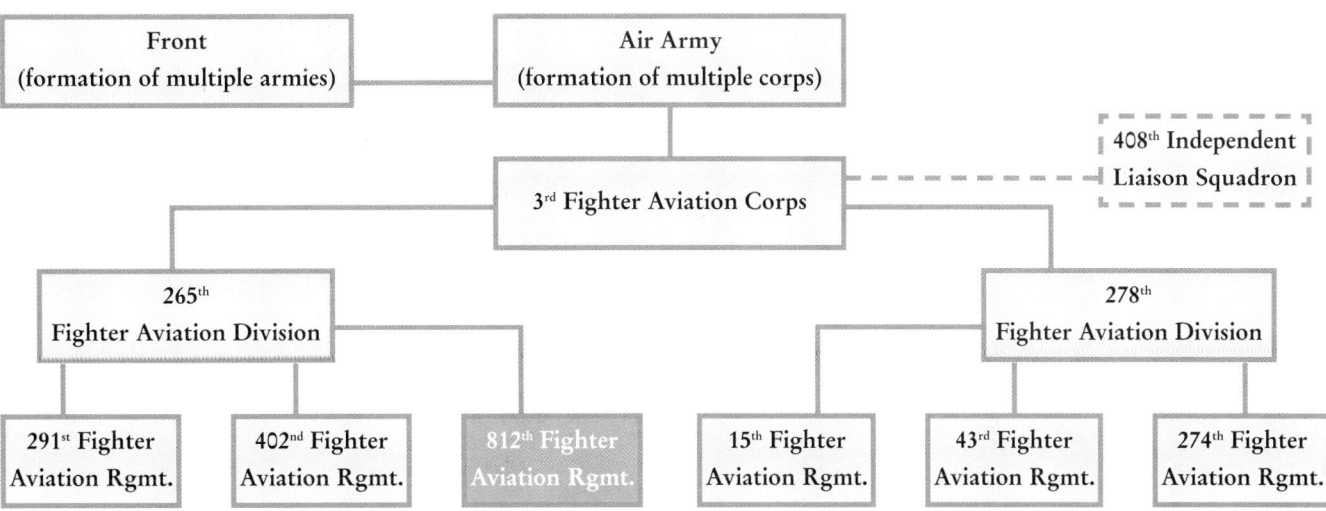

Each Fighter Aviation Regiment comprises 3 squadrons referred to officially as the 1st, 2nd, and 3rd Squadron within the regiment.

Appendix 2

Victories of the 812th IAP pilots on the Kalinin Front (263rd IAD) – 26 July through 15 September 1942

No.	Date	Time	Pilot	Score	Downed (of type)	Location of aerial combat
1	29.07.42	19:10	St. Leytenant Nezolya, P.G. Leytenant Tolkachev, N.A.	-	Fw189	Aleshki Village, 13 km northwest of Klimovo
2	31.07.42	18:23~19:22	Kapitan Solyannikov, I.K. (1)	1	Ju88	Mikhaylovskoye
3	02.08.42	12:07~13:15	Kapitan Solyannikov, I.K. (2)	2	Bf109	3 km northeast of Rzhev
4	02.08.42	18:58~20:05	Kapitan Yuzhakov, I.M. Leytenant Prikhodko, A.M. Ml. Leytenant Chekanikhin, V.K. Serzhant Kvitko, B.A. Serzhant Koledov, V.G.	1/5 1/5 1/5 1/5 1/5	Bf109	Rzhev area
5	02.08.42	18:58~20:05	Kapitan Yuzhakov, I.M. Leytenant Prikhodko, A.M. Ml. Leytenant Chekanikhin, V.K. Serzhant Kvitko, B.A. Serzhant Koledov, V.G.	1/5 1/5 1/5 1/5 1/5	Ju88	Rzhev area
6	03.08.42	7:52~8:45	Kapitan Yefremov, A.A.	1	Bf109	Novo-Semyenovskaya - Polunino
7	03.08.42	7:52~8:45	Kapitan Yefremov, A.A.	2	Bf109	"
8	03.08.42	7:52~8:45	Serzhant Baranov, V.G.	1	Bf109	"
9	03.08.42	7:52~8:45	Serzhant Matveyev, N.G.	1	Bf109	"
10	03.08.42	9:43~10:45	St. Leytenant Limarenko, L.S.	1	Bf109	"
11	03.08.42	9:43~10:45	St. Leytenant Veremeyenko, V.	1	Bf109	"
12	03.08.42	9:43~10:45	Kapitan Solyannikov, I.K. St. Leytenant Veremeyenko, V.	-	Bf109	"
13	03.08.42	17:50~19:15	Kapitan Yuzhakov, I.M.	1	Bf109	"
14	03.08.42	18:55~20:15	Kapitan Solyannikov, I.K. (3)	3	Bf109	"
15	03.08.42	18:55~20:15	St. Leytenant Veremeyenko, V.	2	Bf109	"
16	03.08.42	18:55~20:15	Serzhant Matveyev, N.G.	2	Bf109	"
17	05.08.42	-	St. Leytenant Nezolya, P.G. St. Serzhant Matveyev, N.G.	-	Ju88	In Pogoreloye Gorodishche area

Appendix 3

Pilot losses of the 812th IAP in combat on the Stalingrad Front

No.	Pilot	Date	Cause / Particulars
1	Serzhant Kvitko, Boris Andreyevich	25.09.1942	Shot down in aerial combat, Altukhov area
2	Sq. Cdr. Kapitan Yuzhakov, Ilya Mikhaylovich	27.09.1942	Did not return from combat mission, Stalingrad oblast
3	Flt. Cdr. Leytenant Prikhodko, Anatoliy Matveyevich	30.09.1942	Shot down in aerial combat, Stalingrad oblast
4	Ml. Leytenant Tolkachev, Nikolay Andreyevich	04.10.1942	Did not return from combat mission, Stalingrad oblast
5	Serzhant Kulayev, Timofey Gavrilovich	26.10.1942	Died while fulfilling service obligation, Stalingrad oblast

Conventions used throughout Appendices

- \- = Information not recorded or nil.
- ☼ = More detailed information was not available to the authors.
- " = Ditto: same information as entered in the preceding row.
- No. – Number: running total of 812th IAP victories. A second column of "No." entries carries the running total per campaign / operation.
- Score – Running total of each individual pilot's victories.

Appendix 4

Victories of the 812th IAP pilots on the Stalingrad Front (283rd IAD) — 23 September through 10 December 1942

No.	No.	Date	Time	Pilot	Score	Downed (of type)	Location of aerial combat
–	–	24.09.42	16:55~18:10	Group	–	Bf109 damaged	Solodcha — Kondrashi
–	–	24.09.42	16:55~18:10	Group	–	Ju87 damaged	Altukhov
18	1	25.09.42	8:45~9:55	Serzhant Suslov Leytenant Prikhodko, A.M.	–	He111	Kotluban
19	2	25.09.42	8:45~9:55	Kapitan Solyannikov, I.K.	4	Bf109	Kotluban
20	3	25.09.42	8:45~9:55	St. Lt. Veremeyenko, V. St. Serzh. Gavrilov, M.T.	?	Ju88	2-3 km southwest of Kotluban
21	4	25.09.42	11:45~12:20	Leytenant Prikhodko, A.M.	1	Ju87	Ivanovka
22	5	25.09.42	11:45~12:20	Leytenant Prikhodko, A.M.	2	Ju87	"
23	6	25.09.42	11:45~12:20	St. Serzh. Koledov, V.G.	1	Ju87	Proletskaya — Stalino
24	7	25.09.42	11:45~12:20	St. Lt. Tolkachev, N.A.	1	Ju87	"
25	8	25.09.42	11:45~12:20	Serzhant Suslov	1	Ju87	Ivanovka
26	9	25.09.42	11:45~12:20	St. Lt. Veremeyenko, V.	2	Ju87	Konnaya — Gumrak
27	10	25.09.42	11:45~12:00	Ml. Lt. Chekanikhin, V.K.	1	Ju87	Ivanovka
28	11	28.09.42	9:43~10:45	Group	–	Bf109	Northern Stalingrad area
29	12	29.09.42	6:45~7:55	St. Lt. Veremeyenko, V.	3	Bf109	Krasniy Oktyabr area (Stalingrad)
30	13	29.09.42	10:37~11:30	Leytenant Prikhodko, A.M.	3	Bf109	Orlovka
31	14	30.09.42	15:30~16:25	St. Lt. Veremeyenko, V.	4	Bf109	Kuzmichi area
32	15	30.09.42	15:30~16:25	Kapitan Yefremov, A.A.	3	Bf109	"
33	16	30.09.42	15:30~16:25	St. Serzh. Lukyanov, I.A.	1	Bf109	"
34	17	01.10.42	7:05~8:05	St. Lt. Veremeyenko, V.	5	Bf109	Kuzmichi area
35	18	01.10.42	7:05~8:05	St. Serzh. Gavrilov, M.T.	1	Bf109	"
36	19	01.10.42	10:35~11:30	Kapitan Solyannikov, I.K.	4	Bf109	"
37	20	01.10.42	10:35~11:30	Leytenant Mishachev, V.A.	1	Bf109	"
38	21	01.10.42	10:35~11:30	St. Serzh. Baranov, V.G.	2	Bf109	"
39	22	02.10.42	6:45~7:45	Kapitan Yefremov, A.A. St. Serzh. Baranov, V.G.	–	Bf109	"
40	23	02.10.42	9:45~10:45	Kapitan Yefremov, A.A. St. Serzh. Baranov, V.G.	–	Bf109	"
41	24	03.10.42	7:25~8:10	Kapitan Yefremov, A.A. St. Serzh. Baranov, V.G.	–	Bf109	"
42	25	08.10.42	8:50~8:55	Mayor Rodin, D.I.	1	Ju87	Altukhov area
43	26	probable 08.10.42*	8:50~8:55	Group of Mayor Rodin	–	Bf109	"
44	27	probable 08.10.42*	8:50~8:55	Group of Mayor Rodin	–	Bf109	"
45	28	probable 08.10.42*	8:50~8:55	Group of Mayor Rodin	–	Bf109	"
46	29	09.10.42	–	St. Lt. Tolkachev, N.A.	2	Bf109	Konnaya
47	30	09.10.42	–	Kapitan Yefremov, A.A. Leytenant Shimbalov	–	Ju87	Kotluban
48	31	09.10.42	–	Kapitan Yefremov, A.A. St. Serzh. Kostrykin, I.Ya.	–	Ju88	Opytnoye Polye
49	32	21.10.42	–	Group of St. Lt. Nezolya, P.G.	–	Ju87	"
50	33	*.10.42	–	–	–	Bf109	–
51	34	*.10.42	–	–	–	Bf109	–
52	35	14.11.42	–	Group of Kapitan Veremeyenko	–	Bf109	2-3 km south of Kletskaya
53	36	28.11.42	–	Group of Kapitan Veremeyenko	–	Bf109F	Baburgin area
54	37	probable 28.11.42*	–	Serzhant Kravtsov	1	Bf109	Gumrak airfield area
55	38	–*	–	–*	–	He111	–
56-61	39-44	–*	–	–*	–	6x Bf109	–

Appendix 5

Combat results for 812ᵗʰ IAP pilots on the Kalinin (263ʳᵈ IAD) and Stalingrad (283ʳᵈ IAD) Fronts in 1942

Pilot	Personal victories	Group victories
Regiment navigator Kapitan Veremeyenko, V.T.	6	2-1/2 2-1/4
2ⁿᵈ Sqn. Cdr, Kapitan Solyannikov, I.K.	5	1-1/2
Deputy 2ⁿᵈ Sqn. Cdr, Kapitan Yefremov, A.A.	3	4-1/2
Flight Cdr. Leytenant Prikhodko, A.M.	3	2-1/5 1-1/2
Pilot St. Serzh. Baranov, V. G.	2	3-1/2
Pilot Ml. Lt. Tolkachev, N.A.	2	1-1/2
Pilot St. Serzh. Matveyev, N.G.	2	1-1/2
Pilot St. Serzh. Gavrilov, M.T.	1	1-1/2
Pilot Serzh. Suslov	1	1-1/2
Pilot Ml. Leytenant Chekanikhin, V.K.	1	2-1/5
1ˢᵗ Sqn. Cdr. Kapitan Yuzhakov, I.M.	1	2-1/5
Pilot Serzh. Koledov, V.G.	1	1-1/5
Pilot Serzh. Lukyanov, I.A.	1	-
1ˢᵗ Sqn. Cdr. (from 28.9.42) Mayor Rodin, D.I.	1	-
Flight Cdr. St. Lt. Limarenko, L.S.	1	-
Flight Cdr. Leytenant Mishachev, V.A.	1	-
Deputy 1ˢᵗ Sqdn. Cdr., Flt. Cdr St. Lt. Nezolya, P.G.	-	2-1/2 1-1/4
Pilot Leytenant Shimbalov	-	1-1/2
Pilot St. Serzh. Kostrykin, I. Ya.	-	1-1/2
Pilot Serzh. Kvitko, B.A.	-	1-1/5

Appendix 6

Pilots of the 812ᵗʰ IAP (283ʳᵈ IAD) transferred to newly formed regiments within the 283ʳᵈ IAD

Pilot	New Regiment
Kapitan Veremeyenko, V.T.	563ʳᵈ IAP
Kapitan Solyannikov, I.K.	520ᵗʰ IAP
Kapitan Nezolya, P.G.	
St. Leytenant Mishachev, V.A.	
St. Serzhant Kravtsov G.S.	
Ml. Leytenant Kostrykin, I. Ya.	
Starshina Gavrilov, M.T.	
Ml. Leytenant Chekanikhin, V.K.	
Serzhant Zhilin V.G.	
Starshina Baranov, V. G.	
Starshina Lukyanov, I.A.	
Serzhant Mishin V.I.	
Serzhant Znatkov V.P.	

by order of the commander of 283ʳᵈ IAD from 6.12.43 due to reorganization to a new structure

Appendix 7

Pilot losses of the 812ᵗʰ IAP in combat in the Kuban (Krymskaya, Krasnodar Kray area)

No.	Pilot	Date	Cause / Particulars
1	Starshina Zaspin, Pavel Arsentyevich, born 1917	20.04.1943	Did not return from combat mission, Krymskaya
2	Deputy Sqn. Cdr, St. Lt. Sorokin, Aleksandr Ivanovich, born 1918	20.04.1943	Did not return from combat mission, Krymskaya
3	Flt. Cdr., Leytenant Morozov, Nikolay Nazarovich, born 1919	20.04.1943	Did not return from combat mission, Krymskaya
4	Serzhant Kovalev, Vladimir Yemelyanovich, born 1923	20.04.1943	Did not return from combat mission, Krymskaya
5	Serzhant Babukin, Viktor Vasilyevich, born 1923	20.04.1943	Did not return from combat mission, Krymskaya
6	Starshina Shirokov, Yuriy Aleksandrovich, born 1923	26.04.1943	Shot down in aerial combat. Yak-1 (bort 47)
7	Deputy Sqn. Cdr., Flt. Cdr. St. Lt. Tyugayev, Dmitriy Aleksandrovich, born 1918	27.04.1943	Did not return from combat mission. Yak-1 (bort 28)
8	Sqn. Cdr., Kapitan Novikov, Timofey Timofeyevich, born 1915	28.04.1943	Shot down in aerial combat. Yak-1 (bort 61)
9	Deputy Sqn. Cdr Leytenant Kramarenko, Grigoriy Vasilyevich, born 1918	29.04.1943	Did not return from combat mission. Yak-1(bort16)
10	Starshina Kukushkin, Ilya Dmitriyevich, born 1922	29.04.1943	Did not return from combat mission. Yak-1 (bort 9)
11	Leytenant Kostenko, Aleksey Grigoryevich , born 1919	29.04.1943	Did not return from combat mission, Krymskaya
12	Starshina Patrakov, Mikhail Lavrentyevich, born 1920	02.05.1943	Did not return from combat mission. Yak-1 (bort 23)
13	St. Serzh. Tarasov, Stepan Georgiyevich, born 1923	03.05.1943	Did not return from combat mission. Yak-1 (bort 25)
14	Starshina Krysov, Sergey Ivanovich, born 1917	06.05.1943	Did not return from combat mission. Yak-1 (bort 35)
15	Sqn. Cdr., Kapitan Batychko, Ivan Dmitriyevich, born 1915	07.05.1943	Did not return from combat mission. Yak-1 (bort 32)
16	Sqn. Cdr., Kapitan Svezhentsev, Fedor Klimentyevich, born 1916	08.05.1943	Rammed Bf109. Shot by enemy fighters while under canopy. Yak-1 (bort 24)

Appendix 8

Victories of the 812ᵗʰ IAP pilots in the Kuban battles (265ᵗʰ IAD) — 20 April through 28 May 1943

No.	No.	Date	Time	Pilot	Score	Downed	Location of aerial battle
62	1	20.04.43	8:50~10:00	Kapitan Svezhentsev, Fedor	1	Bf109	Novorossiysk — Myskhako
63	2	20.04.43	8:50~10:00	Kapitan Svezhentsev, Fedor	2	Fw189	"
64	3	20.04.43	8:50~10:00	Leytenant Tyugayev, Dmitriy	1	Bf109	"
65	4	20.04.43	8:50~10:00	Leytenant Tyugayev, Dmitriy	2	Fw189	"
66	5	20.04.43	8:50~10:00	Kapitan Batychko, Ivan	1	Ju88	"
67	6	20.04.43	8:50~10:00	Mayor Yeremin, Aleksey Leytenant Tishchenko, Aleksandr Starshina Patrakov, Mikhail	1/3	Ju88	"
68	7	20.04.43	08:50~10:00	Kapitan Batychko, Ivan	2	Ju88	"
69	8	20.04.43	10:50~12:00	Kapitan Nikolayenkov, Dmitriy	1	Bf109	Novorossiysk – Krymskaya
70	9	20.04.43	10:50~12:00	Starshina Lugovoy, Vasiliy	1	Bf109	"
71	10	20.04.43	10:50~12:00	Starshina Shirokov, Yuriy	1	Bf109	"
72	11	20.04.43	10:50~12:00	Kapitan Novikov, Timofey	1	Bf109	"
73	12	20.04.43	-	Kapitan Novikov, Timofey	2	He111	Novorossiysk
74	13	20.04.43	16:45~18:00	Kapitan Naumchik, Nikolay/42 GIAP	-	Bf109	"
75	14	21.04.43	-	Mayor Yeremin, Aleksey	1	Bf109	Neberdzhayevskaya
76	15	23.04.43	-	Starshiy Serzhant Martynenko, Ivan	1	Bf109	Novorossiysk
77	16	23.04.43	-	Kapitan Svezhentsev, Fedor	3	Bf109	Novorossiysk – Krymskaya
78	17	23.04.43	-	Leytenant Tishchenko, Aleksandr	1	Bf109	Novorossiysk – Krymskaya
79	18	25.04.43	09:05~10:05	Starshina Patrakov, Mikhail	1	Bf109G with underwing cannons	Krymskaya – Abinskaya
80	19	26.04.43	~18:10	Starshiy Serzhant Fedorov, Ivan	1	Bf109	Krymskaya – Abinskaya
81	20	26.04.43	-	Starshiy Serzhant Churakov, Georgiy	1	Bf109	Troitskoye
82	21	27.04.43	10:00~10:20	Starshina Kalugin, Serafim	1	Hs126	Krymskaya
83	22	27.04.43	-	Kapitan Novikov, Timofey	3	Hs126	Southeast of Krymskaya
84	23	28.04.43	-	Kapitan Novikov, Timofey	4	He111	Krymskaya
85	24	28.04.43	13:00~13:58	Mayor Yeremin, Aleksey	2	Bf109	"
86	25	28.04.43	13:00~13:58	Starshina Patrakov, Mikhail	2	Bf109	"
87	26	28.04.43	13:00~13:58	Starshiy Serzhant Kosov, Nikolay	1	Bf109	"
88	27	28.04.43	13:00~13:58	Starshiy Serzhant Tarasov, Stepan	1	Bf109	"
89	28	28.04.43	-	Starshiy Serzhant Shirobokov, V.	1	Bf109	West of Krymskaya
90	29	29.04.43	06:15~07:32	Kapitan Svezhentsev, Fedor	4	Bf109	Krymskaya
91	30	29.04.43	06:15~07:32	Kapitan Svezhentsev, Fedor	5	Bf109	"
92	31	29.04.43	06:15~07:32	Starshina Kukushkin, Ilya	1	Bf109	"
93	32	29.04.43	-	Starshina Kukushkin, Ilya	2	Bf109	"
94	33	29.04.43	06:15~07:32	Leytenant Kostenko, Aleksey	1	Bf109	"
95	34	29.04.43	06:15~07:32	Starshiy Serzhant Martynenko, Ivan	2	Bf109	"
96	35	29.04.43	08:35~09:15	Ml. Leytenant Adamchuk, K.	1	Bf109	"
97	36	29.04.43	08:35~09:15	Group victory	-	Bf109	"
98	37	29.04.43	09:00~09:20	Mayor Nikolayenkov, Dmitriy	2	Bf109	"
99	38	29.04.43	09:10~09:20	Mayor Nikolayenkov, Dmitriy	3	Bf109	"
100	39	29.04.43	10:35~11:35	Leytenant Kramarenko, Grigoriy	1	Fw190	"
101	40	29.04.43	~13:15	Kapitan Batychko, Ivan	3	Ju87	"
102	41	29.04.43	~13:15	Starshina Patrakov, Mikhail	3	Ju87	"
103	42	29.04.43	~13:15	Starshina Balabanov	1	Ju87	"
104	43	29.04.43	~13:15	Starshina Krysov, Sergey	1	Ju87	"
105	44	29.04.43	~13:15	Starshina Lugovoy, Vasiliy	2	Ju87	"
106	45	02.05.43	~13:20	Kapitan Batychko, Ivan	4	Ju88	Nov. Bakanskaya
107	46	02.05.43	-	Starshina Mashenkin, Aleksey	1	Fw189	Neberdzhayevskaya
108	47	02.03.43	-	Kapitan Svezhentsev, Fedor	6	Bf109	Krymskaya
109	48	03.05.43	~08:50	Leytenant Tumanov, Aleksandr	1	Bf109	Krymskaya
110	49	03.05.43	~14:05	Starshina Lugovoy, Vasiliy	3	Bf109	"
111	50	03.05.43	~14:05	Kapitan Svezhentsev, Fedor	7	Bf109G-2	"
112	51	03.05.43	~17:00	Leytenant Tishchenko, Aleksandr	2	Bf109	"

Victories of the 812ᵗʰ IAP pilots in the Kuban battles (265ᵗʰ IAD) — 20 April through 28 May 1943

No.	No.	Date	Time	Pilot	Score	Downed	Location of aerial battle
113	52	03.05.43	-	Kapitan Batychko, Ivan	5	Bf109	"
114	53	04.05.43	~08:00	Kapitan Svezhentsev, Fedor	8	Ju87	Krymskaya
115	54	04.05.43	~08:00	Starshiy Serzhant Kosov, Nikolay	2	Ju87	"
116	55	04.05.43	-	Kapitan Batychko, Ivan	6	Bf109	"
117	56	04.05.43	~16:10	Leytenant Tishchenko, Aleksandr	3	Bf109	Neberdzhayevskaya
118	57	04.05.43	~16:10	Kapitan Svezhentsev, Fedor	9	Bf109	Neberdzhayevskaya
119	58	04.05.43	~16:10	Starshina Mashenkin, Aleksey	2	Fw189	Neberdzhayevskaya
120	59	05.05.43	-	Kapitan Batychko, Ivan	7	Ju87	Krymskaya
121	60	05.05.43	-	Ml. Leytenant Churakov, Georgiy	2	Ju87	Krymskaya
122	61	05.05.43	-	Leytenant Kalugin, Serafim	2	Ju87	Krymskaya
123	62	05.05.43	-	Leytenant Mashenkin, Aleksey	3	Ju87	Krymskaya
124	63	05.05.43	-	Leytenant Krysov, Sergey	2	Bf109	Krymskaya
125	64	05.05.43	-	Kapitan Svezhentsev, Fedor	10	Bf109	Krymskaya
126	65	05.05.43	-	Leytenant Kalugin, Serafim	3	Bf109	Krymskaya
127	66	05.05.43	-	Leytenant Mashenkin, Aleksey	4	Bf109	Krymskaya
128	67	05.05.43	-	Leytenant Mashenkin, Aleksey	5	Bf109	Abinskaya
129	68	06.05.43	-	Leytenant Tumanov, Aleksandr	2	Ju87	"
130	69	06.05.43	-	Leytenant Kosov, Nikolay	3	Ju87	"
131	70	07.05.43	-	Kapitan Batychko, Ivan	8	Bf109	"
132	71	07.05.43	-	Leytenant Lugovoy, Vasiliy	4	Bf109	"
133	72	07.05.43	-	Leytenant Kalugin, Serafim	4	Bf109	"
134	73	07.05.43	~11:50	Leytenant Tishchenko, Aleksandr	4	Bf109	"
135	74	08.05.43	-	Kapitan Svezhentsev, Fedor	11	Bf109 by ramming	Krymskaya
136	75	08.05.43	~14:24	Leytenant Kosov, Nikolay	4	Bf109	"
137	76	09.05.43	~11:40	Leytenant Fedorov, Ivan	2	Fw189	Moldavanskaya
138	77	10.05.43	16:35~17:40	Leytenant Fedorov, Ivan	3	Bf109	Abinskaya
139	78	10.05.43	16:35~17:40	Leytenant Fedorov, Ivan	4	Bf109 by ramming	Abinskaya
140	79	26.05.43	-	Kapitan Tarasov, Pavel	13	Bf109	Krymskaya -Kievskoye
141	80	26.05.43	-	Kapitan Tarasov, Pavel	14	Fw190	Krymskaya - Kievskoye
142	81	26.05.43	-	Leytenant Kalugin, Serafim	5	Bf109	Krymskaya - Kievskoye
143	82	26.05.43	18:15~19:05	Leytenant Vasilyev	1	Bf109	Krymskaya
144	83	26.05.43	18:15~19:05	Leytenant Tumanov, Aleksandr	3	Bf109	Krymskaya
145	84	26.05.43	18:15~19:05	Leytenant Ivanov, Aleksandr	1	Bf109	Krymskaya
146	85	27.05.43	-	Leytenant Loginov	1	Fw190	Kievskoye
147	86	27.05.43	-	Ml. Leytenant Churakov, Georgiy	3	Fw190	Kievskoye
148	87	27.05.43	-	Kapitan Tarasov, Pavel	15	Bf109	Kievskoye
149	88	28.05.43	~07:25	Kapitan Tarasov, Pavel	16	Ju87	Kievskoye
150	89	28.05.43	~07:25	Leytenant Kalugin, Serafim	6	Ju87	Kievskoye
151	90	28.05.43	~07:25	Ml. Leytenant Churakov, Georgiy	4	Ju87	Kievskoye
152	91	28.05.43	~07:40	Kapitan Tarasov, Pavel	17	Bf109	Kievskoye
153	92	28.05.43	-	Kapitan Tarasov, Pavel	18	Bf109 forced to land on airfield	Slavyanskaya
154	93	28.05.43	~07:40	Leytenant Kalugin, Serafim	7	Bf109	Kievskoye
155	94	28.05.43	~07:40	Leytenant Tumanov, Aleksandr	4	Bf109	Kievskoye
156	95	28.05.43	-	Group victory	-	Bf109	Kievskoye

Appendix 9 Pilot losses of the 812ᵗʰ IAP in the South Ukraine battles — 9 September through 31 December 1943

No.	Pilot	Date	Cause / Particulars
1	3ʳᵈ Sqn, Ml. Leytenant Kondyakov, Petr Ivanovich, born 1922	18.09.1943	Did not return from combat mission, Yak-1 (bort 35)
2	Serzhant Belous, Mikhail Vasilyevich, born 1916	18.09.1943	Did not return from combat mission
3	3ʳᵈ Sqn, Ml. Leytenant Rusakov, Anatoliy Sergeyevich, born 1922	18.09.1943	Did not return from combat mission , Yak-1 (bort 37)
4	Dpty. Sqn. Cdr, Lt Churakov, Georgiy Pavlovich, born 1918	19.09.1943	Shot down in aerial combat, Yak-9 (bort 53)
5	Serzhant Konovalov, Nikolay Andreyevich, born 1921	01.10.1943	Did not return from combat mission, Yak-9 No. 0362
6	Ml. Leytenant Maksimov, Ivan Aleksandrovich, born 1922	29.10.1943	Shot down in aerial combat, Yak-7 (bort 3) No. 5103
7	Ml. Leytenant Kashirin, Mikhail Ivanovich, born 1922	28.11.1943	Shot down in aerial combat, Yak-1 (bort 21)

Appendix 10

Victories of the 812ᵗʰ IAP pilots in the South Ukraine battles (265ᵗʰ IAD)

No.	No.	Date	Time	Pilot	Score	Downed	Location of aerial combat
157	1	06.09.43	7:20	Ml. Lt. Peskarev, Petr	1	He111	East of Makeyevka
158	2	06.09.43	7:20	Flt. Cdr., Lt. Kalugin, Serafim	8	He111	East of Makeyevka
159	3	19.09.43	~ 15:00	Deputy Sqn. Cdr., Lt. Churakov, Georgiy	5	Bf109	Pokrovskoye
160	4	19.09.43	~ 15:00	Deputy Sqn. Cdr., Lt. Churakov, Georgiy	6	Bf109	Pokrovskoye
161	5	21.09.43	8:00	Ml. Lt. Maksimov, Ivan	1	Ju88	Yanchekrak
162	6	21.09.43	12:30	Sqn. Cdr., Kapitan Ankudinov, Yegor	2	He111	Shcherbakovka
163	7	21.09.43	12:30	Deputy Sqn Cdr., Lt. Fedorov, Ivan	5	He111	Shcherbakovka
164	8	21.09.43	12:30	Ml. Lt. Maksimov, Ivan	2	Bf110	Shcherbakovka
165	9	21.09.43	13:10	Ml. Lt. Tikhomirov, Fedor	1	Ju88	West of Zherebets
166	10	21.09.43	13:10	Ml. Lt. Tikhomirov, Fedor	2	Ju88	10 km west of Zaporozhye
167	11	21.09.43	13:10	Flt. Cdr., Lt. Martynenko, Ivan	3	Ju88	Stepnaya
168	12	21.09.43	13:10	Ml. Lt. Kuznetsov, Andrey	1	Ju88	West of Shcherbakovka
169	13	21.09.43	13:10-13:15	Ml. Lt. Kashirin, Mikhail	1	Ju88	West of Zherebets
170	14	25.09.43	8:10	Deputy Sqn Cdr., Lt. Fedorov, Ivan	6	He111	West of Bolshoy Tokmak
171	15	25.09.43	15:10-16:20	Sqn. Cdr., St. Lt. Tishchenko, Aleksandr	5	Bf109	Kopani
172	16	25.09.43	15:10-16:20	Ml. Lt. Vasilevskiy, Sergey	1	Ju87	Kopani
173	17	25.09.43	16:40	Deputy Sqn Cdr., Lt. Fedorov, Ivan	7	He111	Southwest of Shcherbakovka (Ognevka)
174	18	25.09.43	17:40	Sqn. Cdr., Lt Mashenkin, Aleksey	6	He111	West of Dmitrovka
175	19	25.09.43	17:40	Navigator, Kapitan Popov, Ivan	1	Bf109	East of Yanchekrak
176	20	26.09.43	7:38	Lt. Shishkin, Vasiliy	1	He111	Mikhaylovka
177	21	26.09.43	12:50-13:05	Ml. Lt. Dergunov, Mikhail	1	Ju87	Bolshoy Tokmak
178	22	26.09.43	12:50	Deputy Sqn Cdr., Lt. Fedorov, Ivan	8	Ju88	15 km west of Kopani (Zelenyy Gay)
179	23	26.09.43	12:50	Flt. Cdr., Lt. Kalugin, Serafim	9	Ju88	Yurtuk
180	24	26.09.43	13:05	Flt. Cdr., Lt. Martynenko, Ivan	4	Bf109	Volnaya (15 km west of Kopani)
181	25	26.09.43	17:25	Ml. Lt. Dergunov, Mikhail	2	Ju87	Bolshoy Tokmak
182	26	26.09.43	17:45	Ml. Lt. Maksimov, Ivan	3	Ju87	Bolshoy Tokmak
183	27	26.09.43	17:50	Lt. Shishkin, Vasiliy	2	Bf109	Zelenyy Gay
184	28	27.09.43	13:40	Deputy Sqn Cdr., Lt. Tumanov, Aleksandr	5	Ju88	3 km west of Kopani
185	29	27.09.43	13:40	Chief of VSS, Kapitan Popov, Ivan	2	Bf109	3 km east of Prishib
–	–	27.09.43	13:40-13:45	Group	–	Ju88 damaged	Prishib – Kopani
186	30	28.09.43	17:30	Sqn. Cdr., St. Lt. Tishchenko, Aleksandr	6	Ju87	West of Neydorf
187	31	01.10.43	11:25	Chief of VSS, Kapitan Popov, Ivan	3	Bf109	East of Mikhaylovka
188	32	01.10.43	13:50	Deputy Sqn Cdr., Lt. Fedorov, Ivan	9	Bf109	Southeast of Burchak
189	33	01.10.43	14:50-15:00	Serzhant Konovalov, Nikolay	1	He111	Voroshilovka – Burchak
190	34	03.10.43	11:40	Navigator, Kapitan Tarasov, Pavel	19	Bf109	N. Andreyevka
191	35	21.10.43	15:05	Deputy Sqn Cdr., Lt. Fedorov, Ivan	10	Bf109	In flight, 2 km east of Krasnyy
192	36	23.10.43	9:35	Deputy Sqn Cdr., Lt. Fedorov, Ivan	11	Hs129	Northwest of Akimovka
193	37	23.10.43	9:45	Lt. Shishkin, Vasiliy	3	Hs129	West of Vladimirovka
194	38	24.10.43	17:30	Zampolit Mayor Pasynok, Timofey	1	Bf109	12 km northwest of Melitopol
195	39	24.10.43	17:30	Deputy Sqn Cdr., Lt. Tumanov, Aleksandr	6	Bf109	12 km northwest of Melitopol
196	40	25.10.43	13:10-13:58	Ml. Lt. Maksimov, Ivan	4	Hs129	10 km west of Akimovka
197	41	25.10.43	16:55	Ml. Lt. Podymov, Nikolay	1	Ju87	Marienfeld
198	42	25.10.43	16:58	Sqn. Cdr., Kapitan Ankudinov, Yegor	3	Ju87	1 km north of Darmshtadt
199	43	25.10.43	17:10	Ml. Lt. Peskarev, Petr	2	Ju87	South of Mariental
200	44	25.10.43	17:10	Chief of VSS, Kapitan Popov, Ivan	4	Ju87	North of Akimovka
201	45	25.10.43	17:10-17:20	Deputy Sqn Cdr., Lt. Fedorov, Ivan	12	Bf109	East of Sharlenfeld
202	46	28.10.43	9:25	Ml. Lt. Tikhomirov, Fedor	3	Bf109	West of Nizhniye Serogozy
203	47	28.10.43	9:00-10:00	Chief of VSS, Kapitan Tarasov, Pavel	20	Hs129	Nizhniye Serogozy
204	48	28.10.43	10:40	Sqn. Cdr., Kapitan Ankudinov, Yegor	4	Bf109	Nova Nikolayevka
205	49	28.10.43	10:40	Deputy Sqn Cdr., Lt. Fedorov, Ivan	13	Fw189	Southwest of Nizhniye Serogozy
206	50	28.10.43	10:30-10:50	Ml. Lt. Maksimov, Ivan	5	Ju87	Akimovka
207	51	28.10.43	16:30	Ml. Lt. Kashirin, Mikhail	2	Ju87	West of Nizhnyaya Torgayevka
208	52	29.10.43	8:20	Chief of VSS, Kapitan Tarasov, Pavel	21	Ju87	Malaya Blagoveshchenka
209	53	29.10.43	8:21	Chief of VSS, Kapitan Tarasov, Pavel	22	Ju87	Malaya Blagoveshchenka – Serogozy
210	54	29.10.43	8:25	Zampolit Mayor Pasynok, Timofey	2	Ju87	Southeast of Torgayevka

Appendix 10 (Continued)

Victories of the 812th IAP pilots in the South Ukraine battles 265th IAD)

No.	No.	Date	Time	Pilot	Score	Downed	Location of aerial combat
211	55	29.10.43	8:25	Zampolit Mayor Pasynok, Timofey	3	Ju87	Southeast of Torgayevka
212	56	06.11.43	13:20–13:50	Ml. Lt. Tikhomirov, Fedor	4	Bf109	Perekop - Dzhankoy
213	57	22.11.43	15:45–15:47	Navigator Kapitan Popov, Ivan	5	Bf109	Northwest of Verkhniy Rogachik (N. Znamenka)
214	58	28.11.43	15:10	Lt. Razumovich, Aleksandr	1	He111	Southern outskirts of Vodyanoye (Belozerka)
215	59	28.11.43	15:20	Lt. Shishkin, Vasiliy	4	Bf109	Northwest of Stakhanov
216	60	28.11.43	16:00	Chief of VSS Kapitan Tarasov, Pavel	23	Bf109	Northeast of Verkhniy Rogachik
217	61	28.11.43	16:00	Lt. Obukhov, V.I.	1	Bf109	Verkhnyaya Ukrainka
218	62	28.11.43	~16:40	Ml. Lt. Serezhenko, Pavel	1	Ju88	North of Bolshaya Belozerka
219	63	20.12.43	13:25	Sqn. Cdr., Kapitan Ankudinov, Yegor	5	Fw190	Southeast of Dneprovka
220	64	31.12.43	-	Sqn. Cdr,. Kapitan Ankudinov, Yegor	6	Hs129	Over Bolshaya Kostromka airfield
-	-	31.12.43	-	Sqn. Cdr., Kapitan Ankudinov, Yegor	-	He111 set fire on the ground	Bolshaya Kostromka airfield
-	-	31.12.43	-	Lt. Shishkin, Vasiliy	-	He111 set fire on the ground	Bolshaya Kostromka airfield
-	-	31.12.43	-	Dpty. Sqn Cdr., Lt Fedorov, Ivan	-	He111 set fire on the ground	Bolshaya Kostromka airfield
-	-	31.12.43	-	Ml. Lt. Podymov, Nikolay	-	Hs129 set fire on the ground	Bolshaya Kostromka airfield

Appendix 11 Combat sorties flown and enemy aircraft destroyed by 812th IAP pilots during the Great Patriotic War (as of the end of December 1943)

Score rank	Pilot	Combat sorties	Kills
1	Mayor Tarasov, Pavel	260	23
2	Starshiy Leytenant Fedorov, Ivan	106	13
3	Leytenant Shishkin, Vasiliy	68	4
4	Kapitan Tishchenko, Aleksandr	93	6/1
5	Kapitan Ankudinov, Yegor	64	6
6	Ml. Leytenant Podymov, Nikolay	39	1
7	Mayor Popov, Ivan	55	5
8	Ml. Leytenant Tikhomirov, Fedor	66	4
9	Starshiy Leytenant Mashenkin, Aleksey	41	6
10	Leytenant Martynenko, Ivan	39	4
11	Leytenant Peskarev, Petr	47 (200 in U-2)	2
12	Ml. Leytenant Stryuk, Ivan	25	-
13	Ml. Leytenant Serezhenko, Pavel	28	1
14	Leytenant Vasilevskiy, Sergey	13	1
15	Ml. Leytenant Razumovich, Aleksandr	34	1
16	Ml. Leytenant Sidorenko, Ivan	18	-
17	Ml. Leytenant Sukhorukov, Nikolay	12	-
18	Ml. Leytenant Kuznetsov, Andrey	41	1
19	Ml. Leytenant Vinogradov, Veniamin	-	-
20	Ml. Leytenant Sharapov, Pavel	-	-
21	Ml. Leytenant Davydov, Yuriy	-	-
22	Ml. Leytenant Sevastyanov	2	-
23.	Ml. Leytenant Karasev, Mikhail	-	-
24	Ml. Leytenant Kureyev, Yuriy	-	-
25	Ml. Leytenant Kononenko	-	-
26	Ml. Leytenant Bartash	-	-

Appendix 12

Combat results of 265th IAD regiments for April 1944

Regiment	291st IAP	402nd IAP	812th IAP	Total
Number of combat sorties	610	760	604	1974
Aerial engagements conducted	26	83	28	146
Enemy aircraft shot down	23	56	30	109
Set on fire on airfields	21	36	19	76
Total Victories	**44**	**92**	**49**	**185***
Division losses				
Shot down in aerial engagements	2	1	3	6
Shot down by antiaircraft fire	1	-	-	1
Did not return to airfield	1	1	1	3
Total Losses	**8**	**4**	**6**	**18**

*-data cannot be considered definitive, since complete analysis was not conducted of combat actions of 291st and 402nd IAPs

Appendix 13

Pilot losses of the 812th IAP in combat during the Crimean operation, 1944

No.	Pilot	Date	Cause / Particulars
1	Ml. Leytenant Obukhov, Yuriy Aleksandrovich, born 1922	09.01.1944	Injured in aircraft accident (04.01.1944). Yak-9T (No. 0238)
2	Flt Cdr., Ml. Lt. Prikhodko, Aleksandr Andreyevich, born 1918	25.01.1944	Did not return from combat mission. Yak-9D
3	Leytenant Tumanov, Aleksandr Ivanovich, born 1921	06.02.1944	Died during strafing (shot down). Yak-9T (No. 0298)
4	Ml. Leytenant Zuyev, Sergey Semenovich, born 1923	12.02.1944	Shot down in aerial combat. Yak-1 (22147)
5	Ml. Leytenant Makarchuk, Vasiliy Ivanovich, born 1923	27.02.1944	Did not return from combat mission. Yak-1 (No. 01142, bort 01)
6	Flt Cdr., Ml. Lt. Podymov, Nikolay Avtonomovich, born 1922	11.03.1944	Did not return from combat mission. Yak-1 (bort 43)
7	Ml. Leytenant Vinogradov, Veniamin Stepanovich, born 1921	11.03.1944	Shot down in aerial combat. Yak-9 (bort 63)
8	Ml. Leytenant Sharapov, Pavel Akakyevich, born 19--	11.03.1944	Did not return from combat mission. Yak-1 (bort 06)
9	Ml. Leytenant Karasev, Mikhail Mikhaylovich, born 1923	14.03.1944	Shot down in aerial combat. Yak-1 (bort 50)
10	Ml. Leytenant Davydov, Yuriy Vasiliyevich, born 1921	17.03.1944	Shot down in aerial combat. Yak-1 (No. 39132, bort 39)
11	Ml. Leytenant Razumovich, Aleksandr Vasiliyevich, born 1921	17.03.1944	Shot down in aerial combat. Yak-1 (bort 37)
12	Flt Cdr., Lt. Tikhomirov, Fedor Mikhaylovich, born 1922	09.04.1944	Shot down over enemy-occupied territory. Yak-9 (1028, bort 28)
13	Flt Cdr., Leytenant Peskarev, Petr Georgievich, born 1921	12.04.1944	Shot down in aerial combat. Yak-9 (1052, bort 52)
14	Ml. Leytenant Kureyev, Yuriy Mikhaylovich, born 1922	12.04.1944	Shot down in aerial combat. Yak-1 (No. 45138, bort 45)
15	Ml. Leytenant Stryuk, Ivan Fedorovich, born 1922	21.04.1944	Did not return from combat mission. Yak-9 (No. 1066, bort 06)
16	Ml. Leytenant Veselov, Konstantin Pavlovich, born 1922	07.05.1944	Died from burns

Appendix 14

Victories of the 812th IAP pilots in the Crimean operation battles (265th IAD)

No.	No.	Date	Time	Pilot	Score	Downed	Location of aerial combat
221	1	10.01.44	13:50-14:00	Sqn. Cdr. St. Lt. Fedorov, Ivan	14	Bf109	Lepetikha airfield area (Voroshilov)
-	-	11.01.44	15:30-15:35	Sqn. Cdr. St. Lt. Fedorov, Ivan	-	He111 set on fire on ground	Lepetikha airfield area (Voroshilov)
-	-	12.01.44	-	Chief of VSS Kapitan Tarasov, Pavel	-	He111 set on fire on ground	Lepetikha airfield area (Voroshilov)
-	-	12.01.44	-	Ml. Lt. Tikhomirov, Fedor	-	He111 set on fire on ground	Lepetikha airfield area (Voroshilov)
222	2	14.01.44	12:50	Mayor Popov, Ivan	6	Bf109	Lepetikha airfield area (Voroshilov)
223	3	14.01.44	12:50	Lt. Peskarev, Petr	3	Bf109	Lepetikha airfield area (Voroshilov)
224	4	14.01.44	12:50	Sqn. Cdr. St. Lt. Tishchenko, Aleksandr	7	Bf109	Lepetikha airfield area (Voroshilov)
225	5	14.01.44	12:50	Ml. Lt. Podymov, Nikolay	2	Bf109	Lepetikha airfield area (Voroshilov)
226	6	14.01.44	16:20	Ml. Lt. Podymov, Nikolay	3	Bf109	Lepetikha airfield area (Voroshilov)
227	7	14.01.44	16:20	Mayor Popov, Ivan	7	Bf109	Lepetikha airfield area (Voroshilov)
228	8	14.01.44	16:20	Sqn. Cdr. Kapitan Ankudinov, Yegor	7	Bf109	Lepetikha airfield area (Voroshilov)
-	-	14.01.44	12:50-16:20	Chief of VSS Kapitan Tarasov, Pavel	-	He111 set on fire on ground	Lepetikha airfield area (Voroshilov)
-	-	14.01.44	12:50-16:20	Ml. Lt. Tikhomirov, Fedor	-	Hs129 set on fire on ground	Lepetikha airfield area (Voroshilov)
-	-	14.01.44	12:50-16:20	Lt. Shishkin, Vasiliy	-	Hs129 set on fire on ground	Lepetikha airfield area (Voroshilov)
-	-	14.01.44	12:50-16:20	Lt. Razumovich, Aleksandr	-	Hs129 set on fire on ground	Lepetikha airfield area (Voroshilov)
-	-	14.01.44	12:50-16:20	Lt. Shishkin, Vasiliy	-	Hs129 set on fire on ground	Lepetikha airfield area (Voroshilov)
-	-	14.01.44	12:50-16:20	Lt. Serezhenko, Pavel	-	Hs129 set on fire on ground	Lepetikha airfield area (Voroshilov)
-	-	14.01.44	12:50-16:20	Lt. Serezhenko, Pavel	-	Hs129 set on fire on ground	Lepetikha airfield area (Voroshilov)
-	-	03.02.44	15:28-16:00	Ml. Lt. Zuyev, Sergey	-	He111 set on fire on ground	Stepnoy (in Nikopol area)
-	-	03.02.44	15:39-17:10	Sqn. Cdr. St. Lt. Fedorov, Ivan	-	Hs129 set on fire on ground	Lepetikha airfield area (Voroshilov)
-	-	05.02.44	-	Sqn. Cdr. St. Lt. Fedorov, Ivan	-	Fi156 set on fire on ground	Northeast of Aleksandrovka
-	-	12.02.44	14:54	Lt. Shishkin, Vasiliy / Lt. Razumovich, Aleksandr	-	Ju87 damaged	Sivash
229	9	25.02.44	-	Lt. Shishkin, Vasiliy	5	Ju87	Chuchak
230	10	27.02.44	17:40	Lt. Peskarev, Petr	4	Ju87	Tomashevka
231	11	27.02.44	17:41	Lt. Peskarev, Petr	5	Bf109	Tomashevka
232	12	01.03.44	14:00	Ml. Lt. Podymov, Nikolay	4	Ju87	South of Chirik
233	13	01.03.44	14:00	Ml. Lt. Tikhomirov, Fedor	5	Ju87	Ruskiy Lake area
234	14	01.03.44	17:35	Sqn. Cdr. St. Lt. Fedorov, Ivan	15	Bf109	Korocha-Kitay
235	15	01.03.44	17:35	Chief of VSS Kapitan Tarasov, Pavel	24	Ju87	Tyuk-Tyube
-	-	01.03.44	-	Ml. Lt. Karasev, Mikhail	-	Bf109 damaged	-
-	-	01.03.44	-	Ml. Lt. Stryuk, Ivan	-	Fw190 damaged	-

Appendix 14 (Continued)

Victories of the 812th IAP pilots in the Crimean operation battles (265th IAD)

No.	No.	Date	Time	Pilot	Score	Downed	Location of aerial combat
236	16	02.03.44	11:30-12:00	Sqn. Cdr. St. Lt. Fedorov, Ivan	16	Bf109	While strafing Rayzendorf airfield
237	17	02.03.44	11:30-12:00	Sqn. Cdr. St. Lt. Fedorov, Ivan	17	Bf109	While strafing Rayzendorf airfield
238	18	02.03.44	11:30-12:00	Ml. Lt. Podymov, Nikolay	5	Bf109	While strafing Rayzendorf airfield
239	19	02.03.44	11:30-12:00	Mayor Popov, Ivan	8	Ju87	While strafing Rayzendorf airfield
-	-	02.03.44	11:30-12:00	Mayor Popov, Ivan	-	He111 set on fire on ground	Rayzendorf airfield
-	-	02.03.44	11:30-12:00	Chief of VSS Mayor Tarasov, Pavel	-	Ju88 set on fire on ground	Rayzendorf airfield
-	-	02.03.44	11:30-12:00	Navigator Kapitan Ankudinov, Yegor	-	Ju87 set on fire on ground	Rayzendorf airfield
-	-	02.03.44	11:30-12:00	Ml. Lt. Kureyev, Yuriy	-	Bf109 set on fire on ground	Rayzendorf airfield
-	-	02.03.44	11:10-12:00	Mayor Popov, Ivan	-	Ju87 set on fire on ground	Rayzendorf airfield
-	-	02.03.44	11:10-12:00	Lt. Shishkin, Vasiliy	-	Ju87 set on fire on ground	Rayzendorf airfield
-	-	02.03.44	11:10-12:00	Ml. Lt. Karasev, Mikhail	-	Ju87 set on fire on ground	Rayzendorf airfield
-	-	02.03.44	11:10-12:00	Ml Lt. Vinogradov, Veniamin	-	Ju87 set on fire on ground	Rayzendorf airfield
-	-	02.03.44	11:10-12:00	Ml. Lt. Podymov, Nikolay	-	Ju87 set on fire on ground	Rayzendorf airfield
240	-	02.03.44	-	Navigator Kapitan Ankudinov, Yegor	8	He111 night victory	Sivash
241	21	11.03.44	10:30	Ml Lt. Vinogradov, Veniamin	1	Fw190	Taub. In crossing area
242	22	11.03.44	10:30	Ml. Lt. Sukhorukov, Nikolay	1	Bf109	Chirik. In crossing area
243	23	11.03.44	13:25-14:25	Ml. Lt. Stryuk, Ivan	1	Bf109	Sivash. In crossing area
244	24	11.03.44	13:25-14:25	Ml. Lt. Sidorenko, Ivan	1	Bf109	Koranki. In crossing area
245	25	11.03.44	13:25-14:25	Lt. Peskarev, Petr	6	Bf109	Tarkhan. In crossing area
246	26	11.03.44	13:25-14:25	Ml. Lt. Tikhomirov, Fedor	6	Ju87	Tarkhan. In crossing area
247	27	11.03.44	13:25-14:25	Ml. Lt. Podymov, Nikolay	6	Fw190	Ishun. In crossing area
248	28	11.03.44	13:25-14:25	Sqn. Cdr. St. Lt. Fedorov, Ivan	18	Fw190	Sivash. In crossing area
249	29	11.03.44	13:25-14:25	Sqn. Cdr. St. Lt. Fedorov, Ivan	19	Ju87	Sivash. In crossing area
250	30	11.03.44	13:25-14:25	Lt. Shishkin, Vasiliy	6	Ju87	Sivash. In crossing area
251	31	13.03.44	12:00-12:45	Sqn. Cdr. St. Lt. Fedorov, Ivan	20	Fw190	Korocha-Kitay. In crossing area
252	32	14.03.44	12:05	Chief of VSS Mayor Tarasov, Pavel	25	Fw190	Tarkhan. In crossing area
253	33	14.03.44	12:05	Sqn. Cdr. St. Lt. Fedorov, Ivan	21	Fw190	Chigory. In crossing area
254	34	14.03.44	14:35-14:40	Chief of VSS Mayor Tarasov, Pavel	26	Bf109	Chigory. In crossing area
255	35	14.03.44	14:35-14:40	Sqn. Cdr., Kptn. Tishchenko, Aleksandr	8	Ju87	South of Russkiy Island
256	36	14.03.44	14:35-14:40	Ml. Lt. Tikhomirov, Fedor	7	Ju87	5 km south of Russkiy Island
257	37	16.03.44	15:50	Sqn. Cdr. St. Lt. Fedorov, Ivan	22	Bf109	Biyuk-Kiyak. In crossing area
258	38	16.03.44	15:51	Sqn. Cdr. St. Lt. Fedorov, Ivan	23	Bf109	Tyuk-Tyube. In crossing area
259	39	17.03.44	10:44	Sqn. Cdr. St. Lt. Fedorov, Ivan	24	Bf109	Kamyshevakha. In crossing area
-	-	17.03.44	15:00-16:00	Sqn. Cdr. St. Lt. Fedorov, Ivan	-	Bf109	Sivash. In crossing area
260	40	18.03.44	~11:25	Sqn. Cdr. St. Lt. Fedorov, Ivan	25	Fw190	Sivash
260	41	18.03.44	11:25	Ml. Lt. Tikhomirov, Fedor	8	Fw190	Sivash
262	42	07.04.44	10:27	Lt. Peskarev, Petr	7	Bf109	Sivash. In crossing area
-	-	07.04.44	16:00-17:10	Mayor Popov, Ivan	-	Ju87 set on fire on ground	Ichki airfield
-	-	07.04.44	16:00-17:10	Chief of VSS Mayor Tarasov, Pavel	-	Ju87 set on fire on ground	Ichki airfield
-	-	07.04.44	16:00-17:10	Sqn. Cdr., St. Lt. Mashenkin, Aleksey	-	Ju87 set on fire on ground	Ichki airfield
-	-	07.04.44	16:00-17:10	Chief of VSS Mayor Tarasov, Pavel	-	Ju87 set on fire on ground	Ichki airfield
-	-	07.04.44	16:00-17:10	Lt. Peskarev, Petr	-	Fw190 damaged on ground	Ichki airfield
-	-	07.04.44	16:00-17:10	Sqn. Cdr. St. Lt. Fedorov, Ivan	-	Fw190 damaged on ground	Ichki airfield
-	-	07.04.44	16:00-17:10	Ml. Lt. Kureyev, Yuriy	-	Fw190 damaged on ground	Ichki airfield
-	-	07.04.44	16:00-17:10	Ml. Lt. Stryuk, Ivan	-	Fw190 damaged on ground	Ichki airfield
-	-	07.04.44	16:00-17:10	Ml. Lt. Kuznetsov, Andrey	-	Fw190 damaged on ground	Ichki airfield
263	43	08.04.44	18:00-19:17	Sqn. Cdr. St. Lt. Fedorov, Ivan	26	Fw190	East of Ichki airfield
-	-	08.04.44	18:00-19:17	Chief of VSS Mayor Tarasov, Pavel	-	Ju87 set on fire on ground	Ichki airfield
-	-	08.04.44	18:00-19:17	Lt. Peskarev, Petr	-	Fw190 damaged on ground	Ichki airfield
-	-	08.04.44	18:00-19:17	Sqn. Cdr., St. Lt. Mashenkin, Aleksey	-	Fw190 damaged on ground	Ichki airfield
-	-	08.04.44	18:00-19:17	Group	-	Fw190 damaged on ground	Ichki airfield
264	44	09.04.44	17:16-18:20	Mayor Popov, Ivan	9	Ju87	Tomashevka
265	45	09.04.44	17:16-18:20	Lt. Peskarev, Petr	8	Bf109	South of Tomashevka
266	46	10.04.44	16:40	Mayor Popov, Ivan	10	Fw190	Tomashevka

Victories of the 812th IAP pilots in the Crimean operation battles (265th IAD)

No.	No.	Date	Time	Pilot	Score	Downed	Location of aerial combat
267	47	10.04.44	18:09-18:50	Mayor Popov, Ivan	11	Ju87	4 km north of Rayzendorf
268	48	10.04.44	18:09-18:50	Chief of VSS Mayor Tarasov, Pavel	27	Fw190	Dzharok
269	49	10.04.44	18:09-18:50	Ml. Lt. Kureyev, Yuriy	1	Fw190	West of Ishun
270	50	10.04.44	18:09-18:50	Sqn. Cdr., Kptn. Tishchenko, Aleksandr	9	Fw190	Voinka
271	51	11.04.44	10:50	Mayor Popov, Ivan	12	Fw190	2 km west of Dzhankoy
272	52	11.04.44	11:47-12:25	Ml. Lt. Belkin, Semen	1	Bf109	In the Sivash crossing area
273	53	11.04.44	11:40-12:47	Navigator Kapitan Ankudinov, Yegor	9	Bf109	Biyuk Neyman
–	–	11.04.44	14:20-15:30	Sqn. Cdr., Kptn. Tishchenko, Aleksandr	–	Ju52 set on fire on ground	Sarabuz airfield
–	–	11.04.44	14:20-15:30	Ml. Lt. Vasilevskiy, Sergey	–	Ju52 set on fire on ground	Sarabuz airfield
–	–	11.04.44	14:20-15:30	Lt. Serezhenko, Pavel	–	Ju52 set on fire on ground	Sarabuz airfield
–	–	15.04.44	05:55-7:10	Lt. Serezhenko, Pavel	–	Ju87 set on fire on ground	Khersones airfield
–	–	15.04.44	05:55-7:10	Sqn. Cdr., Kptn. Tishchenko, Aleksandr	–	Ju87 damaged on ground	Khersones airfield
–	–	15.04.44	05:55-7:10	Ml. Lt. Veselov, Konstantin	–	Ju87 damaged on ground	Khersones airfield
274	54	15.04.44	13:40	Sqn. Cdr., St. Lt. Mashenkin, Aleksey	7	Fw190	North of Makenziya (Sevastopol)
275	55	15.04.44	14:50-15:50	Chief of VSS Mayor Tarasov, Pavel	28	Bf109	North of Inkerman
276	56	15.04.44	14:50-15:50	Ml. Lt. Stryuk, Ivan	2	Fw190	South of Makenziya
277	57	17.04.44	17:10	Mayor Popov, Ivan	13	Bf110	Sevastopol – 6th Versta airfield
278	58	19.04.44	16:35	Mayor Popov, Ivan	14	Bf109	2 km southeast of Cape Fiolent
279	59	19.04.44	16:40	Lt. Vasilevskiy, Sergey	2	Fw190	South of Dzhanishev
–	–	19.04.44	18:30-19:30	Sqn. Cdr. St. Lt. Fedorov, Ivan	–	Ju87 set on fire on ground	6th Versta airfield
–	–	19.04.44	18:30-19:30	Sqn. Cdr. St. Lt. Fedorov, Ivan	–	Ju87 set on fire on ground	6th Versta airfield
–	–	19.04.44	18:30-19:30	Mayor Popov, Ivan	–	Ju52 set on fire on ground	6th Versta airfield
–	–	19.04.44	18:30-19:30	Chief of VSS Mayor Tarasov, Pavel	–	Ju52 set on fire on ground	6th Versta airfield
–	–	19.04.44	18:30-19:30	Ml. Lt. Stryuk, Ivan	–	Ju52 set on fire on ground	6th Versta airfield
280	60	21.04.44	14:45	Chief of VSS Mayor Tarasov, Pavel	29	Fw190	Khersones area
281	61	21.04.44	14:50	Ml. Lt. Sukhorukov, Nikolay	2	Fw190	East of Khersones
282	62	21.04.44	14:50	Mayor Popov, Ivan	15	Fw190	Southeast of Khersones
–	–	22.04.44	~8:26	Sqn. Cdr., Kptn. Tishchenko, Aleksandr	–	Fw190 damaged	Karan
283	63	22.04.44	10:30	Navigator Kapitan Ankudinov, Yegor	10	Fw190	Sevastopol
284	64	22.04.44	19:25	Sqn. Cdr. St. Lt. Fedorov, Ivan	27	Fw190	4 km west of Cape Khersones
285	65	22.04.44	19:30	Sqn. Cdr., St. Lt. Mashenkin, Aleksey	8	Fw190	Khersones area
–	–	23.04.44	5:50-6:40	Sqn. Cdr. St. Lt. Fedorov, Ivan	–	Ju52 set on fire on ground	6th Versta airfield
–	–	23.04.44	5:50-6:40	Ml. Lt. Sukhorukov, Nikolay	–	Ju52 set on fire on ground	6th Versta airfield
–	–	23.04.44	5:50-6:40	Sqn. Cdr., St. Lt. Mashenkin, Aleksey	–	Ju52 set on fire on ground	6th Versta airfield
–	–	23.04.44	5:50-6:40	Ml. Lt. Sivko, Lev	–	Ju52 set on fire on ground	6th Versta airfield
286	66	24.04.44	8:45-9:40	Sqn. Cdr., Kptn. Tishchenko, Aleksandr	10	Bf109	Sevastopol – 6th Versta airfield
–	–	24.04.44	12:30	Mayor Popov, Ivan	–	Fw200 set on fire on ground	Khersones airfield
287	67	24.04.44	17:40	Mayor Popov, Ivan	16	Fw190	Balaklava
288	68	24.04.44	17:40	Mayor Popov, Ivan	17	Fw190	Balaklava
289	69	24.04.44	17:40	Chief of VSS Mayor Tarasov, Pavel	30	Bf109	Nov. Shuli
290	70	24.04.44	18:15	Sqn. Cdr., Kptn. Tishchenko, Aleksandr	11	Bf109	Sevastopol – 6th Versta airfield
291	71	24.04.44	18:15	Navigator Kapitan Ankudinov, Yegor	11	Bf109	Sevastopol – 6th Versta airfield
292	72	05.05.44	12:05-12:57	Mayor Popov, Ivan	18	Bf109	Khersones area
293	73	05.05.44	15:37-16:40	Navigator Kapitan Ankudinov, Yegor	12	Fw190	6th Versta airfield
294	74	05.05.44	15:37-16:40	Ml. Lt. Belkin, Semen	2	Fw190	South of 6th Versta airfield
295	75	06.05.44	17:20	Sqn. Cdr. St. Lt. Fedorov, Ivan	28	Bf109	South of Kacha
–	–	07.05.44	9:00	Sqn. Cdr., Kptn. Tishchenko, Aleksandr	–	Fw190 damaged	Belbek
–	–	09.05.44	7:55-8:45	Mayor Popov, Ivan	–	Ju52 set on fire on ground	Khersones airfield
–	–	09.05.44	12:20-13:20	Mayor Popov, Ivan	–	Fw200 set on fire on ground	6th Versta airfield
–	–	09.05.44	14:37-15:43	Ml. Lt. Sukhorukov, Nikolay	–	Fw190 set on fire on ground	Khersones airfield
–	–	09.05.44	14:37-15:43	Sqn. Cdr., St. Lt. Mashenkin, Aleksey	–	Fw190 set on fire on ground	Khersones airfield
–	–	09.05.44	19:22-19:45	Mayor Popov, Ivan	–	Fw200 set on fire on ground	Khersones airfield
–	–	11.05.44	9:00-9:25	Sqn. Cdr., St. Lt. Mashenkin, Aleksey	–	Ju52 set on fire on ground	Khersones airfield

Appendix 14 (Continued)

Victories of the 812th IAP pilots in the Crimean operation battles (265th IAD)

No.	No.	Date	Time	Pilot	Score	Downed	Location of aerial combat
–	–	11.05.44	11:05–11:30	Navigator Kapitan Ankudinov, Yegor	–	Ju52 set on fire on ground	Khersones airfield
–	–	11.05.44	12:35	Ml. Lt. Belkin, Semen	–	Ju52 set on fire on ground	Khersones airfield
296	76	12.05.44	8:05–8:50	Sqn. Cdr., St. Lt. Mashenkin, Aleksey	9	Bf110	Southwest of Khersones
–	–	12.05.44	8:35–9:10	Navigator Kapitan Ankudinov, Yegor	–	Bf110 damaged	Southwest of Khersones
–	–	13.05.44	3:25	Sqn. Cdr. St. Lt. Fedorov, Ivan	–	He111 damaged	East of Yevpatoriya

Appendix 15

812th IAP airfields — from March 1942 through June 1944

Period	Subordination				Airfield
March – May 1942	Moscow Military District				Lyubertsy (Moscow oblast)
May – June 1942	Moscow Military District				Shumino (Moscow oblast)
July – August 1942	263rd IAD			Kalinin Front	Dulovo (Kalinin oblast)
September 1942	283rd IAD			Moscow Military District	Stepygino (Moscow oblast)
Sept. – Dec. 1942	283rd IAD		16th VA	Stalingrad Front	Altukhov (Stalingrad oblast)
Dec. 1942 – Feb. 1943	8th ZIAD		3rd ZAB	Pri-Volga Military District	Bagay-Baranovka (Saratov oblast)
March – April 1943	265th IAD / 3rd IAK			Moscow Military District	Malino, Stepygino (Moscow oblast)
April – June 1943	265th IAD / 3rd IAK		4th VA	North Caucasus Front	Krasnoarmeyskaya (from 19.04), Novotitarovskaya, Tikhoretsk (Kuban)
June – August 1943	265th IAD / 3rd IAK		15th VA Reserve VK	Steppe Front	Lipetsk, Trubetchino (Ryazan oblast)
September 1943	265th IAD / 3rd IAK		8th VA	Southern Front	Shakhty, Oktyabrskiy (Rostov oblast)
Sept. – Oct. 1943	265th IAD / 3rd IAK		8th VA	Southern Front	Gulyaypolye, Kharkovo (Zaporozhye oblast)
October 1943	265th IAD / 3rd IAK		8th VA	4th Ukrainian Front	Astrakhanka (from 13.10) (Zaporozhye oblast)
Oct. – Nov. 1943	265th IAD / 3rd IAK		8th VA	4th Ukrainian Front	Chekhograd (from 27.10), Komsomolskiy (from 30.10) Krestovskiy (from 02.11.) Krasnoarmeyskiy (Zaporozhye oblast)
Nov. 1943 – Jan. 1944	265th IAD / 3rd IAK		8th VA	4th Ukrainian Front	Uspenskoye (07.11) Nizhnyaya Torgayevka (from 08.11) Gogolevka, Agayman (from 28.11), (Kherson oblast)
Jan. – April 1944	265th IAD / 3rd IAK		8th VA	4th Ukrainian Front	Veseloye [Khutor Veselyi] (from 20.01) Forward airfields: Zakharovka and Pokrovka, (Kherson oblast)
April – May 1944	265th IAD / 3rd IAK		8th VA	4th Ukrainian Front	Rayzendorf (11.04), Sarabuz (12.04), Adzhi-Bulat (14.04) (Crimea)
June 1944	265th IAD / 3rd IAK				Orel (through 21.06)

Appendix 16

265th IAD commanders during the Great Patriotic War

Commander	Period in position
Podpolkovnik Minayev, Aleksey Vasilyevich	09.06.1942 – 10.03.1943 - transferred to position of commander, 257th SAD
Podpolkovnik (from 23.05.43 - Polkovnik) Korobkov, Pavel Terentyevich	11.03.1943 – 26.06.1943 - transferred to position of commander, 320th IAD
Podpolkovnik (from 04.02.44 - Polkovnik) Koryagin, Aleksandr Aleksandrovich	27.06.1943 – 09.05.1945

Appendix 17

VVS ranks and equivalents during the Great Patriotic War

VVS	Luftwaffe	USAAF	RAF
Enlisted			
Krasnoarmeyets	Flieger	Private	Aircraftsman
Yefreitor	Gefreiter	Private 1st Class	Senior Aircraftsman
none	Obergefreiter	Corporal	Junior Technician
none	Hauptgefreiter	*none*	*none*
NCOs			
Mladshiy Serzhant	Unteroffizier	Staff Sergeant	Corporal
Serzhant	Unterfeldwebel	Sergeant	
Starshiy Serzhant	Feldwebel	Technical Sergeant	
Starshina	Oberfeldwebel	Master Sergeant	Flight Sergeant
Commissioned Officers			
Mladshiy Leytenant	*none*	*none*	*none*
Leytenant	Leutnant	2nd Lieutenant	Pilot Officer
Starshiy Leytenant	Oberleutnant	Lieutenant	Flying Officer
Kapitan	Hauptmann	Captain	Flight Lieutenant
Mayor	Major	Major	Squadron Leader
Podpolkovnik	Oberstleutnant	Lieutenant Colonel	Wing Commander
Polkovnik	Oberst	Colonel	Group Captain
General Officers			
General Mayor	Generalmajor	Brigadier General	Air Commodore
General Leytenant	Generalleutnant	Major General	Air Vice-Marshal
General Polkovnik	General	Lieutenant General	Air Marshal
General Armiy	Generaloberst	(4 star) General	Air Chief Marshal
Marshal Sovetskogo Soyuza	Generalfeldmarschall	(5 star) General of the Army	Marshal of the Royal Air Force
none	Reichsmarschall	*none*	*none*

The Officer Candidate / Warrant Officer classification is not given here as there is no VVS equivalent rank

Appendix 19

Combat results of the 812th IAP during the GPW

Period of combat actions	Combat sorties	Combat sortie hours	Number of victories over enemy aircraft	Particulars
29.07.1942 – 08.08.1942	141	142	1/	**14** aerial engagements
22.09.1942 – 09.12.1942	856	746	44	**52** aerial engagements
19.04.1943 – 29.06.1943	462	453	95	Data about number of aerial engagements conducted is not available
01.09.1943 – 31.12.1943	1156	1241	64 (+4[1])	**83** aerial engagements
01.01.1944 – 12.05.1944	1710	1605	76 (+64[1])	Data about number of aerial engagements conducted is not available Distribution of combat sorties: - for coverage of ground forces – **1194** - for reconnaissance of enemy forces – **55** - for escort of bombers – **152** - for strafing of enemy forces – **185** - for strafing of airfields – **31** - for interception and air superiority – **93**
20.06.1944 – 10.09.1944	1240	1137	40 (+23[1])	**50** aerial engagements Distribution of combat sorties: - for coverage of ground forces – **509** - for reconnaissance of enemy forces – **316** - for free hunt – **275** - for escort of shturmoviks and bombers – **109** - for interception and air superiority – **31**
08.01.1945 – 09.05.1945	1970	1030	96 (+27[1])	**247** aerial engagements Distribution of combat sorties: - for coverage of ground forces – **1650** - for reconnaissance of enemy forces – **167** - for free hunt – **84** - for escort of shturmoviks and bombers – **69**
Totals	**7535**	**6354**	**432 (+118[1])**	

(1) destroyed on enemy airfields during strafing attacks.

Appendix 18

Aces of the 812th IAP — 1942 - 1945

Ranking	Pilot	Victories P+G
1	Fedorov, I.V.	37
2	Tarasov, P.T. [1]	30+1
3	Popov, I.F.	24
4	Dzhabidze, D.V. [2]	20+2
5	Tishchenko, A.T.	18+2
6	Ankudinov, Ye.Ye.	15
7	Melnikov, V.I.	12
8	Svezhentsev, F.K.	11
9	Mashenkin, A.M.	11
10	Lopatin, N.V.	10 + 1 balloon
11	Kalugin, S.P.	9+1
12	Peskarev, P.G.	8
13	Tikhomirov, F.M.	8
14	Kablukov, V.	8
15	Batychko, I.D.	7+1
16	Veremeyenko, V.	6+4
17	Tumanov, A.I.	6+1
18	Churakov, G.P.	6
19	Shishkin, V.D.	6
20	Podymov, N.A.	6
21	Belkin, S.V.	6
22	Viktorovich, I.D.	6
23	Shuvalov, D.A.	6
24	Shcheglov, P.T.	6
25	Solyannikov, I.K.	5+1
26	Maksimov, I.A.	5
27	Martynenko, I.N.	5
28	Sukhorukov, N.F.	5
29	Kuznetsov, A.	5

(1) 18 personal victories while assigned to 812th IAP
(2) 9 personal victories while assigned to 812th IAP

Yak-1 1/48 scale

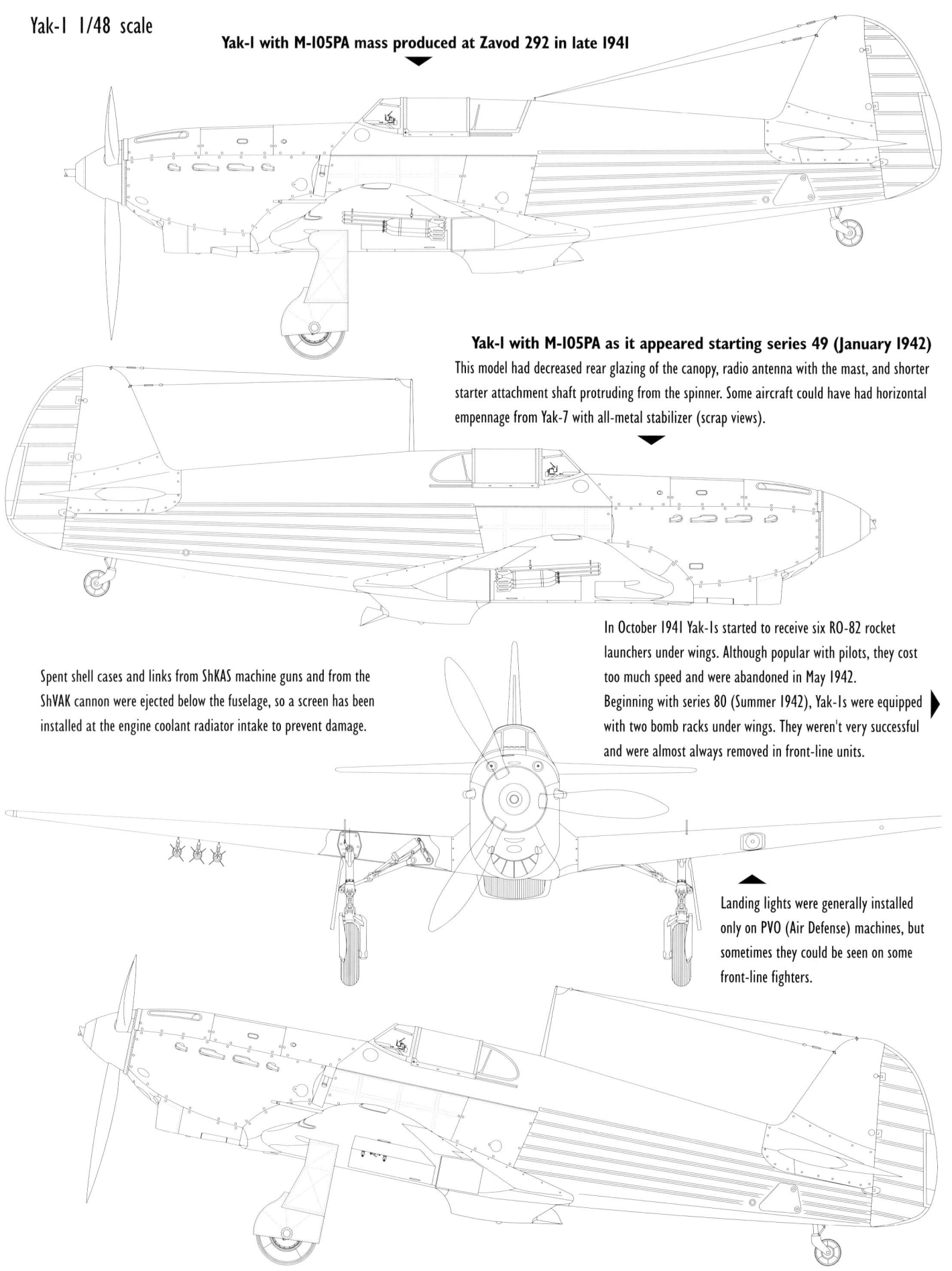

Yak-1 with M-105PA mass produced at Zavod 292 in late 1941

Yak-1 with M-105PA as it appeared starting series 49 (January 1942)
This model had decreased rear glazing of the canopy, radio antenna with the mast, and shorter starter attachment shaft protruding from the spinner. Some aircraft could have had horizontal empennage from Yak-7 with all-metal stabilizer (scrap views).

Spent shell cases and links from ShKAS machine guns and from the ShVAK cannon were ejected below the fuselage, so a screen has been installed at the engine coolant radiator intake to prevent damage.

In October 1941 Yak-1s started to receive six RO-82 rocket launchers under wings. Although popular with pilots, they cost too much speed and were abandoned in May 1942.
Beginning with series 80 (Summer 1942), Yak-1s were equipped with two bomb racks under wings. They weren't very successful and were almost always removed in front-line units.

Landing lights were generally installed only on PVO (Air Defense) machines, but sometimes they could be seen on some front-line fighters.

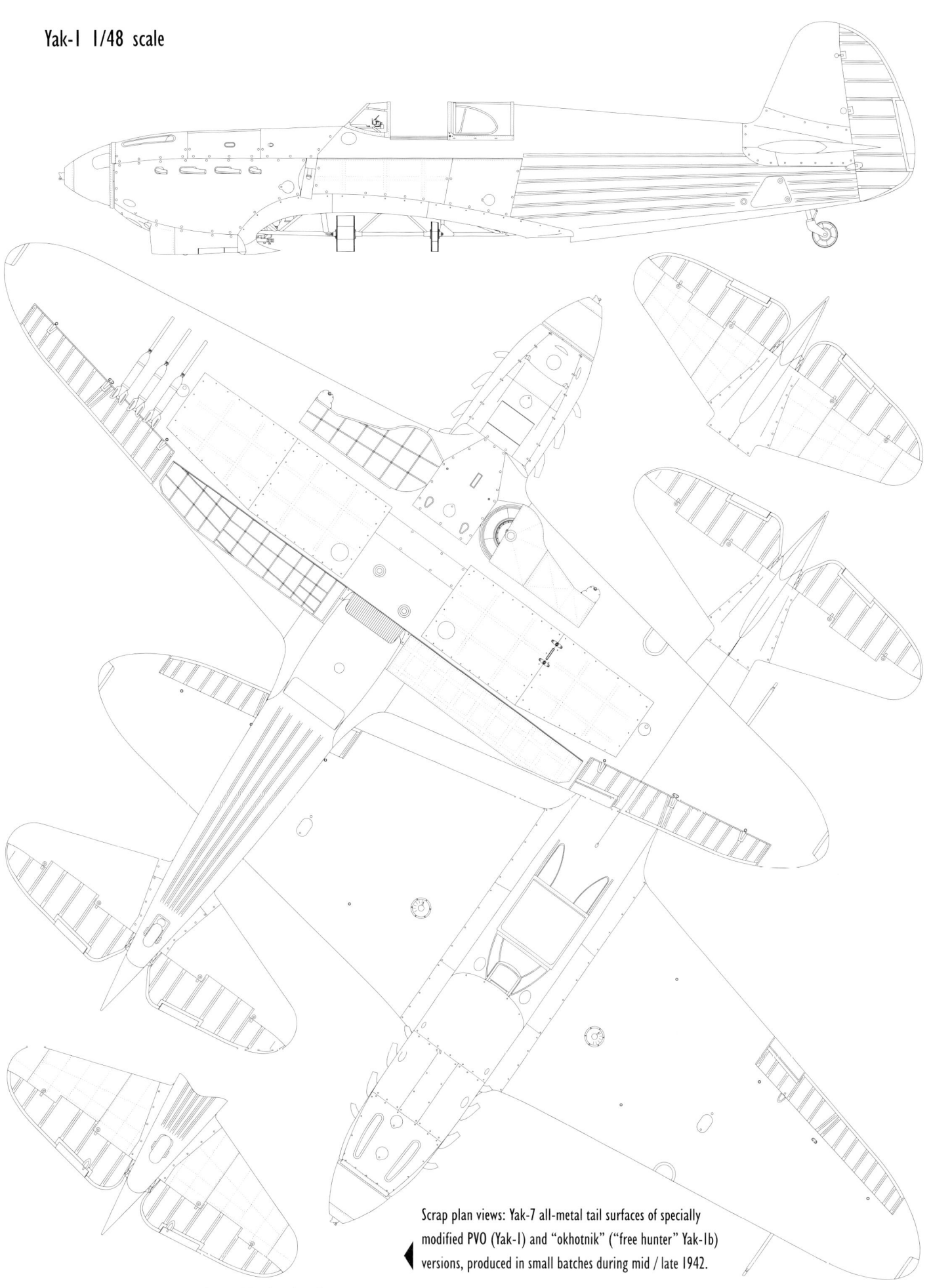

Scrap plan views: Yak-7 all-metal tail surfaces of specially modified PVO (Yak-1) and "okhotnik" ("free hunter" Yak-1b) versions, produced in small batches during mid / late 1942.

Yak-1b 1/48 scale

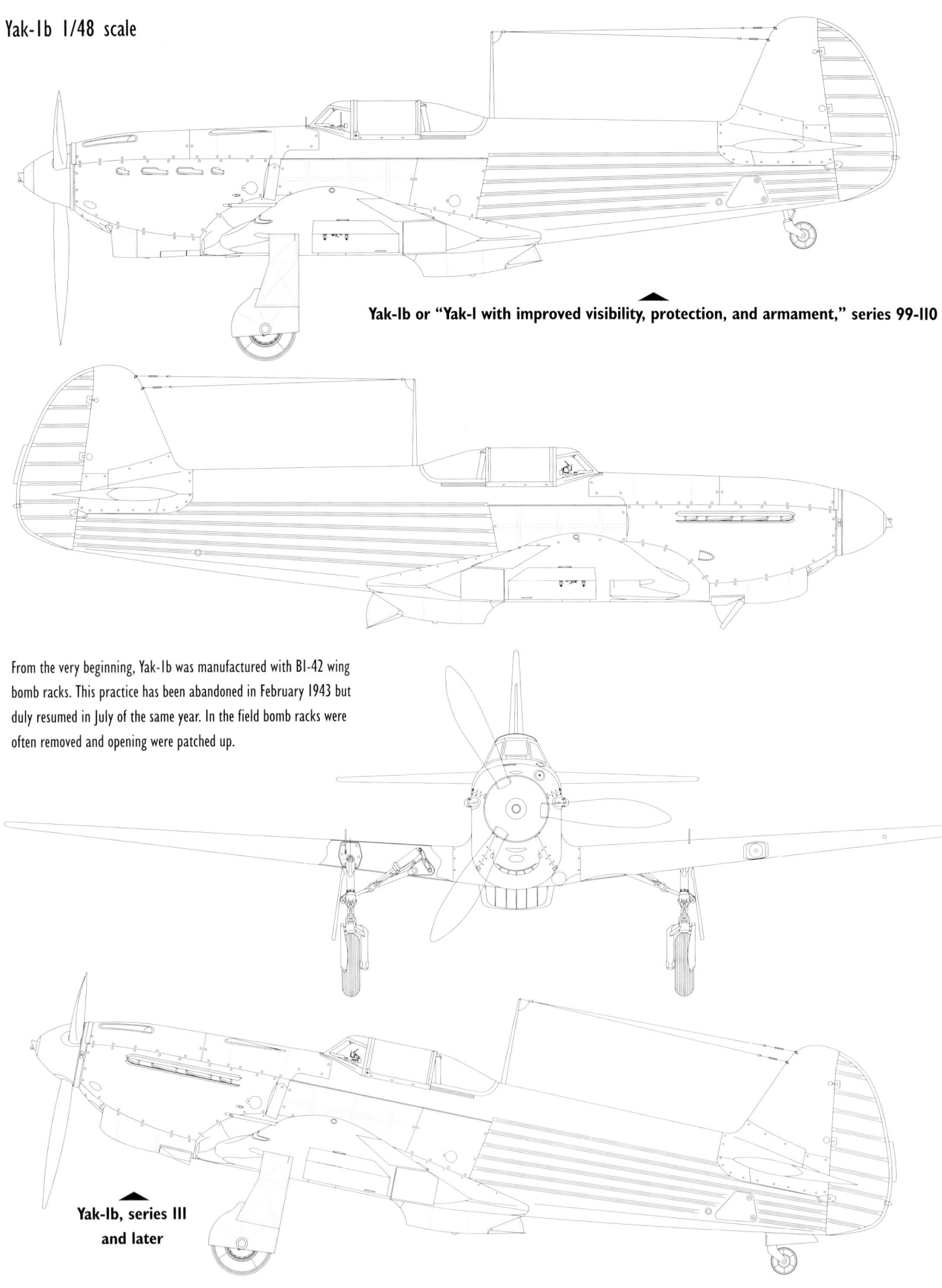

Yak-1b or "Yak-1 with improved visibility, protection, and armament," series 99-110

From the very beginning, Yak-1b was manufactured with B1-42 wing bomb racks. This practice has been abandoned in February 1943 but duly resumed in July of the same year. In the field bomb racks were often removed and opening were patched up.

Yak-1b, series III and later

Yak-1b 1/48 scale

Alternative sliding parts of the canopy seen on Yak-1b ▶

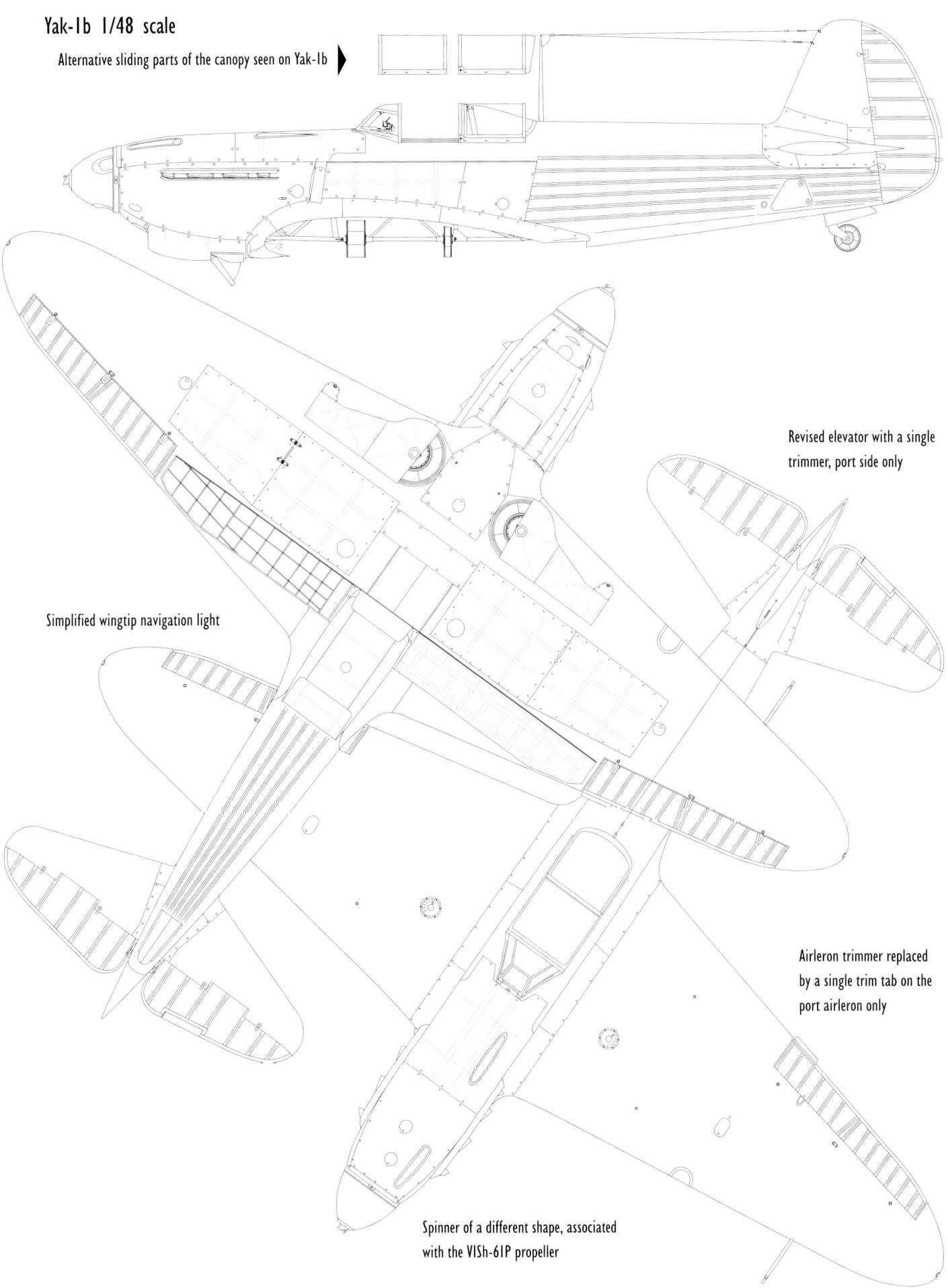

Revised elevator with a single trimmer, port side only

Simplified wingtip navigation light

Airlreron trimmer replaced by a single trim tab on the port airlreron only

Spinner of a different shape, associated with the VISh-61P propeller

Yak-7 1/48 scale

Yak-7V trainer that was manufactured from
5.1942 to 12.1943 in parallel with fighter version

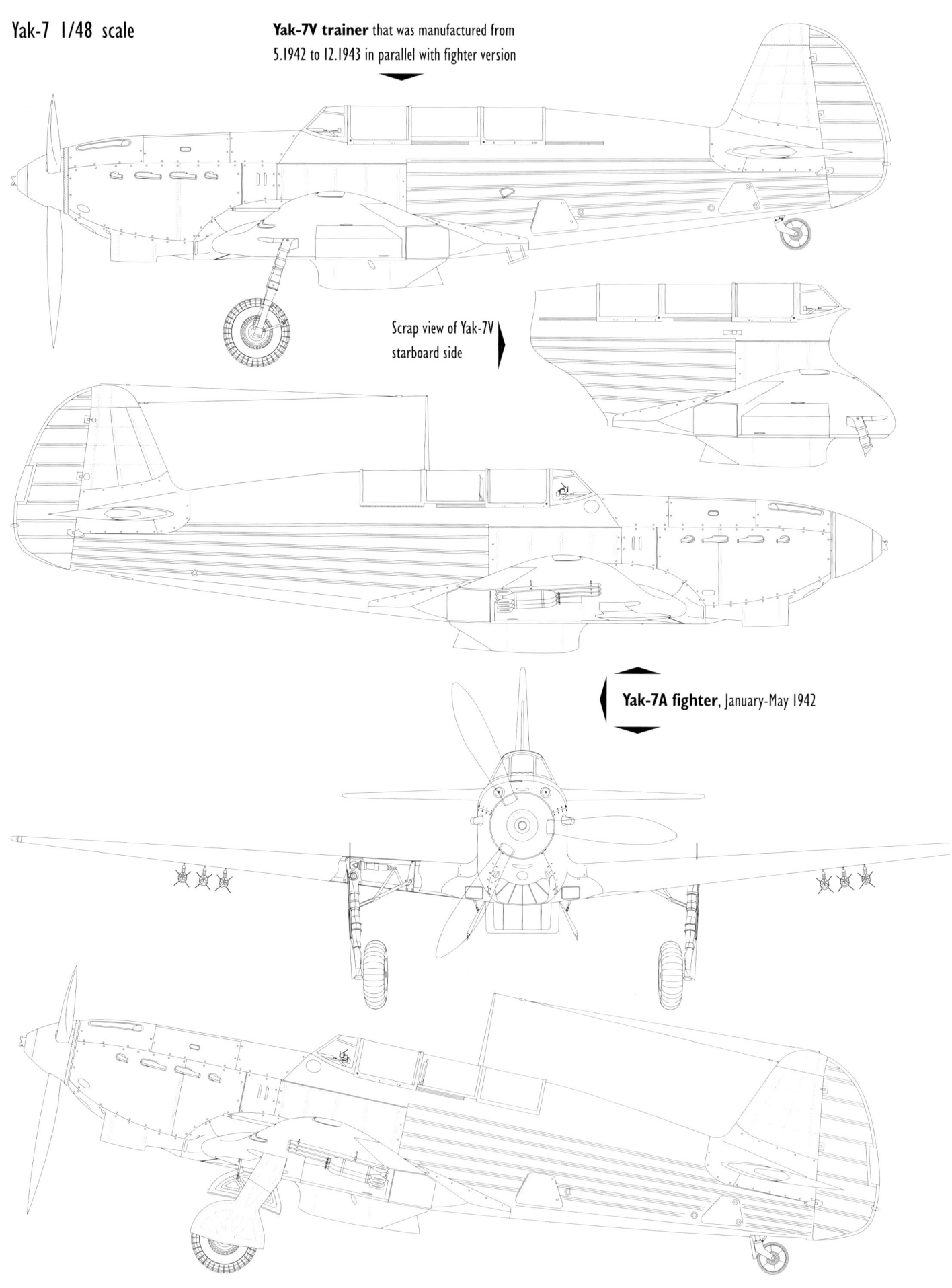

Scrap view of Yak-7V
starboard side

Yak-7A fighter, January-May 1942

Yak-7 1/48 scale

Yak-7UTI, initial trainer version April - September 1941

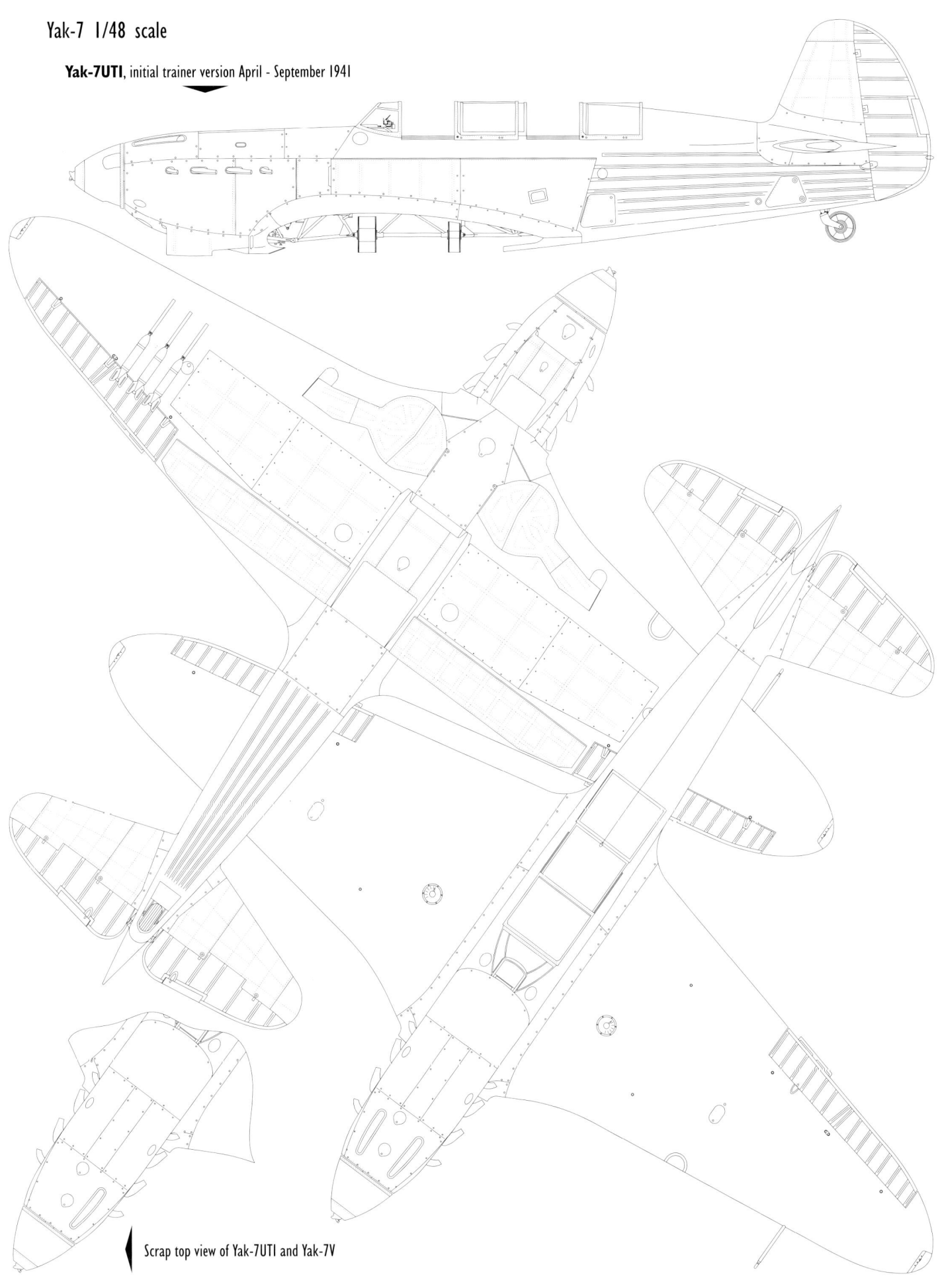

Scrap top view of Yak-7UTI and Yak-7V

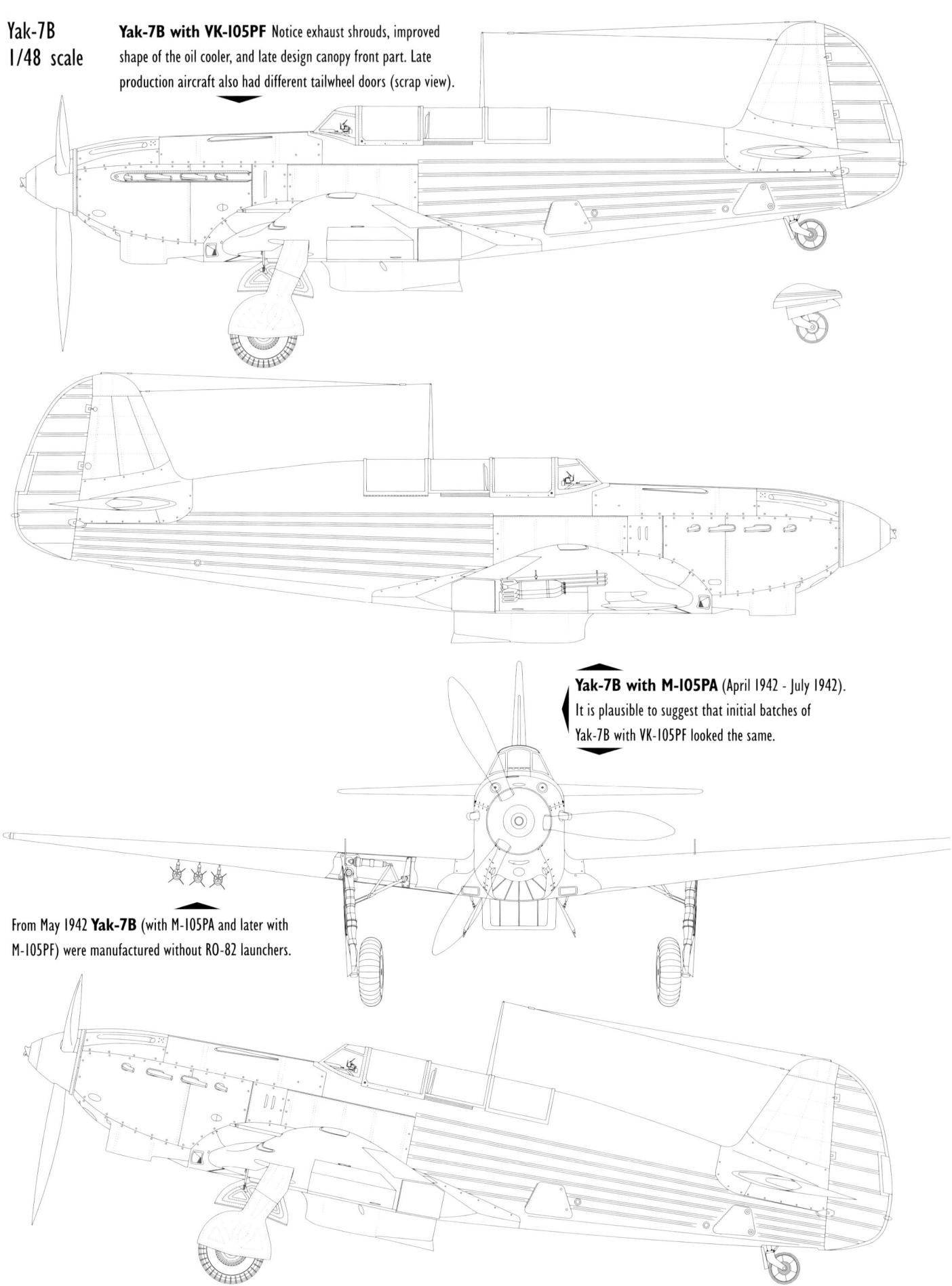

Yak-7B
1/48 scale

Yak-7B with VK-105PF Notice exhaust shrouds, improved shape of the oil cooler, and late design canopy front part. Late production aircraft also had different tailwheel doors (scrap view).

Yak-7B with M-105PA (April 1942 - July 1942). It is plausible to suggest that initial batches of Yak-7B with VK-105PF looked the same.

From May 1942 **Yak-7B** (with M-105PA and later with M-105PF) were manufactured without RO-82 launchers.

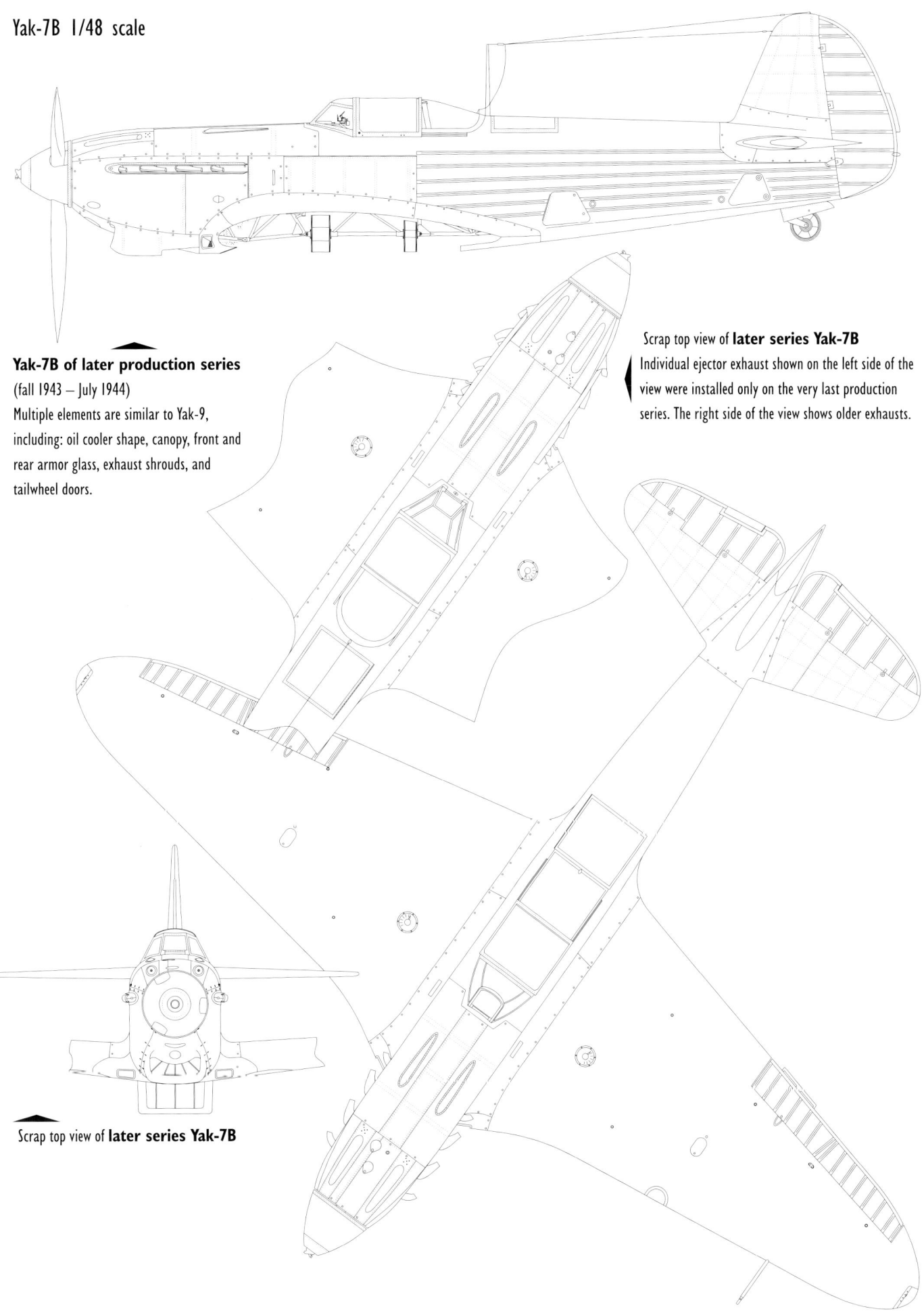

Yak-7B 1/48 scale

Yak-7B of later production series
(fall 1943 – July 1944)
Multiple elements are similar to Yak-9,
including: oil cooler shape, canopy, front and
rear armor glass, exhaust shrouds, and
tailwheel doors.

Scrap top view of **later series Yak-7B**
Individual ejector exhaust shown on the left side of the
view were installed only on the very last production
series. The right side of the view shows older exhausts.

Scrap top view of **later series Yak-7B**

Yak-9 1/48 scale

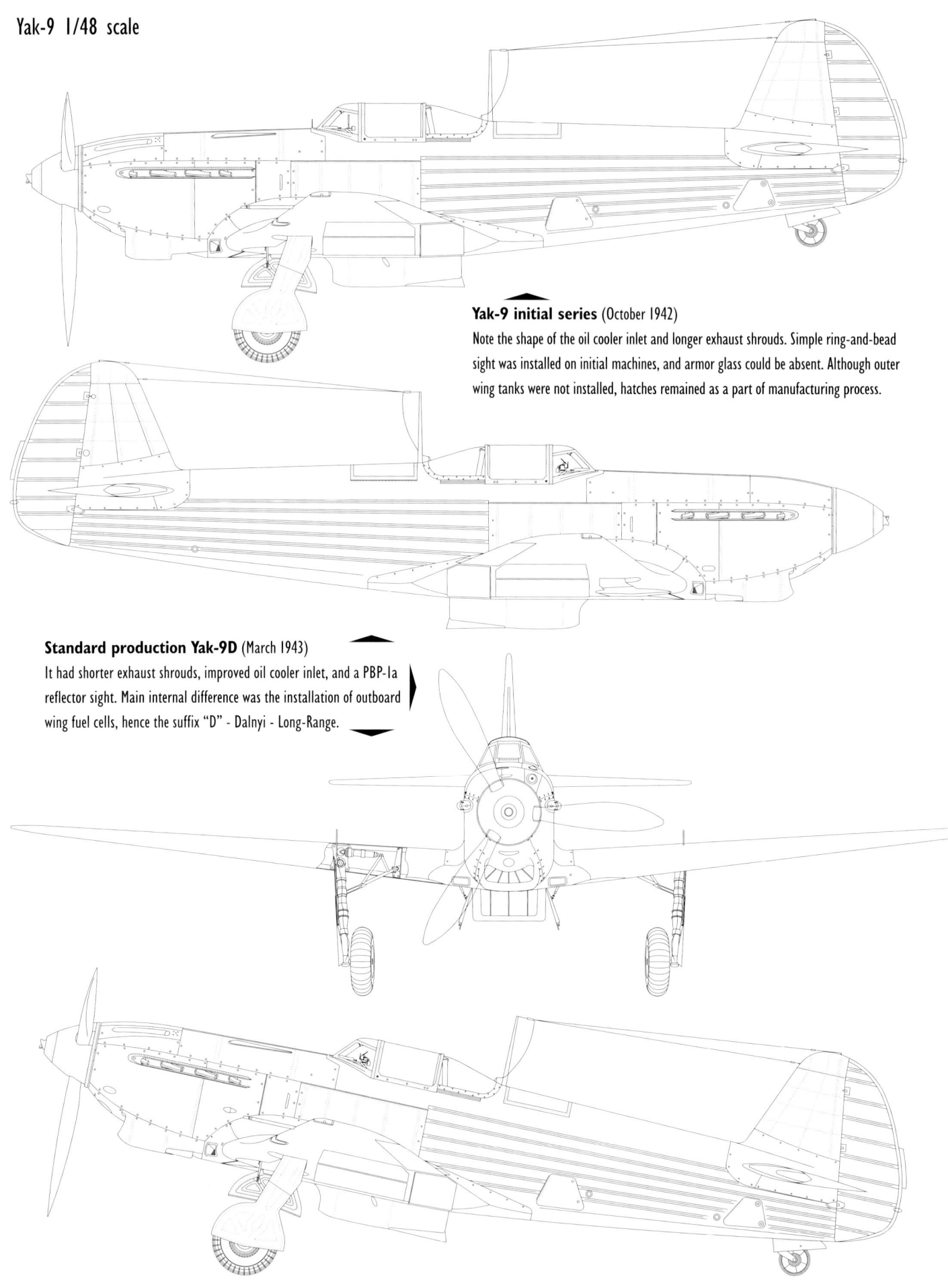

Yak-9 initial series (October 1942)
Note the shape of the oil cooler inlet and longer exhaust shrouds. Simple ring-and-bead sight was installed on initial machines, and armor glass could be absent. Although outer wing tanks were not installed, hatches remained as a part of manufacturing process.

Standard production Yak-9D (March 1943)
It had shorter exhaust shrouds, improved oil cooler inlet, and a PBP-1a reflector sight. Main internal difference was the installation of outboard wing fuel cells, hence the suffix "D" - Dalnyi - Long-Range.

Yak-9 1/48 scale

Yak-9B (Yak-9L) fighter-bomber (March 1944)
Had elongated rear canopy which could be removed for loading of four vertical bomb bays.

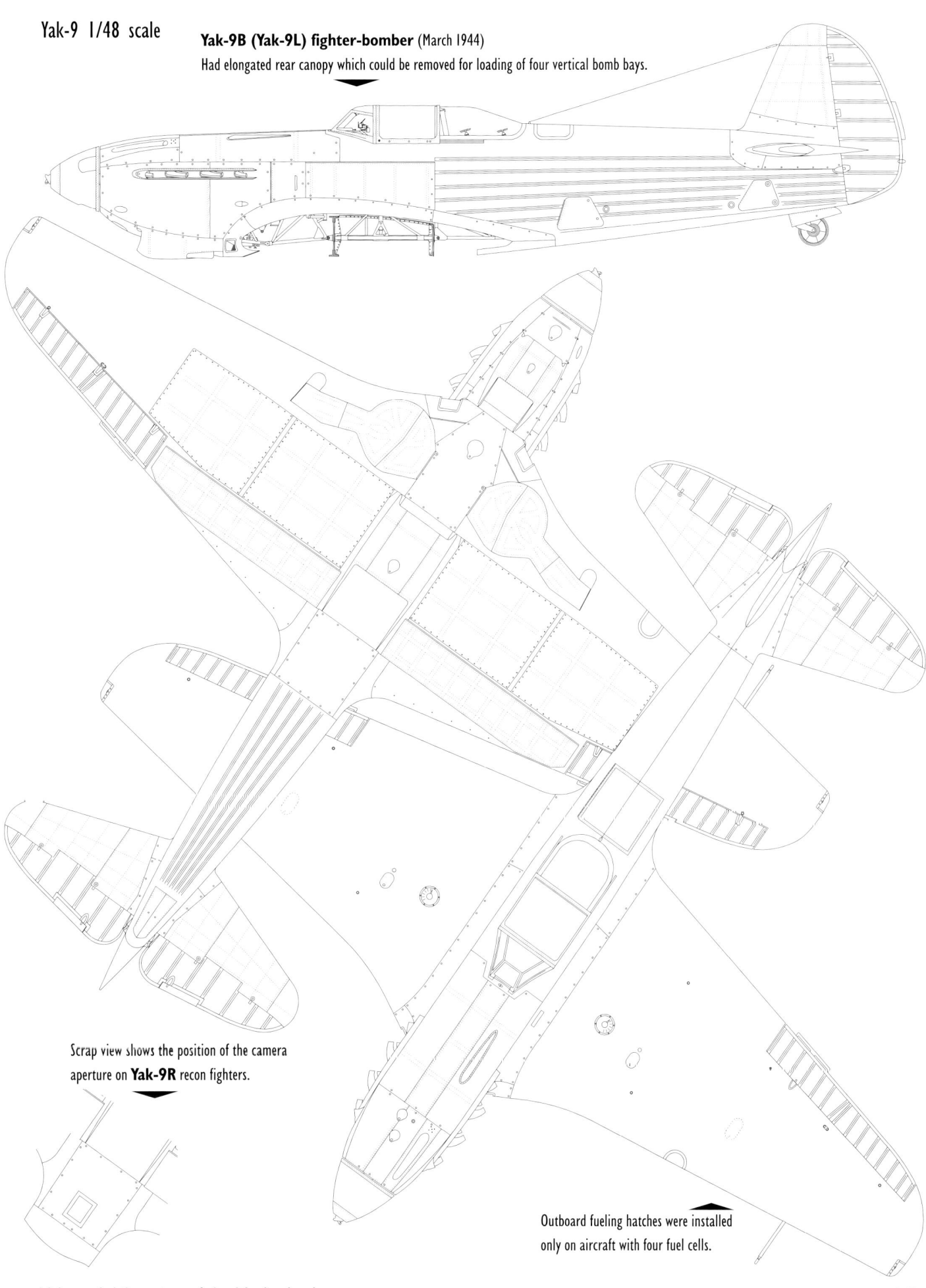

Scrap view shows the position of the camera
aperture on **Yak-9R** recon fighters.

Outboard fueling hatches were installed
only on aircraft with four fuel cells.

Yak-9T and M 1/48 scale

Later series Yak-9T based on **Yak-9M** airframe and sometimes referred to as Yak-9DT (May 1944 and later), Note more rounded spinner, doors in wingroot intakes, and full set of armor glass. These later series -9Ts had all four fuel cells installed.

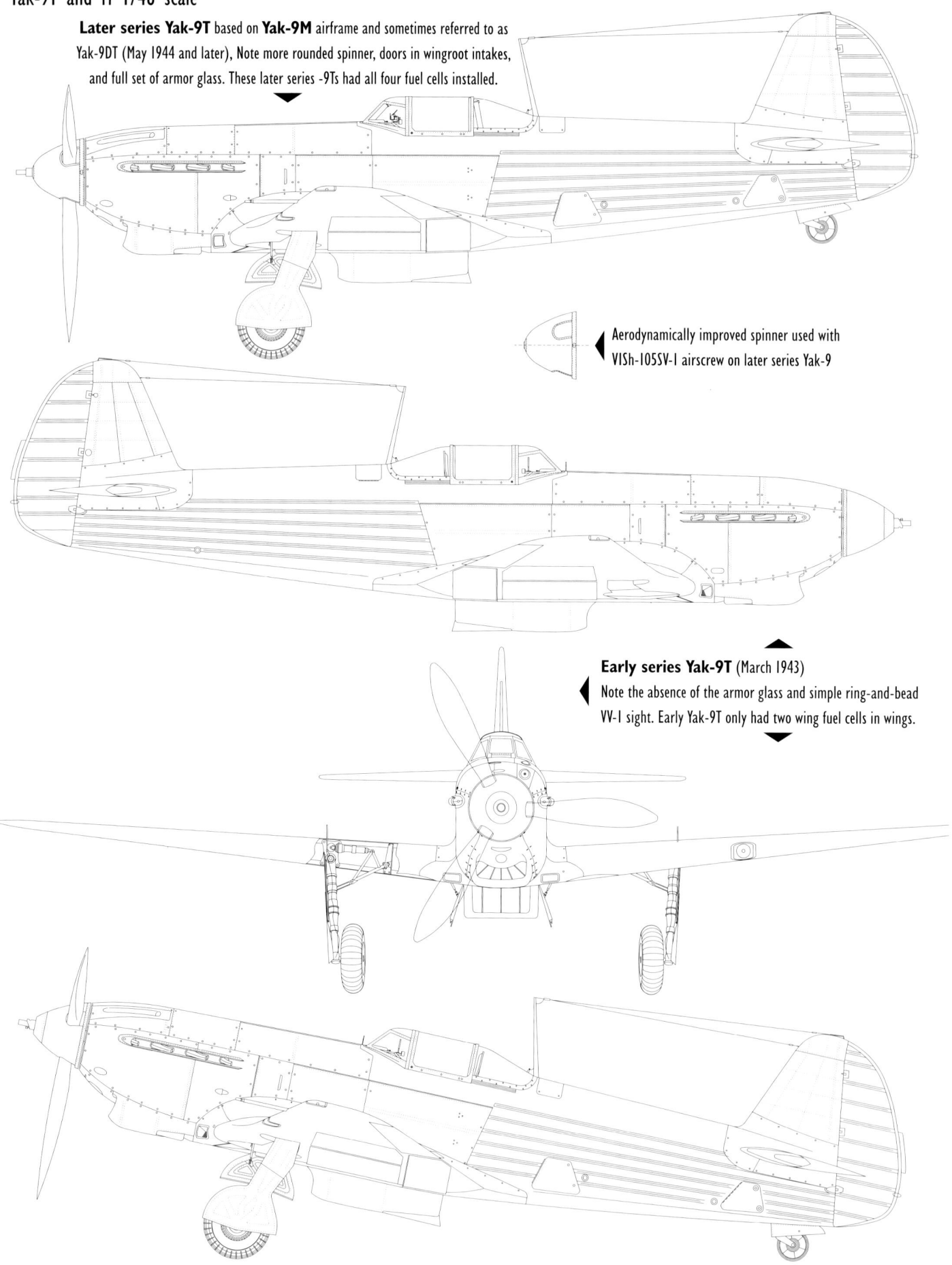

Aerodynamically improved spinner used with VISh-105SV-1 airscrew on later series Yak-9

Early series Yak-9T (March 1943)
Note the absence of the armor glass and simple ring-and-bead VV-1 sight. Early Yak-9T only had two wing fuel cells in wings.

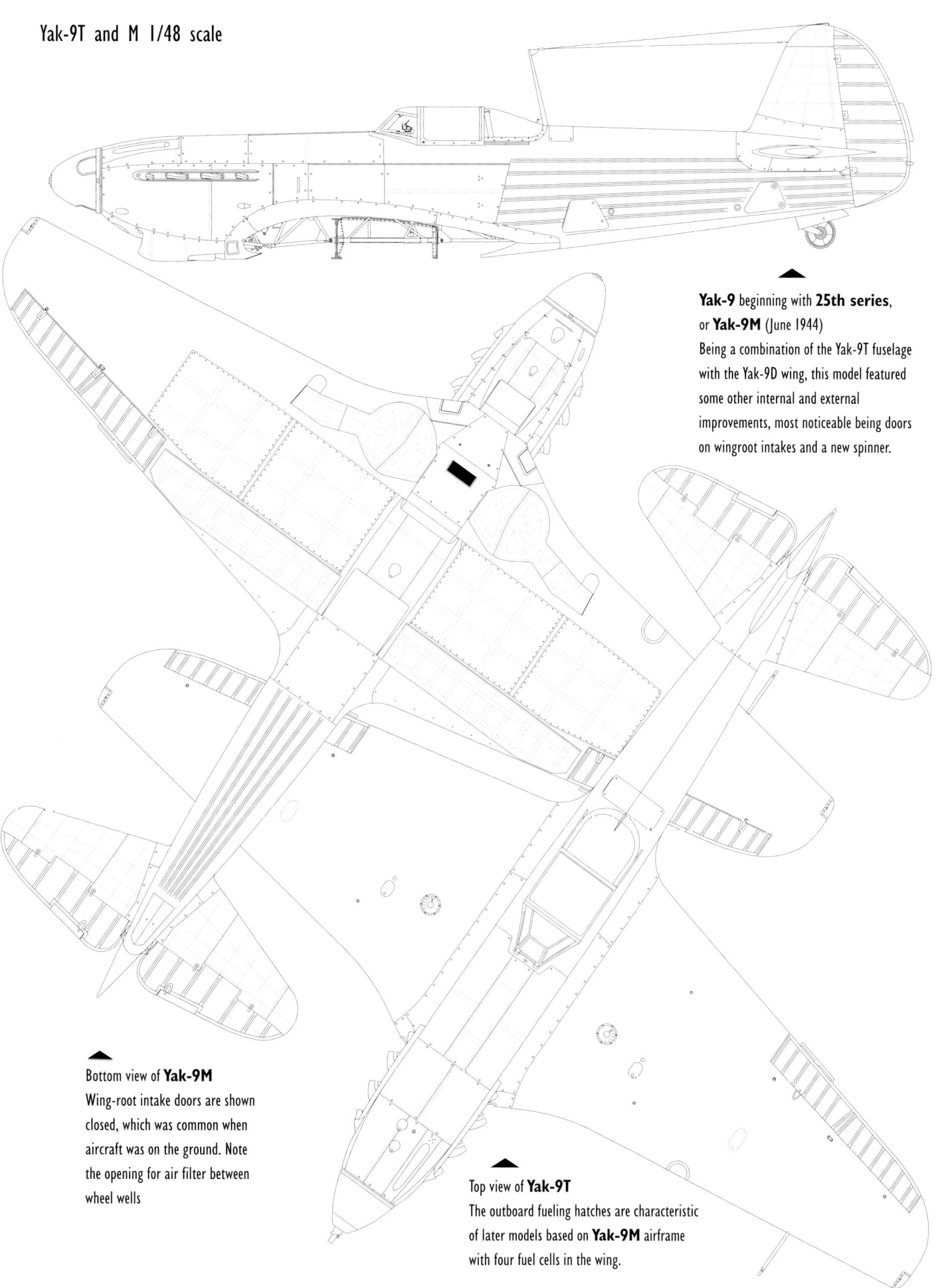

Yak-9 beginning with **25th series**, or **Yak-9M** (June 1944)
Being a combination of the Yak-9T fuselage with the Yak-9D wing, this model featured some other internal and external improvements, most noticeable being doors on wingroot intakes and a new spinner.

Bottom view of **Yak-9M**
Wing-root intake doors are shown closed, which was common when aircraft was on the ground. Note the opening for air filter between wheel wells

Top view of **Yak-9T**
The outboard fueling hatches are characteristic of later models based on **Yak-9M** airframe with four fuel cells in the wing.

The 812ᵗʰ IAP in dates and events through to May 1944

1942

26.03.1942 — C-in-C VVS Red Army signs the order for the formation of the 812ᵗʰ IAP

26.07.1942 — the 812ᵗʰ IAP goes to the Kalinin Front and begins combat work as part of 263ʳᵈ IAD

29.07.1942 — regiment's first aerial victory in Great Patriotic War — Fw189 reconnaissance aircraft

31.07.1942 — regiment's first aerial victory over a Ju88

02.08.1942 — regiment's first aerial victory over a Bf109

03.08.1942 — regiment pilots down 11 Bf109s

09.09.1942 — the 812ᵗʰ IAP is withdrawn from the front to the VVS reserve

24.09.1942 — the regiment is committed to battle at Stalingrad as part of 283ʳᵈ IAD (16ᵗʰ VA)

25.09.1942 — the regiment's first aerial victory over He111 and Ju87 bombers, and its first combat loss — B.A. Kvitko is shot down in combat

30.09.1942 — St. Lt. V Veremeyenko is the first to reach 5 personal victories, becoming the regiment's first ace

01.12.1942 — the 812ᵗʰ IAP turns over its aircraft to other regiments and leaves for reformation at the 3ʳᵈ ZAB

12.12.1942 — 32 pilots of the 534ᵗʰ IAP are transferred from the Far East to the 8ᵗʰ ZIAP (Povolzhye), fully replacing the original 812ᵗʰ IAP pilots who have been reassigned to other aviation units

1943

Jan.-Feb. 1943 — "Far Easterners" lacking combat experience (new personnel of 812ᵗʰ IAP) transition from I-16 and I-153 to Yak-1. Regiment assigned to 265ᵗʰ IAD, 3ʳᵈ IAK RVGK

17.04.1943 — regiment pilots fly from the Moscow area to the Kuban area on 29 Yak-1s

20.04.1943 — 812ᵗʰ IAP "Far Easterners baptism of fire" occurs in the Kuban air campaign; regiment pilots down 12 enemy aircraft, losing 5 of their own pilots

27.04.1943 — the regiment's first aerial victory over an Hs126

29.04.1943 — Kapitan F.K. Svezhentsev achieves 5 personal victories, becoming the regiment's first Kuban era ace. Altogether the regiment downed 16 enemy aircraft, losing 3 pilots

— the regiment's first aerial victory over an Fw190; regiment achieves 100ᵗʰ aerial victory

03.05.1943 — squadron commander Kapitan I.D. Batychko becomes an ace, achieving his 5ᵗʰ personal victory

05.05.1943 — squadron commander Kapitan F.K. Svezhentsev is the first in the regiment to reach 10 personal victories

— Lt. A.M. Mashenkin becomes an ace, achieving his 5ᵗʰ personal victory

08.05.1943 — regiment's first aerial victory by ramming (Yak-1 vs. Bf109)

— regiment loses its 17ᵗʰ pilot during battles in Kuban

10.05.1943 — regiment's second aerial ramming (Yak-1 vs. Bf109)

26.05.1943 — Lt. S.P. Kalugin becomes an ace, achieving his 5ᵗʰ personal victory

28.05.1943 — Kapitan P.T. Tarasov forces Bf109G-4/R6 (W.Nr.14997) to land. pilot is captured; regiment achieves its 95ᵗʰ aerial victory (the last in the Kuban campaign)

16.06.1943 — 9 pilots remaining after heavy fighting in Kuban are taken to Trubetchino airfield, Lipetsk oblast, for rest; regiment is in the rear; regiment is reconstituted with personnel and receives new fighters

July-August 1943 — Mayor D.Ye. Nikolaenkov becomes regiment commander; the regiment receives 26 new young pilots and is the first to receive the new 37mm cannon armed Yak-9T fighter

28.08.1943 — 812ᵗʰ IAP personnel see their regiment banner for the first time

06.09.1943 — the regiment begins combat work on Southern Front

18.09.1943 — "Black Saturday": three young pilots of the regiment die in combat with eight Bf109s

19.09.1943 — Lt. G.P. Churakov achieves his 5ᵗʰ personal victory, is shot down in the same battle, and dies after landing

21.09.1943 — RUS-2 "Pegmatit" radar is used to vector the regiment's fighters onto aerial targets

— Lt. I.V. Fedorov becomes an ace, achieving his 5ᵗʰ personal victory

— the regiment's pilots shoot down 8 enemy bombers (6 Ju88s and 2 He111s), and achieve their first victory over the Bf110.

25.09.1943 — St. Lt. A.T. Tishchenko becomes an ace, achieving his 5ᵗʰ personal victory

— squadron commander Lt. A.M. Mashenkin is shot down in aerial combat and captured by the enemy

26.09.1943 — Lt. A.I. Tumanov becomes an ace, achieving his 5ᵗʰ personal victory

27.09.1943 — disastrous "demonstration" aerial battle with enemy bombers

Oct. 1943 — the regiment's pilots begin to actively employ "free hunt" method with strafing of enemy ground targets and reconnaissance of enemy rear area

01.10.1943 — the regiment's third aerial ramming (Yak-9 vs. He111)

21.10.1943 — Lt. I.V. Fedorov achieves his 10ᵗʰ personal victory

23.10.1943 — the regiment's first aerial victory over an Hs129

25.10.1943 — the regiment's pilots down six enemy aircraft and achieve the unit's 200ᵗʰ aerial victory

28.10.1943 — regiment chief of aerial gunnery, Kapitan P.T. Tarasov, achieves his 20ᵗʰ personal victory; Ml. Lt. I.A. Maksimov becomes an ace, achieving his 5ᵗʰ personal victory

29.10.1943 — Kapitan P.T. Tarasov and Mayor T.Ye. Pasynok down four Ju87 dive bombers

— Ml. Lt. I.A. Maksimov is shot down in combat, is buried by regiment commissar Mayor T. Ye. Pasynok, who also was shot down and forced to land near place of Maksimov's death

Nov. 1943 — the regiment's pilots begin successful long-range reconnaissance flights in two Yak-9D fighters

22.11.1943 — regiment navigator Kapitan I.F. Popov becomes an ace, achieving his 5ᵗʰ personal victory

11-14.12.1943 — Kapitan P.T. Tarasov from the 812ᵗʰ IAP makes a formal presentation at the 8ᵗʰ VA "hunters" fighter pilot conference

20.12.1943 — squadron commander Ye.Ye. Ankudinov becomes an ace, achieving his 5ᵗʰ personal victory

31.12.1943 — Bolshaya Kostromka airfield is subjected to strafing attack, this is the first time during the war that the regiment's pilots conduct a strafing attack on an enemy airfield

1944

10.01.1944 — Lt. I.V. Fedorov finds the enemy airfield at Lepetikha (Voroshilovka) while on a reconnaissance sortie and supports the launching of a series of strafing attacks against it

11.01.1944 — regiment navigator Mayor I.F. Popov is named commander of 812ᵗʰ IAP

14.01.1944 — a group of fighters led by regiment commander Popov conducts two successful strafing attacks against Lepetikha (Voroshilovka) airfield without losses, in the process destroying seven Bf109s in aerial battles and six Hs129s plus one He111 on the ground

06.02.1944 — squadron commander St. Lt. A.I. Tumanov executes a fiery ramming attack, guiding his damaged aircraft into an enemy troop column

21.02.1944 — having fled from captivity, St. Lt. A.M. Mashenkin returns to the regiment

25.02.1944 — Lt. V.D. Shishkin becomes an ace, achieving his 5ᵗʰ personal victory

27.02.1944 — Lt. F.G. Peskarev becomes an ace, achieving his 5ᵗʰ personal victory

01.03.1944 — Ml. Lt. F.M. Tikhomirov becomes an ace, achieving his 5ᵗʰ personal victory; St. Lt. I.V. Fedorov achieves 15ᵗʰ personal victory

02.03.1944 — Ml. Lt. N.A. Podymov becomes an ace, achieving his 5ᵗʰ personal victory

— combined fighter group led by Mayor I.F. Popov strikes one of the most effective strafing attacks on an enemy airfield—nine enemy aircraft are destroyed on the ground and four in the air at Rayzendorf airfield

— the regiment's navigator Kapitan Ye.Ye.Ankudinov was the first in the regiment to achieve night victory, shooting down an He111

11.03.1944 — regiment loses three pilots over the Sivash crossing sites and destroys 10 enemy aircraft in aerial battles. One of the downed Ju87s is 50ᵗʰ of this type destroyed by regiment since the beginning of the war

— Lt. V.D. Shishkin shot down a Ju87 over the Sivash and the regiment achieves its 250ᵗʰ aerial victory

13.03.1944 — squadron commander I.V. Fedorov achieves his 20ᵗʰ personal victory

14.03.1944 — Mayor P.T. Tarasov achieves his 25ᵗʰ and 26ᵗʰ personal victories

18.03.1944 — St. Lt. I.V. Fedorov achieves 25ᵗʰ personal victory

07.04.1944 — the regiment's pilots conduct routine effective strafing attacks on enemy airfields—9 enemy aircraft are destroyed and damaged on the ground at Ichki airfield

10.04.1944 — regiment commander I.F. Popov achieves his 10th and 11th personal victories, and in all regiment downs five enemy aircraft

13.04.1944 — Mayor P.T. Tarasov is the first in the regiment to be awarded Hero of the Soviet Union

15.04.1944 — the regiment's pilots straff Khersones airfield for first time, destroying three enemy aircraft on the ground and three more in the air

19.04.1944 — strafing of enemy airfield at "6ᵗʰ versta"; two enemy aircraft are destroyed in aerial combat and five on the ground, one of which becomes the 50ᵗʰ aircraft destroyed on the ground during strafing attacks on enemy airfields

21.04.1944 — regiment commander Mayor I.F. Popov raises his score to 15 personal victories

22.04.1944 — regiment navigator Kapitan Ye.Ye. Ankudinov achieves 10ᵗʰ personal victory

24.04.1944 — Mayor P.T. Tarasov achieves his 30ᵗʰ personal victory, and squadron commander Kapitan A.T. Tishchenko achieves his 10ᵗʰ personal victory

09.05.1944 — strafing of Khersones airfield; five enemy aircraft destroyed on the ground

11.05.1944 — strafing of Khersones airfield; eight enemy aircraft destroyed on the ground

12.05.1944 — squadron commander St. Lt. A.M. Mashenkin achieves his 9ᵗʰ personal victory, which becomes the last (76ᵗʰ) regiment victory in the battle for Crimea

14.05.1944 — For active participation in battles around Sevastopol, by Supreme High Command Order No.136 aviation the regiment is granted honorific title "Sevastopolskiy"

End of May 1944 — the 812ᵗʰ IAP, as part of 265ᵗʰ IAD, is withdrawn to Orel for replenishment of personnel and equipment